Archeology in Cultural Systems

Archeology in Cultural Systems

Sally R. Binford &
Lewis R. Binford

Routledge
Taylor & Francis Group
LONDON AND NEW YORK

First published 1968 by Transaction Publishers

Published 2017 by Routledge
2 Park Square, Milton Park, Abingdon, Oxon OX14 4RN
711 Third Avenue, New York, NY 10017, USA

Routledge is an imprint of the Taylor & Francis Group, an informa business

Library of Congress Catalog Number: 2008018476

Library of Congress Cataloging-in-Publication Data

Binford, Sally R.
Archeology in cultural systems / Sally R. Binford and Lewis R. Binford.
p. cm.
Originally published: Chicago : Aldine Pub. Co., [1968].
Includes bibliographical references and index.
ISBN 978-0-202-36237-3
1. Ethnoarchaeology. 2. Social archaeology. 3. Cultural property.
I. Binford, Lewis Roberts, 1930- II. Title.

CC79.E85B56 2008
930.1—dc22 2008018476

ISBN 13: 978-0-202-36237-3 (pbk)

Since historical events and essential social divisions of prehistoric peoples don't find an adequate expression in material remains, it cannot be right to try to arrive at a knowledge of them through archaeological interpretation.—M. S. SMITH.

With the proper approach it should be possible to discover and document a great deal about social systems and the political and religious organizations for most prehistoric . . . cultures. There must be limits, kinds of information we cannot reconstruct, but until we have tried we shall not know these limits are.—W. H. SEARS.

Preface

Most of the papers in this volume were presented at an all-day symposium entitled "The Social Organization of Prehistoric Communities" held at the 64th Annual Meeting of the American Anthropological Association at Denver in November, 1965. The symposium was organized by the editors, prompted by a conversation the previous spring with Stuart Struever and William Longacre. All of us were engaged in archeological research which represented a departure from conventional studies, and we were aware of the fact that there were many other archeologists in the country also working toward the same ends, utilizing various theoretical and methodological approaches. It was felt that the time was ripe to present the findings of some of these workers, both to inform non-archeologists of what was going on in our sub-field and to stimulate discussion of common problems between archeologists and cultural anthropologists.

The list of participants in the symposium was not exhaustive of those engaged in new kinds of research and should not be taken to represent any "school" of archeological thinking. The participants were selected with an eye toward maximizing areal and temporal coverage and diversity of innovation in method. Albert C. Spaulding and Paul S. Martin were asked to be chairmen of the symposium's two sessions since they are senior men in the field who have consistently encouraged and inspired many of us and have aided greatly the development and acceptance of new ideas.

The plans for organizing the symposium papers and comments into publishable form were made at the Denver meetings. Since then there have been many changes in specific contributions as well as in the overall plans for presentation. Most of the symposium papers have been substantially revised, and five papers have been added which were not included in the original symposium. The introductory paper here, "Archeological Perspectives," was written especially for this volume to provide a background against which the substantive papers might be viewed. Spaulding's paper was presented at the 1965 meeting of the American Association for the Advancement of Science and was solicited for this book by the editors. Cowgill's paper was read at the Denver meeting of the American Anthropological Association but was not included in the symposium because of lack of time. The paper by Longacre and Ayres was presented to the 1966 meeting of the Society for American Archaeology at Reno. Williams' paper was especially written for this volume at the request of the editors. The organization of the entire volume was worked out between the editors and Alexander J. Morin of Aldine Publishing Company.

There were major contributions of individuals and organizations which made publication of this book possible. The tapes of discussants' comments at the symposium were transcribed by Mrs. Karla Maddox, who also had the unenviable task of riding herd on the authors to complete revisions on their manuscripts. We are very grateful to Mrs. Maddox for her herculean efforts. Richard Humphrey of the University of California, Santa Barbara, prepared some of the illustrative material, and we are appreciative of his work.

Funds used in the preparation of manuscripts, photographic work, and clerical assistance were provided to the editors by a grant from the Graduate Council of the University of California, Santa Barbara, and additional assistance has been given by the Department of Anthropology, University of California, Los Angeles.

The Wenner-Gren Foundation for Anthropological Research provided a grant to support the publication of this work. We are most grateful to Mrs. Lita Osmundsen, Director of Research, and to the Board of the Wenner-Gren Foundation for their generous and gracious assistance.

SALLY R. BINFORD

LEWIS R. BINFORD

Contents

PART I

Archeological Theory and Method

Archeology is neither history nor anthropology. As an autonomous discipline, it consists of a method and a set of specialized techniques for the gathering or "production" of cultural information (Taylor, 1948, p. 44).

It has been said that archaeology, while providing data and generalizations in such fields as history and general anthropology, lacks a systematic body of concepts and premises constituting archaeological theory. According to this view, the archaeologist must borrow his theoretical underpinning from the field of study his work happens to serve, or do without. Whether the latter alternative be an admissible one does not seem to be an arguable point. Acceptable field work can perhaps be done in a theoretical vacuum, but integration and interpretation without theory is inconceivable. . . . It seems to us that American archaeology stands in a particularly close and, so far as theory is concerned, dependent relationship to anthropology (Willey and Phillips, 1958, p. 1).

These quotations voice a common opinion regarding the degree to which archeology can be said to make use of a body of theory which is unique or even specific to itself. Taylor defines archeology as a method and set of specialized techniques; Willey and Phillips accept this view, at least in part, in stating that it is possible to do field work in a vacuum, but they add that interpretation is dependent upon theory, in this case anthropological theory. In the papers that follow it will be argued that scientific methods and techniques can be developed only when they are relevant to certain aims and only with regard to the properties of the empirical data utilized. A. C. Spaulding has stated:

> Archaeology can be defined minimally as the study of the interrelationships of form, temporal locus, and spatial locus exhibited by artifacts. In other words, archaeologists are always concerned with these interrelationships, whatever broader interests they may have, and these interrelationships are the special business of archaeology (1960, p. 439).

Accepting Spaulding's minimal definition of what archeology is, we can go a step further and specify its aim as the explanation of the observed interrelationships; in other words, as an explanation of the order we observe in the archeological record. Archeological theory consists of propositions and assumptions regarding the archeological record itself—its origins, its sources of variability, the determinants of differences and similarities in the formal, spatial, and temporal characteristics of artifacts and features and their interrelationships. It is in the context of this theory that archeological methods and techniques are developed.

Since artifacts are cultural data and since they once functioned as elements of a cultural system, many of the explanations we might offer for observations made on the archeological record will refer to organizational features of past cultural systems. On the other hand, the archeologist might explain an observed pattern in his data by citing sampling error. The former situation is no more justification for saying the archeologist is a technician in the service of anthropology than is the latter for calling him a technician in the service of probability statistics. The archeologist *is* an anthropological scientist, but this does not imply that there is no body of theory specific to his specialty. On the contrary, advances in archeological theory are prerequisite to the achievement of broader anthropological goals. It is through theoretical advances and sound arguments of relevance that we can link our observations on the archeological record to particular questions on the operation of past cultural systems.

Archeology shares with other anthropological sciences the aim of explaining differences and similarities among cultural systems. We are, therefore, concerned with cultural theory and processual arguments which treat problems of the interrelationship of cultural (and any other relevant class of) variables which have explanatory value.

If archeological theory attempts to develop arguments of relevance for archeological data to past conditions, then it should develop arguments on the explanatory relevance of cultural and ecological variables to differences and similarities among cultural systems. Archeological anthropologists must try to advance both of these complementary areas. We might be able to demonstrate the relevance of our observations to certain past conditions, but if these conditions are irrelevant for measuring either cultural change or variability, then our accomplishments would be (as Deetz cautions) "sterile methodological virtuosity." On the other hand, advances in cultural theory which place crucial explanatory value on variables not previously considered challenge the archeologist to develop arguments of relevance so that he may make use of these advances. In such a case the hope would be that archeological data could be used in testing hypotheses drawn from theories of general anthropological interest. The ability of archeologists to maximize advances in culture theory depends on the existence of a viable and progressive body of archeological theory and method.

There are five papers in the first portion of this book, and they are arranged in a progression from more exclusively theoretical-methodological discussions to specific consideration of archeological materials. In the final paper of this first part, a particular cultural-historical period is discussed in terms of many of the points treated theoretically in the preceding papers. It should be pointed out that there are disagreements and incompatibilities in some of the archeological theory and method discussed in these papers. This volume is not a monolithic presentation of any particular school of archeological thought; there are common interests and many points of agreement among the authors, but there is also diversity of opinion on several points. It is these points which we can expect to be the focus of research interest in the coming years.

References

SPAULDING, ALBERT C. 1960. The dimensions of archaeology. In Gertrude E. Dole and Robert L. Carneiro (Eds.), *Essays in the science of culture: in honor of Leslie A. White*. New York: Thomas Y. Crowell.

TAYLOR, WALTER W. 1948. A study of archeology. Memoir no. 69, *American Anthropologist*, 50(3), Part 2.

WILLEY, GORDON R., and PHILLIP PHILLIPS. 1958. *Method and theory in American archaeology*. Chicago: University of Chicago Press.

ONE

LEWIS R. BINFORD

Archeological Perspectives

A book whose title proclaims something new immediately challenges the reader to verify the claim to novelty or innovation. The purpose of this paper is to justify this book's title by making explicit what is new and, also, how familiar ideas and arguments gain a new significance when viewed in the perspective being developed.

This paper does not attempt an exhaustive historical analysis of the field of archeology but is rather the selective treatment of several general areas of archeological concern put into historical perspective. It is hoped that this background will offer the reader a greater depth of field against which to view the substantive papers which follow.

The Aims of Archeology

> The most profitable inquiry [of archeology] is the search for the origin of epoch-making ideas in order to comprehend the history of civilization (Mason, 1893; p. 403).

> Archaeology, by etymology the study of beginnings, has historical reconstruction for its objective (Kroeber, 1937, p. 163).

These early statements summarize the generally accepted view on the aims of archeology. Taylor (1948, pp. 26, 207) has thoroughly documented the fact that reconstruction of culture history was widely accepted as the end of archeological research. Since Taylor's publication, this aim has been reiterated frequently and continues to be stated in very recent publications (Rouse, 1965, p. 2; Meggers, Evans, and Estrada, 1965, p. 5; Willey, 1966, pp. 2–3; Deetz, 1967a, p. 3).

If seeking origins and tracing the history of culture was one task of archeology, some researchers considered a further aim to be the reconstruction of the lifeways of the peoples responsible for the archeological remains. Such an aim appears early in the literature—for example, in H. I. Smith (1910) and Sollas (1924). Concern with the reconstruction of lifeways of extinct peoples has been expressed by many, but probably the most influential advocate for more attention toward this end has been Taylor:

> The conjunctive approach . . . has as its primary goal the elucidation of cultural conjunctives, the associations and relationships, the "affinities," within the manifestation under investigation. It aims at drawing the completest possible picture of past human life in terms of its human and geographic environment (1948, pp. 95–96).

Most archeologists would agree that we should not lose sight of "the Indian behind the artifact" (Braidwood, 1959, p. 79) and would accept as a major aim of archeology the reconstruction of lifeways.

While these aims of reconstructing culture history and lifeways cannot be said to have been satisfactorily achieved, a few archeologists during the 1930's began to suggest aims reaching far beyond these:

> Some day world culture history will be known as far as archaeological materials and human intelligence permit. Every possible element of culture will have been placed in time and space. The invention, diffusion, mutation and association of elements will have been determined. When taxonomy and history are thus complete, shall we cease our labors and hope that the future Darwin of Anthropology will interpret the great historical scheme that will have been erected? . . . Candor would seem to compel the admission that archaeology could be made much more pertinent to general cultural studies if we paused to take stock of its possibilities. Surely we can shed some light not only on the chronological and spatial arrangements and associations of elements, but on conditions underlying their origin, development, diffusion, acceptance and interaction with one another. These are problems of cultural process . . . (Seward and Setzler, 1938, pp. 5–7).

And one year earlier a Scandanavian archeologist also urged that his colleagues take stock of where they have been and where they were going:

> It appears that archaeology, in spite of its remarkable achievements, has got into a cul-de-sac. . . . The whole subject consists merely of a comparison of forms and systematization. . . . Brilliant systematization, regarded as exact, has not led to and does not lead to an elucidation of the organic structure of the whole life of the period studied, to an understanding of social systems, of economic and social history. . . . Forms and types . . . have been regarded as much more real and alive than the society which created them and whole

needs determined these manifestations of life. . . . Have we reached a crisis where the procedure and aim of our science must be revised? (Tallgren, 1937, pp. 154–55).

Statements urging archeologists to concern themselves with problems of process appeared with increasing frequency in the literature of the next twenty years (Steward, 1942, p. 139; Bennett, 1943, p. 208; Childe, 1946, p. 248; Clark, 1953a, 1953b; Barth, 1950; and especially Caldwell, 1959). As recently as 1958 this concern with process was still being defined and distinguished from other aims of archeology:

> So little work has been done in American archaeology on the explanatory level that it is difficult to find a name for it. . . . In the context of archaeology, processual interpretation is the study of the nature of what is vaguely referred to as the culture-historical process. Practically speaking, it implies an attempt to discover regularities in the relationships given by the methods of culture-historical integration. . . . On this explanatory level of organization . . . we are no longer asking merely what but also how and even why (Willey and Phillips, 1958, pp. 5–6).

Willey and Phillips' statement about so little work having been done on the explanatory level was made despite such efforts as Steward's (1937) investigation of settlement patterns which were later elaborated on in the Viru Valley project. Willey himself had expressed great optimism about the possibilities for "processual interpretation" as well as for the reconstruction of cultural institutions (Willey, 1953, p. 1). Some of the other efforts made between the late 1930's and the late 1950's toward gaining an understanding of cultural process were White's arguments on the role of energy in the evolution of culture (White, 1943, pp. 335–56), Steward's "Cultural Causality and Law . . . " (1949), and Steward and Wittfogel's study of irrigation (Steward *et al.*, 1955).

In his 1962 Presidential Address to the American Anthropological Association, Willey again commented on the lack of progress in gaining a processual understanding of culture history:

> Certainly the answers to the . . . causal questions as to why the ancient American civilizations began and flourished as they did and when they did still elude us, and what I can offer . . . will do little more . . . than describe and compare certain situations and series of events (Willey, 1962, p. 1).

There began to appear in the literature a general dampening of enthusiasm of those who some twenty years earlier had called for the archeologist to turn his attention to processual investigations. There was a similar pessimism expressed in the writing of British scholars despite the work of such authors as Childe (1936), Crawford (1953), and Clark (1951, 1953):

> We have lost the confidence of the nineteenth century, and are children of an age of doubt. . . . We must recognize that in archaeology . . . there are no

> facts other than those which are . . . "observational data." . . . What we have at our disposal, as prehistorians, is the accidentally surviving durable remnants of material culture, which we interpret as best we may and inevitably the peculiar quality of this evidence dictates the sort of information we can obtain from it (Piggott, 1965b, pp. 4–5).

The linking together of the limits of archeological interpretation with the fragmentary nature of the archeological record is a phenomenon we examine in some detail later (see pp. 18–23), but the points to be made here are: (1) there was general acceptance of the three aims of archeology—reconstruction of culture history, reconstruction of lifeways, and the delineation of cultural process; and (2) there has been increasing despair over the feasibility of achieving the third aim.

The Methods of Archeology—Traditional Approaches

This section examines the methods traditionally used in attempts to achieve the aims of archeology. We shall deal with each of the aims separately, attempt to describe the methods employed, and analyze some of the problems underlying the application of method to problem.

RECONSTRUCTING CULTURE HISTORY

Reconstructing culture history consists of arranging cultural units in a way which accurately reveals their generic affinities. Archeologists have generally operated on the basis of the following two assumptions:

1. The degree of genealogical affinity between two cultural units varies directly with the similarities they exhibit in generically related characteristics (for example, whole culture traits or complexes, design elements on artifacts, etc.).
2. The degree of genealogical affinity between two cultural units can be measured by the ratio of shared generically related characteristics to the number of such traits not shared.

It is evident that each culture trait tabulated in obtaining the ratio which measures degree of genealogical affinity must be evaluated to determine whether the similarity between traits arose as a function of lineal transmission, diffusion between cultural units, or independent development within each cultural unit. It is here that a basic, unsolved problem lies: How can archeologists distinguish between homologous and analogous cultural similarities?

As early as 1896 E. B. Tylor concerned himself with this problem and suggested a procedure for analyzing observed similarities by

> . . . division into constituent elements showing so little connection with one another that they may be reasonably treated as independent. The more numerous such elements, the more improbable the recurrence of the combination (1896, p. 66)

In other words, Tylor suggests that one might calculate the probabilities of independent occurrences of identical combinations among a set of independently varying characteristics.

Other workers worrying over the same problem offered similar suggestions. For example, Graebner (1911) cites two criteria for evaluating cultural similarities: the criterion of form, and that of quantitative coincidence. For Graebner the criterion of form consisted of the degree to which there was a coincidence of characteristics which did not necessarily stem from "the nature of the objects compared"; the criterion of coincidence lay in determining whether or not the trait or item under study occurred as an isolated similarity or as an element of a greater cultural complex. On the basis of the criterion of form, this greater cultural complex could not reasonably be viewed as having arisen independently.

Robert Lowie pointed out some of the shortcomings of Graebner's reasoning: "The comparison of form can never do more than establish the identity of forms; that such identity is to be explained by genetic relationship is an hypothesis . . . " (1912, p. 28). He also noted that Graebner's quantitative criterion was not probabalistic as was Tylor's but was simply the criterion of form raised to a higher level of abstraction and was therefore not an independent criterion for judgment (1912, p. 27).

A recent evaluation of the applications of Tylor's probability method notes that probability calculations of concrete cases have seldom been performed accurately, and in many instances the apparent accuracy of probability reasoning has been a semantic rather then a methodological addition to the anthropological literature (Erasmus, 1950, pp. 374–75). A more basic flaw in Tylor's procedure is the assumption of a worker's ability to recognize constitutent elements which are in fact independent variables. This problem has been discussed (Erasmus, 1950, pp. 375–87; Rands and Riley, 1958; and indirectly by Sackett, 1966), but no methods have been advanced for the solution of the problem other than the intensive analysis of the distribution and patterns of covariation demonstrable among selected characteristics. Such studies have rarely been conducted by archeologists and certainly have never been a routine analytical component of the works of archeologists proposing historical reconstructions. This particular problem has been the almost exclusive concern of ethnographers, and is one of which archeologists involved in reconstructions of culture history have seemed deliciously unaware.

Lowie (1912, pp. 24–27) pointed out another problem in method—that while some workers have attempted to identify similarities which arose from generic connections between cultural units, no one had considered the means for evaluating the alternative of independent development, except by lack of ability to demonstrate historical connections. Without first gaining some understanding of laws of cultural development, such independent means for evaluating particular cases will continue to be lacking.

Despite these unsolved problems of method and our consequent inability to distinguish accurately between analogies and homologies, archeologists have continued to formulate reconstructions using the procedures set forth by Tylor and Graebner on a common sense level, often adding distributional criteria. The principles of interpretation which have guided archeologists' reconstructions of culture history can be summarized as follows:

1. The probability of diffusion having taken place increases directly with the degree of formal resemblance between items and traits (Jennings, 1957, p. 265; Linton, 1936, p. 372) and with the degree of componential complexity of the traits compared (Linton, 1936, p. 372).
2. The probability of diffusion having taken place decreases with the amount of temporal and spatial separation between the traits being compared (Linton, 1936, p. 370; for relevant discussions see Wallis, 1928; Meggers, Evans, and Estrada, 1965, pp. 157–78; and Rowe, 1966, pp. 334–37).

Such guides to interpretation ignore the inherent unsolved problems of method and epistemology, and most taxonomic schemes proposed as aids to historical reconstruction also fail to cope with them. For example, McKern in his discussion of the Midwestern Taxonomic System made it quite clear that classifications are to be made with respect to a list of culture traits undifferentiated as to the likelihood of their representing analogies or homologies:

> All the traits characteristic of a given culture manifestation comprise the culture complex for that manifestation. . . . In any comparison of this manifestation with another, made for purposes of classification, certain traits may be demonstrated as present in both complexes, and these linked traits [serve] to show cultural similarity between the two culture variants (1939, p. 205).

Numerous cases of the application of the Midwestern Taxonomic System (Smith, 1940; Cole and Deuel, 1937, pp. 207–219; Griffin, 1943; Morse, 1963) demonstrate that there was no attempt made to distinguish between analogous and homologous traits. (It should be pointed out, however, that the McKern system is internally consistent and logical; most of the problems with it have arisen from those who have misused it.) Other schemes have also employed summations of observations whose relevance to discussions of cultural phylogeny and contact might well be questioned (Gladwin, 1934; Colton, 1939). Rouse (1955) recognized the difference between classification based on gross measures of similarity and "genetic correlations"; he went on to suggest that for the purpose of historical reconstruction

> . . . it would seem advisable first to eliminate all those resemblances which

> do not appear to have been accompanied by contact. Next, one must decide which of the remaining resemblances are due to genetic connection rather than to some other factor such as adaptation to a similar environment or attainment of the same level of cultural development. Only then will it be safe to choose from among two various possible forms of genetic connection . . . (1955, p. 719).

However, Rouse offers no guidelines for deciding which traits are generically related and which ones might exhibit similarity from other causes. In short, Rouse's statement shows an awareness of many of the shortcomings of taxonomic schemes but offers no solution to one of the major underlying methodological problems.

It is argued here that the accomplishment of the reconstruction of culture history is predicated upon an overhaul of method and theory, that traditional methodology and analytical procedures are inadequate for the successful achievement of the stated aims of the field. Given our current sophistication in dating techniques, we can fairly accurately place archeological remains in their proper chronological relationships to one another. We can inventory the remains and discuss additions, deletions, and "hybridizations" in the inventories of sites through time. We can also formulate classifications of assemblages on the basis of summary measures of formal similarities between recovered items (see Ford, 1954); we can also measure likenesses by comparing the total composition of the sample of recovered materials (see Bordes, 1953). Arguments can then be formulated about the probability of one such taxon being the cultural ancestor, descendant, or collateral relative of another taxon (see Hodson *et al.*, 1966; Doran and Hodson, 1966), or whether another unit might be more appropriately considered (see Warren, 1967, pp. 168–85; Sanger, 1967, pp. 186–97; Aikens, 1967, pp. 198–209; and Schlesier, 1967, pp. 210–22).

These procedures, however, do not help to achieve the stated aims of archeology. An accurate and meaningful history is more than a generalized narrative of the changes in composition of the archeological record through time (see, for example, Griffin, 1967); it is also more than a reconstruction from that record using interpretive principles such as those discussed above which can be shown to have inherent flaws. If we hope to achieve the aim of reconstructing culture history, we must develop means for using archeological remains as a record of the past and as a source of data for testing propositions which we set forth regarding past events, rather than as a record we can read according to a set of a priori rules or interpretive principles whose application allow the skilled interpreter to "reconstruct" the past. We know much too little about both archeological data and processes of cultural development to make "reading the archeological record" anything but a shallow and suspicious pastime. What we seek to investigate is cultural process, and only with an understanding of such processes can we reconstruct the events which form the context in which the archeological record was produced.

RECONSTRUCTING PAST LIFEWAYS

The reconstruction of the lifeways of extinct peoples is the second aim of archeology which we will examine in order to evaluate traditional methods. The standard operating procedure for achieving this aim is set forth in the following quotation:

> Everyone is aware of the fact that is is impossible to explain and to give absolute meaning to all the discoveries which are made while digging ancient villages. All we can do is to interpret what we find in the light of our knowledge of modern . . . [peoples]. . . . In this way, it is possible to moderate our conjectures, and piece them together by means of reasonable imagination. Thus, the cold, unrelated and often dull archaeological facts are vivified and the reader may have some sort of reconstruction in his mind's eye of what [past peoples] . . . were like and how they lived. (Martin and Rinaldo, 1939, p. 457. [This statement is one of the first in the literature of American archeology that deals with the reconstruction of lifeways. Paul Martin was in the avant-garde of archeological thought in the 1930's, and he still is today. This quotation should in no way be considered a statement of his current views, which have grown and changed remarkably in thirty years—EDS.]).

Most archeologists would agree with this statement (see Willey, 1966, p. 3; Chang, 1967a, p. 109; Ascher, 1961). Analogy to living peoples has been the traditional answer to the question of how one goes about reconstructing lifeways (see Randall-MacIver, 1932, pp. 6–7; Hawkes, 1954, pp. 157–58; Vogt, 1956, p. 175; Piggott, 1965b, p. 12; Rouse, 1965, p. 10; Willey, 1966, pp. 3–4). The major controversy has concerned the appropriateness of a given ethnographically known group or set of conditions as a model for the lifeways of the groups under archeological study (see Lowie, 1940, pp. 369–70; Slotkin, 1952; S. R. Binford, 1968).

Given the method of analogy to living peoples, appeals have been made by archeologists to explore the record in search of units which can be meaningfully compared in analogies to living peoples. One obvious plea has been for archeologists to excavate the remains of entire communities, to concern themselves with the comparative study of settlement, as well as with the internal organization of sites. Taylor (1948), in appealing for archeologists to study in detail the contextual relationships among the archeological remains, asked for a search for order demonstrable among the elements in an archeological deposit. Willey (1953, 1956), Chang (1958, 1967a), and Trigger (1967) among others, have stressed the desirability of the investigation of settlement patterns, since these are observable among living peoples and are said to be informative about social organization.

Pleistocene archeologists also are increasingly viewing sites as the remains of activities conducted by social units; this kind of data collection is stressed in the search for living floors and in attempts at fairly complete excavation of sites.

> The living places of Pleistocene peoples are capable of yielding the same kind of evidence as to the behavior and ecology as do those of much later times when the appropriate techniques of exposure and excavation are applied to their recovery. . . . Such field studies . . . of . . . Paleolithic sites [are] infinitely more rewarding and significant, as can be . . . appreciated from papers . . . relating to living floor excavation (Clark and Howell, 1966, pp. v–vi).

Another aspect of data collection which has been dealt with in recent years is the problem of sampling. There has been frequent discussion of the use of sampling techniques which are designed to increase the probability that archeological samples taken are in fact representative of what remains from the past (see L. R. Binford, 1964; Rootenburg, 1964).

Along with these refinements in data collection, there has been a growing interest in the study of living peoples by archeologists (Crawford, 1953; Kleindienst and Watson, 1956; Thompson, 1958; Ascher, 1962; Watson, 1966). Such studies have as their aim the delineation of behavioral correlates for material items (Chang, 1958; Robbins, 1966), and the purpose of archeologists undertaking such research has been to maximize their interpretive powers by increasing their knowledge of living peoples —that is, to make more secure the analogies they draw between lifeways of peoples known archeologically and those known ethnographically.

While we applaud all attempts to increase the reliability of data collected archeologically, and while we certainly favor a firmer basis for determining the behavioral correlates of material culture, both refinements in data collection and increased ethnographic knowledge cannot by themselves increase our knowledge of the past. Facts do not speak for themselves, and even if we had complete living floors from the beginning of the Pleistocene through the rise of urban centers, such data would tell us nothing about cultural process or past lifeways unless we asked the appropriate questions. We can infinitely expand our knowledge of the lifeways of living peoples, yet we cannot reconstruct the lifeways of extinct peoples unless we employ a more sophisticated methodology. Fitting archeological remains into ethnographically known patterns of life adds nothing to our knowledge of the past. In fact, such a procedure denies to archeology the possibility of dealing with forms of cultural adaptation outside the range of variation known ethnographically (see S. R. Binford, 1968). In view of the high probability that cultural forms existed in the past for which we have no ethnographic examples, reconstruction of the lifeways of such sociocultural systems demands the rigorous testing of deductively drawn hypotheses against independent sets of data.

This perspective is in marked contrast to the epistemological basis of traditional method, whose implications can readily be seen in a recent statement:

> As to analogy, archaeology as a whole is analogy, for to claim any knowledge other than the objects themselves is to assume knowledge of patterns in culture and history and to apply these patterns to the facts (Chang, 1967a, p. 109).

I have criticized this view elsewhere (L. R. Binford, 1967a, 1967b, 1968) and would state here that so long as we insist that our knowledge of the past is limited by our knowledge of the present, we are painting ourselves into a methodological corner. The archeologist must make use of his data as documents of past conditions, proceed to formulate propositions about the past, and devise means for testing them against archeological remains. It is the testing of hypotheses that makes our knowledge of the past more certain, and this is admittedly a difficult business. Archeology as part of anthropology and anthropology as a social science are often guilty of the charges made against them by the "harder" scientists:

> The most important feature about a hypothesis is that is is a mere trial idea . . . [and] until it has been *tested*, it should not be confused with a *law*. . . . The difficulty of testing hypotheses in the social sciences has led to an abbreviation of the scientific method in which this step is simply omitted. Plausible hypotheses are merely set down as facts without further ado (Wilson, 1952, pp. 26–27).

Traditional archeological methodology has not developed this final link in scientific procedure. For this reason, reconstruction of lifeways has remained an art which could be evaluated only by judging the competence and honesty of the person offering the reconstruction (Thompson, 1956).

THE STUDY OF CULTURAL PROCESS

Different authors have referred to different phenomena in their discussions of culture process. The phrase has been used to refer to the dynamic relationships (causes and effects) operative among sociocultural systems, to those processes responsible for changes observed in the organization and/or content of the systems, or to the integration of new formal components into the system. The term cultural process has been used by others to refer to patterns or configurations in the temporal or spatial distributions of the archeological materials themselves (see Wauchope, 1966, pp. 19–38). The first set of meanings—that of dynamic relationships operative among cultural systems—is the one used by this author and by the other authors in this volume.

Let us examine the methods and procedures traditionally followed in seeking an understanding of culture process, regardless of the meaning given to the term. Most often, the procedure has been to equate process to a transformational sequence of forms, normally summarized in a stage classification. A second, or sometimes an alternative, procedure has been to pursue a comparative study of temporal and spatial changes of archeologically known cultural forms, to note certain trends or regularities. These trends are then stated as empirical generalizations which, in turn, are taken as statements regarding culture process (see Steward, 1949; Braidwood, 1952, 1960; Braidwood and Reed, 1957; Willey and Phillips, 1958; Willey, 1960; Beardsley *et al.*, 1956). The criticism to be offered here is that any stage classification is simply an ordinal scale for measurement. The application of such a scale to innumerable empirical cases, or even the ultimate systematization of all archeological materials, can never provide us with an understanding of the processes operative in the past which resulted in the stadial sequence. An empirical generalization of data—no matter how accurate it is—is never an explanation for the data. The ordering of forms of life, the end-products of evolution, by Linnaeus, did not describe or define the process of organic evolution.

Steward has suggested that the comparative study of distribution of cultural forms in space and through time will reveal certain trends, regularities, or patterns for which historical or generic interpretations are appropriate; he suggests further that these trends or patterns reflect cultural process (Steward, 1949, p. 3). This suggestion is, however, predicated on our ability to discriminate between cultural analogies and homologies. As pointed out above (pp. 8–11), methods for such discrimination have yet to be developed. Even if we were capable of making this distinction, the demonstration of empirical "regularities" simply documents similarities which need to be explained; it is to be hoped that the explanations offered would deal with cultural or ecological processes operative in the past.

Rouse (1964, 1965) has offered archeologists an "out," and his ideas undoubtedly have great appeal for those who would like to study cultural processes but lack the methods for doing so. He states that since we recognize a difference between the *process* of evolution and the *products* of evolution, that the study of the process should properly be the domain of ethnologists, "who are able to observe change as it is still going on" (Rouse, 1964, p. 465). He suggests further that the archeologists might more appropriately study the products of evolution in systematic terms—by descriptive taxonomic and distributional schemes. In this view, processes of cause and effect cannot legitimately be studied by archeologists, since they are not part of the archeological record, cannot be dug up, and are not available for direct observation.

Others, working within the traditional framework, have stated that archeologists *can* gain understanding of cultural process, and that the means for doing so is to interpret data from the past in the light of our understanding of the present. An example of this approach can be seen in what Willey and Phillips term "developmental interpretation"—a process which allows the archeologist to "abstract . . . certain characteristics that seem to have significance from the point of view of the general development of . . . culture" (Willey and Phillips, 1958, p. 77).

However, the decisions as to which characteristics are significant in the general development of culture do not derive from the data themselves; they are given meaning by the ideas we hold about the processes of cultural development. If we simply employ these ideas for interpreting archeological remains, then no new information can be gained from the archeological record about processes which operated in the past. In short, traditional archeological studies have often recognized the desirability of investigating process, but methods for successfully conducting such studies have not been developed. It is toward this end that much of the thought and work of the authors in this volume have been directed.

Archeological Theory and Method—New Perspectives

We have offered a brief review of the methods commonly employed for achieving the stated aims of archeology. In this section we hope to compare and contrast some aspects of traditional method and theory with very recent developments in the field which are substantively illustrated in this book. This discussion of theory and method will be conducted under several problem headings.

INDUCTION AND DEDUCTION

One striking feature of traditional archeological method, regardless of the aims of the research, has been the lack of any rigorous means of testing, and thereby gaining confidence in, propositions about the past. Statements about the historical, functional, or processual significance of observed characteristics of the archeological record have been evaluated by two criteria: (1) the degree to which our knowledge of contemporary peoples might justifiably be projected back to extinct sociocultural systems, and (2) the degree to which we might have confidence in the professional competence and intellectual honesty of the archeologist advancing interpretations (see Thompson, 1956, p. 33). Traditional methodology almost universally espouses simple induction as the appropriate procedure, and the archeological record is viewed as a body of phenomena from which one makes inductive inferences about the past. Such inferences are to be guided by our knowledge of contemporary peoples and also by certain principles, such as mechanical principles which govern the fracture of flint. The application of ethnographic knowledge and of guiding principles are the traditional means for increasing confidence in our inferential generalizations about the past.

Inference is the key or the methodological pivot of archaeology, for it is only

> through inference that inanimate objects are reassembled into the milieu of life. Inferences are drawn from analogies. . . (Willey, 1966, p. 3).

> At the inferential level, the archaeologist is at last providing the flesh for the bare bones of his data, and, if done with care and imagination, such a procedure makes possible the delineation and ultimate understanding of past cultures (Deetz, 1967a, p. 11).

The changes in archeology which are documented in this book are more than simply new methods and new theories; the changes consist of theories and methods developed in the context of a new epistemological perspective on such basic issues as the appropriate scientific procedures to be followed in investigating the past. In this perspective, a central point to be made concerns the role of induction in science:

> There can be no general rules of induction; the demand for them rests on a confusion of logical and psychological issues. . . . What determines the soundness of a hypothesis is not the way it is arrived at (it may have been suggested by a dream or a hallucination), but the way it stands up when tested, i.e., when confronted with relevant observational data (Hempel, 1965, p. 6).

In stressing induction and the drawing of sound inferences, then, the stress falls on the psychological issue, as pointed out by Hempel, of how to make meaningful statements about archeological remains and what they represent from the past. What is argued here is that the generation of inferences regarding the past should not be the end-product of the archeologist's work. While an awareness of as great a range of variability in sociocultural phenomena as possible and the citation of analogy to living peoples are not belittled here, the main point of our argument is that independent means of testing propositions about the past must be developed. Such means must be considerably more rigorous than evaluating an author's propositions by judging his professional competence or intellectual honesty.

We assert that our knowledge of the past is more than a projection of our ethnographic understanding. The accuracy of our knowledge of the past can be measured; it is this assertion which most sharply differentiates the new perspective from more traditional approaches. The yardstick of measurement is the degree to which propositions about the past can be confirmed or refuted through hypothesis testing—not by passing judgment on the personal qualifications of the person putting forth the propositions. The role of ethnographic training for archeologists, the use of analogy, and the use of imagination and conjecture are all fully acknowledged. However, once a proposition has been advanced—no matter by what means it was reached—the next task is to deduce a series of testable hypotheses which, if verified against independent empirical data, would tend to verify the proposition.

The shift to a consciously deductive philosophy, with the attendant emphasis on the verification of propositions through hypothesis testing, has far-reaching consequences for archeology. As an example of such consequences I will discuss briefly two topics commonly treated in presentations on archeological theory and method: the limitations of the archeological record, and the appropriate units of archeological observation.

LIMITATIONS OF THE ARCHEOLOGICAL RECORD

The arguments on this topic generally begin by citing the fact that much of the material content of an ongoing sociocultural system is lost through decay or the action of other physical agents (such as fire) before the time the archeologist can make his observations. It is then asserted that our knowledge of the past is limited to those classes of data which survive and that, depending on variations in past behavior, our knowledge of the operation of the sociocultural system in question may be enormously distorted (see, for example, Piggott, 1965a, p. 8). Such arguments also frequently take the form of asserting that since we can never know what is missing from the archeological record, we can never correctly evaluate what *is* present. How can we know that an empirical generalization about archeological data is accurate, since there may be pertinent and nonconforming evidence that has been lost? (See M. A. Smith, 1955, p. 6; Heider, 1967, p. 62; Deetz, 1968.)

An excellent example of reasoning of this kind is found in a recent discussion of the proper historical interpretation of distributions of African art styles:

> It is a curious fact that, with certain exceptions in Tanganyika, little rock art in the form of either painting or engraving, has been found north of the Zambezi. . . . It would appear that there is an almost complete break between the painting and engraving traditions of southern Africa and those of the Sahara. If this is so it makes the similarity between the two groups . . . appear as a striking example of parallel development. This would be a very hard case to prove . . . in view of the practice in many parts of the world of painting and engraving on such perishable substances as wood. . . . Indeed there is no reason to suppose that Late Stone Age man in East Africa and in the Congo did not paint or draw or engrave, simply because his work has not been preserved. . . (Allchin, 1966, p. 41).

Allchin's dilemma arises directly and inevitably from the fact that she is offering an empirical generalization directly from the data and makes use of an a priori principle for interpreting the historical-cultural significance of the generalization. In this case the unstated principle would be that an interrupted distribution signifies a cultural boundary and independence for the two traditions represented. If one accepts the interpretive principle, the only possible way of invalidating the interpretation is to question the validity of the empirical generalization itself (namely, that there is a geographical break between the painting and engraving traditions of southern Africa and those of the Sahara). The validity of the generalization can be destroyed by citing an empirical case to the contrary (an instance of painting or engraving in the "empty zone"). The generalization can also be challenged, and this is what Allchin does, by suggesting the possibility of such an empirical case to the contrary.

The possibility of an undocumented case to the contrary normally takes the form used in Allchin's argument—speculation about conditions under which data might be destroyed, overlooked, or "hidden." The validity of all generalizations may be questioned if this procedure is followed, since the possibilities for speculation about "hidden data" are infinite. Further, the validity of the interpretive principle itself can never be independently tested, since its accuracy is tested only by reference to the empirical generalization it is said to cover. Extension of the generalization to cover new cases simply provides more instances for which the principle might be relevant; it in no way tests the principle itself. Cases to the contrary of the generalization only show that the data generalized are inappropriate to the principle employed; they in no way serve to test the principle itself. This is one of the crucially weak points of a purely inductive methodology. Thus, Allchin's principle implicitly used for interpretation of her generalization cannot, with the methodology employed, be validated or refuted, and the generalization itself can always be questioned by the possibility of citing hidden data or the incompleteness of the archeological record.

The procedure we would advocate as a way out of Allchin's dilemma would be as follows:

Observations:

1. There is a geographical break in the archeological distribution of rock paintings and engravings between southern Africa and the Sahara.
2. The style of paintings and engravings from the two areas are very similar.

Proposition:

The geographic break is the result of there having been two independent cultural traditions in the respective areas.

Deduction:

Therefore, the similarity in form of painting and engraving is the result of parallel development.

Prediction:

We would expect a similar break in the distribution of stylistic attributes of other items—for example, bead forms, decoration on bone implements, projectile point forms, etc.

Bridging Arguments:

Here we would attempt to establish the relevance of some classes of archeological data to our deduction and prediction. We would try to establish that certain formal characteristics of artifacts, other than rock paintings and engravings, were stylistic and would therefore vary as a function of tradition.

Hypothesis:

The distribution of the data whose relevance has been argued will exhibit interrupted distributions between southern Africa and the Sahara.

If the hypothesis were confirmed, then arguments about hidden data would be irrelevant since the existence of cultural boundaries would have been established by independent data. If the hypothesis were refuted, arguments of hidden data, while possibly relevant to the original generalization, would in no way place limits on our ability to gain knowledge of cultural boundaries from the archeological record.

High-probability statements covering a broad range of phenomena are the aim of science, not empirical generalizations which can be destroyed by the citation of a single empirical case to the contrary. The endless search for data in harmony with empirical generalizations is a wasteful procedure at best, and the data can never serve to validate the generalization. Propositions can be evaluated by deducing hypotheses which must be tested against independent data. The argument of hidden data can always be made about generalizations, but it is significant only insofar as it prompts testing the validity of propositions made regarding the significance of the generalization. The citation of possible hidden data has no inherent value as a statement of limitation of our knowledge of the past, nor it is applicable to the truth or falsity of propositions. Confidence in any given proposition can be evaluated only with respect to the history of hypothesis formulation and with testing relevant to that proposition.

Another common argument on the limitations of the archeological record asserts that the reliability of conclusions reached by an archeologist varies directly with the degree to which the subject is removed from discussions of artifacts themselves (see MacWhite, 1956, pp. 4–6; Hawkes, 1954, p. 161; M. A. Smith, 1955, pp. 3–4; Piggott, 1965a, pp. 10–11).

> Artifacts and the study of artifacts—including typologies—are placed at the lowest level, and historic interpretations based upon such studies are considered to be of the greatest reliability. Moving into the socio-cultural system is moving up the levels of abstraction with increased use of inferences, and moving down the ladder of reliability. . . . Those who want to make inferences and to step beyond the limitations of archaeological remains can do so and engage in the fancy game of socio-cultural reconstruction (Chang, 1967a, pp. 12–13).

A frequent way of stating this argument is to propose a formal ladder of reliability:

> 1. To infer from the archaeological phenomena to the techniques producing them I take to be relatively easy. . . .
> 2. To infer to the subsistence-economies of the human groups concerned is fairly easy. . . .
> 3. To infer to the socio/political institutions of the groups, however, is considerably harder.
> 4. To infer to the religious institutions and spiritual life . . . is the hardest inference of all (Hawkes, 1954, pp. 161–62).

These statements are predicated upon two major premises: first, that the archeological record is incomplete, that many items of the material culture have been lost through decay, destruction, etc.; second, that the archeological record is lacking in all the non-material features of the sociocultural system under study. The conclusion is then drawn that the reliability of our interpretations will vary directly with the degree to which we can justify the acceptance of a partial record as representative of the total material culture, and also with the degree to which we can believe that the non-material components of any sociocultural system are reflected in the imperfectly preserved material items.

This reasoning is functionally linked to a methodology that limits the archeologist to generalizing about the "facts" he uncovers. Since preservation is always imperfect, inferences from the facts of material culture to statements about the non-material culture move us away from the primary data and thus diminish the reliability of our statements.

There has been a wide range of opinion expressed on this latter point—the degree to which non-material aspects of culture can be inferred from material facts; the ultraconservative range of this spectrum can be seen in the following statement:

> Since historical events and essential social divisions of prehistoric peoples don't find an adequate expression in material remains, it cannot be right to try to arrive at a knowledge of them through archaeological interpretation (M. A. Smith, 1955, p. 7).

Most of the authors in this volume would take strong exception to this statement. In the first place, the argument that archeologists must limit their knowledge to features of material culture is open to serious question; and second, the dichotomy between material and non-material aspects of culture itself and the relevance of this dichotomy for a proposed hierarchy of reliability have also been the subject of critical discussion (Service, 1964; L. R. Binford, 1962, 1965). It is virtually impossible to imagine that any given cultural item functioned in a sociocultural system independently of the operation of "non-material" variables. Every item has its history within a sociocultural system—its phases of procurement of raw material, manufacture, use, and final discarding (see Deetz, this volume). There is every reason to expect that the empirical properties of artifacts and their arrangement in the archeological record will exhibit attributes which can inform on different phases of the artifact's life history.

Many different determinants which were operative in the past might be cited as proper explanatory variables for archeologically recovered items. For example, pottery vessels manufactured in two different communities for use in identical tasks may vary significantly in form, depending on local habits of ceramic manufacture and on local design and decorative concepts. On the other hand, different forms of vessels made for different uses (for example, cooking *vs.* storage) might be produced with the same techniques and have similar decorative elements. In this latter case, the formal properties of the vessels relating to use would vary independently of formal properties relating to local ceramic techniques. It is conceivable that many other independently varying classes of attributes in combination might characterize the final form of any given class of item. Each kind of independently varying attribute might be relevant to a different set of determinants and would thus require independent explanation for their form and distribution in the archeological record. Each such independent explanation would, upon verification, inform us about the operation of different variables in the cultural system under study. It is highly improbable that the multiple, independent variables which determined the form of any item or the distribution of items should be restricted to only one component of a cultural system. This means that data relevant to most, if not all, the components of past sociocultural system *are* preserved in the archeological record (L. R. Binford, 1962, pp. 218–19).

Our task, then, is to devise means for extracting this information from our data, and this demands more than making summary generalizations about items of material culture. There is no reason to expect that our explanations of the archeological record should necessarily refer to the same order of phenomena as that being explained. If this is so, it follows that we cannot be restricted to the knowledge of "material culture"; rather, to explain our observations from the archeological record, we must deal with the full range of determinants which operate within any sociocultural system, extant or extinct.

There has been as yet no attempt to assess the limitations of the archeological record for yielding different kinds of information; nor does there seem to be the means of accurately determining these limits short of total knowledge of all the systematic relationships which characterized past cultural systems. Thus, present discussions of limitations of reliability are inappropriate and are based on speculation. And it is speculation which the more conservative exponents of such arguments have sought to avoid!

The position being taken here is that different kinds of phenomena are never remote; they are either accessible or they are not. "Non-material" aspects of culture are accessible in direct measure with the testability of propositions being advanced about them. Propositions concerning any realm of culture—technology, social organization, psychology, philosophy, etc.—for which arguments of relevance and empirically testable hypotheses can be offered are as sound as the history of hypothesis confirmation. The practical limitations on our knowledge of the past are not inherent in the nature of the archeological record; the limitations lie in our methodological naiveté, in our lack of development for principles determining the relevance of archeological remains to propositions regarding processes and events of the past.

UNITS OF OBSERVATION AND UNITS OF RELEVANCE: A BASIS FOR ANALYSIS

The shift to a rigorous hypothetico-deductive method with the goal of explanation implies changes also in our perception and use of the archeological record. Archeologists have normally accepted certain observational units—such as the item, the industry, or the assemblage—as the appropriate units for comparative investigation. Such investigation generally proceeds by breaking down archeological remains into categories based on raw materials: bone, stone, ceramics, basketry, etc. Or, in other cases, the investigator may use functional classes, such as projectile points, knives, axes, etc. Whatever the breakdown used, such analysis serves only to clarify information already available; it cannot increase our knowledge. After his initial comparative analysis, the archeologist may offer descriptive generalizations regarding his analytical categories; he may also offer some kind of synthetic statement, assigning categories to proposed events which presumably were the context in which the materials in question were produced. The end-product of this kind of analysis is normally comparison, either by verbal generalizations or summary statistics, among a series of sites in order to evaluate differences and similarities which are then used to reconstruct culture history or formulate statements about culture process.

One of the assumptions underlying such a procedure is that the analytical categories used are adequate and useful components of a nominal scale for measuring cultural differences and similarities. By definition the categories of a nominal scale are mutually exclusive and presumably part of an exhaustive scale which can accomodate all archeological observations (see Siegel, 1956, pp. 21–30; Blalock, 1960, pp. 11–16, for a discussion of scales for measurement). One other linked assumption is that information tabulated by such a scale is additive (this is well documented in Thompson *et al.*, 1956, pp. 42–45). Stated another way, the assumption is that culture consists of a single class of phenomena which can be accurately measured by our analytical units and about which accurate summary statements, based on those analytical units, can be made. When we compare the summary statements or statistics from a number of sites and observe differences or similarities, these are generally taken as indicators of degrees of cultural relationship.

We can criticize this kind of analysis on two grounds. First, it is highly questionable that the analytical categories used by archeologists actually measure a single class of phenomena; we would argue that they are measuring along several dimensions simultaneously, that culture is neither simple nor additive. Second, intuitively established analytical units, whose significance is not specified, can at best be of limited utility in testing hypotheses. For in hypothesis testing we must always be able to justify our observations as relevant measures of the variables identified in the propositions we have formulated (see Nagel, 1967, p. 10).

With respect to the first criticism—that culture is not additive and consists of more than summed traits—we would argue further that culture is a system of interrelated components. The archeological record must be viewed as the byproduct of the operation of such a system, and any single facet of that record can be referred back to multiple variables or components of that system. The determinants which operated to produce one part of the archeological record need not be, and probably are not, the same determinants which produced another part of the archeological record.

We may explain changes or differences in certain attributes of artifacts or features in terms of variations in prehistoric economy; such explanations may be largely irrelevant for explaining variations in motor habits as documented in the same artifacts. If we treat both these kinds of variation as undifferentiated measures of cultural difference, we are scarcely getting reliable information about past cultural systems. This same criticism is applicable to consideration of a single attribute and also to generalizations about summed attributes. A single characteristic observed in the archeological record might well be the compounded byproduct of a number of codeterminant variables.

An example of the confusion produced by treating independent variables as though they were one compounded variable can be seen if we take the case of measuring attributes of people rather than of artifacts. Let us assume that what we wish to explain is variation in human size, and the attribute we select as informing most economically on size is that of volume. We might proceed to measure a large number of people and even work out a taxonomy based on variation as measured by volume. The next step would be to attempt to explain variability in size and the distribution of size among human groups. We might investigate the degree to which size as measured by volume tends to covary with other variables such as environment, diet, disease, etc. Any such attempt would necessarily be doomed to failure, since at least two independent variables —height and weight—were being observed compounded into a single variable—volume. Someone who is 6½ feet tall and very thin might yield an identical value for volume as someone who is 5 feet tall and exceedingly stout. In studying the archeological record, there is no reason to expect that our units of observation are, in their form and distribution, referrable to the operation of a single variable in the past.

The crucial question for archeology is the relationship of our observations to the operation of past cultural systems. What are we measuring when we apply various scales to the archeological record: either nominal scales (typologies) or ordinal scales (stage classifications)? Do our stone tool typologies, for example, measure function or style, or do the attributes which define types involve two or more variables? At each juncture of explaining observations from the archeological record, we must question anew to what variables operative in the past our observations refer. Any explanatory proposition must be reasoned in terms of relevance to the operation of the cultural system under study (see Spaulding, 1957, p. 87). These arguments of relevance frequently result in the modification of our analytical units and the generation of further analytical categories. This procedure insures the expansion of our knowledge of the past, since it facilitates the testing of propositions. With the acceptance of a hypothetico-deductive method for archeology and the use of a multiple-stage scientific procedure—observation and generalization, formulation of explanatory propositions, testing these against the archeological data—it becomes evident that the analytical units employed in the initial stage may not be very useful during the final stages of testing. The sets of phenomena selected for observation, from the infinite number of possible observations, are not most profitably determined by the formal structure of the archeological record itself. On the contrary, they are data which we must justify as relevant to the particular propositions advanced and as useful for hypothesis testing. A crucial role is thus given to the development of analytical techniques and to the generation of increasingly accurate analytical units for measuring cultural and environmental variables. During the past thirty years archeologists have warned against the mixing of levels and inaccurate partitioning of archeological deposits; the warning offered here is against the analytical mixing of variables and against the partitioning of our observational universe into irrelevant analytical units.

Relevance is established by reference to the propositions being advanced and by the theoretical context of those propositions. We can anticipate that progress toward achieving the goals of archeology will be marked by continued refinement of the units of observation by which the archeological record can be summarized and by the development of more accurate and less multivariate scales for measurement.

Conclusions

I have attempted to point out rather specifically what is new about the new perspectives. In doing so, I have made several points of contrast with more traditional approaches. I have noted that most archeologists of whatever theoretical persuasion would agree on the triple aims of the discipline—reconstruction of culture history, reconstruction of extinct lifeways, and the delineation of culture process. There are, however, major differences among archeologists when it comes to theory and method, and it is argued that revamping traditional theory and method is essential for achieving any or all of the generally agreed-upon aims of the field.

The major methodological and theoretical points of contrast involve distinctions between cultural analogies and homologies, between culture viewed as a summation of traits and culture viewed as a system, between units of observation and units of analysis, between inductive and deductive approaches to the archeological record. A basic underlying problem involves the use of scales of measurement. It was argued that traditional archeological measures compound variables which probably operated independently in the past, and that a solution of the problem of measuring along several dimensions simultaneously must be reached in order to determine just what it is we *are* measuring. Despite remarkable advances in data collection techniques and in techniques of analysis, so long as the data from the past are considered within the framework of traditional theory, they can bring nothing new to bear on our knowledge of the past. It is a concern with the nature of knowledge, with the testing and verification of hypotheses, and with the relevance of questions asked that distinguishes much of the work in this book. We assume that the past is knowable; that with enough methodological ingenuity, propositions about the past are testable; and that there are valid scientific criteria for judging the probability of a statement about the past besides ad hominem arguments or "common sense."

The problems raised by the relationship of theory, method, and question-asking were elegantly dealt with fifteen years ago by Sherwood L. Washburn. Although Washburn was writing specifically about physical anthropology, his statement seems uncannily relevant for archeology in the 1960's:

> The assumption seems to have been that description (whether morphological or metrical), if accurate enough and in sufficient quantity, could solve problems of process, pattern, and interpretation. . . . But all that can be done with the initial descriptive information is to gain a first understanding, a sense of problem, and a preliminary classification. To get further requires an elaboration of theory and method along different lines (Washburn, 1953, pp. 714–15).

The elaboration of theory and method which characterizes much of the recent work in archeology consists minimally of two elements: First, the active search for understanding variability in the archeological record—all of the variability and not just that judged a priori to be significant; second, an attempt to explain variability scientifically, rather than by conjecture or by "hunch." Some variability may be more apparent than real and may reflect sampling error, partial erosion, redeposition, etc. Only with the self-conscious use of sophisticated method can this "noise" be factored out. Many kinds of variation will be shown to be the result of the normal functioning of internally differentiated cultural systems; others may document evolutionary changes within cultural systems. Still other kinds of variation may reflect changes in content within an essentially stable cultural system. In our search for explanations of differences and similarities in the archeological record, our ultimate goal is the formulation of laws of cultural dynamics.

Many of the authors in this volume would agree that advances in achieving the aims of archeology necessitate the enforced obsolescence of much of traditional theory and method, and thus many of the papers in this book are radical in the original sense of the word. If we are successful, many traditional archeological problems will prove to be irrelevant, and we will see an expansion of the scope of our question-asking which today would make us giddy to contemplate. Despite a recent statement that one should not speak of a "new archeology" since this alienates it from the old (Chang, 1967a, p. 3), we feel that archeology in the 1960's is at a major point of evolutionary change. Evolution always builds on what went before, but it always involves basic structural changes.

In a rather caustic analysis of the field of archeology, Spaulding has stated that apparently

> . . . truth is to be determined by some sort of polling of archaeologists, that productivity is doing what other archaeologists do, and that the only purpose of archeology is to make archaeologists happy (Spaulding, 1953, p. 590).

We think that this statement was more appropriate in 1953 than it is today, and its inappropriateness today is a rough measure of the extent to which our field has advanced.

References

AIKENS, C. MELVIN. 1967. Plains relationships of the Fremont Culture: a hypothesis. *American Antiquity,* 32(2): 198–209.

ALLCHIN, BRIDGET. 1966. *The stone tipped arrow, late Stone Age hunters of the tropical Old World.* New York: Barnes and Noble.

ASCHER, ROBERT. 1961. Analogy in archaeological interpretation. *Southwestern Journal of Anthropology,* 17(4): 317–25.

——. 1962. Ethnography for archeology: a case from the Seri Indians. *Ethnology,* 1(3): 360–69.

BARTH, FREDRIK. 1950. Ecologic adaptation and cultural change in archaeology. *American Antiquity,* 15(4): 338–39.

BEARDSLEY, R. K. *et al.* 1956. Functional and evolutionary implications of community patterning. In Robert Wauchope (Ed.), *Seminars in archaeology*: a special publication of *American Antiquity,* 22(2), Part 2: 129–57.

BENNETT, JOHN W. 1943. Recent developments in the functional interpretation of archaeological data. *American Antiquity,* 8(2): 208–219.

BINFORD, L. R. 1962. Archaeology as anthropology. *American Antiquity,* 28(2): 217–25.
——. 1964. A consideration of archaeological research design. *American Antiquity,* 29(4): 425–41.
—— 1965. Archaeological systematics and the study of culture process. *American Antiquity,* 31(2): 203–210.
——. 1967a. Smudge pits and hide smoking: the role of analogy in archaeological reasoning. *American Antiquity,* 32(1): 1–12.
——. 1967b. Comment on K. C. Chang's "Major aspects of the interrelationship of archaeology and ethnology." *Current Anthropology,* 8(3): 234–35.
——. 1968. Methodological considerations of the archeological use of ethnographic data. In Richard B. Lee and Irven DeVore (Eds.), *Man the hunter.* Chicago: Aldine Publishing Company.
BINFORD, SALLY R. 1968. Ethnographic data and understanding the Pleistocene. In Richard B. Lee and Irven DeVore (Eds.), *Man the hunter.* Chicago Aldine Publishing Company.
BLALOCK, HUBERT M., JR. 1960. *Social statistics.* New York: McGraw-Hill.
BORDES, FRANÇOIS. 1953. Essai de classification des industries "moustériennes." *Bulletin de la Société Préhistorique Française,* 50(7 and 8): 457–66.
BRAIDWOOD, ROBERT J. 1952. The Near East and the foundations for Civilization. Condon Lectures. Eugene: University of Oregon.
——. 1959. *Archeology and the evolutionary theory.* In *Evolution and anthropology: a centennial appraisal,* pp. 76–89. Washington, D.C.: Anthropological Society of Washington.
——. 1960. Levels in prehistory, a model for the consideration of the evidence. In Sol Tax (Ed.), *The evolution of man* (Vol. 2 of *Evolution after Darwin*). Chicago: University of Chicago Press.
BRAIDWOOD, ROBERT J., and CHARLES REED. 1957. The achievement and early consequences of food production. *Cold Spring Harbor Symposia in Quantitative Biology,* 22: 19–31.
CALDWELL, JOSEPH R. 1958. The new American archeology. *Science,* 129 (3345): 303–307.
CHANG, KWANG-CHIH. 1958. Study of the Neolithic social grouping: examples from the New World. *American Anthropologist,* 60(2): 298–334.
——. 1967a. *Rethinking archaeology.* New York: Random House.
——. 1967b. Major aspects of the interrelationship of archaeology and ethnology. *Current Anthropology,* 8(3): 227–34.
CHILDE, V. GORDON. 1936. *Man makes himself.* London: Watts and Co.
——. 1946. Archaeology and anthropology. *Southwestern Journal of Anthropology,* 2(3): 243–51.
CLARK, GRAHAME. 1951. *Star Carr.* Cambridge: Cambridge University Press.
——. 1953a. The economic approach to prehistory. *Proceedings of the British Academy,* 39: 215–38.
——. 1953b. Archaeological theories and interpretation: Old World. In A. L. Kroeber (Ed.), *Anthropology today.* Chicago: University of Chicago Press.
CLARK, J. DESMOND, and F. CLARK HOWELL. 1966. Preface. In J. Desmond Clark and F. Clark Howell (Eds.), *Recent studies in paleoanthropology,* a special publication of the *American Anthropologist,* 68(2), Part 2.
COLE, FAY-COOPER, and THORNE DEUEL. 1937. *Rediscovering Illinois.* Chicago: University of Chicago Press.
COLTON, HAROLD S. 1939. Prehistoric culture units and their relationships in northern Arizona. *Bulletin* 17. Flagstaff: Museum of Northern Arizona.

CRAWFORD, O. G. S. 1953. *Archaeology in the field.* London: Phoenix House.

DEETZ, JAMES. 1967. *Invitation to archaeology.* Garden City, N.Y.: American Museum Science Books, Natural History Press.

——. 1968. The archeological visibility of food-gatherers. In Richard B. Lee and Irven DeVore (Eds.), *Man the hunter.* Chicago: Aldine Publishing Company.

DORAN, J. E., and F. R. HODSON. 1966. A digital computer analysis of Palaeolithic flint assemblages. *Nature,* 210 (5037): 688–89.

ERASMUS, CHARLES J. 1950. Patolli, parchisi, and the limitation of possibilities. *Southwestern Journal of Anthropology,* 6(4): 369–87.

FORD, J. A. 1954. The type concept revisited. *American Anthropologist,* 56 (1): 42–54.

GLADWIN, HAROLD S. 1934. A method for designation of cultures and their variations. *Medallion Papers,* (15). Globe, Ariz.: Gila Pueblo.

GRAEBNER, FRITZ. 1911. *Methode der Ethnologie.* Heidelberg: Universitätsbuchhandlung.

GRIFFIN, JAMES B. 1943. *The Fort Ancient aspect.* Ann Arbor: University of Michigan Press.

——. 1967. Eastern North American archaeology: a summary. *Science,* 156 (3772): 175–91.

HAWKES, CHRISTOPHER. 1954. Archeological theory and method: some suggestions from the Old World. *American Anthropologist,* 56(1): 155–68.

HEIDER, KARL G. 1967. Archaeological assumptions and ethnographical facts: a cautionary tale from New Guinea. *Southwestern Journal of Anthropology,* 23(1): 52–64.

HEMPEL, CARL G. 1965. *Aspects of scientific explanation.* New York: The Free Press.

HODSON, F. R., P. H. A. SNEATH, and J. E. DORAN. 1966. Some experiments in the numerical analysis of archaeological data. *Biometrika,* 53(3 and 4): 311–24.

JENNINGS, JESSE D. 1957. Danger Cave. Memoir of the Society for American Archaeology no. 14, *American Antiquity,* 23(2), Part 2.

KROEBER, A. L. 1937. Archaeology. In *Encyclopedia of the Social Sciences,* Vol. 2.

KLEINDIENST, MAXINE R., and PATTY JO WATSON. 1956. Action archeology: the archeological inventory of a living community. *Anthropology Tomorrow,* 5 (1): 75–78.

LINTON, RALPH. 1936. *The study of man.* New York: Appleton-Century-Crofts.

LOWIE, ROBERT H. 1912. The principle of convergence in ethnology. *Journal of American Folk-Lore,* 25(45): 24–42.

——. 1940. *An introduction to cultural anthropology.* (2d ed.) New York: Farrar and Rinehart.

MCKERN, W. C. 1939. The Midwestern taxonomic method as an aid to archaeological culture study. *American Antiquity,* 4(2): 301–313.

MACWHITE, EOIN. 1956. On the interpretation of archeological evidence in historical and sociological terms. *American Anthropologist,* 58(1): 3–25.

MARTIN, PAUL S., and JOHN RINALDO. 1939. Modified Basket Maker sites Ackmen-Lowry area southwestern Colorado. *Anthropological Series, Field Museum of Natural History,* 23(3), Publication 444: 307–444.

MASON, OTIS T. 1893. The birth of invention. In *Annual Report Smithsonian Institution for 1892.* Washington, D.C.: Smithsonian Institution.

MEGGERS, BETTY J., CLIFFORD EVANS, and EMILLIO ESTRADA. 1965. Early form-

ative period of coastal Ecuador: the Valdivia and Machalilla phases. *Smithsonian Contributions to Anthropology*, Vol. 1. Washington, D.C.: Smithsonian Institution.
MORSE, DAN F. 1963. The Steuben village and mounds: a multicomponent late Hopewell site in Illinois. *Anthropological Papers*, no. 21. Ann Arbor: Museum of Anthropology, University of Michigan.
NAGEL, ERNEST. 1967. The nature and aim of science. In Sidney Morganbesser (Ed.), *Philosophy of science today*. New York: Basic Books.
PIGGOTT, STUART. 1965a. *Ancient Europe: from the beginnings of agriculture to classical antiquity*. Chicago: Aldine Publishing Company.
——. 1965b. *Approach to archaeology*. New York, Toronto: McGraw-Hill Paperbacks, Harvard University Press.
RANDALLH-MACIVER, DAVID. 1932. Archaeology as a science. *Antiquity*, 7(1): 5–20.
RANDS, ROBERT L., and CARROLL L. RILEY. 1958. Diffusion and discontinuous distribution. *American Anthropologist*, 60 (2): 274–97.
ROBBINS, MICHAEL C. 1966. House types and settlement patterns: an application of ethnology to archaeological interpretation. *The Minnesota Archaeologist*, 28(1): 3–35.
ROOTENBERG, S. 1964. Archaeological field sampling. *American Antiquity*, 30 (2): 111–88.
ROUSE, IRVING. 1955. On the correlation of phases of culture. *American Anthropologist*, 57(4): 713–22.
——. 1964. Archaeological approaches to cultural evolution. In Ward Goodenough (Ed.), *Explorations in cultural anthropology*. New York: McGraw-Hill.
——. 1965. The place of "peoples" in prehistoric research. *Journal of the Royal Anthropological Institute*, 95(1): 1–15.
ROWE, JOHN HOWLAND. 1966. Diffusionism and archaeology. *American Antiquity*, 31(3): 334–37.
SACKETT, JAMES R. 1966. Quantitative analysis of Upper Paleolithic stone tools. In J. Desmond Clark and F. Clark Howell (Eds.), *Recent studies in paleoanthropology*, a special publication of the *American Anthropologist*, 68(2), Part 2: 356–94.
SANGER, DAVID. 1967. Prehistory of the Pacific northwest plateau as seen from the interior of British Columbia. *American Antiquity*, 32(2): 186–97.
SCHLESIER, KARL H. 1967. Sedna Creek: report on an archaeological survey of the arctic slope of the Brooks Range. *American Antiquity*, 32(2): 210–24.
SERVICE, ELMAN R. 1964. Archaeological theory and ethnological fact. In Robert A. Manners (Ed.), *Process and pattern in culture: essays in honor of Julian H. Steward*. Chicago: Aldine Publishing Company.
SIEGEL, SIDNEY. 1956. *Nonparametric statistics for the behavorial sciences*. New York: McGraw-Hill
SLOTKIN, J. S. 1952. Some basic methodological problems in prehistory. *Southwestern Journal of Anthropology*, 8(4): 442–43.
SMITH, BENJAMIN L. 1940. The Midwestern taxonomic method and its application to an eastern Massachusetts group. *Bulletin of the Massachusetts Archaeological Society*, 2(1): 1-13.
SMITH, H. I. 1910. Prehistoric ethnology of a Kentucky site. *Anthropological Papers*, 6(2). New York: American Museum of Natural History.
SMITH M. A. 1955. The limitations of inference in archaeology. *Archaeological Newsletter*, 6: 3–7.
SOLLAS, W. J. 1924. *Ancient hunters and their modern representatives*. (3d rev. ed.) New York: Macmillan.

SPAULDING, A. C. 1953. Review of "Measurements of some prehistoric design developments in the southeastern states" by James A. Ford. *American Anthropologist,* 55(4): 588–91.

——. 1957. Review of "Method and theory in American archaeology," by Gordon R. Willey and Philip Phillips. *American Antiquity,* 23 (1): 85–87.

STEWARD, JULIAN H. 1937. Ecological aspects of southwestern society. *Anthropos,* 32: 87–114.

——. 1942. The direct historical approach to archaeology. *American Antiquity,* 7(4): 337–43.

——. 1949. Culture causality and law: a trial formulation of the development of early civilizations. *American Anthropologist,* 51(1): 1–28.

——. 1960. Evolutionary principles and social types. In Sol Tax (Ed.), *The evolution of man* (vol. 2 of *Evolution after Darwin*). Chicago: University of Chicago Press.

STEWARD, JULIAN H., and FRANK M. SETZLER. 1938. Function and configuration in archaeology. *American Antiquity,* 4(1): 4–10.

STEWARD, JULIAN H., *et al.* 1955. Irrigation civilizations: a comparative study. *Social Science Monographs I.* Washington, D.C.: Pan American Union.

TALLGREN, A. M. 1937. The method of prehistoric archaeology. *Antiquity,* 11(42): 152–61.

TAYLOR, WALTER W. 1948. A study of archeology. Memoir No. 69. *American Anthropologist,* 50(3), Part 2.

THOMPSON, RAYMOND H. 1956. The subjective element in archaeological inference. *Southwestern Journal of Anthropology,* 12(3): 327–32.

——. 1958. Modern Yucatan Maya pottery making. Memoirs of the Society for American Archaeology, no. 15, *American Antiquity,* 23(4), Part 2.

TRIGGER, BRUCE G. 1967. Settlement archaeology–its goals and promise. *American Antiquity,* 32(2): 149–59.

TYLOR, E. B. 1896. On American lot-games as evidence of Asiatic intercourse before the time of Columbus. *Internationales Archiv für Ethnographie,* Vol. 9.

VOGT, EVON Z. 1956. An appraisal of "Prehistoric settlement patterns in the New World." In Gordon R. Willey (Ed.), *Prehistoric settlement patterns in the New World.* Viking Fund Publications in Anthropology No. 23. New York: Wenner-Gren Foundation for Anthropological Research.

WALLIS, WILSON D. 1928. Probability and the diffusion of culture traits. *American Anthropologist,* 30(1): 94–106.

WARREN, CLAUDE N. 1967. The San Dieguito complex: a review and hypothesis. *American Antiquity,* 32(2): 168–85.

WASHBURN, S. L. 1953. The strategy of physical anthropology. In A. L. Kroeber (Ed.), *Anthropology today.* Chicago: University of Chicago Press.

WATSON, PATTY JO. 1966. Clues to Iranian prehistory in modern village life. Philadelphia: University Museum of the University of Pennsylvania.

WAUCHOPE, ROBERT. 1966. Archaeological survey of northern Georgia, with a test of some cultural hypotheses. *American Antiquity,* 3(5), Part 2. Memoir no. 21.

WHITE, LESLIE A. 1943. Energy and the evolution of culture. *American Anthropologist,* 45(3): 335–56.

WILLEY, GORDON R. 1953. Prehistoric settlement patterns in the Viru Valley, Peru. *Bureau of American Ethnology Bulletin 155.* Washington, D.C.: Smithsonian Institution.

——. 1956. (Ed.) Prehistoric settlement patterns in the New World. Viking Fund Publications in Anthropology No. 23. New York: Wenner-Gren Foundation for Anthropological Research.

——. 1960. Historical patterns and evolution in native New World cultures. In Sol Tax (Ed.), *The evolution of man* (Vol. 2 of *Evolution after Darwin*). Chicago: University of Chicago Press.
——. 1962. The early great styles and the rise of the Pre-Columbian civilizations. *American Anthropologist*, 64(1): 1–14.
——. 1966. *An introduction to American archaeology*. Vol. 1: *North and Middle America*. Englewood Cliffs, N.J.: Prentice-Hall.
WILLEY, GORDON R., and PHILIP PHILLIPS. 1958. *Method and theory in American archaeology*. Chicago: University of Chicago Press.
WILSON, E. BRIGHT, JR. 1952. *An introduction to scientific research*. New York: McGraw-Hill.

TWO

ALBERT C. SPAULDING

Explanation in Archeology

My intention here is to produce an argument or, stated more cautiously, a sketch of an argument to the general effect that the papers in this volume and the remarks of the commenters are clear examples of the convergence of the theoretical underpinnings of archeologists and social anthropologists. The argument turns on (1) the abandonment in effect by both groups of the notion of historical explanation as a valid category of intellectual activity and, with even more force, of scientific activity, and (2) the explicit recognition by social anthropologists of the technically imperfect nature of social systems. A careful argument of this nature would present a voluminous and fully documented history of anthropology to support these assertions, but owing to limitations of space and ambition I will rely instead on what I hope are persuasive allusions to well-known main trends in anthropological theorizing. Some characteristic items exemplifying these trends are such statements as: by and by, anthropology will be history or it will be nothing; culture areas have lost most (or all) of the theoretical significance formerly ascribed to them, but they remain convenient devices for organizing data; anthropology, like astronomy, belongs in the category of historical sciences; the present can be understood only in terms of the past; culture history is for dilettantes, and it contributes nothing to real anthropology; and so on. The major import of these statements seems to be that there are, or were, two kinds of anthropologists with rival claims to anthropological truth. One kind asserts that satisfactory understanding of anthropological data is a matter of historical explanation, the other that understanding lies rather in generalizations derived from analyses of functioning social systems. The remainder of this paper is an attempt to show that a consideration of the nature of explanation, history, historical science, and anthropology leads to the dismissal of these rival claims and to a satisfactory theoretical foundation for interrelating all types of anthropological data.

My discussion of explanation is derived from a selective scanning of the work of various philosophers of science, among whom the topic seems to be a lively one. It is not true, however, that an appeal to philosophers is an appeal to ultimate authority; the task of philosophy of science is to describe in general terms what scientists do, not to legislate on what they can or cannot do. But it is true that philosophers are impressively skillful at their special business and that the problem at hand involves generalizations that are squarely within this area of special competence. The discussion that follows is an attempt to apply a point of view especially associated with the work of Carl G. Hempel, and the essential features of the matter are set out in Hempel (1962), Brodbeck (1962), Kaplan (1964), and references cited by these authors.

The issue which seems directly relevant here is whether or not there are two kinds of explanations of the way in which the world works—historical explanation with its appropriate body of data, and scientific explanation with a second kind of associated data. If there are two fundamentally different kinds of serious explanation, it may well be that both are appropriate for anthropology, depending on the nature of the data considered, and there may be two anthropologies linked only by a common interest in customary human behavior. If there is only one kind, then the interrelationships of the various kinds of anthropology will have to be analyzed on some other ground.

The view which I find convincing is attractively simple: there is only one kind of serious explanation, the nomological or covering-law explanation. All serious explanations relate the circumstance to be explained to relevant general laws or at least to empirical generalization. Explanations may be deductive, in which case the covering law admits of no exceptions, or they may be probabilistic-statistical (or inductive, if you prefer), in which case the covering law has the form of a frequency distribution. Explanations may be causal (when they identify some more or less complex set of antecedent circumstances as sufficient to produce that which is to be explained) or they may not be causal (when they refer to some law of coexistence rather than to a law of succession; for example, the laws on the volume, temperature, and pressure of gases, or the laws on the length and period of a pendulum). Explanations may be complete, as in the case of the universal covering laws of nomological-deductive explanations (all relevant variables are taken into account), or they may be partial, that is, account for the occurrence of the general class of circumstance to be explained but not of the narrow class to which the circumstance belongs. The idea of completeness here refers only to some selected aspect or aspects of the event or thing to be explained; the notion of a complete explanation of any particular event is self-defeating for obvious reasons.

What has become of the historical explanation? The leading candidate for a peculiarly historical explanation, the so-called "genetic explanation," can be shown to be nomological in character; the mere recitation of a list of successive events is not an explanation at all unless there are implicit laws or empirical generalizations linking the events. The list of prior events which explains something must have been selected with some criterion of relevance if the explanation is to be successful. "There is no such thing as 'historical' explanation, only the explanation of historical events" (Brodbeck, 1962, p. 254).

If this disposal of the historical explanation is accepted, we can turn to the problem of history, historical science, and anthropology with a new point of view. As a first observation, it is not possible to link anthropology and history on the basis of the common possession of a special kind of explanation, nor is it possible to separate them on the ground that they use different kinds of explanation. In fact, it is not possible to distinguish between history and science at all by means of broad types of explanation, and we can ask on what ground, if any, they can be distinguished. The answer, is, I think, that history and science can be distinguished by the degree of explicitness of the covering laws (or empirical generalizations) which make explanation possible. History and science share a set of techniques for producing warranted or intersubjectively verifiable knowledge, but the explanatory generalizations of history are characteristically matters of common knowledge on human dispositions or motivations, and they are quite properly implicit rather than explicit in the historical narrative. It is for this reason that skillful historical narratives are so immediately satisfying; the historian and the reader possess in common the implicit generalizations that make sense of the narrative. Science, on the other hand, has as its avowed goal the production of explicit, formal laws to provide a basis for the deductive explanation of particular things and events. In history, the stock of explanatory generalizations is given as primitive concepts; in science, the search for increasingly broad explanatory generalizations is the characteristic preoccupation. History has a particularizing quality (note the phrase "for historical reasons"); science, a generalizing one.

All of this leads directly to the question of whether or not anthropology is a science. There seems to be general agreement among anthropologists that it is, at least by intention and aspiration, however short it may fall of the deductive elegance of physics. The goal of anthropology is presumably the explanation of the similarities and differences of customary behavior in all possible pairs of societies, past and present, and common knowledge of human dispositions is clearly not equal to this task. Although it may be true that anthropologists have not advanced very far toward the goal of deductive elegance, it seems plain enough that they are trying to point in this direction. Anthropologists are devising objective measuring instruments, looking for association, and thinking about connecting generalizations.

Granted that anthropology is a science, what are the implications of the old idea that it is a historical science as opposed to some other kinds of science? If "historical science" means a science in which successive transformations of things and classes of events over a substantial span of time is of fundamental importance, then it is apparent that anthropology is a historical science, as Kroeber, Sapir, and others pointed out. The contrast here is with laboratory science; the materials of anthropology are complex and the processes are slow. The implication is that they must be observed in the field and that description must be elaborate because of the complicated interaction of the many variables in every social situation. Laboratory sciences, on the other hand, can isolate relevant variables and duplicate processes under controlled conditions. Taken in this sense, there is no reason to quarrel with the characterization of anthropology as a historical science. The only point to be made is that a historical science is no less a science for being historical.

There is a second sense in which the adjective "historical" can be applied to anthropology. In this sense, the implication is that anthropology is like history not only because of its preoccupation with successive events but also because, as is the case with history, already well-understood human dispositions are adequate for explanation. This position in effect either denies the status of a science to anthropology, as I have done with history, or claims that there is no possibility of developing further explanatory generalizations, whatever the intentions of anthropologists may be. In the second case, anthropology would be in a state of permanently arrested development; new data would be simply more of the same thing appropriately presented in particularistic, historical fashion. This latter claim is a factual one; it can be refuted only by the discovery of more laws or empirical generalizations. Social anthropology and the papers of this symposium are representative attempts to refute this claim.

Anthropology, like social science in general, can be contrasted with that paradigm of science, classical mechanics, in terms of other aspects of explanation. Clearly, anthropological explanations are characteristically probabilistic-statistical rather than deductive, and they are partial rather than complete. This is the penalty for dealing with anything so multidimensional and unwieldy as human behavior, and there is no easy remedy. Anthropologists are not forbidden, however, to struggle toward covering generalizations with greater powers of prediction and retrodiction. They can strive to sharpen statements of the frequency distributions underlying probabilistic explanations, to make explanations more complete. In the case of causal vs. non-causal explanations, have little to say simply because I cannot think of any examples of non-causal explanations in anthropology. In short, anthropology is a science not because it is just like physics in every respect. It is a science because, or insofar as, it examines its data with the object of discovering systematic interrelationships therein, and it is a successful science insofar as it is able to explain its data by means of these interrelationships.

I turn now to the question of whether or not there are profound differences among the various activities conventionally embraced by the term "anthropology" as it is used in the United States. I have excluded the possibility of distinguishing between activities on the basis of whether or not historical explanation is a characteristic instrument by arguing that there are no historical explanations and that probably all anthropological explanations are causal, partial, and probabilistic. It is nevertheless true that some aspects of anthropology appear to be historical in some meaningful sense of the concept while others do not. Prehistoric archeology, with its explicit interest in chronology and its heavy content of particularistic description, is the obvious choice to represent the historical branch of anthropology. Social anthropology, with its stated lack of interest in history and its interest in functional relationships, is an equally obvious candidate for a non-historical anthropology.

Certainly archeologists consider their subject to have a strong historical component. Archeology is, after all, the study of the past. The connection with history is revealed by the term "prehistory" and by the linking of anthropological and undoubted historical research through the common employment of the technique called "archeology." And it is archeologists who keep asserting that the present can be understood only through the past, although I am not aware that anyone making this claim has produced a respectable explanation of why we can understand the present only in terms of the past or even an explanation of just what is meant by the assertion. It seems that a discussion of the place of archeology within anthropology might better begin by reversing the dictum and asserting that the past can be understood only through the present. All studies of the past are conducted by taking present objects (or present memories) as relics of the past and drawing inferences as to past events from them. The premises by means of which the inferences are drawn are based on observations of present things, events, and relationships. Moreover, the implied claim that the past influences the present has the magical quality of action at a distance unless it is carefully qualified. All of this being the case, archeologists must be regarded as primarily consumers rather than producers of anthropological knowledge and theories. They illuminate the past through application of this knowledge, and they are successful insofar as there is a good stock of knowledge to apply to their relics and insofar as they are diligent in seeking out and applying this knowledge.

Despite this undeniably dependent role, however, archeologists are not merely passive consumers of anthropological knowledge. This is so because they also apply non-anthropological knowledge to their relics to produce plausible inferences as to relative and absolute age, ecological circumstances, and other relevant dimensions of cultural variation. In so doing, they contribute independent data to theories of sequence of forms and rate of change of at least some aspects of customary behavior. The chronological data are clues to the identification of antecedent and consequent conditions in slow-moving cultural transformations. I conclude that prehistoric archeology is indeed historical in the sense of having a primary interest in objects of the past, but that this historicism is a beneficent state that does not imply that archeology should be cast out from either science or anthropology. Archeology is scientific to the degree that it is anthropological, and it is anthropological to the degree that anthropology can provide cogent premises for inferences about archeological data. In fact, archeology as such is simply a technique (essentially digging holes in the ground or stooping over to pick up objects) which can be employed in the service of anthropology, history, or amusement.

Social anthropology, or an idealized version of social anthropology, is a much closer approach to our polar type of non-historical science. In purest form, the units of study are existing human societies, and the attributes or variables in terms of which the societies are studied are the class of behavioral events directly concerned with interpersonal relationships. In conventional terms, social anthropologists study kinship and social organization. A central activity of social anthropologists is the intensive study of a society to produce a description of the social structure and an analysis of the functions performed by the various elements of the structure, although completely satisfactory explications of the concepts of structure and function do not seem to have been attained. It appears that the goal of social anthropology is to achieve through comparative studies a typology of social organization together with transformation rules for successions of types. There are indications of a claim of logical priority of social analysis, presumably on the ground that explanations of societies are what anthropology is really about and that social organization is the heart of the matter. There are (or were) also indications of a goal of closure: an attempt to treat social organization as a closed system, a system which could be described and explained solely in terms of interacting social variables. This goal excludes historical (particularistic) studies of efficient causes; identification of individual circumstances connected with a social innovation are unimportant. What is important is why the innovation is incorporated into the social system. Social anthropology as a program for research is beyond criticism. If its researches succeed in demonstrating an independent order of social phenomena explicable in their own terms, then social anthropology is a new science. It might then perhaps be considered a historical science in the sense that its phenomena are not endlessly repeatable in a laboratory, but its historicism would not constitute any important link with archeology. Archeologists do not dig up social structures, and social anthropologists would not speak of artifacts or relationships among artifacts.

This discussion can be ended on a question of fact. As I interpret the results of a hundred years of anthropology and something like forty years of social anthropology, there is abundant evidence that social systems are not closed systems. Instead, they are articulated at almost every point with biologically and environmentally oriented behavior. Social anthropology is a research specialty and a research program, not an independent science. Social anthropologists speak of subsistence techniques and economic principles because they must if they are to have adequate explanations of social phenomena. Cultural ecology and cross-cultural investigations of associations between social and technological behavior are the necessary link between the poles of archeology and social anthropology, between artifacts and behavior.

The papers in this volume are clear examples of explicit attempts to explain observed regularities in archeological data by means of observed regularities in social processes. The remarks of the commenters suggest that the attempts do offer hope of an enriched science of anthropology.

References

BRODBECK, MAY. 1962. Explanation, prediction, and "imperfect" knowledge. In Herbert Feigl and Grover Maxwell (Eds.), *Scientific explanation, space and time*. Minneapolis: University of Minnesota Press. Minnesota Studies in the Philosophy of Science, Vol. 3.

HEMPEL, CARL G. 1962. Deductive-nomological *vs.* statistical explanation. In Herbert Feigl and Grover Maxwell (Eds.), *Scientific explanation, space and time*. Minneapolis: University of Minnesota Press. Minnesota Studies in the Philosophy of Science, Vol. 3.

KAPLAN, ABRAHAM. 1964. *The conduct of inquiry*. San Francisco: Chandler.

The Inference of Residence and Descent Rules from Archeological Data

The recent interest in the reconstruction of prehistoric social systems has served to call attention to the nature and possible causes of patterning as it is seen in archeological materials. Whether inferences are drawn concerning social institutions based on settlement pattern, tool groupings which indicate patterning that suggests particular activities, or the clustering of attributes indicative of the nature of social units, they all stem from an awareness, perhaps implicit, of consistent and meaningful patterning of certain modular units—houses, tools, or attributes. The purpose of this paper is to make explicit the types of patterning encountered in archeological data, to suggest possible applications of these types to the refinement of method, and to explore, in a preliminary way, the nature and significance of patterning at the level of individual behavior as it relates to the inference of rules of residence and descent.

It is generally agreed that meaningful inference from the archeological record concerning the cultural systems responsible for its existence depends on an understanding of the manner in which culture is reflected in its products. Behavior is a product of culture which is perishable and therefore beyond recovery to the archeologist in a direct sense, but the products of this behavior—sites, structures, artifacts—reflect behavior in a systematic manner. By acknowledging how different levels and types of behavior might affect their products, one is provided with valuable insights regarding the behavioral significance of archeological assemblages. Four levels of behavior, and their archeological equivalents, can be defined and shown to have particular relevance to four types of inferential problems.

The first of these levels is that of the *individual.* Individual behavior is reflected at the attribute level, since the patterning of attributes exhibited by a group of similar artifacts results from similar patterned behavior on the parts of a number of individuals. While this behavior is shared by these individuals, as it would have to be if a pattern were to exist, it is the individual alone who is responsible for combining, for example, side notching with basal concavity on a projectile point. It is unlikely that more than one individual was responsible, in a direct sense, for the attribute configuration of any given artifact of the type commonly encountered in archeological analysis. For this reason, patterning of attributes at the level of individual activity, is archeology's only case of perfect association. Neither rodent activity, incorrect excavation procedure, nor improper laboratory sorting can destroy the association of cord-impressed decoration and lip thickening on a rim sherd. This perfection of association does not obtain with such an absolute guarantee at any of the three higher levels of patterning to be considered.

The second level of patterning is that which results from the actions of members of various minimal groups of interacting individuals—lineages, families, hunting groups, males, or females. Individuals grouped into such aggregates share in sets of behavioral patterns which can be seen in the patterned combination of artifacts as coordinate groups, as well as in the attributes of these artifacts. Such artifact complexes result either from individual or group action. Therefore, while only individuals are responsible for attribute groupings, both individuals or groups of individuals can produce artifact clusters. Unlike attribute groupings, artifact groupings are vulnerable to mixing and imperfect recovery due to field and laboratory procedural error.

The third level of patterning, that of the community, reflecting behavior of a face-to-face group of individuals, and including in most cases a number of minimal groupings as described above, is most frequently observed in the patterning of individual sites at the level of a single component. For example, the spatial arrangement of houses and the form of their architecture are a function of behavior at the community level, although one must also consider patterning at the individual and minimal-group levels in forming coherent inferences.

The fourth level is that of the entire society as a coordinate unit, and behavioral patterning at this level is a function of those patterns which are universal to the society as a whole. This level is seen archeologically in settlement pattern, as the term is used by Chang (1958) distinct from community pattern, as well as in certain aspects of patterning at the three lower levels.

Examples of each of these four levels will make their definition more clear. At the level of the individual, recent studies of attribute patterning in ceramics (Deetz, 1965; Longacre, 1964) have demonstrated that tight clustering of attributes might result from the orderly transmission of behavioral pattern relating to pottery manufacture along female lines, permitting the postulation of matrilocal residence, a social convention which expectably would lead to such a phenomenon. Patterning of individual behavior manifested in attribute patterning can also provide information concerning culture-contact situations. During the excavation of a tanning vat complex at La Purisima Mission, Lompoc, California (Deetz, 1963), a series of beamers was recovered from the vat floors. These had been used in the removal of hair from hides tanned for use in the mission ships, a technology introduced to the Chumash neophytes living at the mission. The particular attribute combination exhibited by these tools is quite illustrative of the nature of aboriginal conversion to European practices. The beamers are made from ribs; bone was a commonly used raw material by pre-Mission Chumash for tool manufacture. While the material was one familiar to the Indians, it was used to make a tool which formed a part of an introduced technological process, although the general form of the implement is similar to native ones used in similar activities, including bone-sweat sticks. The ribs used, however, were from cattle, an introduced animal. The pattern here is that of an aboriginally used raw material (bone) from an introduced animal (cow) to fashion an aboriginally known tool (bone beamer or scraper) to accomplish an introduced technological process (hair removal for vat tanning).

Patterning in artifact groupings is demonstrated by several recent studies. At La Purisima Mission during the nineteenth century, male Chumash neophytes were employed in a complex of roles introduced by Europeans—farming, cattle herding, and various crafts in the mission shops—while female neophytes continued in an occupational tradition not dissimilar from the aboriginal one, involving food preparation and the production of artifacts involved in this and related activities. Excavations in the neophytes' quarters (Deetz, 1963) produced data which provide a striking demonstration of this differential shift in roles according to sex. While it is known that nuclear families resided in the barracks, a classification of the aboriginal artifacts according to activity by sex reveals that all artifacts associated with male activities had vanished from the inventory of the missionized Chumash, while female-associated artifacts were as numerous as they had been in pre-contact and contemporary aboriginal sites. Baskets, mortars, pestles, manos, metates, and comales formed the vast majority of the aboriginal assemblage, while scrapers, projectile points, arrow-shaft straighteners, and chert flakes resulting from the manufacture of stone implements were exceedingly rare. It was possible to determine that one portion of the barracks had been used earlier in time, and this earlier occupation produced almost all of the few male-associated artifacts recovered. One other aspect of these data is of significance to those inferences regarding acculturation on a sexually differential basis. When one considers the nature of the complete assemblage from the barracks structure, including European and aboriginal artifacts, it is obvious that in the case of female material culture change, this was an additive process. European objects such as pottery, scissors, and knives were added to the aboriginal female tool kit, resulting in a complex actually somewhat richer than before, while change in male material culture was largely substitutive, with the European objects replacing rather than supplementing aboriginal items.

Other examples of this level of patterning are to be seen in the recent analysis of Mousterian sub-assemblages by Sally Binford (1965 and in this volume) and in Longacre's analysis of materials from the Carter Ranch Site in eastern Arizona (Longacre, 1964). That the level of minimal group behavior depends in part on individual behavior is shown by Longacre's demonstration that different ceramic attribute groups which are a function of individual behavioral patterning have spatial significance, in that attribute clusters resulting from different modal individual behavior tend to group in artifact clusters which are a function of the shared behavior of segments of the community.

Examples of the third level of patterning are provided by those artifacts which represent an entire community, and are usually encountered in settlement-pattern studies. The artifacts in this case are usually structures, and their number and arrangement provide an indication of community behavior. The clustering of houses and storage pits within tightly formed defensive moats and palisades seen in the Middle Missouri Region late in the eighteenth century reflects defensive behavior in the part of the community as a whole.

Chang's study (1958) of the correlation between certain social systems, classified according to residence and descent rules, and community layout is another case which demonstrates the manner in which community behavior might be expected to reflect in the physical arrangements of material objects.

At the fourth level of behavioral patterning, that common to an entire society, emphasis shifts to the nature of patterning of whole communities into larger groups. The patterning seen in contemporary archeological sites in a region is a reflection of the manner in which the society represented by those sites grouped its community units on the landscape, a form of patterning which in its formal analysis might reasonably be expected to reflect certain aspects of the behavior of the members of the society in certain universal categories. Examples would include the nature of ceremonial center distribution in Middle America or the relationship between seasonal camps and semipermanent villages in the Santa Barbara Channel region of southern California. In the latter case, small camps in the area inland from the foreshore suggest a seasonal division of the larger communities into smaller more economically efficient units during part of the year, probably during the dry summer months and early fall.

The brief examples cited above are intended only to serve as an indication of the nature of the four levels of patterning inherent in archeological data. What is of primary importance is the realization that different levels require somewhat different analytical approaches, and that certain questions are better answered at certain levels of analysis. Basic to inferential method based on the analysis of patterning is that the very term *pattern* denotes repetition. Unless a number of examples of similarly patterned phenomena can be produced, sound inferences cannot be drawn, since the patterning must be demonstrated by numerous cases.

The remainder of this paper will be concerned with patterning at the lower two levels as it might permit the inference of rules of residence and descent in prehistoric societies. While it can be argued with considerable effect that to concentrate on the aspects of descent and residence in a social system is at least potentially dangerous, in that it can lead to an undesirable narrowing of perspective, certain recent archeological analyses have been directed at the inference of either or both of these institutions. For this reason, it is perhaps advisable at this time to inquire into the possibility as well as the feasibility and practicality of such efforts. As has been suggested above, residence might be expected to be inferred from the individual level of patterning, that of attribute-clustering phenomena. While unilocal residence is in a sense a group activity, the effect which this practice might have on material objects would be the production of a series of similar artifacts resulting from family-based microtraditions of style, reflected in the attribute patterns produced by the individual. This assumption underlies both Deetz's (1965) and Longacre's (1964) recent ceramic studies. It is also demonstrated by the patterning observed in assemblages from historic Chumash sites in southern California. In this case, objects manufactured by males, particularly projectile points, exhibit a high degree of stylistic similarity within single sites, although intersite formal variation is high. While one might explain such variation as the result of different functions served by projectile points at different sites, our knowledge of Chumash subsistence patterns would suggest a highly homogeneous tradition within the area represented by the sites in question. This is almost certainly true of two of the sites, which are but ten miles apart, and located in identical environmental situations. At most, functional differences would only be a matter of virtually identical problems being met with alternate solutions and, as a result, explaining the variation as primarily due to social factors is more economical and efficient. In contrast to chipped-stone implements, made and used by males, milling equipment and basketry are strikingly similar throughout the entire range of the Chumash as they were known during the early nineteenth century. This pattern of high intersite variability but low variation within an assemblage shown by projectile points, and of the converse pattern seen in basketry and milling equipment is at least in agreement with the known facts of Chumash social organization, which was characterized by patrilocal residence and community exogamy. In this case, highly distinctive microtraditions of projectile-point manufacture might have been preserved by patrilocality, and similar isolated microtraditions in female manufacture prevented by a continuous circulation of females between communities.

This example serves to place emphasis on one important aspect of inferring residence rules from modes of attribute patterning. It would seem to be most urgent that one investigate patterning in objects known or thought to have been manufactured by both sexes or, lacking this, to investigate the nature of patterning of single-sex traditions over time. By doing this, one avoids the difficult question: How much is enough? That is, to what degree must one demonstrate clustering to be certain that matrilocality or patrilocality has been reasonably established? A simple statement that the patterning can be shown not to be random is not sufficient, since theoretically one might expect a significant degree of attribute association to result from bilocality, particularly if combined with a unilineal descent rule, which might tend to bias residence in either an uxorilocal or virilocal direction. Most bilocal situations could reasonably be expected to produce significant attribute clustering in both male and female manufactures, particularly if accompanied by bilateral descent and a nearly even distribution of uxorilocal and virilocal modes of residence. To infer relatively rigid unilocality of either type in the absence of a controlled chronological series, one must not only demonstrate clustering of attributes in the products of one sex, but also a corresponding lack of clustering in the products of the opposite sex. In this sense, unilocal residence is an asymmetrical institution, and the existence and degree of asymmetry must be shown.

An alternative approach to the problem is provided by an analysis of change in patterning in ceramic attributes among protohistoric Arikara (Deetz, 1965). In this instance, although patterning in only female cultural objects was considered, it was shown that over time this patterning became more random, and was accompanied by a reduction in house size. Furthermore, a reasonably sound historical reconstruction of later Arikara kinship change was made to provide the necessary control. Even in this case, however, one cannot say with certainty that residence was the sole causal factor in attribute clustering, nor to what degree clustering must occur to demonstrate matrilocality conclusively. The study does demonstrate that as matrilocality became less frequent, association of attributes became more random. No inference was formed from the data alone regarding residence; two simultaneous aspects of change were demonstrated, and their probable systematic relationship suggested. Relative degrees of clustering and association are indicated, but absolute frequencies cannot be postulated as reliable indicators of unilocality.

Inference of descent from archeological data, at least in terms of patterning, is a much more difficult and complex problem. Unlike residence, descent is a group function, and therefore fits the level of group behavioral patterning described above. As such, it requires more meticulous care in handling the data, since this level is subject to the problems of mechanical mixing discussed earlier. Furthermore, descent is a subunit of residence, in a sense, since some but not all unilocal societies have a consistent residence rule Therefore the demonstration of residence rule should be firmly established prior to the postulation of a rule of descent. The study of unilineal descent systems is, of course, the focus of much of ethnological theory, and many of the classics of ethnological writing treat the subject. As yet, there is not unanimous agreement on just what is meant by unilineal descent, or what purpose it serves in those societies which utilize it. It is very likely that there has been a confusion of cause and effect underlying much of the controversy in this area, and it can be suggested that unilineal descent is but a manifestation of another process, that of the formulation of clear-cut corporate groups which are structured in such a way as to function efficiently in a certain rather special social context. It is highly unlikely that a member of the most highly unilineal society would in fact deny *biological* descent from both parents, but at the same time, he would indicate that certain corporate rights and responsibilities reach him through either his mother's or his father's side. In this sense, descent is but a means to an end of corporate group formation, and perhaps if the term *descent* had not become one of general usage, clearer understandings would have been forthcoming more rapidly. Part of the cause is historical; the first workers concerned with unilineal descent worked in those areas, particularly Africa, where it was most clearly developed, and only later did it become apparent that there is more than one type of corporate kin group, and that unilineal descent is an organizing principle of only some.

If unilineal descent is seen as a mechanism by which sharply bounded corporate units are formed, then what must be demonstrated archeologically is a group concept of corporate participation. Even if a means of accomplishing such an end were devised, it would not necessarily indicate unilineal descent, but only corporate membership in one or another social group, organized on the basis of residence, descent, or voluntary participation, to name but three possibilities. Conversely, the presence of an extended family unit in the same dwelling over a long period of time, using similar artifacts and perhaps sharing in a subsistence pattern from the same parcel of land, does not necessarily indicate the existence of a corporate concept. Unlike residence, which can be described in terms of purely *physical* and *spatial* relationships between people and objects, descent, at least in its corporate sense, involves in its description certain essential *conceptual* relationships between people and objects *held by the people* and, as a result, there is a dimension of patterning which may well not be reflected in the tangibles of archeological data.

In conclusion, it is perhaps legitimate to ask why we are so concerned with the reconstruction of prehistoric social systems at all. There is always the danger of a certain method or area of inquiry becoming an end unto itself. The true value of such inferences would seem to lie in the direction of the ultimate benefit to general anthropological theory; the elucidation of system and orderly process in culture, past and present. Until and unless this type of inquiry is joined in a systematic fashion to the main body of ethnological theory, the danger is always present of such reconstructions entering the realm of ultimately sterile methodological virtuosity. This *should* not happen, but it must be kept in mind at all times that such a pursuit must relate in some way or another to the attainment of a broader understanding of culture. There is every reason to be confident that such will in fact take place but, at the same time, the possible pitfalls should be kept in mind. At the present point in our progress in this direction, perhaps the most significant value of recently gained understanding is that they indicate the nature of articulation between objects and people, and man's behavior in the larger sense. If this behavior is social, all well and good, but it must be studied regardless of the realm of culture it relates to. Studies such as those cited above, particularly in relationship to residence patterns, are of less value in their present imperfect state to social reconstruction than they are to indicating the nature of patterning and process in prehistoric cultures as shown by their material remains. Only with refinement will they become truly incisive and truly useful in the detailing of extinct social systems. However, though the route will be a long and difficult one, the longest journey must begin with a single step, and these first steps seem to lie in the right direction.

References

BINFORD, SALLY R. 1965. Social groupings and settlement systems in the Mousterian. Presented at the Amercian Anthropological Association annual meeting. (Unpublished.)

CHANG, K. C. 1958. Study of the Neolithic social groups: examples from the New World. *American Anthropologist*, 60: 298–399.

DEETZ, JAMES. 1963. Archaeological investigations at La Purisima Mission. *Annual Report 1962–63*, UCLA Archaeological Survey.

——. 1965. *The dynamics of stylistic change in Arikara ceramics.* Urbana: University of Illinois, Series in Anthropology, no. 4.

LONGACRE, WILLIAM. 1964. Archaeology as anthropology. *Science*, 144(3625): 1454–55.

FOUR

SALLY R. BINFORD

Variability and Change in the Near Eastern Mousterian of Levallois Facies

As anthropologists we are concerned with cultural differences and similarities. The most impressive schemes for the *description* of differences and similarities in flint assemblages have developed in Old World prehistory, partly as a function of the academic context of prehistory in Europe, where it is considered a natural science and students are trained in the basic skills of the natural sciences—among which is systematics (see Sackett's paper, this volume, for a complete discussion of this point). To those trained in North America and familiar with the relatively unsystematic treatment of projectile points and the lack of systematic treatment of other kinds of flint materials, work such as that of the Bordes (Bordes, 1953a, 1961; deSonneville-Bordes, 1960) in France in dealing with total flint assemblages in clearly defined, repeatable ways is all the more impressive. Morphological and technological criteria have been explicitly and consistently applied, so that total assemblage differences and similarities can be expressed in precise, quantitative terms.

Problems arise, however, in the *explanation* of differences and similarities and in understanding changes through time. All too often prehistorians view flint industries "evolving" through time, as though they contained genetic materials and were capable of mutation. It is on the explanatory level that anthropological concepts are particularly valuable. Our basic concept is culture, and it is to the understanding of functional variability and change within cultural systems that we wish to direct attention. Because of the nature of the preserved material from Paleolithic sites, systematic and consistent typologies are essential. But the description, however detailed, of assemblages does not constitute an *explanation* of differences and similarities. Certainly one of the most productive aspects of prehistoric research in recent years has been the feedback and mutual stimulation between European and American prehistorians. The benefits to both groups and to prehistory have far outweighed the few moments of misunderstanding and asperity between them.

The major thesis of this paper is that assemblage variability does not necessarily indicate either fixed local traditions (style) or evolutionary change within cultural systems. The alternative of *functional* variability must be considered. The distinction between stylistic and functional differences, on the one hand, and evolutionary change, on the other, must not only be a logical one but must be made operational through the development of the appropriate methods of analysis.

Two aspects of Paleolithic assemblages in the Near East will be dealt with: first, variation within a single cultural level; second, change from one cultural level to another. In examining variability between assemblages of the same broad culture type, our main purpose will be to suggest an explanation for the observed variability which is not predicated upon immutable local traditions. In the examination of evolutionary change, we shall offer an explanatory hypothesis which does not require assumptions about the genetic qualities of stone artifacts or invoke migrations of populations.

Variability

If we view lithic assemblages as sets of tools designed to perform specific tasks, then differences between assemblages on the same broad cultural level can be interpreted as reflecting: (1) differences in the jobs being performed (Kleindienst, 1961a, 1961b); (2) differential site utilization—that is, a different settlement type (Beardsley *et al.*, 1956); (3) replacement of one functional unit of the assemblage for another—what is commonly termed stylistic variability (L. R. Binford, 1963); or (4) sampling error.

The specific use which we infer for a set of tools must necessarily be tentative, but it is maintained that a functional view of artifactual material is more in keeping with reality than a view in which variability is interpreted as lithic mutation. A functional approach further forces us to cope with several variables simultaneously when interpreting variability. The determinants of the nature of a specific assemblage, or of its components, are related in a complex way, and our mode of analysis must be geared to dealing with multivariate causation.

Factor analysis (Fruchter, 1954; Harmann, 1961) is designed to express just such multivariate relations. It is designed to isolate from a matrix of many variables those which consistently share mutual determinants. With lithic assemblages we assume that these mutually determined units represent functional categories of tools, their specific functions being inferred from the nature of the working edge of the implements and/or from known ethnographic examples.

In the summer of 1964 a factor analysis study was undertaken by L. R. Binford and the author (Binford and Binford, 1966a) of one specific kind of Mousterian assemblage—the Mousterian of Levallois facies (Bordes, 1953a, 1953b)—to determine what units might be isolated as "tool-kits" and how these varied in their distribution.

The data we used were the stone implements from Couches 2–8 of Shelter I at Jabrud, Syria (Rust, 1950; Bordes, 1955) and from Mugharet es-Shubbabiq, a cave site near Tiberias, Israel (S. R. Binford, 1966). Jabrud was excavated by Rust and the lithic material reanalyzed by Bordes; Shubbabiq was excavated by the author and the tools analyzed with Bordes' assistance. They are, to the best of my knowledge, the only Near Eastern assemblages of the Mousterian of Levallois facies which have thus far been completely analyzed using the same criteria so that intersite comparisons are possible.

Despite the often bitter disputes about correlations of the Mousterian sequence in Western Europe and the Near East (Bordes, 1955, 1960, 1962; Garrod, 1953, 1956, 1963; Howell, 1959, 1961), there is general agreement that the Mousterian of Levallois facies is relatively late in the Middle Paleolithic of the Near East. Thus, in our selection of data we were able to hold three variables constant: typological consistency, general geographical area, and relative time.

The limitations of the data we used are: first, the absence of published faunal material from Jabrud, the deeply stratified site in our sample. Second, the major portion of the artifacts from Shubbabiq came from a midden deposit in the rear chamber of the cave; thus, only one small sample of artifacts could be tied in with features such as fire layers, which could serve as a check on functional hypotheses. Despite these limitations, our results provided useful information which can serve as a basis for the formulation of hypotheses to be tested against more complete data in the future.

The factor analysis separated the 63 Mousterian artifact types (Bordes, 1953a) into five clusters. Factor I, the most inclusive of the factors, consists of sixteen artifact types; those sharing the greatest degree of mutual determinancy are: borers, becs, endscrapers, atypical burins, and naturally backed knives. Due to the absence of elements which seem to be associated with hunting or butchering and the absence of heavy-duty tools, plus our as-yet-undemonstrated proposition that when this factor is dominant we have a base-camp type of settlement, we have interpreted this factor as representing activities carried out around the home base—manufacture of secondary tools and perhaps hide-finishing.

Factor II appears to be the hunting and butchering tool kit; the dominant types are points of all kinds, as well as almost every type of side-scraper.

The types diagnostic of Factor III which exhibit a high order of mutual determinancy are: backed knives, naturally backed knives, end-notched pieces, typical and atypical Levallois flakes, and unretouched blades. All of these types, with the exception of end-notched pieces, can be seen as fine-cutting implements, and their association with fire layers suggests that this group of tools might have been used in the preparation of food.

Factor IV has the most obvious relation to one of Bordes' subtypes of Mousterian assemblage, the denticulate (Bordes, 1953a, 1963). The elements in this factor are: denticulates and notched tools, scrapers with abrupt retouch, raclettes, and truncated flakes. The specific use of this group of tools is difficult to guess at; Bordes (1963, p. 47) suggests that the denticulate Mousterian is associated with the processing of plant materials.

Factor V's tightly associated elements are: elongated Mousterian points, discs, scrapers on the ventral surface, typical burins, and unretouched blades. The fact that only one kind of point and one kind of sidescraper are represented in the diagnostic cluster suggests that this group represents a more specialized hunting and butchering factor than was seen in Factor II.

The percentages in Figure 1 represent the degree to which the variability in each assemblage can be accounted for by a single factor. At Shubbabiq, with the exception of one small group of artifacts (Unit 8), the assemblage as a whole is quite internally consistent, with the major part of the variation being accounted for by Factor I and the rest shared by Factors II and III. Units 5 and 6 exhibit a small degree of determinancy by the denticulate factor (Factor IV), but otherwise fit the general pattern well. Unit 8, with its very high loading on Factor III, the fine-cutting or food preparation factor, is from a remnant deposit in the front of the cave where there were three small fire lenses. The homogeneity of the other units confirms the original hypothesis about Shubbabiq (S. R. Binford, 1966), based on Bordes' method of analysis and on Chi-square testing of samples—that the cave was intensively occupied but that a relatively short period of time seems to be involved.

The hypothesis that Factor I would be associated with a base-camp type of settlement is supported in this case by the consistent co-occurrence of Factors I and III, as well as by the nature of the site itself. The cave is large, well-lighted, and well-protected against wind and remains dry during the rainy season. The area within the limits of natural light

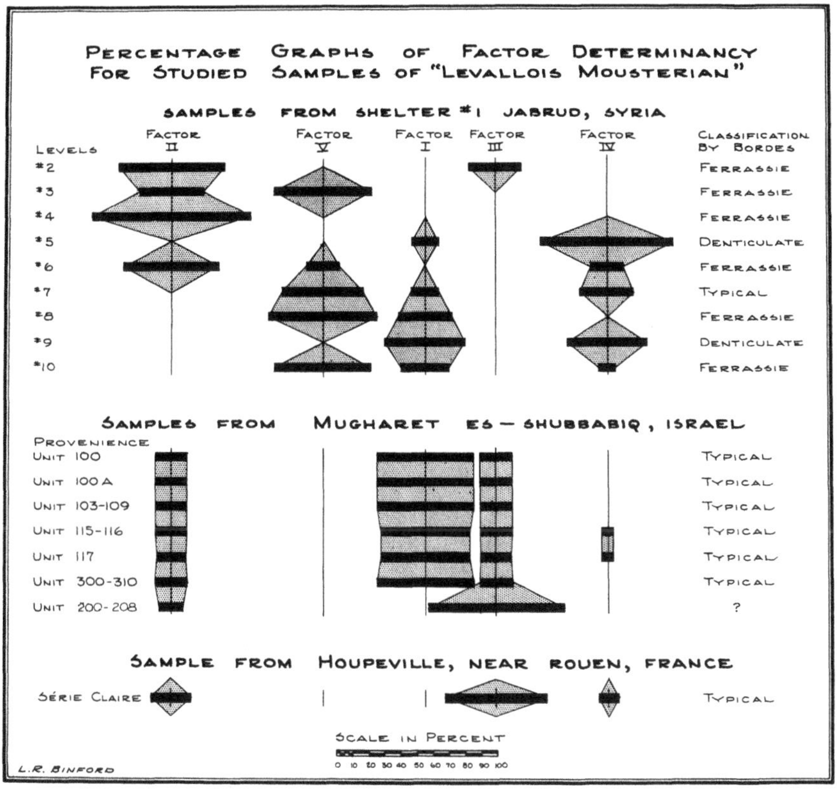

Figure 1.

consists of almost 300 square meters of floor space.

The samples from Jabrud were recovered from a trench averaging 3 meters in width and running the length of the shelter for about 22.5 meters (Rust, 1950; Plates 3 and 4). We estimate that approximately half of the living space of the shelter at the time of the occupations of Couches 2–8 is represented. The determinants of the variability in the assemblages from these levels exhibit a great deal more variance than can be observed at Shubbabiq. There are also striking differences in the factors represented at the two sites. Nowhere in Jabrud does Factor I play the dominant role it does at Shubbabiq; in Jabrud, Factors II, IV, and V account for most of the variance. Factor III is absent in all the levels except Couche 2, and this is the only level for which Rust mentions the presence of fires (1950, p. 61). The entire configuration of the factors in Jabrud 2–8 suggests various kinds of temporary occupations of the shelter by specific work groups, and the large role played by Factors II and V would seem to suggest that the site was used for small hunting encampments. The relatively open nature of the site, its relatively small size (an estimated average of 175 sq. m. of floor space at the time of these occupations), and the nature of the determinants of the observed variance all support the hypothesis that Shelter I served as a temporary work camp, rather than as a base camp.

There is a general trend observable in the variation of Couches 2–8—the replacement through time of Factor V by Factor II. Since both of these factors suggest hunting and butchering, this trend could be interpreted as the replacement of one functional unit by another—that is, stylistic change. However, since Factor II is a less complex tool kit, this trend might also signify changes in hunting behavior along with the development of more specialized tools. The current work at Jabrud being done by Dr. Ralph Solecki should yield faunal data to confirm or refute our current hypotheses.

The factor analysis results from Jabrud and Shubbabiq demonstrate that variability in a single culture type can profitably be examined within a functional frame of reference. Variability *between assemblages at the same site* may well represent activity variants, not necessarily "culture change" or occupations by bearers of different "traditions," and we must develop analytical tools for distinguishing between these phenomena. Variability *between sites* may represent differences in settlement type, not necessarily regional traditions, and we must also make a distinction between these.

Change

Let us turn to the second problem mentioned above—that of interpreting change from one major culture type to another. The data under discussion are those pertaining to the Middle-to-Upper Paleolithic transition in the Near East.

Dorothy Garrod has stated that the Emiran culture is transitional between the Levallois-Mousterian and Upper Paleolithic in the Palestinian region of the Near East and asserts that the Emireh point is the hallmark of this culture (Garrod, 1951, 1955). The type site consists of three shelters in Wadi Amud, Israel, two of which yielded the artifacts by which Garrod defines the Emiran.

The Emireh point is known from several sites in the Palestinian area. It is always made on a Levallois point, which may or may not be marginally retouched, and it is characterized by the removal of small, subparallel flakes at the base of the point on the bulbar side. The point always occurs in very low frequencies and is known in several different contexts.

At Abu Halka, Lebanon, there is some ambiguity about context. The example there occurs in Layer IVf, which is termed Upper Paleolithic *because of the presence of the Emireh point* (Haller, 1946, pp. 6–7). All the artifacts illustrated from the level in question appear to be typical of the Levallois-Mousterian (Haller, 1946, Plate I), but the percentages of burins and endscrapers reported are exceedingly high for a Mousterian assemblage. The possible interpretations of this situation are: (1) two archeological horizons were mixed during excavation; (2) errors were made in typology; or (3) this does in fact represent a "transitional" industry.

Ewing reported the presence of Emireh points at Ksar 'Akil, Lebanon, one of which occurred in this site below the zone which Ewing termed transitional; it was in the upper portion of the Levallois-Mousterian (Ewing, 1947, p. 191).

Two Emireh points were recovered from Mugharet es-Shubbabiq (S. R. Binford, 1966)—one from a disturbed level which yielded artifacts ranging from Mousterian stone tools to Early Bronze sherds, the second from an unmixed horizon of Mousterian of Levallois facies.

Five Emireh points from el-Wad are illustrated in *The Stone Age of Mount Carmel* (Garrod and Bate, 1937, Plate XXVI, Nos. 1–3, Plate XXVII, Nos. 7 and 8). Three were in layer G, originally called Lower Aurignacian, and two in Layer F, which was identified as Upper Levallois-Mousterian. The report states that in places layer G was indistinguishable in appearance from F, which immediately overlay it, and, as it contained a small proportion of Lower Aurignacian implements, it "cannot be regarded as quite free from disturbance" (Garrod and Bate, 1937, p. 23).

After the identification of Emireh points at Abu Halka and Ksar 'Akil, Garrod was led to reexamine her findings from el-Wad (Garrod, 1951). The reexamination consisted of treating the lithic materials from layers F and G as if they represented "an archaeological horizon containing an industry with the same mixed characters as those of the Lebanese sites" (Garrod, 1951, p. 121). The average thickness of layer F is 10 cms. while layer G varies from 40 cms. to over 7 meters (Garrod and Bate, 1937, p. 23). The interpretation of materials from over 7 meters of possibly disturbed deposits as though they represented a single archeological horizon seems a doubtful procedure and one which would obscure rather than clarify differences.

Garrod's original interpretation of the type site, the Emireh shelters, excavated forty years ago under far from ideal conditions (Turville-Petre, 1927), was that the deposits were disturbed. Yet the collection from these shelters was made the type assemblage for the Emirán (Garrod, 1955, p. 21). After field inspection of the remaining deposits in the large shelter at Emireh, I am strongly inclined to agree with Garrod's original interpretation of the site—that the deposits are disturbed and mixed, and that at least two components are present.

In summary, at the sites under discussion the Emireh point occurs at two locations—Ksar 'Akil and Shubbabiq—in clear Mousterian context.

At two other sites—el-Wad and Emireh—there is a good probability of disturbance and/or mixing. Only at Abu Halka can there be said to be anything "transitional" about the context. Skinner (personal communication, 1964) in his examination of this question has drawn up an even longer list of Emiran ambiguities. In view of this, the value of the Emireh point as a *fossile directeur* is open to serious question.

It is further suggested here that the traditional emphasis on "transitional industries" is open to question. If we view the change from Middle to Upper Paleolithic in an adaptive framework, we can observe that several significant shifts occur. Anatomically modern man (*Homo sapiens sapiens*) puts in his first appearance. New and more economical ways of utilizing raw material rapidly become dominant—the consistent manufacture of implements by punch-blade technique and a marked increase in frequencies of composite tools. It is hypothesized that these changes were predicated on new kinds of relationships between man and his environment, both physical and social, and that the changing relationships occurred within the latter part of the Middle Paleolithic itself. The emergence of new biological and cultural forms is the end-product of adaptive change, and it is in the nature of the basic adaptive changes that we will begin to understand why and how new forms appeared.

Although the currently available data are limited, the kinds of changes which occurred within the social environment can profitably be examined by techniques such as factor analysis which allow us to make inferences as to settlement systems and the structuring of work groups. If new methods of data collection and analysis are employed, we can certainly learn much more about both the internal divisions of local groups and between-group relations and how these might have changed throughout the Middle Paleolithic.

Changes in man's relations to his physical environment will be reflected in subsistence activities, and there is an intriguing hint of such a shift at Skhūl, one of the Mount Carmel caves (Garrod and Bate, 1937). Accepting Howell's relative dating of Tabūn and Skhūl (1957), Tabūn being the earlier of the two, a marked change in the exploitation of game can be observed through time.[1] Tabūn yielded a fauna characterized by a wide variety of species with no evidence of preference for any single form, but with an increase in *Bos* fragments in the Upper Levallois-Mousterian levels (Garrod and Bate, 1937, pp. 143–50). Skhūl, the more recent site, is described as follows:

> The most striking character of the collection from this deposit is the extremely large number of *Bos* (Garrod and Bate, 1937, p. 149).

Certainly this suggests a shift from generalized to specific hunting, and it is the systematic exploitation of a single species of herd mammals which

[1] This is set forth in a more playful manner in Binford and Binford 1966b.

characterizes much of the Upper Paleolithic. It is Skhūl which also yielded the remains of the Neanderthals which Howell terms "sapien-sized" (1957).

It is suggested that the place to see a "transition" is in the basic adaptation itself and not in the technological means developed within the framework of the new adaptation. The shift to specialized exploitation of specific kinds of game and the emergence of anatomically modern man were probably achieved over a considerable period of time, whereas the adoption of a more efficient mode of tool production might well have been change of a quick, replacive nature.

In dealing with lithic assemblages, we must distinguish between *stylistic* change and *functional* change. The battleship curve is an excellent model for dealing with style change, but the kind of technological changes reflected in the assemblages of the Middle to Upper Paleolithic of the Near East is of a completely different order and cannot be understood in terms of the same model. Man does not continue to use less efficient tools when newer and better ones are readily available. The steel-point pen very quickly replaced the quill, and modern commercial airlines do not continue to purchase piston engine planes instead of jets because of "tradition." These are two examples of more efficient technological means quickly replacing older forms, and there is no reason to believe that Paleolithic man made his artifacts half by Levallois-Mousterian techniques and half by Upper Paleolithic techniques because of cultural conservatism. The isolation of the archeological horizons where the technological change occurred will not only be very difficult; it will tell us almost nothing about how and why the underlying adaptive shifts took place.

Even more basic questions might be raised with respect to "transitional" industries when the problem is understanding the change from one major culture type to another. The assumptions underlying the search for transitional industries appear to be not only that stone tools themselves somehow evolve but also that changes are more or less evenly distributed through time and do not cluster. The first assumption and the problems it raises are discussed by Sackett in this volume. The latter assumption is often made explicit by American anthropologists in the form of statements to the effect that culture is a continuum. The analytical problems arising from such an assumption have been discussed by Spaulding (1957, pp. 86–87), who points out that while space and time are indeed continua, cultural phenomena are characterized by their tendency to cluster in space and time:

> I am of the opinion that clustering of this sort is generally characteristic of cultural data and that the development of adequate scaling and analytical techniques for its study is the most important methodological problem confronting archeologists (1957, p. 87).

The pressing need for the development of scaling and analytical techniques for studying the kind and degree of culture change involved between Middle and Upper Paleolithic can be readily seen in the extant literature. A recent example is the article by Pradel (1966) and the comments published with the article which exhibit the futility of attempting to explain the observed differences in terms of migrations (Gallus, 1966, pp. 39–40; Echegaray, 1966, p. 41), transitional industries (Garrod, 1966, pp. 40–41; Freund, 1966, pp. 38–39), and lithic mutation (Brace, 1966, p. 37; Smith, 1966, p. 44). Almost all prehistorians agree that the Mousterian and the early Upper Paleolithic are somehow different; some see little difference (Bordes, 1961) and therefore assume lineally related populations responsible for the two kinds of assemblage, while others (Vogel, 1966, p. 46–47) assert that the change in lithic industries is so marked and rapid that different populations must be involved.

Until the Mousterian and the early Upper Paleolithic are both analyzed in terms of units which are relatable to human activities (that is, tool-kits) and their spatial distribution (settlement types and patterns), we have no means for accurately measuring the degree of difference between Mousterian and Upper Paleolithic cultural systems. The rapid adoption of new technological means for flint-tool manufacture may mask underlying similarities and differences in subsistence base, settlement pattern, and social organization. It is only when these differences and similarities are measured and compared that we can hope to explain the kind and degree of change which took place.

Two problems have been discussed—variability within a single culture type and change from one culture type to another. It is important to distinguish between these phenomena, since they are radically different yet are often treated as though they were the same. Variability within the same broad culture type, defined in terms of lithic assemblages, has often been interpreted as reflecting culture change or as the expression of regional traditions. It is suggested here that such variability must be investigated functionally—in terms of the activities represented and the structure of settlement systems. If structural change can be demonstrated in these aspects of behavior in the past, then we have the basis for developing processual models for understanding changes in lithic assemblages.

References

Beardsley, R. K., *et al.* 1956. Functional and evolutionary implications of community patterning. *American Antiquity*, 22(2), Part 2: 130–57.

Binford, L. R. 1963. Red ocher caches from the Michigan area: a possible case of cultural drift. *Southwestern Journal of Anthropology*, 19(1): 89–108.

Binford, Sally R. 1966. Mugharet es-Shubbabiq: a Mousterian cave in Israel. *Journal of the Israeli Exploration Society*, 16(1 and 2): 18–32, 96–103.

BINFORD, L. R., and SALLY R. BINFORD. 1966a. A preliminary analysis of functional variability in the Mousterian of Levallois facies. *American Anthropologist*, 68(2), Part 2: 238–95.

——. 1966b. The predatoray revolution: a consideration of the evidence for a new subsistence level. *American Anthropologist*, 68(2), Part 1: 508–512.

BORDES, F. H. 1953a. Essai de classification des industries "moustériennes." *Bulletin de la Société Préhistorique Française*, 50(8): 457–66.

——. 1953b. Levalloisien et Moustérien. *Bulletin de la Société Préhistorique Française*, 50(4): 226–35.

——. 1955. Le paléolithique inférieur et moyen de Jabrud (Syrie) et la question du pré-Aurignacien. *L'Anthropologie*, 59(5 and 6): 486–507.

——. 1960. Le pré-Aurignacien de Yabroud (Syrie), et son incidence sur la chronologie du Quaternaire en Moyen Orient. *Bulletin of the Research Council of Israel*, 9G(2 and3): 91–103.

——. 1961. *Typologie du paléolithique ancien et moyen*. Bordeaux: Imprimerie Delmas.

——. 1962. Sur la chronologie du paléolithique au Moyen Orient. *Quaternaria*. 5: 57–69.

——. 1963. Le moustérien à denticulés. *Arheološki Vestnik*, 14: 43–49.

BRACE, C. L. 1966. Comments on Pradel's paper. *Current Anthropology*, 7(1): 37.

ECHEGARAY, J. G. 1966. Comments on Pradel's paper. *Current Anthropology*, 7(1): 41.

EWING, J. F. 1947. Preliminary note on the excavations at the Palaeolithic site of Ksâr 'Akil, Republic of Lebanon. *Antiquity*, 21(84): 186–96.

FREUND, G. 1966. Comments on Pradel's paper. *Current Anthropology*, 7(1): 38–39.

FRUCHTER, B. 1954. *Introduction to factor analysis*. Princeton: D. van Nostrand.

GALLUS, A. 1966. Comments on Pradel's paper. *Current Anthropology*, 7(1): 39–40.

GARROD, D. 1951. A transitional industry from the base of the Upper Palaeolithic in Palestine and Syria. *Journal of the Royal Anthropological Institute*, 81: 121–30.

——. 1953. The relations between south-west Asia and Europe in the Later Palaeolithic Age. *Cahiers d'Histoire Mondiale*, 1: 13–38.

——. 1955. The Mugharet el-Emireh in Lower Galilee: type station of the Emiran industry. *Journal of the Royal Anthropological Institute*, 85: 1–22.

——. 1956. Acheuléo-Jabroudien et "Pré-Aurignacien" de la grotte de Taboun (Mont Carmel); étude stratigraphique et chronologique. *Quaternaria*, 3: 39–59.

——. 1963. The Middle Palaeolithic of the Near East and the problem of Mount Carmel Man. The Huxley Memorial Lecture, 1962. *Journal of the Royal Anthropological Institute*, 93: 232–59.

——. 1966. Comments on Pradel's paper. *Current Anthropology*, 7(1): 40–41.

GARROD, D., and D. BATE. 1937. *The stone age of Mount Carmel*, Vol. 1. Oxford: Clarendon Press.

HALLER, J. 1946. Notes de préhistoire phénicienne: l'Abou Halka. *Bulletin du Musée de Beyrouth*, 6: 1–20.

HARMANN, H. H. 1961. *Modern factor analysis*. Chicago: University of Chicago Press.

HOWELL, F. CLARK. 1957. The evolutionary significance of variation and varities of "Neanderthal" man. *Quarterly Review of Biology*, 32(4): 330–47.

——. 1959. Upper Pleistocene stratigraphy and early man in the Levant. *Proceedings of the American Philosophical Society*, 103: 1–65.
——. 1961. Stratigraphie du Pleistocene supérieur dans l'Asie du sud-ouest. *l'Anthropologie*, 65: 1–20.
KLEINDIENST, M. R. 1961a. Components of the East African Acheulian assemblage: an analytic approach. *Actes de 4e Pan-Africain Congres de Préhistorie*. (Leopoldville, 1959): 81–111.
——. 1961b. Variability within the late Acheulian assemblage in East Africa. *South African Archaeological Bulletin*, 16: 35–50.
PRADEL, L. 1966. Transition from Mousterian to Perigordian: skeletal and industrial. *Current Anthropology*, 7(1): 33–50.
RUST, A. 1950. *Die Höhlenfunde von Jabrud (Syrien)*. Neumünster.
DESONNEVILLE-BORDES, D. 1960. *Le paléolithique supérieur en Périgord*. Bordeaux: Imprimerie Delmas.
SMITH, P. E. L. 1966. Comments on Pradel's paper. *Current Anthropology*, 7(1): 44–45.
SPAULDING, A. C. 1957. Review of "Method and theory in American archaeology." *American Antiquity*, 23(1): 85–87.
TURVILLE-PETRE, F. 1927. *Researches in prehistoric Galilee 1925-26*. London: British School of Archaeology in Jerusalem.
VOGEL, J. C. 1966. Comments on Pradel's paper. *Current Anthropology*, 7(1): 46–47.

FIVE

JAMES R. SACKETT

Method and Theory of Upper Paleolithic Archeology in Southwestern France

The aims of this essay are to review the present state of method and theory in Upper Paleolithic archeology and to examine some of the problems that must be met in attempting to design its future research strategy.[1] Like the other essays in this volume, it is based upon the assumption that the growing alliance between archeology and cultural anthropology will not only prove mutually beneficial, but that indeed it will play a determinant role in the future development of both disciplines. Unhappily, despite the enormous wealth and importance of the cultural data for which it is responsible, Upper Paleolithic archeology is less a part of this alliance than any other major field of prehistory. Few of its actual practitioners have but the most generalized notions of either modern culture theory or the substantive data of ethnography, while most anthropologists in turn know no more of it than is provided by brief summaries in outdated textbooks. Although directed primarily toward archeologists, the following discussion will—it is hoped—suggest to both of these almost mutually exclusive audiences that a synthesis of their respective formula-

[1] A short draft of this paper was read at the annual meeting of the American Anthropological Association, Denver, 1965. Several developments since the present version was written (June, 1966) indicate that much of its argument is not as original as I believed. Particularly relevant is the appearance of Philip Smith's *Le Solutréen en France* (1966), which proposes many aspects of the research strategy advocated here.

tions and analytic approaches may well be of profit to the scientific study of culture history.

The Upper Paleolithic (late Old Stone Age) consists of a relatively diverse block of hunting and gathering cultures that occupied Europe and the Near East during the latter half of the Final or Würm Glacial period, Late Glacial extensions of which penetrated as far as western North Africa and northern Asia. Although their precise genetic connections remain undefined, all of these cultures appear to be historically related by their common possession of distinctive stone-tool industries that are usually dominated by advanced blade technologies. Wherever it appears, the Upper Paleolithic seems to represent a qualitative advancement in regional culture history as measured by elaboration of artifactual remains and density of sites. The disparity between it and the preceding Mousterian period is nowhere more dramatically expressed than in the periglacial zone extending across mid-latitude Europe from the Atlantic Ocean to the South Russian Plain. Here Upper Paleolithic societies seem to have achieved levels of economic success and cultural complexity that were not to recur until Neolithic times in the Old World and that have been rivaled among historic hunters and gatherers perhaps only by such groups as the maritime cultures of the Pacific Northwest Coast.

In this paper we shall deal systematically with only one segment of this Upper Paleolithic climax—the classic archeological sequence of the Périgord region of southwestern France, centering upon the modern department of the Dordogne.[2] This regional restriction will preclude examination of some of the most important achievements of Upper Paleolithic archeology, such as the refined analysis of extremely informative open-air sites in Russia (Boriskovski, 1965) and central Europe (Klima, 1962; Rust, 1958), and even some of the most advanced research being conducted in France itself (for example, Leroi-Gourhan, 1963; Leroi-Gourhan and Brésillon, 1964; Escalon de Fonton, 1961). However, since the Dordogne has traditionally played a leading role in the development of archeological theory and method, this discussion should prove to be of at least general relevance to Upper Paleolithic investigations throughout mid-latitude Europe.

Figure 1 provides an extremely simplified version of the Dordogne sequence within its climatic and geological framework. The chronology is based upon a radiocarbon regime that is very incomplete; subsequent to 20,000 B.C., the assigned dates may be no more than a millenium off, but their likely range of error increases markedly for earlier periods. It should be noted that the somewhat inconsistent terminology of cultural periods

[2] The primary source for the Dordogne is de Sonneville-Bordes (1960), which in both content and method furnishes the indispensible point of departure for all research in this region.

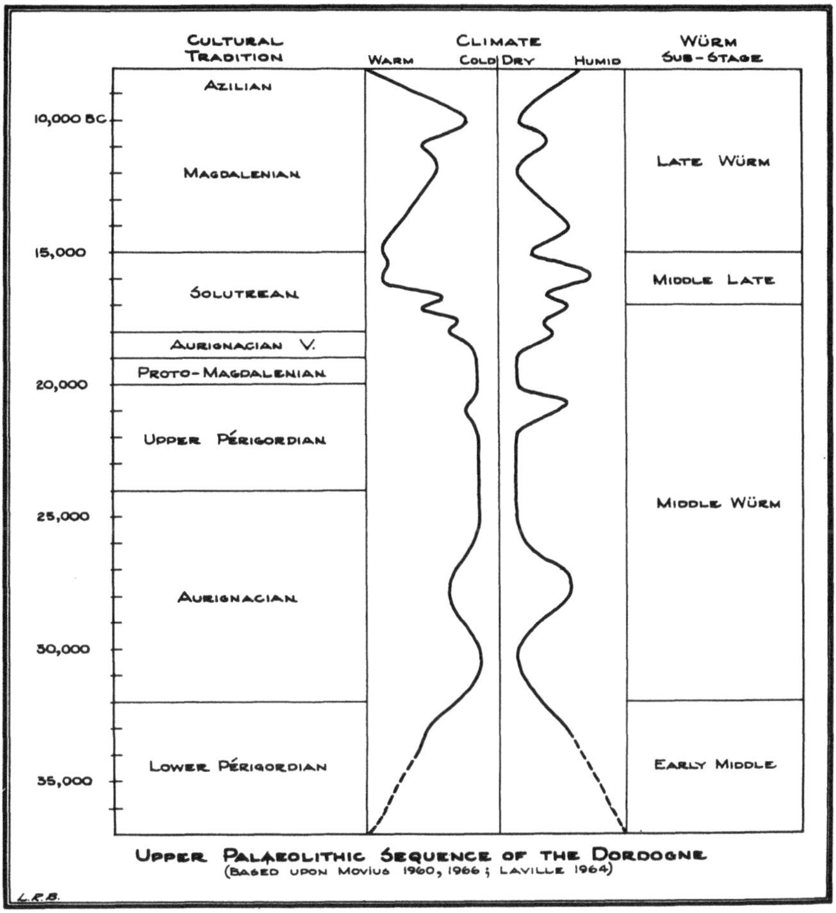

Figure 1.

and traditions partially reflects older historical interpretations that are now widely questioned.

The Dordogne sequence is based upon what is at present the world's richest concentration of Upper Paleolithic sites. The bulk of these are rock-shelter or *abri* stations which have been uncovered in the talus of limestone cliffs that dominate many of the valleys in this region. Although intensive exploration has been restricted to the Dordogne and Vézère river valleys, more than 150 such sites have been at least partially excavated—a number that probably represents but a small fraction of those that remain to be discovered. These sites often yield several meters' thickness of occupation levels containing many thousands of stone implements and vast quantities of kitchen and industrial garbage. Residence seems to have continued the year-round in many of the levels, and often apparently involved several neighboring rock-shelters simultaneously; in localities such as the Gorge d'Enfer and the Les Eyzies cliffs, buried occupation zones may actually extend more or less continuously for almost a kilometer. Moreover, the region is richly endowed with open-air sites and painted and engraved caves, both of which are ascribed to the same peoples who inhabited the rock-shelters. In view of the sheer volume and elaboration of their cultural remains, there can be little doubt that Upper Paleolithic societies in the Dordogne achieved one of the most successful hunting and gathering adaptations in culture history.

The factors accounting for this success presumably stemmed from an almost ideal combination of exploitative skills and environmental resources enjoyed by Upper Paleolithic men in this region. Though serious gaps and ambiguities remain in our knowledge of their technology, especially with regard to perishable manufactures and in specific areas such as food storage and preservation, their extant artifacts and pictorial art strongly suggest that Upper Paleolithic men possessed almost the entire range of techniques and equipment found among historic hunters and gatherers aside from those items that have only recently diffused from semi-industrialized societies. This range seems to have included in at least many cultural phases all of the specialized technology required for intensive semi-Arctic land and riverine exploitation, such as tailored skin clothing, refined missile systems involving the throwing board and bow and arrow, and fishing harpoons, leisters, and gorges.[3]

The environmental side of the equation was dominated by an extremely high biomass that apparently greatly exceeded the present carrying capacity of Arctic and sub-Arctic tundras and steppes, which today exist only at much higher latitudes (Butzer, 1964, p. 374). This mainly consisted of large populations of herbivores such as reindeer, horse, and bison, in addition to a variety of birds and fish, the latter including anadromous forms like salmon. The region also provided rich sources of workable stone, housing in the form of numerous rock-shelters immediately accessible to water, and a variegated landscape that was particularly well suited for pedestrian big-game hunting. This heterogeneous topography of wind-swept plateaus and sheltered valleys may itself have been a dominant factor in the economic success of Paleolithic hunters. Exposed simultaneously to generally severe continental and relatively mild oceanic weather conditions, it apparently accomodated a variety of contiguous micro-environments among which the principal game animals could usu-

[3] See J. G. D. Clark (1952) for a general survey of Upper Paleolithic technology from the perspective of subsequent culture history.

ally find suitable conditions for regional occupation regardless of seasonal variations and even the long-range climatic oscillations represented in Figure 1 (Bouchud, 1959).

While the preceding may be a reasonably valid sketch of Upper Paleolithic man-land relationships in the Dordogne, one can only speculate about the details of the economic practices involved and the broader cultural contexts within which they operated. For there exists no significant body of literature that is directly concerned with the systematic analysis of Old Stone Age cultural patterns and the processes that determined them. Frequent and occasionally penetrating cultural inferences are in fact drawn by most archeologists, but these generally remain isolated and particularistic, most often based upon archeological facts taken out of context and explained in terms of ethnographic facts equally out of context. Their emphasis moreover is heavily oriented toward "humanistic" considerations of the more spectacular artifactual remains such as burials, Venus figurines, and cave art. Little rigorous analysis is devoted to such areas as the functions of stone and bone tools, demography, and the seasonal distribution and availability of food resources—precisely those topics that must first be understood if prehistoric cultures are to be reconstructed (much less, if their art and ideology are to be interpreted in a meaningful context). As a result, the more basic questions of Upper Paleolithic life remain unanswered and, in fact, seldom asked. For example, what precisely were the subsistence techniques of Upper Paleolithic foragers, what population sizes and densities might they support, and with what kinds of settlement patterns were they associated? Or again, do the successive Upper Paleolithic artifact complexes refer to distinct types of economic and social organization, or do they merely reflect stylistic variations within a single cultural tradition? Indeed, were it not for their apparent associations with distinct types of hominids, most archeologists would be hard pressed even to suggest a testable hypothesis accounting for the obviously different levels of economic success achieved by the Mousterian and Upper Paleolithic cultures in general (however, see Bordes, 1960).

Now, it could be argued that the deficiencies of current archeological interpretation in the Upper Paleolithic, as in other fields of prehistory, largely indicate no more than that other research tasks have necessarily had greater priority. In fact, the artifactual and stratigraphic complexity of the Dordogne have necessitated that primary concern be given to purely descriptive classification, that is, typological definitions of archeological assemblages and the construction of a regional sequence of cultural phases. Nevertheless, this alone cannot explain the general lack of interest in the kinds of questions raised above. For archeologists have not even obtained the organized data upon which interpretations of cultural pattern and process could be systematically tested once the basic requirements of descriptive classification are met. Only a handful of artifact assemblages representing all of the rock-shelters that have been excavated to date are in any manner complete, well documented, or accompanied by adequate provenience and paleoenvironmental information. Hence, regardless of what research objectives may be given priority, it would seem that prehistorians in the Dordogne have generally failed to employ a culturally meaningful frame of reference for either the collection or interpretation of their data.

This of course does not mean that research has evolved in a theoretical vacuum, but rather that its primary frame of reference has traditionally lain in another area. From the pioneer work of Gabriel de Mortillet (1869) down through World War II, research strategy was strongly influenced by the notion that the archeological record was best approached in the same manner that earlier had proven successful in interpreting the fossil record. Just as paleontologists subdivided organic history according to successive forms of index fossil organisms, so prehistorians attempted to define and order their archeological data in terms of artifact *fossiles directeurs*—qualitatively diagnostic tool forms whose restricted stratigraphic distributions were believed to delineate major culture blocks and their principal evolutionary subdivisions. In the hands of gifted typologists (Bourlon, Bouyssonie, and Bouyssonie, 1912), a refined excavator (Peyrony, 1933), or a subtle culture historian (Breuil, 1912), this approach furnished a useful classificatory tool through which the French sequence became established as the model for Upper Paleolithic research throughout the Old World. Yet regardless of its general utility in space-time systematics, the continued acceptance of this approach undoubtedly retarded the development of sophisticated cultural reconstruction and interpretation.

First, the similar manner in which archeological and paleontological *fossiles* were conceived inevitably fostered the assumption that culture history was amenable to an organic, or at least a *natural*, evolutionary model. This was clearly implicit in even the classificatory schemes of Denis Peyrony, the Dordogne's most brilliant traditional prehistorian. In his revolutionary *Les industries "aurignaciennes" dans le bassin de la Vézère* (1933) and continuing to dominate his subsequent papers (for example, 1939, 1948) was the attempt to equate artifact *fossiles*, cultural stages, and geological horizons as narrowly as possible into mechanical systems whose parts articulated with almost robotic precision. Further, when the patterns of culture dynamics reflected in these schemes could not be "explained" as concomitant expressions of change in the natural universe, they were attributed to behavioral expressions of biological differences among human groups. Thus Peyrony maintained that a racial split within *Homo sapiens* was sufficient to account for the simultaneous occupation of the Dordogne by two distinct cultural traditions over several millenia.[4] Hence, it is not surprising that the writings of Peyrony and his contemporaries nevertheless expressed strong if particularistic interest in archeological evidences of art and ritual. A "humanistic" concern with prehistoric ideology and esthetics was in effect predictably the focus (and extent) of traditional interest at the detailed level of cultural inference, as it was precisely these aspects of culture that most obviously eluded systematic explanation within an organic frame of reference.

A second and equally unfortunate consequence of the *fossile* approach was that, by assuming a one-to-one correlation between cultural and natural stratigraphy, it led prehistorians to underestimate grossly the complexity of the archeological record. The minimum excavation unit recognized by the best researchers was no less than an entire archeological *couche*, an artifact-bearing zone of distinct sedimentary composition that very often incorporates a number of discrete occupational subdivisions. At the same time, sampling techniques concentrated only upon the data that were required to obtain a sequential ordering of *couche*-specific archeological horizons: artifact assemblages were collected with no regard to vertical and horizontal tool distributions within strata, and little paleoenvironmental data were systematically recovered other than the macrofaunal remains that were considered to be primary chronological indicators. Moreover, there was a strong tendency to overlook the more *banal* areas of typology in favor of the established *fossiles* that were believed capable of providing at once an adequate definition of both the formal contents and genetic affiliations of assemblages—a procedure that of course only intensified the analytic circularism inherent in traditional systematics. Thus the application of sampling techniques designed to meet only the limited requirements of *fossile* classification prevented accumulation of the organized body of information that we previously noted must underlie culturally meaningful analysis in archeology.

However, during the past fifteen years, a number of fundamental innovations in the techniques of data collection and analysis undoubtedly signal a dramatic shift in the research strategy of Upper Paleolithic archeology. Under the leadership of François Bordes, excavation techniques have approached the limits of micro-stratigraphic control in which complete and fully documented artifact assemblages are segregated according to the minimal sedimentary components that can be discerned in archeological *couches* (for example, Bordes, 1958, Fig. 2). At some sites, as in the ambitious research program conducted by Hallam Movius at the Abri Pataud (see below), detailed stratigraphic control is complemented by

[4] Even more extreme organic models were adopted during this era for earlier cultural stages, as in the so-called parallel phyla theory of Lower and Middle Paleolithic evolution. Here the confusion of biology and culture often became intense, with divergent hominid lines being held responsible for distinct cultural traditions at the same time that archeological terminology frequently hinted at the practice of sexual relations among stone tools.

horizontal dissection aimed toward determining the spatial relations of tool distributions and architectural features over occupational surfaces. Refined techniques are now available for obtaining detailed ecological information from sedimentology (Bonifay, 1957; Laville, 1965) and palynology (Lavocat, 1966), while paleontological analysis has been extended both to micro-faunal remains and to such problems as the reconstruction of hunting practices as these are reflected in the age and sex structures of butchered animal assemblages (Bouchud, 1961). Equally revolutionary advances have been made in descriptive classification. Of supreme importance here has been the replacement of traditional systematics by *comprehensive* typologies in which the entire range of artifactual variation found in the Upper Paleolithic may be codified, and the use of descriptive statistical techniques for assessing and ordering archeological assemblages. First introduced into Upper Paleolithic studies by de Sonneville-Bordes and Perrot (1953) as an extension of techniques earlier applied by François Bordes to the Mousterian Complex (1950), numerical taxonomy has rapidly become established as the foundation of archeological classification throughout Western Europe.[5] To date it has provided the most thoroughgoing revision of traditional schemes in the Dordogne itself, as is summarized in de Sonneville-Bordes' monumental *Le Paléolithique supérieur en Périgord* (1960).

It is to be hoped that one day the results of these several lines of investigation will be synthesized in an extensive literature devoted to cultural interpretation in the Upper Paleolithic. No doubt this will emerge only gradually, due to the vast expenditure of time and money that is demanded by the new techniques of excavation and laboratory analysis. Equally important, however, it will require the development of a more viable interest in research strategy than is now apparent in the writings of most archeologists. Aside from purely descriptive reviews of the new techniques, there is presently almost no concern expressed in print with regard to general questions of theory and method. This silence is so profound that an outside observer might well conclude either that archeologists are naively assuming that their data—when available in sufficient quantities—will automatically fall into culturally meaningful patterns or, conversely, that there actually has been no rejection of the traditional goals of *fossile* strategy. As for the latter, one prehistorian in an allied field (Moberg, 1961, p. 26) suggests that nothing really has changed: the quantitative procedures used in ordering assemblages, for example, simply represent the introduction of techniques that are current in the natural sciences, and are perhaps intended to reflect the same kinds of patterning. And, in fact, the most ambitious attempt in the last decade to explain Upper Paleolithic culture history is grounded upon an extreme

[5] Escalon de Fonton and de Lumley, 1955; Bohmers, 1956; Laplace, 1964; Ronen, 1966.

organic model whose mechanisms are allegedly verified by the facts of primate history, the early Tertiary radiation of fissiped carnivores, and I. Vavilov's epicenter theory of plant domestication (Laplace, 1961, p. 66).

Nonetheless, even a modest familiarity with the current literature indicates that such examples are no more than individual expressions of continuity in the evolution of present research from that of the past. It is no doubt true that interest in method and theory has been diverted by pragmatic emphasis upon the immediate gain in refined descriptive classification that is provided by the new techniques. But the general climate of opinion is one of ambivalence rather than reaction; the traditional frame of reference has been discarded by most students, but its successor has not yet clearly emerged. Therefore, the remainder of this discussion will be devoted to a programmatic statement that will attempt to define the nature of cultural interpretation in Upper Paleolithic archeology and the kind of research strategy it might entail. What should be our research objectives, and with what analytic techniques and interpretive frameworks ought we to be concerned in order to begin approaching them?

With regard to the former, the design of future research strategy should focus upon the complementary goals of (1) reconstructing the content and structure of Upper Paleolithic cultural systems, and (2) elucidating the processes that determined their form and mode of change. The term *system* is employed here in L. R. Binford's (1964) sense to emphasize the view that prehistoric cultures were more than complexes of discrete archeological traits and that to be understood they must be analyzed structurally as systems of functionally interrelated elements. A cultural system is posited by the archeologist from the sum total of his inferences regarding the component technological, social, and ideological aspects of all the activities that can be referred to it. Activities are culturally patterned segments of human behavior that have received ordered expressions in the archeological record. They are isolated and analyzed in terms of clusters of associated elements—more specifically, the presence of nonrandom variation in the complementary distributions of attributes and/or classes of what Spaulding (1960) has called the "dimensions" of archeology: space, time, and form. Time and space define the loci of activities, while the activities themselves are formally expressed by artifacts—concrete manifestations of human behavior such as implements and architectural features—and by paleoecological remains.[6] An "activity" is a purely relative analytic unit that may range in scope from the manufacture of a single artifact to the total lifeway of a community, and hence the

[6] While it is convenient to distinguish a paleoenvironmental order of formal data, it should be noted that most if not all of its elements concretely express prehistoric behavior patterns and are therefore artifactual in the strict sense of the term. Thus a faunal assemblage recovered from an archeological site invariably reflects selective cultural agents and does not provide a random sample of the animal communities that actually existed in nature when the site was occupied.

activities that can be identified with a specific prehistoric culture are neither additive nor mutually exclusive categories. It is of course for this reason that a systemic approach is required, since our analysis must obviously focus as much upon the functional articulations that once related a variety of cross-cutting and overlapping activities as upon the contents of the activities themselves.

Aside from its emphasis upon a systemic view of culture, the above is of course no more than an explicit description of what archeologists have always done. The difference between one area or phase of prehistoric research and another simply depends upon the kinds of activities that receive paramount attention and the manner in which they are analyzed. Therefore our problem may be stated as follows: assuming that present data-gathering techniques provide reasonably complete information on all cultural activities that are archeologically represented in the Upper Paleolithic, upon what activities should cultural interpretation primarily focus and in terms of what method and theory should their analysis be conducted? An answer to this question must begin with the assumption of a theoretical attitude regarding the nature of culture and the terms in which it can most profitably be interpreted. The approach advocated here is that of *cultural ecology,* which is based upon the proposition that the content and structure of a cultural system are primarily, if not wholly, determined by the technological procedures and sociodemographic arrangements employed by its members in exploiting their environment. Defined in its modern form by Julian Steward (1955), cultural ecology has proved to be efficacious in a variety of interpretive studies in both ethnology and archeology (see Sahlins, 1962; Helm, 1962). Due to its wealth of materials directly reflecting man's technological exploitation of his environment, the Dordogne Upper Paleolithic should be particularly amenable to analysis and interpretation oriented in terms of this approach.

Given the perspective of cultural ecology, the initial focus of our proposed research strategy should be directed toward those activities that can be distinguished as primarily economic tasks; these by definition involve the extraction of raw materials and their consumption either in the form of food or implemental manufacture. Analysis of the artifactual and paleoenvironmental components of such activities in the light of their spatial distributions within and between archeological sites should enable us to identify in at least general terms the nature of the tasks performed and the composition of the groups undertaking them. Gradually from such analysis should emerge a paradigm of the ecological adaption of the cultural system under consideration, expressing how its integral tasks were functionally related within a settlement pattern and population demography through the year-round cycle of environmental exploitation and occupation. This formulation should provide a background against which non-economic activities may then be projected for analysis, and in turn related to each other and to the more explicit patterns of subsistence and settlement. Ultimately, with continual readjustment to accomodate newly incorporated information, the paradigm may be expanded to embrace the total range of inferences that can be deduced concerning the economic, social, and ideological aspects of the prehistoric cultural system.

Although the precise form such an approach will take must remain obscure until adequate materials become available for testing, it is possible to anticipate some of the methodological problems that will be involved. Obviously it will require an interdisciplinary effort in which parallel studies in natural sciences like palynology and paleontology are coordinated with each phase of the archeological investigation. This synthesis has already begun to emerge in the Dordogne (for example, Bouchud, 1961), and excellent precedents are available from other areas of Paleolithic research (J. D. Clark, 1960; J. G. D. Clark, 1954). Equally important, however, it will require a sophisticated use of the data and theory of anthropology, especially as these relate to foci of cultural ecological interpretation such as the demographic (Birdsell, 1968), residential (Chang, 1964), and social (L. R. Binford, 1964) correlates of subsistence pursuits. Here of course the problems of research design will be especially formidable. Anthropologists themselves are only just beginning to achieve some amount of detailed predictive control in explaining living societies, while—even at the level of cultural reconstruction—past failures have revealed the dangers inherent in attempting to isolate specific ethnographic analogues for Upper Paleolithic societies. However, this phase of the investigation can still proceed on the assumption of cultural uniformitarianism—the theoretical position that the basic form and articulations of prehistoric activities were at least analogous to those found in modern cultural systems and that both can be accounted for in terms of similar processes. Unlike students of earlier Stone Age phases, we are concerned with the cultural by-products of essentially modern forms of *Homo sapiens* whose behavioral capabilities were presumably at least equal to those found in the present races of men.

In any event, it must be stressed that our analytic procedures will themselves differ fundamentally from those of ethnography or social anthropology. While the investigation of an extant culture invariably proceeds in a systemic frame of reference, any one of its various components or aspects may still be discretely identified and interpreted by independent observations of human behavior. Thus, ethnographers apparently seldom find it necessary to work with more variables than can be intuitively controlled at one time. A prehistoric cultural activity, however, is much more difficult to isolate as a discrete entity, due to the incompleteness of the archeological record and the inherent ambiguity of its data. The definition and interpretation of an activity must therefore depend as much upon an analysis of its relations to other activities as upon its artifactual contents. Conversely, the validity with which it has been formulated must itself be measured largely in terms of its analytic feedback, that is, the consistency it (or additional formulations based upon it) may exhibit in articulating with these same activities in the paradigm of a cultural system. It is obvious, therefore, that our investigation might profitably be conducted within a framework of multivariate statistical analysis, without which it would be impossible to order systematically the large numbers of variables whose covariance expresses the presence of activities and their mutual relations.

The kind of analytic approach suggested here is not unknown in other fields of prehistoric research. Many of the essays in this volume provide detailed examples of refined ecological interpretation, some of which in addition incorporate multivariate procedures whereby activities are analyzed in terms of statistically significant associations among artifact classes, or between artifacts and classes of paleobiological data, that appear in different loci which make up the settlement patterns of prehistoric cultures. However, the most suggestive examples for Upper Paleolithic research are recent studies by the Binfords (S. R. Binford, this volume, 1965; Binford and Binford, 1966) and Leslie Freeman (1966) in which factor analysis is used to partition Mousterian artifact assemblages into a number of "tool-kits" that seemingly refer to aggregates of exploitative and maintenance economic tasks and their associated residence patterns which were to some extent spatially segregated. Redefined in this manner, the assemblage types making up Bordes' (1953) Mousterian Complex may be viewed as primarily representing complementary *structural poses* in the year-round subsistence pursuits of a single cultural system. The capabilities for meaningful interpretation inherent in such an approach are especially apparent in the most recent phase of this investigation (Binford and Binford, 1966). In their recent unpublished research the nature of the activities involved is more precisely defined by incorporating faunal and botanical evidence into the multivariate analysis, and ethnographic inference is used in conjunction with the archeological data in an attempt to outline the social and demographic correlates of economic activities in a paradigm of Mousterian cultural ecology.

At present there is available only one attempt to apply similar techniques to the Upper Paleolithic: Robert Whallon's (1963) unpublished master's thesis on Dordogne Aurignacian I stone-tool assemblages. While extremely provocative, Whallon's results are nevertheless inconclusive, at least in part because they are based on inadequate data that mainly derive from *fossile*-oriented excavations. However, the accumulation of large quantities of new evidence by modern data-gathering techniques will not in itself guarantee that the Upper Paleolithic can be successfully analyzed by the kind of research strategy proposed here. For there remain at least three problems in method and theory that must first be overcome before we can be assured either that the new data are properly ordered or even that they can provide the kinds of information that will be needed for culturally meaningful analysis.

First, the classifications and analytic procedures that are now used in ordering artifactual data must be fundamentally revised. The available comprehensive stone-tool typologies obviously mark a distinct advance over traditional *fossile* classifications, and their quantitative application has brought considerable refinement to both the comparison of archeological assemblages and the construction of space-time ordering schemes. But it is questionable whether any of them is in fact capable of systematically codifying the varieties of formal patterning inherent in archeological assemblages that must be controlled if activities are to be consistently isolated and interpreted. Taxonomists, perhaps still influenced by the traditional paleontological model, appear to assume that artifact types are in some manner natural units like species, and that consequently a single typology is capable of serving all purposes. At the same time, the question of what precisely types represent in behavioral terms is largely ignored and the investigation of their functional employment is even discouraged (Tixier, 1963, p. 17).

No doubt such attitudes are both an effect and cause of the fact that typologies continue to be designed solely by intuitive sorting procedures that are incapable of systematically controlling the extremely subtle kinds of patterning that are inherent in stone tools. This is apparent even in the taxonomic structure of the typologies themselves. For example, detailed typological subdivisions are usually recognized among "two-dimensional" tool families like burins, whose formal variation may be codified in terms of simple geometric relations on a single plane; but even more variable "three-dimensional" tools, like the carinate-nosed family of scrapers on elevated blocks, usually receive only minimal subdivision.

The best solution available to this problem entails replacing intuitive type design by an approach known as *attribute-cluster analysis,* which isolates typological categories by means of an explicit quantitative analysis of the patterns in which formal attributes segregate non-randomly (that is, cluster) among artifact samples.[7] Although the specific statistical techniques employed are quite different, attribute-cluster typology is pursued in a framework of multivariate analysis which is basically similar to that used in isolating cultural activities; indeed, a type defined by this approach is in reality no more than a particularly discrete variety of cultural activity. While attribute-cluster analysis has had several trials in the New World, its only comprehensive application to the Upper Paleolithic is found in an unpublished thesis on the Dordongne Aurignacian

[7] The term "statistical typology" is used frequently by Upper Paleolithic archeologists, but it refers to the quantitative applications of typologies in ordering assemblages and not to type design itself.

tradition (Sackett, 1965). A brief article is however available on Aurignacian endscraper typology that summarizes the major features of the method and theory involved (Sackett, 1966). The study is based upon a version of Spaulding's (1953) non-parametric approach to isolating attribute clusters, to which is added a procedure for controlling the higher order interaction effects in multivariate analysis that presumably reflect multiple-attribute contingencies. Although the application of such techniques requires a considerable expenditure of effort, it does seem to yield considerably enhanced refinement in typological discrimination when compared with the intuitive procedures now used in designing artifact classifications.

For example, this analysis demonstrates that the Aurignacian endscraper categories recognized in the current typologies largely fail to equate with the attribute clusters revealed by statistical analysis, even when the attributes subjected to analysis are precisely those that were used in defining the current types. Some of the latter appear to be intuitively idealized trait configurations that actually recur among only a minority of endscrapers, while others either fail to constitute mutually exclusive units or express no more than random combinations of attribute segregation. A second conclusion is that it should be possible to distinguish between what may be called stylistic and functional typological variation, and that these to a great extent seem to provide cross-cutting bases for type definition. Hence there is no single typology inherent in endscrapers, and the manner in which these tools are classified must depend upon the way in which their typological categories are to be employed in subsequent phases of research. Thus an endscraper typology designed for space-time systematics would presumably be based upon stylistic variables, as these provide the most sensitive reflections of historic relations among archeological assemblages. On the other hand, an analysis of economic activities among archeological sites would require an endscraper classification that systematically controlled functionally significant typological variation. A third conclusion is that the behavior of lithic attributes was strongly influenced by complex networks of mechanical contingencies that seemingly originated in the raw materials and techniques involved in stone-tool maufacture. In other words, a large degree of attribute clustering in stone tools reflects neither stylistic nor functional patterning, and in fact is not typologically significant in the usual sense of the term.

The last point is of particular interest, both because it greatly increases the statistical difficulties of isolating meaningful stone-tool types and because it would appear to call for a reexamination of some of the theoretical assumptions that are currently employed in interpreting the meaning of typologies. With regard to the latter, the type concept may not be valid to the degree it involves the notion that types are the material expression of mental models or templates, since lithic patterning seems to involve mechanical factors—as well presumably as motor habits—of which the artisan himself may not have been aware. Hence, while it is possible to isolate culturally meaningful typological patterns by attribute-cluster analysis, their precise behavioral significance may in many cases remain obscure.

Similar and considerably more refined cluster analysis must of course be pursued before a substantial body of new typologies can be designed or before it can even be concluded that the varieties of patterning observed in Aurignacian assemblages recur elsewhere. It is quite possible that the interplay of stylistic, functional, and purely mechanical attribute contingencies may in fact vary considerably among the Upper Paleolithic cultural traditions over and above their more obvious differences in form and relative frequencies of tools. In addition, it will be necessary to define much more precisely the meaning of stylistic and functional variation in stone tools and the manner in which these are to be identified in attribute clustering.[8] The question of tool function is especially crucial in view of the emphasis a cultural ecological approach places upon the reconstruction of economic tasks. Aside from the search for relevant ethnographic parallels, what little analysis of tool function there is at present concentrates solely upon formal variation within artifact assemblages themselves. Examples of this are Semenov's (1964) microscopic investigation of the stigmata of cutting-edge wear and the writer's ongoing statistical analysis of breakage patterns in different categories of stone tools. While considerably more work must be done along these lines, it would appear that the results of such investigations are most often equivocal unless independent confirmation is available. Obviously, the study of tool function must be extended to *contextual* analyses that will focus upon the manner in which attributes and classes of implements spatially covary both with each other and with architectural features and paleoecological remains on the living floors of archeological sites. If valid inferences are to be drawn concerning the functional roles of tools in cultural activities, the tools must ultimately be viewed in the actual matrix in which they were manufactured and used.

A second prerequisite for the proposed research strategy is a revision of the present taxonomies and procedures that are used in the space-time ordering of archeological assemblages. Unlike the Mousterian Complex, which may be sufficiently uniform for all of its manifestations to be

[8] One aspect of this definition must obviously concern the relativistic natures of style and function themselves. For example, a split-based bone javelin head may be considered a functional class of early Aurignacian assemblages; however, from the viewpoint of the Upper Paleolithic in general, it might be regarded as but one stylistic variant of this class—which it isomorphically shares with Gravette points, Magdalenian harpoons, etc. Moreover, within any given tool, a single attribute may behave either as a stylistic or as a functionable variable (aside from its mechanical contingencies with other such variables), depending upon the context within which it is analyzed. Thus marginal retouch on Aurignacian endscraper samples appears to be almost as sensitive to temporal and spatial factors as a design element in ceramics.

profitably analyzed in terms of a single ideal culture type, the Upper Paleolithic seems to incorporate extreme formal heterogeneity over time and space that strongly suggests the presence of both a number of distinct types of cultural systems and a considerable amount of micro-evolutionary change within systems. However, it may be questioned whether these could be isolated with sufficient precision by current ordering techniques even if adequate data and refined typologies were available. Although assemblages are presently ordered on the basis of quantitative assessment of their artifact inventories, the statistical methods involved are of limited value. They are restricted to purely descriptive techniques such as graphs and tabled artifact percentages, while the analysis of interassemblage frequency variation remains a purely qualitative operation that allows only intuitive control over the effects of sampling error. Another weakness in the current approach is that the artifact-type frequencies used in ordering are usually calculated as percentages of the total artifact assemblage. Yet the latter often may not be representative of their respective levels, since most assemblages are the product of restricted and somewhat arbitrarily placed excavations within occupation zones whose tools are by no means horizontally distributed at random. Hence the interassemblage frequency variations that are used in ordering may be due as much to differential sampling as to temporal and spatial factors. Finally, it should be noted that the principles of seriation are incompletely appreciated by many taxonomists, who—when direct stratigraphic evidence is lacking—often design essentially organic schemes of culture change in which temporally sensitive artifact frequency shifts are attributed to a speciation model of evolutionary radiation (*évolution buissonnante*).

Experiments with the Aurignacian materials discussed previously (Sackett, 1965, 1966) suggest that fairly rigorous space-time ordering can be obtained for lithic assemblages which is at least analogous to, if not as refined as, those which New World archeologists have designed for ceramic traditions. Aside from employing an artifact typology that was specifically designed to reflect what is presumably stylistic formal variation, the approach adopted in this study differs from current systematics in two fundamental ways. First, relative artifact-type frequencies are calculated not from the total assemblage but rather from restricted groups of tools that—it is hoped—refer to the same broad functional category. In other words, the popularity of a specific endscraper type is measured in terms of the frequencies of other endscrapers, and is completely unaffected by the numbers of such tools as burins and points. This procedure serves both to reduce the effects of skewed assemblage sampling noted above and to provide a basis for confirming assemblage variations by means of a number of independent tests (since endscrapers, burins, points, etc., are treated as distinct statistical universes). Second, assemblage comparison and ordering are conducted in terms of a quantitative measure of formal likeness and tested within a framework of statistical inference. This is achieved by combining the seriation matrix technique designed by Robinson (1951) and Brainerd (1951) with the use of independent Chi-square goodness-of-fit tests for determining the role of sampling error in the frequency variations of each pair of assemblages indexed in the matrix. By these means it is possible to obtain simultaneously both a precise mathematical expression of the formal differences among assemblages and a statement of the degree to which each of these differences is statistically significant.

While such procedures may never attain the level of control required for delimiting the archeological expressions of self-conscious social groups, they still afford considerably greater refinement in assemblage ordering than is now generally available. Moreover, they also provide important auxilliary information about cultural continuities and discontinuities and the demographic patterns of settlement that help elucidate many problems of cultural interpretation. For example, assuming that the rate of stylistic change was constant, the results of the above study suggest that Aurignacian societies underwent no marked temporal changes in the intensity of their occupation of the Dordogne. This conclusion directly contradicts both the traditional and most current ordering schemes, which indicate a progressive diminution of the numbers of Aurignacian sites over time—a result of assuming that the postulated stages of Aurignacian evolution were of equal length. In reality, two-thirds of all Dordogne Aurignacian temporal variation falls within stage I, while stages III and IV cannot statistically be distinguished either from each other or from stage II.[9] The spatial aspects of social demography may also be illuminated by these techniques. In this case the Aurignacian results suggest that it may be possible to define subregional stylistic zones that correlate highly with river valley systems, presumably a reflection of both the areal distributions of some kind of social frontiers and the ecological factors that may have determined them.

Finally, aside from sophisticated typologies and space-time ordering, the analysis of Upper Paleolithic cultural systems will require a body of evidence that is not only well documented but moreover representative. Although current excavation techniques are sufficiently refined to guarantee the former, there remains the question of sampling procedure: how are we to ensure that our evidence represents the full range of activities archeologically expressed in Upper Paleolithic societies? This undoubtedly will call for systematic investigation of the spatial distributions of activities both within individual sites and among the site complexes that make up the settlement patterns of cultural systems.

[9] Excluded from this analysis is the enigmatic Aurignacian V stage, known at present from a single assemblage (Laugerie-Haute). Aside from the fact that it stratigraphically succeeds the entire Upper Périgordian block, its tools fail to equate with the attribute cluster types which accomodate all other Aurignacian assemblages from the Dordogne that have been tested.

Our understanding of the localization of activities within sites is extremely limited because of the excavation techniques that were traditionally employed in *fossile*-oriented research. While archeologists have long been aware that artifacts and features are not randomly distributed within occupation levels, there are few examples—such as the Solutrean "hut" excavated by Peyrony (1932) at Fourneau du Diable—in which horizontal patterning was systematically recognized and described. However, this kind of information is of extreme importance to cultural interpretation since there is much evidence to suggest that Upper Paleolithic rock-shelter occupations may simultaneously have incorporated most of the activities that were segregated among a number of different localities in Mousterian times. Thus, in comparison with those of the Mousterian, Upper Paleolithic sites tend to be considerably larger in extent and more often occupied the year-round; their associated tool assemblages at once indicate both exploitative and maintenance economic activities; and certain tasks that one might expect to have been carried on elsewhere—such as reindeer butchering—often took place in the habitation sites themselves. In fact, the only food preparation task that has been clearly demonstrated not to have occurred in the rock-shelters is salmon cleaning and drying (J. G. D. Clark, 1948, p. 48).

The wealth of information that is actually to be found in rock-shelters is indicated by preliminary reports of the excavations at the Abri Pataud (Movius, 1965). Although no detailed review has yet appeared concerning the full range of activities represented at this site, initial study of the hearth and artifact distributions at least reveals that their residential associations may vary dramatically from one level to the next. In the Périgordian VI level, for example, hearths are aligned in 2-meter intervals to form so-called "long house" patterns of occupation, while in underlying Aurignacian horizons occupational debris tends to concentrate about isolated hearths that are more or less randomly distributed. Furthermore, Movius has been able to demonstrate how the relative frequencies of exotic raw materials and manufacturing debris complement the age and sex structures of butchered reindeer assemblages in indicating that the various residence types at this site appear to represent different patterns of seasonal exploitation.

Future investigation may similarly demonstrate that considerable variation exists in the spatial distributions of economic tasks and residence patterns that make up the settlement systems of Upper Paleolithic cultures. This is suggested by what appear to be marked differences in the intensity and localization of rock-shelter occupation in the various Dordogne cultural traditions. Summarizing information provided by de Sonneville-Bordes (1960), the Lower Périgordian is represented by relatively thin and areally dispersed layers, while the Aurignacian replaces it massively with intensive occupations and a tendency to cluster in more or less contiguous rock-shelters in narrow valleys or cliff faces. The Upper Perigordian in turn appears in somewhat thinner occupation levels that are generally evenly dispersed throughout the region. The Solutrean exhibits an especially interesting temporal development, being represented by relatively few but intensive occupations in its earlier phases and them seemingly fragmenting into dispersed settlements later on (see also Smith, 1964, p. 91). Finally, the Magdalenian recurs intensively in a great number of sites, many of which were previously unoccupied, with perhaps a progressive trend toward settlement along low-lying riverbanks.[10]

In addition to much more detailed information of this kind, an understanding of Upper Paleolithic settlement patterns will also require consideration of the numerous open-air sites in the Dordogne, which only recently have begun to receive systematic attention. Excavation of open stations in the Bergerac area by F. Bordes and J. Guichard (Bordes and de Sonneville-Bordes, 1966), and in the Isle Valley by J. Gaussen (1965), are revealing a hitherto unsuspected dimension of Upper Paleolithic economics and demography. In this connection, it may prove that the development of new techniques for isolating and interpreting prehistoric activities will depend largely upon such sites. This is due to their mode of habitation, which presumably involved shorter occupation spans and less spatial restriction than was the case in rock-shelters, and which resulted in considerably more explicit horizontal patterning of artifact complexes. Spatial segregation of activities is particularly clearcut in the Isle Valley sites, whose artifacts associate with cobblestone "pavements" that obviously define regular architectural features (Sackett, 1967).

Now, since Upper Paleolithic settlement patterns varied over space and time, and since most of our archeological assemblages probably express a variety of different kinds of activities, we are faced with extremely complex decisions about excavation procedure. Should we concentrate upon the complete recovery of a relatively few occupation levels in order to refine our techniques for distinguishing the multiple activities that were engaged in by individual residence groups? Or, rather, ought we to concentrate upon randomly sampling a large number of sites hoping to increase our knowledge of the total variety of activities and demographic patterns that occurred in the Upper Paleolithic as a whole? Circumstances and the personal inclinations of individual students will probably dictate both courses. Nevertheless, given the enormous cost in funds and time that is required for refined excavation, the development of culturally meaningful sampling techniques is of paramount importance in the design of future research strategy.

Especially when outlined so briefly, a programmatic statement such as this can intend only to provoke further discussion, not wholesale agreement. Indeed, in a field as viable and diverse as Upper Paleolithic archeology, it should neither be expected nor desired that research strategy will

[10] The Aurignacian V and Proto-Magdalenian phases are presently known from but a single and two occupations respectively.

develop according to any single formula. It is to be hoped, however, that this paper has demonstrated that long-range goals are of immediate concern. The present absorption of archeologists in data collection and descriptive classification is obviously not wrong in itself, as these must necessarily precede meaningful cultural analysis. At the same time, however, it should be equally apparent that both the methodology and degree of sophistication with which these more fundamental tasks are approached are determined by the kinds of assumptions we make regarding the nature of Upper Paleolithic cultural systems and the means we plan to use in pursuing their interpretation.

References

Binford, Lewis R. 1962. Archaeology as anthropology. *American Antiquity,* 28: 217–25.

——. 1964. A consideration of archaeological research design. *American Antiquity,* 29: 425–41.

Binford, Sally R. 1965. Social groupings and settlement systems in the Mousterian. Presented at the American Anthropological Association annual meetings. (Unpublished.)

Binford, Lewis R., and Sally R. Binford. 1966. A preliminary analysis of functional variability in the Mousterian of Levallois facies. In J. Desmond Clark and F. Clark Howell (Eds.), *Recent studies in paleoanthropology. American Anthropologist,* 68(2), Part 2: 238–95.

Birdsell, Joseph. 1968. Some predictions for the Pleistocene based upon equilibrium systems among recent hunters. In Richard B. Lee and Irven DeVore (Eds.), *Man the hunter.* Chicago: Aldine Publishing Company.

Bohmers, A. 1956. Statistics and graphs in the study of flint assemblages. *Palaeohistoria,* 5: 1–6.

Bonifay, Eugene. 1957. Les sédiments détritiques grossiers dans les remplissages des grottes. Méthode d'analyse morphologique et statistique. *L'Anthropologie,* 60: 477-61.

Bordes, François. 1950. Principes d'une méthode d'étude des techniques de débitage et de la typologie du Paléolithique ancien et moyen. *L'Anthropologie,* 54: 19–34.

——. 1953. Essai de classification des industries "moustériennes." *Bulletin de la Société Préhistorique Française,* 50: 457–66.

——. 1958. Nouvelles fouilles à Laugerie-Haute Est. Premiers résultats. *L'Anthropologie,* 62:205–44.

——. 1960. Evolution in the Paleolithic cultures. In Sol Tax (Ed.), *The evolution of man* (Vol. 2 of *Evolution after Darwin*). Chicago: University of Chicago Press.

Bordes, François, and Denise deSonneville-Bordes. 1966. Protomagdalénien ou Périgordien VII? *L'Anthropologie,* 70: 113–22.

Boriskovski, P. J. 1965. A propos des récents progrès des études paléolithiques en U.R.S.S. *L'Anthropologie,* 69: 5–30.

Bouchud, Jean. 1959. Le milieu et la vie pendant le Paléolithique moyen et supérieur. *Bulletin de la Société d'Etudes et de Recherches Préhistoriques et Institute Pratique de Préhistorie.* Les Eyzies. 9: 10–5.

——. 1961. Etude de la faune du gisement des Cottés (Haute-Vienne). *L'Anthropologie*, 65: 258–70.

Bourlon, M., A. Bouyssonie, and J. Bouyssonie. 1912. Grattoirs carénés, rabots et grattoirs nucléiformes. Essai de classification des grattoirs. *Revue Anth·opologique*, 22: 473–86.

Brainerd, G. W. 1951. The place of chronological ordering in archaeological analysis. *American Antiquity*, 16: 301–13.

Breuil, Henri. 1912. Les subdivisions du Paléolithique supérieur et leur signification. *Compte-Rendu* de la XIVe Session, Congrès International d'Anthropologie et d'Archéologie Préhistoriques, Geneva. Lagny: E. Grevin.

Butzer, Karl. 1964. *Environment and archeology*. Chicago: Aldine Publishing Company.

Chang, Kwan-chih. 1962. Typology of settlement and community patterns. *Arctic Anthropology*, 1: 28–41.

Clark, J. D. 1960. Human ecology during Pleistocene and later times in Africa south of the Sahara. *Currnt Anthropology*, 1: 307–24.

Clark, J. G. D. 1948. Fishing in prehistoric Europe. *Antiquaries Journal*, 28: 45–85.

——. 1952. *Prehistoric Europe: the economic basis*. London: Cambridge University Press.

——. 1954. *Excavations at Star Carr: an early Mesolithic site at Seamer near Scarborough, Yorkshire*. London: Cambridge University Press.

Escalon de Fonton, Max. 1961. Informations archéologiques: Montpellier (Grotte de La Salpetrière). *Gallia Préhistoire*, 4: 291–95.

Escalon de Fonton, Max, and H. de Lumley. 1955. Les civilisations de la Mediterranée septentrïonale et leurs intercurrences. Le complexe Montadien. *Bulletin de la Société Préhistorique Française*, 51: 379–94.

Freeman, Leslie G. 1966. The nature of Mousterian facies in Cantabrian Spain. In J. Desmond Clark and F. Clark Howell (Eds.), *Recent studies in paleoanthropology*, a special publication of the *American Anthropologist*, 68(2) Part 2: 230–37.

Gaussen, Jean. 1965. Le Paléolithique supérieur de la Basse Vallée de l'Isle. *Centenaire de la Préhistoire en Périgord* (1864–1964). Numéro Special du Bulletin de la Société Historique et Archéologique du Périgord, pp. 47–54.

Helm, June. 1962. The ecological approach in anthropology. *American Journal of Sociology*, 67: 630–39.

Laplace, Georges. 1961. Recherches sur l'origine et l'évolution des complexes Leptolithiques. Le problème des Périgordiens I et II et l'hypothese du synthétotype aurignaco-gravettien. Essai de typologie analytique. *Quaternaria*, 5: 153–240.

——. 1964. Essai de typologie systématique. *Annali dell'Universita di Ferrara*, Sezione XV, 1: 2.

Laville, Henri. 1964. Recherches sédimentologiques sur la paléoclimatologie du Wurmien recent en Périgord. *L'Anthropologie*, 68: 1–48, 219–52.

Lavocat, R., *et al.* 1966. Faunes et flores préhistoriques de l'Europe occidentale. "L'Homme et ses origines," *Atlas de Préhistoire*, vol. III. Paris: Boubée.

Leroi-Gourhan, André. 1963. Chatelperronien et Aurignacien dans le Nord-Est de la France (d'après la stratigraphie d'Arcy-sur-Cure, Yonne). *Bulletin de la Société Méridionale Spéleologie et de Préhistoire*, 6–9: 74–84.

Leroi-Gourhan, André, and M. Brésillon. 1964. Le site Magdalénien de Pincevent (Seine-etMarne). *Bulletin de l'Association Française pour l'Etude du Quaternaire*, 1: 59–64.

MOBERG, CARL-AXEL. 1961. Mangder av Fornfynd, Kring Actuella Tendenser I Arkeologisk Metodik, *Acta Universitatis Göthburgensis,* LXVII: I. (Summary: Trends in the present development of quantitative methods in archeology).

DE MORTILLET, GABRIEL. 1869. Essai d'une classification des cavernes et des stations sous abri fondée sur le produit de l'industrie humaine. *Bulletin de la Société Géologique de France,* 2: 583–87.

MOVIUS, HALLAM L., JR. 1960. Radiocarbon dates and upper Paleolithic archeology in central and western Europe. *Current Anthropology,* 1: 155–91.

——. 1965. Upper Perigordian and Aurignacian hearths at the Abri Pataud, Les Eyzies (Dordogne). *Miscelanea en Homenaje au Abate Henri Breuil,* II: 181–96.

——. 1966. The hearths of the Upper Périgordian and Aurignacian horizons at the Abri Pataud, Les Eyzies (Dordogne), and their possible significance. In J. Desmond Clark and F. Clark Howell (Eds.), *Recent studies in paleoanthropology. American Anthropologist,* 68(2) Part 2: 296–325.

PEYRONY, DENIS. 1932. *Les gisements préhistoriques de Bourdeilles (Dordogne).* Archives de l'Institut de Paléontologie Humaine, Mémoire 10.

——. 1933. Les industries "aurignaciennes" dans le bassin de la Vézère. Aurignacien et Périgordien. *Bulletin de la Société Préhistorique Française,* 30(10): 543–59.

——. 1939. Les Grimaldiens en Périgord. *L'Anthropologie,* 49(6): 702–8. 708.

——. 1948. Le Périgordien, l'Aurignacien, et le Solutréen en Eurasie d'après les dernières fouilles. *Bulletin de la Société Préhistorique Française,* 45 (9–10) : 305–28.

PRADEL, LOUIS. 1961. La Grotte des Cottés, commune de Saint-Pierre-de-Maille (Vienne). *L'Anthropologie,* 65: 229–70.

ROBERTS, J. H. *Zuñi daily life.* Laboratory of Anthropology, Notebook, deposits. *American Antiquity,* 16: 293–301.

RONEN, AVRAHAM. 1965. Observations sur l'Aurignacien. *L'Anthropologie,* 69: 465–86.

RUST, ALFRED. 1958. *Die Jungpalaolithischen Zeltangen von Ahrensburg.* Neumünster.

SACKETT, JAMES R. 1965. Aurignacian culture in the Dordogne: a study in archeological systematics. Unpublished Ph.D. thesis, Harvard University.

——. 1966. Quantitative analysis of Upper Paleolithic stone tools. In J. Desmond Clark and F. Clark Howell (Eds.), *Recent studies in paleoanthropology,* a special publication of the *American Anthropologist,* 68(2) Part 2: 356–94.

——. 1967. Solvieux: an Upper Paleolithic open-air site in southwestern France. In preparation.

SAHLINS, MARSHALL D. 1964. Culture and environment. In Sol Tax (Ed.), *Horizons of anthropology.* Chicago: Aldine Publishing Company.

SEMENOV, S. A. 1964. *Prehistoric technology.* Translated by M. W. Thompson. London: Cort, Adams and MacKay.

SMITH, PHILLIP. 1964. The Solutrean culture. *Scientific American,* 211: 86–94.

——. 1966. *Le Solutréen en France.* Publications de l'Institut de Préhistoire de l'Université de Bordeaux, Mémoire No. 5. Bordeaux: Imprimeries Delmas.

DE SONNEVILLE-BORDES, DENISE. 1960. *Le Paléolithique supérieur en Périgord.* 2 vols. Bordeaux: Imprimeries Delmas.

DE SONNEVILLE-BORDES, DENISE, and J. PERROT. 1953. Essai d'adaptation des méthodes statistiques au Paléolithique supérieur. Premiers resultats. *Bulletin de la Société Préhistorique Française,* 50: 323–33.

——. 1954–56. Lexique typologique du Paléolithique supérieur. *Bulletin de la Société Préhistorique Française,* 51: 327–35; 52: 76–79; 53: 408–412, 547–59.

SPAULDING, ALBERT C. 1953. Statistical techniques for the discovery of artifact types. *American Antiquity,* 18: 305–313.

——. 1960. The dimensions of archaeology. In Gertrude E. Dole and R. L. Carneiro (Eds.), *Essays in the science of culture: in honor of Leslie A. White.* New York: Thomas Y. Crowell.

STEWARD, JULIAN H. 1955. *Theory of culture change.* Urbana: University of Illinois Press.

TIXIER, JACQUES. 1963. Typologie de l'Epipaléolithique du Maghreb. Centre de Recherches Anthropologiques Préhistoriques et Ethnographiques, *Mémoir* 2.

WHALLON, ROBERT. 1963. A statistical analysis of some Aurignacian I assemblages from southwestern France. Unpublished master's thesis, University of Chicago.

PART II

Investigating Variability in the Archeological Record: A Single Occupation Unit

The papers in this section all focus on the analysis of archeological remains from a single site. Concern is primarily with the recognition, measurement, and explanation of variability in the form and distribution of a site's cultural remains. The authors argue that internal variability is to be expected and that it derives from the differential composition and distribution of the societial segments represented at the site. These segments were distinguished by their activities and tasks and by their cultural means of relating to one another.

All of the papers deal with analytical techniques that facilitate the demonstration of non-random distributions and associations among units of archeological observation. The isolation and definition of ordered relationships in the archeological record are necessary for empirical generalizations about the record; these generalizations then can serve as the referents for our explanations. An assumption basic to this process is that the archeological deposits are undisturbed and have been investigated in a manner which takes sampling error into account, and that order in the record derives from the systematic relationships which characterized the social life of the cultural unit under study. Explanations for order therefore take the form of propositions as to the organizational and/or behavioral characteristics of the sociocultural unit represented. If these propositions are verified, they may then account for the observations made on the archeological record.

Most of the papers in this section emphasize the initial, exploratory phase of analysis. This emphasis is probably due to an enthusiasm on the part of archeologists free to explore their data for classes of order not considered before. These classes of order are not to be seen in the "self-evident" units of observation, nor would they be seen by those who proclaim our knowledge of the past limited by the incompleteness of the archeological record. These papers are examples of some of the directions in which our knowledge of the past can expand, given the new perspectives developing in archeology.

The papers by Longacre, Hill, and Cowgill are concerned with the analysis of the archeological record at a single site. Problems related to data collection, handling, and analysis are discussed—problems which could arise only when the archeological record is viewed as a complex of structured relationships arising out of the organizational and dynamic characteristics of extinct cultural systems. Pursuit of the arguments of relevance presented by these authors can result in the development of general systems of measurement of cultural variables in the operation of any number of cultural systems. It is here that much of the excitement of this kind of archeology lies: By developing archeological theory and verifying arguments of relevance to past conditions, we can gradually build up a battery of measurement scales for the comparative study of behavior or of cultural and ecological variables. The crucial link here is the development of sound, verifiable arguments of relevance. However, the comparative study of archeological observations can bring us understanding of the operation of past cultural systems only insofar as our observations can be shown to be relevant to stated classes of cultural variables.

The papers by Ayres and Longacre and the paper by Williams explore the feedback that can be developed between archeological and ethnographic problems. The expected relationships between material items and behavioral features of cultural systems are frequently most economically analyzed and tested with non-archeological data. Similarly, many problems originating in the investigation of non-archeological data may be efficiently tested by the use of archeological data. These papers exemplify both these cases and demonstrate kinds of research which will be more frequently taken up in the future.

The grouping of these papers under a single section heading is not meant to imply that the authors have failed to consider the relevance of the particular site under study to broader regional and more general anthropological considerations. But one lesson to be drawn from the papers presented is that without a rigorous investigation of the meaning of the internal variablity at a single site and the contexts in which such variability is produced, comparisons of differences and similarities between sites can be very misleading. Comparisons made on such a basis can frequently obscure variability within a stable system and change from one kind of system to another (see S. R. Binford's paper, this volume). The arrangement of these papers in the book is the work of the editors and does not reflect the context in which individual authors developed their arguments. Thus, some of the arguments offered here as to processes of culture change and the significance of ecological relationships should more appropriately be considered in the context of the discussion of the following section, Part III.

Some Aspects of Prehistoric Society in East-Central Arizona

This paper discusses a series of archeological investigations conducted in east-central Arizona (Fig. 1) directed toward elucidating the nature of cultural stability and change in the extinct societies of the region.[1] The primary focus is on the Carter Ranch Pueblo (*ca.* A.D. 1050–1200), where we attempted to isolate and explain certain organizational features of the sociocultural system as an initial step toward gaining a better understanding of adaptive changes made by the society to environmental stress. This report must be viewed as a case study and the research as a somewhat crude and initial effort. It is our hope that as the field advances our

[1] The field work that provided the data for this report was carried out in eastern Arizona during the summers of 1959-62. This work was supported in large measure by grants from the National Science Foundation to the Chicago Natural History Museum, Paul S. Martin, Principal Investigator. I thank Dr. Martin and his colleague, J. B. Rinaldo, for their encouragement and help both in the field and at the Museum. Most of the statistical operations were undertaken with the help of the IBM 7094 computer at the University of Chicago. A grant to the Chicago Natural History Museum by the Wenner-Gren Foundation for Anthropological Research made these operations possible. The work reported here formed the basis for my doctoral dissertation at the University of Chicago (Longacre, 1963). I acknowledge and thank the members of my dissertation committee: L. R. Binford, Director; Fred Eggan; L. A. Fallers; and P. S. Martin. This paper grew out of a shorter one presented by J. N. Hill and myself at the 64th annual meeting of the American Anthropological Association, Symposium on Prehistoric Social Organization, Denver, in 1965.

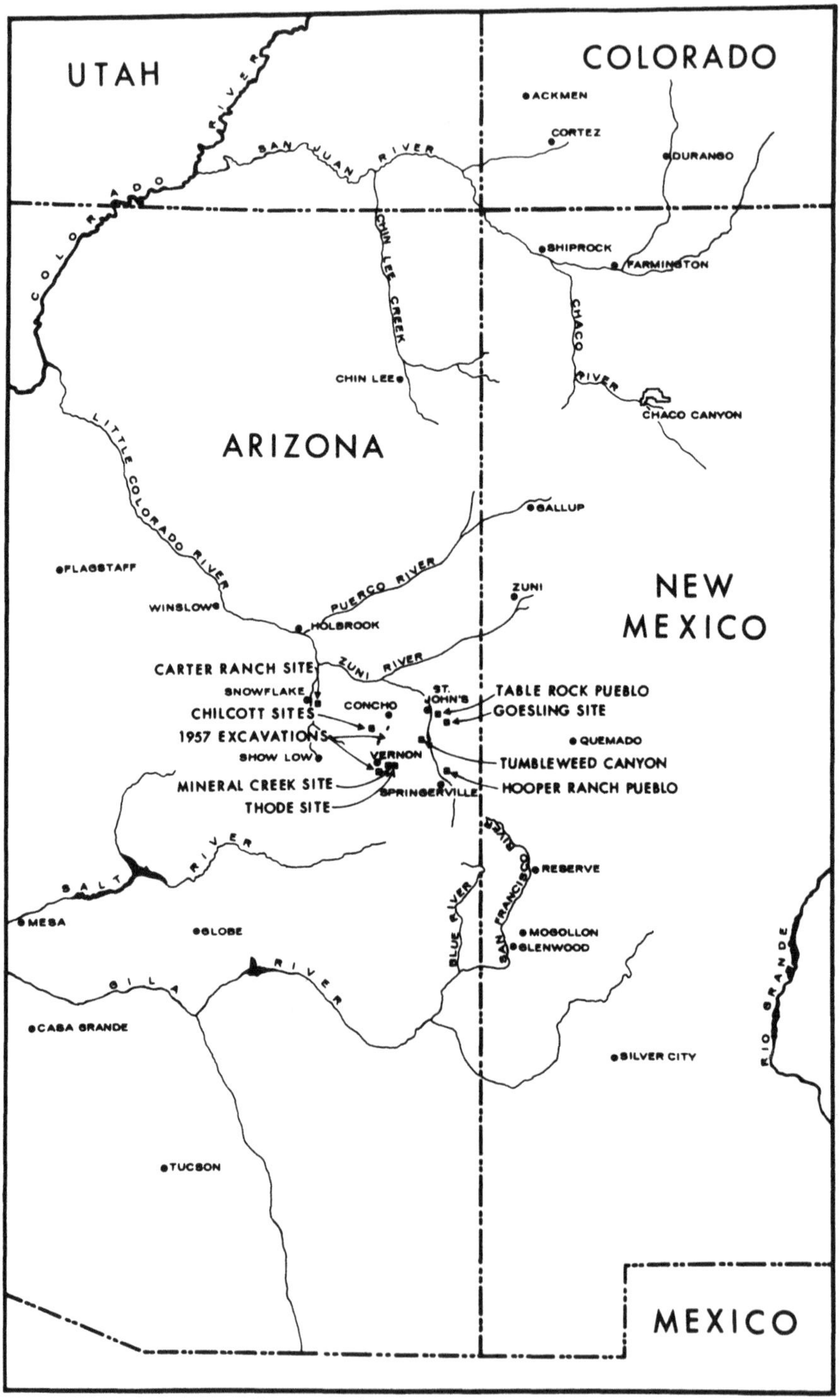

Figure 1. Area of investigations.

findings will be rendered obsolete by refinement and growth of methods of data collection and analysis.

In the undertaking of this research we were guided by several assumptions of a basic theoretical nature. First, we adopted a perspective which views culture as a systemic whole composed of interrelated subsystems, such as the social system, the technological system, the religious system, etc. This view of culture has been discussed and described by L. R. Binford (1962, 1965). Such a perspective compels the paleoanthropologist to focus on the nature and interrelations of the component parts of the cultural system under study, and to work within an ecological frame of reference. The aim is to isolate and define cultural processes, the means by which cultures remain stable or change.

The second assumption underlying this work is that the patterning of material remains in an archeological site is the result of the patterned behavior of the members of an extinct society and that this patterning is potentially informative as to the way the society was organized. Our first task, then, is to define the structure of the archeological remains at a site and to offer hypotheses as to the organization of the society and associated patterns of individual behavior. The patterned relationships among classes of artifacts should document the context in which they were made, used, and lost or abandoned. It is essential to measure the mutual covariation among all classes and types of archeological data; the structure of this covariation, once delimited, should reflect the organizational and behavioral aspects of the society that produced it.

We will begin by discussing the environmental and cultural setting of the prehistoric pueblo under consideration, and this will be followed by a description of the archeological structure delimited at the site. We then offer some propositions as to the nature of the society represented and the cultural processes operative in the region.

Sociocultural Background and the Environmental Setting

This section consists of a brief synthesis of environmental and cultural changes which occurred in east-central Arizona before A.D. 1200 in order to provide a background for the period under study. Data for this synthesis come from excavation and survey (Martin *et al.*, 1964, pp. 201–215).

The area today is environmentally transitional between the White Mountains and the Colorado Plateau. It is a semi-arid, topographically rugged region in the upper drainage of the Little Colorado River. The landscape is dotted with basalt-capped mesas, cinder cones, deep river valleys, and numerous arroyos. This area was occupied from at least 1500 B.C. until approximately A.D. 1350, at which time permanent occupations became restricted to the deepest stream valleys such as Silver Creek and the Little Colorado itself.

At the present time the region is marginal for most forms of agriculture;

the most important economic activity is stock-raising. The only economically significant agricultural lands are the irrigated lowlands in the deep stream valleys such as those at Taylor and Shumway on Silver Creek where corn and other cultigens grow readily. The lack of upland agriculture cannot be explained simply by a lack of water; the critical factor seems to be the absence of a regular growing season of at least 120 frost-free days. In the upland town of Vernon, individuals who maintain irrigated garden plots tell us they are lucky to get a crop of corn to mature once every three or four years. It is significant that these upland regions are dotted with prehistoric sites dating from about A.D. 700 to about 1000 and we know that occupants of the sites were dependent upon corn agriculture. Obviously there must have been some important changes in the local environment.

The study of fossil pollens has been a significant part of the investigation of the degree and kind of climatic change which has occurred. Schoenwetter (Martin *et al.*, 1962, pp. 191–94) and Hevley (1964) can find no palynological evidence of major climatic change in the area. Both workers, however, indicate that there are subtle and critical shifts in the nature of the environment. It is argued here that these minor shifts necessitated major adaptive changes on the part of the area's prehistoric inhabitants. The nature of these changes must be seen against the preceding centuries of gradual development.

The period from about A.D. 600–700 to about 1000 or 1100 shows a basic trend suggesting continuity despite numerous stylistic changes in material remains. After the initial appearance of established village farming communities in the region, there was a regular and impressive increase in the population, resulting in a network of small agricultural communities (Martin *et al.*, 1964, pp. 205–209). Village distribution was linked to the presence of arable lands in the alluvium of the many small streams in the area, streams which today are arroyos. Pueblo architecture appears later, but community size remains unchanged—small hamlets of from three or four to fifteen or twenty rooms replaced the earlier pit house villages. Rectangular or circular kivas are sometimes associated with these small pueblo villages. When the population of a village reached a critical size, budding-off seems to have occurred, and this process resulted in the establishment of increasing numbers of small agricultural communities in previously unoccupied habitats. The newly founded villages probably maintained kinship and ritual ties with the mother community for several generations, but there are indications that through time these ties became attenuated.

Cohesion within the villages was probably maintained along kin lines and might have been reinforced by the emergence of non-kin-based membership groups, a ceremonial sponsorship system, or both. There is no evidence suggesting strong multi-community integration during this period.

At about 1000 or 1100, or perhaps earlier in the eastern portion of the region, there is evidence of major structural change in these cultural systems. The palynological data reflecting minor but critical environmental shifts are correlated with these cultural changes. Schoenwetter (Martin *et al.*, 1962, pp. 194–206) argues that the pollen spectra suggest a minor shift in rainfall pattern beginning about A.D. 1000. His report hints also that about 1350 there might have been a slight decrease in the mean annual temperature. Subsequent work by Hevley (1964) supports this suggestion and points to a drop in mean annual temperature of about 2°–3°F. at about 1300. This order of change may appear to be insignificant, but it was of sufficient magnitude to have jeopardized the subsistence base of the local people. The small temperature drop would have meant a shorter growing season which, in turn, made corn agriculture hazardous. As modern environmental conditions were reached, the uplands were abandoned and there was a convergence of the prehistoric populations in the deeper valleys, where the lower elevations meant mean temperatures 2°–3°F. higher. The importance of these conditions can be seen today if the agricultural productivity at Taylor and Shumway is compared with the marginal agricultural activity in the uplands.

The coincidental occurrence of changes in critical climatic variables and changes in location and size of settlements suggests that the local populations underwent rather striking adaptive responses. Some of the changes are readily apparent in the data; others are more difficult to delimit.

Two main trends can be detected. First, the beginning of population convergence, with small, single-residence-unit villages coalescing to form larger communities of more than one residence grouping; second, the appearance of Great Kivas at a few sites at about A.D. 1000–1100 documents an attempt to integrate a number of villages via a religious mechnism such as a ceremonial sodality. This pattern of convergence continued and culminated in the presence of a few very large towns composed of units which had previously formed single villages.

This aggregation forming larger population units posed certain integrative problems. A community composed of residence units with strongly traditional kinds of internal cohesion had built-in sharp lines of cleavage. Some of the means available for a new level of integration were religious; some might have involved sodalities such as curing societies which crosscut residence units; mutual interdependence among social groups could have been created through reciprocal exchange of goods and services.

Carter Ranch Pueblo was investigated in order to determine more precisely the nature of the environmental and cultural changes of this region between A.D. 1050 and 1200.

Description of the Carter Ranch Site

The Carter Ranch Site consists of a U-shaped block of rooms which face a courtyard with various activity areas such as cooking and storage facilities

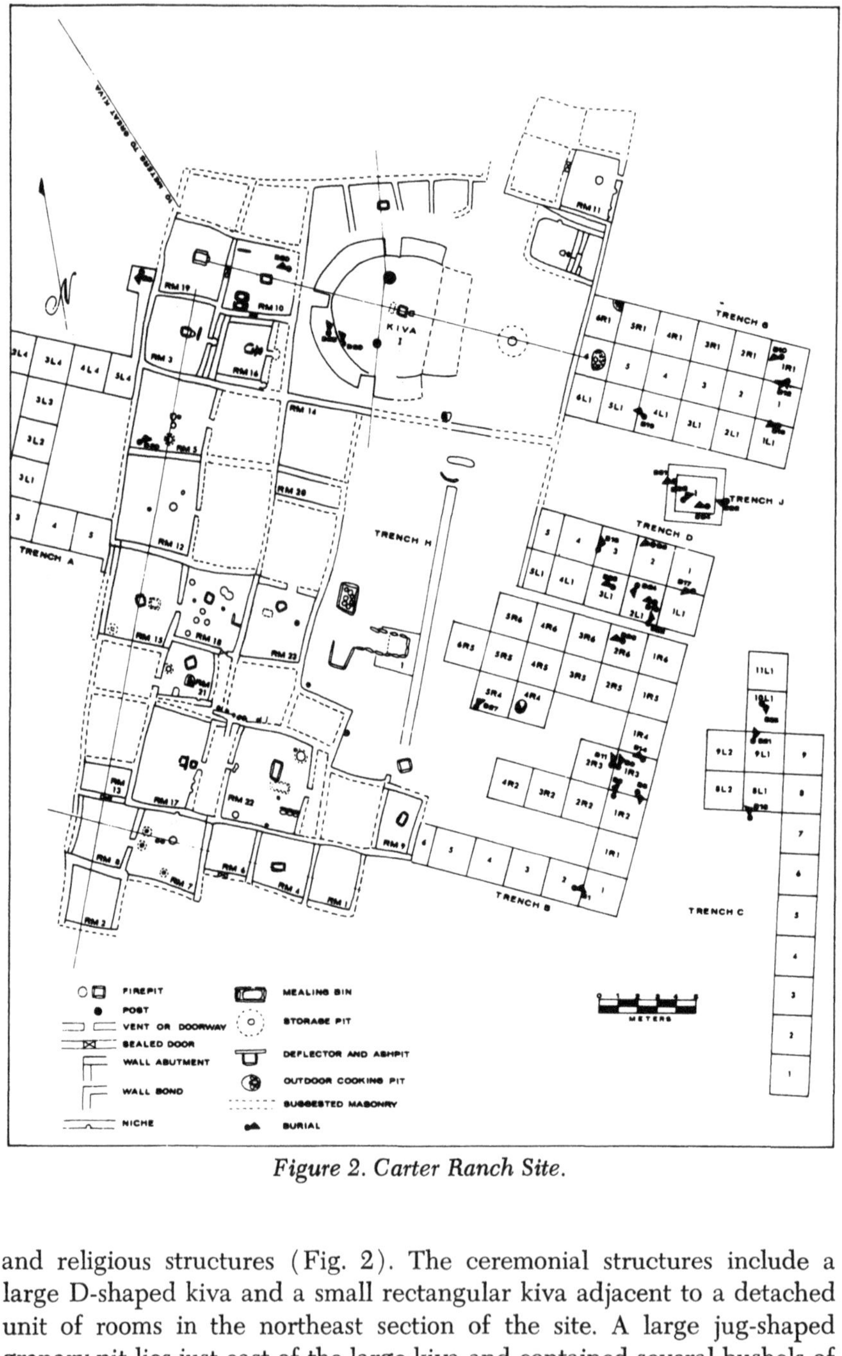

Figure 2. Carter Ranch Site.

and religious structures (Fig. 2). The ceremonial structures include a large D-shaped kiva and a small rectangular kiva adjacent to a detached unit of rooms in the northeast section of the site. A large jug-shaped granary pit lies just east of the large kiva and contained several bushels of charred corn. A detached circular Great Kiva is located about 10 meters northwest of the north wing. This kiva is approximately 18 meters in diameter and has a long lateral entry ramp to the east.

A mound of trash of considerable size occurred just east of the site; this midden yielded a number of burials which clustered in three distinct areas. The burials in the northern cluster were oriented east-west; those in the southern area were oriented north-south; burials in the central area were mixed with respect to orientation.

The site as a whole is oriented toward the east. The interior features of the kivas and most of the rooms are lined up from west to east, and the Great Kiva is also oriented in the same direction, 7°30′ south of true east. This angle corresponds with the angle of sunrise in this location during the first week of March, two weeks before the vernal equinox.[2] Although we have been unable to correlate this orientation with any specific celestial phenomena, such as solstice, eclipses, or constellations, it remains clear that the measuring devices of the site's inhabitants allowed a high order of accuracy in that the Great Kiva and the community itself are aligned exactly.

SEQUENCE OF CONSTRUCTION

The first rooms to be built at the site were in the north end of the central section: rooms 19, 3, 5, 12, 15, 18, 16, and 10. There were four later periods of construction, and the pueblo expanded mainly to the east and the south. The last addition was probably the detached unit in the northeastern part of the site.[3]

THE ASSEMBLAGE

Thousands of potsherds, whole vessels, whole and partial tools of stone and bone as well as ornaments and other kinds of cultural items were recovered. They are described in detail elsewhere (Martin *et al.*, 1964).

SUMMARY

The arrangement of the site is that of a "front-facing" plan (Reed, 1956). The nature of the cultural items from the site suggests that it is stylistically affiliated with what Rinaldo (1964) has called "Late Mogollon" culture. The easterly orientation of the site is support for this interpretation.

Formal and Spatial Correlational Analysis

Forming the initial archeological work at the Carter Ranch Site in 1961, a statistical analysis of a portion of the data was undertaken by L. G.

[2] This was done with the help of Dr. Frank Jettner of the Adler Planetarium in Chicago.

[3] Details of the sequence of construction and the supporting evidence are given by Rinaldo (Martin *et al.*, 1964, pp. 49—51).

Freeman and James Brown (Martin *et al.*, 1964; Brown and Freeman, 1964). Frequencies of ceramic types and their distribution were subjected to bivariate regression analysis using a Univac computer at the University of Chicago.

Frequencies of fourteen pottery types in eighteen floor and subfloor samples from twelve features were used in the analysis; frequencies of each of these pottery types was analyzed against each of the other thirteen types. The results showed a strong mutual correlation among certain of the pottery types, a non-random distribution of these covarying ceramic classes among distinct classes of rooms. There were four such clusters of pottery types which varied independently of one another. Brown and Freeman (1964) were able to discard temporal variation in pottery styles as a possible explanation for the observed independence and for the related differential distribution of the ceramic classes among different room types. An alternative explanation was advanced—that of functional independence for the ceramic classes. This functional hypothesis was supported by the strong association between the ceramic classes and room types; the defining attributes for the room types were the presence or absence of features such as hearths, mealing bins, etc. The findings indicate that the correlated differences in features and pottery reflect different kinds of activities localized in different kinds of rooms.

Excavations were continued at the Carter Ranch Site during 1962 with finer control of provenience employed. The newly gathered data on ceramic types and their distributions were subjected to multiple regression analysis using the IBM 7094 computer at the University of Chicago. In addition, non-ceramic artifact frequencies and distributions from both the 1961 and 1962 seasons were analyzed in the same way. Multiple regression analysis (IBM Bimed 34) proved to be a more powerful analytical technique and resulted in some refinement of the findings.

The four classes of pottery types originally suggested were expanded to five; these five classes are presented in Table 1. One major point of interest concerns class number three which contains a number of smudge types. This corresponds to a class proposed by Freeman and Brown (Martin *et al.*, 1964, pp. 129*ff.*) which was noted to occur in high frequency in a ceremonial context (that is, kiva floors and burials). This same correlation was demonstrated in the second multiple regression analysis (Great Kiva and burials) and confirmed the association of this ceramic class with ceremonial activities.

Artifact frequencies by location were also subjected to multiple regression analysis. A number of clusterings were defined, but there was a great deal of overlapping between them. Generalized tools would probably have been used in a number of tasks, and this might account for the less tight artifact clusters when compared to ceramics.

Table 1. Pottery Constellations from Floors of Rooms 18–23 and Great Kiva, Carter Ranch Site.

I. Snowflake Black-on-White, Snowflake variety.
Alma Plain.
McDonald Corrugated, indented.

II. Snowflake Black-on-White, Carterville variety.
St. Johns Polychrome.
McDonald Corrugated, plain.

III. St. Johns Black-on-Red.
Plain Brown Corrugated.
Brown Indented Corrugated, smudged interior.
Plain Brown Corrugated, smudged interior.
Patterned Corrugated.

IV. Snowflake Black-on-White, Hay Hollow variety.
Show Low Black-on-Red.
Brown Indented Corrugated.

V. Plain Brown Corrugated.
Show Low Black-on-Red.
St. Johns Polychrome.

There were, however, two strong associations, each between two classes of artifacts. First, the class called "ceremonial" and the weaving implements were highly correlated. Since weaving today is a male activity associated with the kiva among the people of the Western Pueblos, this correlation is consistent with the ethnographic data from the area.

Second, there was an unusually tight association between the chopping artifacts and those used in the manufacture of arrow-shafts. Since both tool kits suggest male activities, this association strengthens the interpretation of a fairly strong division of labor and functionally specific male and female activity areas at the site.

The Distribution of Design Elements and Element Groups

Our pre-excavation research design involved the formulation of a series of testable hypotheses. One of these concerned post-marital residence patterns. Briefly, the argument might be stated as follows: if there were a residence rule which led to related females living in the same locale through several generations, then ceramic manufacture and decoration would be learned and passed down within the context of this residence unit (assuming female potters). Non-random preference for certain designs might reflect this social pattern.[4]

One hundred seventy-five design elements and element groups were defined, using more than 6,000 sherds and a number of whole vessels.[5] The first analytical step involved the plotting of distribution of relative frequencies for each design on a site plan. This suggested that there was a non-random distribution, but the technique was crude at best. It was decided, therefore, to refine the analysis by using multiple regression analysis. In this operation, actual counts were used rather than relative frequencies.

The counts from each floor were run against every other floor sample. Floors were correlated on the basis of the frequencies of occurrence of the 175 design elements and element groups. The same was done for some of the fill samples. Fourteen floor proveniences were used, and the following clusters emerged: (1) Rooms 2, 4 (both floors), 7, and 8 (both floors) form a tight group; (2) Rooms 3, 5, 10 (both floors), 12, 15, and Kiva I form an equally tight group. Room 11 consistently shows associations with the first group.

When the location of these rooms is noted on the site plan (Fig. 2), the significance of these clusters becomes clear. The first group consists of a block of adjacent rooms at the south end of the pueblo. The second group is a block of rooms with an adjacent kiva at the north end of the pueblo. Room 11, which associates with the first group, is in the northeastern portion of the site and is part of a group of unexcavated rooms.

The analysis of room fill was less successful, but there were similarities among the fills of Rooms 3, 5, 12, 15, and Kiva I. This suggests continuity in the pattern of design similarities in the floor distributions and argues for the consistent production of similar designs in the northern part of the village, probably over several generations of potters. Therefore, our hypothesis on the spatial distribution of design elements correlating with residence unites received support.

The Burial Analysis

Thirty-four burials were excavated at the Carter Ranch Site; most were in the trash east of the pueblo. Grave goods were associated with male and infant burials, while interments of females yielded few or no associated goods.

[4] The first demonstration of a correlation between changes in residence and the distribution of design attributes of pottery was made by Deetz (1960, 1965), by utilizing data from the historic period in the Plains. The usefulness of the distribution of design elements and element groups as a tool for sociological interpretation in prehistory was first realized by Cronin (Martin *et al.*, 1962, pp. 105 *ff.*). It was out of the initial research by Cronin that the hypothesis reported here developed.

[5] This was done by two Chicago Natural History Museum artists, Mr. and Mrs. Stevens Seaberg. I am grateful to Dr. Anna O. Shepard for excellent suggestions regarding design terminology (personal communications, 1965).

The burials occurred in three clusters: the north and south clusters each had eight burials, and there were nine in the central area. Seven of the eight burials in the northern clusters were oriented east-west; all eight in the southern group were oriented north-south. Orientation of burials in the central area was mixed.

The design elements and element groups of the mortuary ceramics were analyzed to see if the burial groups could be related to the architectural units of the site. Our results showed that the northern burial area had pottery with designs that occurred in the northern cluster of rooms at the site, and the southern burial group was similarly linked to the southern group of rooms. The central area was mixed with respect to design distribution, although there are more affinities to the northern block of rooms.

There were many respects in which the central burial cluster differed from the other two. This group was mixed in orientation and in the distribution of design elements and element groups. Further, almost all of the ceremonial items included as grave offerings came from this cluster of interments. There is also a non-random distribution of ceramic vessels in the center cluster:

	North	*Center*	*South*
Vessels	19	32	20
Burials	8	9	8

The mixed orientations of the central burials, together with the large number of ceremonial items and vessels, suggest that the central cluster represents high-status individuals from the residence units. It would appear that each of the residence units maintained its own burial area but that a separate portion of the cemetery was reserved for high-status individuals.

Summary and Conclusions

At the Carter Ranch Pueblo, 175 design elements and element groups were analyzed in terms of their distribution in rooms, kivas, burials, and trash. The designs clustered in association with two major architectural units at the site. Kivas, discrete burial areas, and trash deposits were also associated with the architectural units. On the assumption that the females were the potters, this patterned distribution argues for post-marital residence in the vicinity of the wife's female relatives, with ceramic decoration learned and passed down within the residence unit. Time depth is demonstrated by the association of designs on pottery in the architectural units and associated trash in deposits of over one meter deep.

The localization of females in architectural units at the site over a period of several generations suggests in turn that non-portable objects, such as rooms and access to a specific mortuary area, were inherited within the residence units and that this inheritance was probably in the female line. The corporate nature of the residence unit is also suggested by the maintenance of a kiva and by associated mortuary practices. A large bell-shaped storage pit was excavated in association with one of the kivas; this large storage facility contained the charred remains of several bushels of corn. This adds support to the inference regarding the corporate nature of the residence units themselves, as it appears to have been a jointly used storage area which must have been maintained by a social unit larger than a single family.

Although it has not been possible to demonstrate the actual lineality of the residence units, it seems likely that they were localized matrilineal descent groups.[6] The inferred corporate nature of the units and the suggested pattern of matrilineal inheritance support this suggestion. In addition, the maintenance of a discrete cemetery with design elements and element groups clustering in terms of residence units argues for a lineage organization and one which reckoned descent in the female line.

Social groups smaller than the residence unit have not been archeologically determined. Arguing from the ethnographic present, one might expect a household to be present, essentially a familial social unit. Among the Hopi and Zuni, households are localized in adjoining rooms and form the basic local unit among the Western Pueblos (Eggan, 1950, pp. 29–31, 297–99; Beaglehole, 1937, pp. 5–6; Titiev, 1944, pp. 7–14; Roberts, 1956, p. 2). There is today a great deal of variation in the number of individuals who compose a household and variability in the number of rooms constituting the spatial unit (cf. Roberts, 1956). The household today is a basic economic unit and is the one which is the land-holding unit.
ently multi-functional, but the strong correlations among the ceramic classes with room types suggest that each room had a primary or more

The households at Carter Ranch Site probably consisted of groups of adjoining rooms which formed residence areas. The rooms were apparusual function. Isolation of specific functions is admittedly difficult, but the ceramic classes themselves offer some clues. The pottery types associated with ritual units such as the kivas are found in relatively low frequencies on habitation room floors. This indicates that some ritual was conducted in some houses, although on a small scale. The same pattern exists among the present day Western Pueblo peoples (Eggan, 1950, pp. 298–99).

Specific groupings of pottery types may indicate certain generalized room functions. Painted pottery never shows signs of having been used for cooking (absence of sooted exteriors), whereas the smaller brown,

[6] Although I refer to these residence units as "localized matrilineal descent groups" in earlier publications (Longacre, 1963, 1964), I have been able to refine my thoughts regarding the difficulty if not the impossibility of getting at descent using archeological data. This refinement is largely due to discussions with David Schneider, University of Chicago; F. K. Lehman, University of Illinois; and James N. Hill, University of California, Los Angeles. Of equal importance have been my students, all of whom are excellent teachers and to whom I extend my gratitude.

textured jars often show such evidence. Brown and Freeman (1964) have noted a high frequency of such brown pottery at the site in rooms with circular floor pits, suggesting that these rooms might have had cooking as their primary function. They were probably also used for storage (many had storage pits), general work (such as manufacture of household articles), and other tasks as well.

Painted ceramics occur as bowls, pitchers, and jars. Since they apparently did not serve as cooking vessels, they were probably used in the preparation of food for cooking and in the serving of food. As Brown and Freeman (1964) point out, a grouping of painted pottery types consisting principally of pitchers and bowls appears to be associated with rooms with square fire pits and mealing bins. This suggests a function of food preparation for rooms with these features. The smaller, featureless rooms were probably used for storage.

The pattern, then, appears to be one of multi-functional uses for each room but with a more common set of activities for each room type. This is precisely the pattern of the modern Western Pueblos (Roberts, 1956). The multi-functional nature of the rooms makes the delimitation of households at Carter Ranch very difficult. Chang (1958, p. 302) has suggested that the fireplace (kitchen) is the most obvious index of a household. His suggestion is, however, based on ethnographic data from tropical or semi-tropical environments. In the more temperate climates, heating fires would also be necessary. It is, therefore, not surprising to find fire pits in so many of the rooms at the Carter Ranch Site. Some of these fires might well have served also for lighting and food preservation.

The Carter Ranch Site stands as a turning point in the prehistory of this particular region of the Southwest. The occupation of the site by two residence units ushers in an era of population aggregation in the area. Prior to this—over a period of more than 500 years—villages consisted of small groups of people approximating the size of one of the residence units of the Carter Ranch Site. This striking shift in the structure of population culminates in a pattern of fewer but considerably larger towns during the fourteenth century.

The process of aggregation coincides with the onset of a period of environmental stress and would seem to be an adaptive response on the part of these extinct societies. The initial set of adaptive changes documented at the Carter Ranch Site are a prelude to the even greater changes that appear in the region by 1300 (cf. Hill, 1966). Many of the adaptive shifts that have been noted appear to be in the direction of a form of cultural system exemplified by the modern Western Pueblos (cf. Longacre, 1964).

The inferences drawn in this report were largely justified by reference to a set of propositions drawn within a particular theoretical context (general systems theory) which served to structure the field research (cf. L. R. Binford, 1965). The implications of our conclusions have not been stressed here, since they are made explicit elsewhere (Longacre, 1963, 1964, 1966). The conclusions offered here are tentative and only further testing and research can strengthen, modify, or replace them.

References

BEAGLEHOLE, ERNEST. 1937. *Notes on Hopi economic life.* Yale University Publications in Anthropology, no. 15. New Haven: Yale University Press.

BINFORD, LEWIS R. 1962. Archaeology as anthropology. *American Antiquity,* 28: 217–25.

——. 1965. Archaeological systematics and the study of culture process. *American Antiquity,* 31: 203–210.

BROWN, JAMES A., and LESLIE G. FREEMAN, JR. 1964. A UNIVAC analysis of sherd frequencies from the Carter Ranch Pueblo, eastern Arizona. *American Antiquity,* 30(2): 162–67.

CHANG, KWANG-CHIH. 1958. Study of Neolithic social groupings: examples from the New World. *American Anthropologist,* 60(2): 298–334.

DEETZ, JAMES D. F. 1960. An archaeological approach to kinship change in eighteenth century Arikara culture. Ph.D. dissertation, Harvard University.

——. 1965. *The dynamics of stylistic change in Arikara ceramics.* Illinois Studies in Anthropology, no. 4. Urbana: University of Illinois Press.

EGGAN, FRED. 1950. *Social organization of the western pueblos.* Chicago: University of Chicago Press.

HEVLY, RICHARD H. 1964. Pollen analysis of Quaternary archeological and lacustrine sediments from the Colorado Plateau. Unpublished Ph.D. dissertation, University of Arizona.

KROEBER, A. L. 1917. *Zuñi kin and clan.* Anthropological Papers, American Museum of Natural History, Vol. 18, Part 2.

LONGACRE, WILLIAM A. 1963. Archaeology as anthropology: a case study. Ph.D. dissertation, University of Chicago.

——. 1964. Archaeology as anthropology: a case study. Science, 144(3625): 1454–55.

——. 1966. Changing patterns of social integration: a prehistoric example from the American Southwest. *American Anthropologist,* 68(1): pp. 94–102.

MARTIN, P. S., J. B. RINALDO, W. A. LONGACRE, C. CRONIN, L. G. FREEMAN, and J. SCHOENWETTER. 1962. Chapters in the Prehistory of eastern Arizona, I. *Fieldiana: Anthropology,* vol. 53.

MARTIN, P. S., J. B. RINALDO, W. A. LONGACRE, L. G. FREEMAN, J. A. BROWN, R. H. HEVLY, and M. E. COOLEY. 1964. Chapters in the prehistory of eastern Arizona, II. *Fieldiana: Anthropology,* vol. 55.

REED, ERIK K. 1956. Types of village-plan layouts in the Southwest. In G. R. Willey (Ed.), *Prehistoric settlement patterns in the New World,* Viking Fund Publications in Anthropology, no. 23. New York: Wenner-Gren Foundation for Anthropological Research.

RINALDO, JOHN B. 1964. Notes on the origins of historic Zuñi culture. *Kiva,* 29(4): 86–98.

ROBERTS, J. H. 1956. *Zuñi daily life.* Laboratory of Anthropology, Notebook, no. 3. Lincoln: University of Nebraska.

TITIEV, MISCHA. 1944. *Old Oraibi, a study of the Hopi Indians of Third Mesa.* Papers of the Peabody Museum of American Archaeology and Ethnology, no. 22. Cambridge.

SEVEN JAMES N. HILL

Broken K Pueblo: Patterns of Form and Function

As the other papers in this volume indicate, there is an increasing tendency among archeologists to be concerned with making inferences about prehistoric human behavior. In addition to the useful and time-honored concerns with developing typologies and studying the spatial and temporal distributions of artifacts, there is an increasing emphasis on trying to find out how prehistoric peoples actually lived. While this concern is by no means new, it is evident that our capabilities of implementing it are being greatly enhanced by recent theoretical, methodological, and technical developments. Most of the contributions along this line have involved examinations of settlement pattern, ceremonial organization, mortuary practices, craft specialization and social status (Sears, 1961). Within the last half-dozen years or so, it has even been possible to describe prehistoric residence patterns (Deetz, 1960, 1965; Longacre, 1963, 1964; Hill, 1965, 1966; Martin, Longacre, and Hill, 1967). In short, we are beginning to develop the means for gaining knowledge of many aspects of prehistoric cultural systems that were formerly considered beyond the limitations of our data and competence.

This paper attempts to describe a limited aspect of a cultural system that existed in eastern Arizona during the thirteenth century A.D.[1] My

[1] The data for this paper were derived from two summers of excavation (1962—63) at Broken K Pueblo, in east-central Arizona. Excavation and analysis were sponsored by the Chicago Natural History Museum (now Field Museum of Natural History), and supported by the National Science Foundation (Grants G16006 and G22028). Computer research was supported by the Wenner-Gren Foundation for Anthropologi-

primary concern is threefold: (1) to describe the locational patterning of various kinds of cultural features at the site, (2) to offer explanations of the demonstrated patterning in terms of past behavior, and (3) to test the accuracy of these explanatory propositions. This is intended as a case study in the demonstration of "activity-areas" or "activity-structure" within prehistoric communities.

This paper also serves as an example of a general methodological approach that should prove useful in nearly all archeological studies, regardless of the kinds of archeological remains being considered (cf. L. R. Binford, 1957). I have attempted to illustrate a means by which it is possible to go beyond merely making inferences about past behavior; we can also test these inferences, and gain confidence (or lose confidence) in their validity. This can be done, even in those cases in which direct ethnographic evidence is not available.

The focus of the analysis is Broken K Pueblo, located eleven miles east of Snowflake, Arizona (excavated by the Chicago Natural History Museum, with National Science Foundation support; cf. Martin, Longacre, and Hill, 1967). The site is a 95-room,[2] single-storied, surface masonry pueblo, dating from about A.D. 1150 to 1280 (Fig. 1). It is the largest and latest site in the Hay Hollow Valley, and it is located in a savanna-woodland vegetation zone. The climate is semi-arid today, and the terrain has been heavily dissected by the prevailing pattern of torrential summer thundershowers.

Since the site was too large to excavate completely, it was necessary to sample it. After extensive wall-trenching had revealed the locations of nearly all of the rooms at the site, it was decided that a system of simple random sampling would be employed; this provided a basis for making probability statements, and permitted an objective evaluation of the representativeness of the sample. Forty-six rooms were excavated in the initial sample, and eight additional rooms were excavated as the importance of doing so became apparent. All unexcavated rooms are shown in Figure 1 as shaded areas. The plaza was scraped with a tractor blade to reveal the major features, and several trenches were dug in that area.

---

cal Research (Grant 1524). The project was directed by Paul S. Martin, Chief Curator of Anthropology at the Museum. Dr. Martin and Dr. John B. Rinaldo (then of the Museum) are responsible for stimulating the research; I have also received help and encouragement from Lewis R. Binford (University of California, Los Angeles), William A. Longacre (University of Arizona) and John M. Fritz (University of Chicago). The pollen analyses were performed by Richard H. Hevly (Northern Arizona University, Flagstaff). I thank all of these individuals and institutions, as well as Mr. and Mrs. James Carter, who graciously permitted us to excavate on their property.

[2] The room-count is complicated by the fact that the initial wall-trenching (to discover all of the rooms in the site prior to sampling) failed to locate all of the rooms accurately. Rooms 31 and 33 should be considered a single room, as should Rooms 35 and 37 (cf. Fig. 1). Room 44 was divided into two rooms (Rooms 44a and 44b); Room 92 (located in the west wing) is numerically out of place because it was not discovered until the simple random sample had already been chosen, thus "freezing" the room numbers.

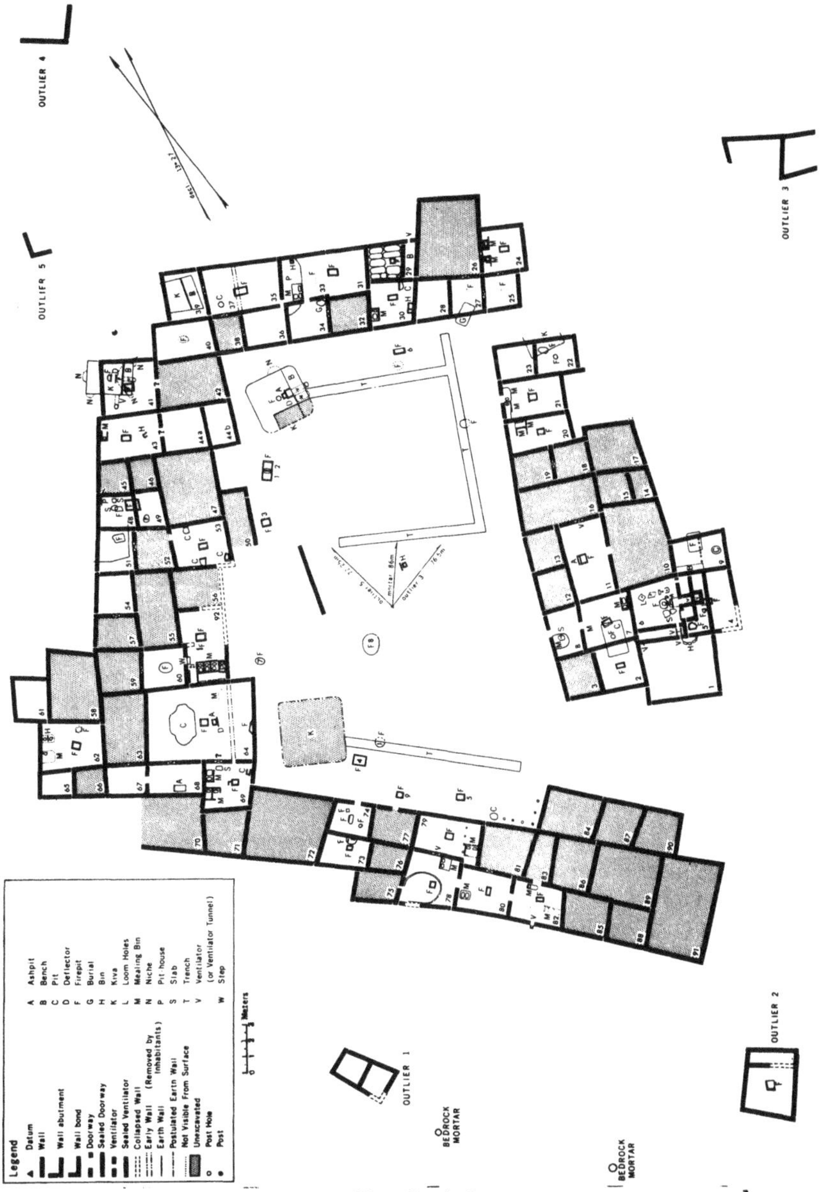

Figure 1. Plan of Broken K Pueblo. Shaded rooms were not excavated.

All levels containing cultural material (except in the plaza) were screened with a 1/4-in. screen in an attempt to ensure comparability of samples. Materials found directly on the floors of the rooms were kept separate from those in the fill levels, since in isolating the functions of the various rooms the materials lying directly on the floors are clearly most informative.

Much of the data was quantified and manipulated statistically; both the Chi-square test of association (Cochran, 1952; Siegel, 1956; Spaulding, 1953) and the Fisher Exact Test (Fisher, 1938) were extensively employed in demonstrating formal variability among the rooms, and in demonstrating associations among attributes of rooms and other categories of cultural remains. Factor analysis (Fruchter, 1954) was employed in discovering non-random clusters of pottery-types.[3] The IBM 7094 computer at the University of Chicago was used to perform this multivariate analysis.

A final item of concern, and a crucial one, involves an evaluation of the degree to which the activities or functions carried out in the rooms at Broken K Pueblo can be expected to have either remained stable or changed during the period the site was occupied. The site was not constructed at a single point in time. Radiocarbon dating, as well as ceramic cross-dating, indicate that the occupation lasted for about 130 years.[4] Architectural and stratigraphic evidence show that in general the southern portion of the site was constructed slightly earlier than the northern portion. There could, of course, have been changes in the kinds of activities performed at the site during this time period, and changes in the kinds of locations in which they were carried out. If so, we should expect this analysis of activity-structure to reveal evidence of two different activity-systems, separated somewhat in time—or perhaps a gradual change in the activity-system through time.

There is some independent evidence, however, which indicates that we can expect no such change to be discovered. The basis for this expectation lies in the fact that both architectural and stratigraphic data provide evidence that people were living in the pueblo throughout its entire extent prior to abandonment. In the first place, there was ample evidence of remodeling in the southern portion of the site, both in terms of constructing new floors and in terms of changes and additions to the walls of rooms. These architectural additions exhibit a style of masonry similar to

[3] Factor analysis is a multivariate statistical technique useful in isolating non-random clusters of materials that "behave" together, or occur together. The results of a factor analysis of pottery-types are reported in this paper. This analysis yielded seven clusters of pottery-types, and each cluster is a "factor."

[4] Pollen data were also found useful in intra-site dating. A pollen chronology for the area (Schoenwetter, 1962; Hevly, 1964) showed a gradual temporal change in the relative proportions of pollen-types, characterized by decreasing percentages of arboreal pollen and increasing percentages of non-arboreal pollen during the period of occupation of the site. Most of the "early" rooms at the site (based on architectural and stratigraphic evidence) had significantly more arboreal pollen (esp. pine) than did the "late" rooms; the late rooms contained more non-arboreal pollen (cf. Hill and Hevly, 1968).

that used in the northern portion of the site. And secondly, many of the rooms in the southern portion had not had trash dumped into them, as might be expected if that area had been abandoned before the northern half was occupied (Hill, 1965). We may thus infer that the entire site was occupied contemporaneously, at least during a portion of its existence. It must be pointed out, however, that even if this were *not* the case, the temporal disparity between the two portions of the site would not mean that there had necessarily been any changes in the kinds of activities carried on, or in their spatial structure.

More detailed discussions of the methodological aspects of the research presented in this paper are given elsewhere (Hill, 1965, 1966; Martin, Longacre, and Hill, 1967).

Variability in Rooms

During the excavation of the site it was noticed that there were differences in the formal characteristics of the rooms. In order to explain this formal variability (in a behavioral or functional sense), it was first necessary to define the differences among the rooms in a clear and rigorous fashion. Traditionally, variability among pueblo rooms has been rather loosely described, and the attributes that are chosen for use in measuring variability are often not made explicit; it is frequently difficult to specify what really distinguishes different kinds of rooms. I have attempted here to describe such differences as rigorously as possible.

Four of the rooms at the site were clearly different from all other rooms and could be distinguished without an involved or complicated analysis. These will be called "special" rooms; Southwestern archeologists would recognize them as kivas (that is, similar to present-day Pueblo ceremonial rooms). They were immediately separated from the analysis of room variability for two reasons: (1) they contained a number of peculiar features not common to the other rooms, including wall niches, benches, and a peculiarly designed firepit-ventilator combination, and (2) there were only four of them, which would have made a statistical description of them difficult to accomplish.[5] Two of them were subterranean (the one in the northwest corner of the plaza and the one beneath Room 41) with inferred roof entrances. The other two were surface rooms with slab-lined floors (Rooms 6 and 29). Thus, while there may have been two types of these special rooms, they did not resemble any of the other rooms at the site.

In dealing with the formal variability among other rooms, however,

[5] The four excavated special rooms include surface Rooms 6 and 29, the subterranean room stratigraphically underlying Room 41, and the subterranean room in the northwest corner of the plaza (Fig. 1). Two additional special rooms were discovered, but they could only be partially excavated (the ones beneath Rooms 22 and 39). A possible seventh special room in the southwest corner of the plaza was excavated (contrary to map designation), but it was not actually a room; it was a large, rectangular prehistoric excavation that may have been intended for use as a special room but had been abandoned prior to completion.

more difficulty was encountered; their similarities and differences were by no means clear. Several classes of attributes were selected as likely measures of these differences:

1. Size (floor-area)
2. Firepits (presence or absence)
3. Mealing bins (presence or absence)
4. Ventilators (presence or absence)
5. Doorways (presence or absence)
6. Height of door sill
7. Masonry style

Size was recognized as important while the excavation was still in progress; some rooms were much larger than others. This size differential indicated that there were probably at least two major kinds of rooms at the site, in addition to the special rooms. In order to check the validity of this bimodal distribution, the floor-area of each excavated room was calculated (in square meters), and the rooms were graphed on an interval scale of size. The distribution proved to be non-random. There was no continuum in size from small to large; instead there were two clear groups of rooms, small and large, with few in between. Approximately half of the rooms were in the small size-mode, containing less than 6.5 square meters of floor-area. They ranged in size from 2.5 to 6.5 square meters, with an average of 5.0 square meters. Most of the large rooms, on the other hand, ranged from 6.6 to 16.0 square meters, with an average of 9.7 square meters. The special rooms also fell within this mode. A similar graphic analysis including the unexcavated rooms at the site yielded almost identical results; the dividing point between the two modes was shifted to 7.0 square meters. It was possible to do this because nearly all of the rooms had been located and mapped prior to excavation.

There was some indication, however, that this size distribution might actually be considered trimodal. Seven of the rooms (Rooms 1, 10, 26, 47, 64, 72, and 91) were larger than most of the rooms in the large size-mode, ranging from 16.0 to 33.5 square meters in area. Unfortunately, there were so few of them that a definite third mode could not be demonstrated. Aside from their large size, they were indistinguishable from the other rooms in the large-size mode, and I have here considered them as belonging to the large-room category. Two of them (Rooms 1 and 64) were excavated in the initial sample. and two more (Rooms 72 and 92) were excavated later in order to obtain a larger sample of these rooms.

Having demonstrated the clustered or non-continuous nature of variability in size, it was desirable to find out whether or not any of the other attributes (above) were associated with one or another of the recognized size classes. An examination of the distribution of sandstone, slab-lined firepits revealed that they were usually found in the large-room category. In fact, out of a total of 23 such firepits, only one of them occurred in a small-size room. This observation was tested by Chi-square, with the result that there is less than one chance in a thousand that the association is not significant (.001 level).

Mealing bins were also found to be associated with the large-room category. Thirteen out of fifteen of these bins occurred in large rooms, and the association was significant at the .05 level (probability of .95). Some large rooms had two or more mealing bins side by side. A similar association was discovered with respect to ventilators; ten of the eleven ventilators were associated with large rooms (.02 level). Further, the ventilators, firepits and mealing bins were associated with one another (in large rooms), with a 95 per cent chance of the association being valid.

The other three attributes (doorways, height of door sill, and masonry style) were not found associated with either of the room-size modes; they appeared to vary randomly with respect to large and small rooms. This suggests, of course, that variability in the locations of these particular attributes had not been determined by the same behavioral determinancies that were responsible for the tight clustering among the first four attributes.

The results of the analysis are clear, however. There were, in addition to the four special rooms, two other kinds of rooms—large rooms containing firepits, mealing bins, and ventilators, and small rooms that did not have such features. While some of the large rooms were *extra* large, they were not associated with any peculiar structural features.

All rooms did not fall neatly into one category or another, however. There were six cases in which classification was difficult (Rooms 9, 27, 40, 48, 60, and 74; Fig. 1). These rooms exhibited some of the attributes of both large and small rooms, and they may actually represent functional overlap. For purposes of analysis, they were placed in the category to which they seemed most similar; Rooms 40 and 48 were considered to be in the large-room category, while Rooms 9, 27, 60, and 74 were included in the small-room category.

The schematic map (Fig. 2) shows the spatial distributions of these formally different kinds of rooms. Of all of the rooms excavated, 26 were large rooms, 24 were small rooms, and 4 were special rooms (Table 1). Representative photographs of these room-classes are presented in Figures 3, 4, and 5.

Table 1. Room Numbers by Category
(See Figure 1)

Large	*Small*	*Special*
1, 2, 4–5, 7, 11, 20, 21, 24, 30, 31–33, 35–37, 40, 41, 43, 48, 53, 62, 64, 69, 73, 78, 79, 80, 82, 92, Outlier 2	8, 9, 19, 22, 23, 25, 27, 28, 34, 36, 39, 44a, 44b, 49, 51, 54, 60, 61, 65, 67, 68, 74, Outlier 1 (a, b)	6, 29, 41 Plaza

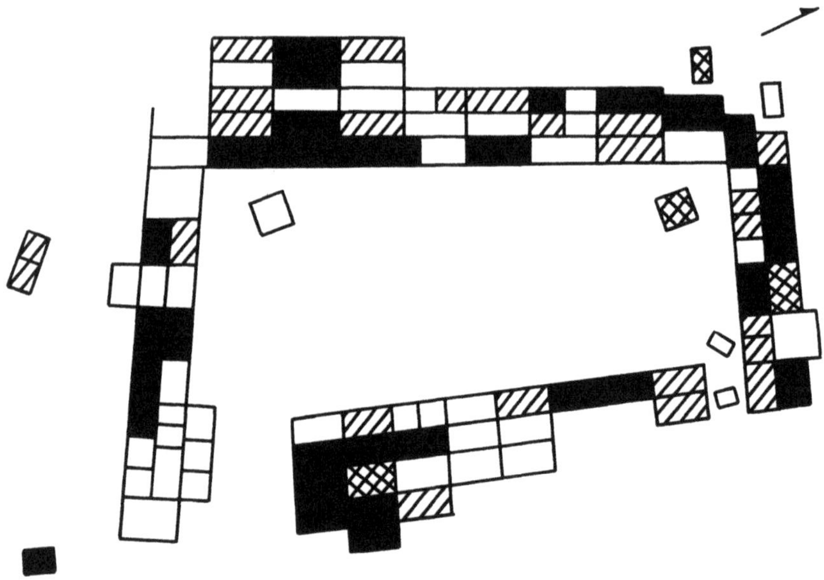

Figure 2. Distribution of room-categories. Black areas represent "large" rooms; hatched areas represent "small" rooms; cross-hatched areas represent "special" rooms. Blank areas are unexcavated.

Explanations of Variability

It is quite clear that variability among rooms at the site must have resulted from the fact that they were designed and built for different purposes, to serve as the loci for different kinds of activities.

The large rooms, for example, may have been built because they were needed to accommodate larger groups of people than the small rooms could accommodate. These may have been the rooms in which families or households carried on most of their indoor activities, such as eating, working, and sleeping. The need for such large areas may also have resulted from the fact that certain kinds of activities required large areas for their performance, or it may be that several different activities were performed in them simultaneously. It may simply be that their large size was determined by the fact that they were to be used more frequently than the other rooms and it was convenient to have ample space in which to move about.

The size of the small rooms, on the other hand, was certainly determined by the fact that they were used in activities not requiring the congregation of large groups of people or a great deal of space, and they may also have been used infrequently. They would appear to have been

Figure 3. A typical "large" room. Note slab-lined firepit and mealing bin with metate.

Figure 4. A typical "small" room.

most suitable for storage purposes—and perhaps other small-scale activities on occasion.

The presence of firepits in the large rooms permits the inference that the activities performed in them required heat, light, or both. It is logical that cooking may have been involved, since these firepits are the only ones that could reasonably have been used in routine cooking activities.[6] Heat and light were not of importance to the activities carried out in the small rooms.

The presence of mealing bins in the large rooms must certainly indicate that corn or other food materials were ground in such rooms. It would thus appear that food preparation (or some of it) was being done in the large rooms, and this lends support to the inference that the firepits were used in cooking. There is no indication that such activities were carried out in the small rooms.

The presence of ventilators in many of the large rooms indicates that the activities involved in these rooms required fresh air or draft. If, as suggested, these rooms were frequented by relatively large numbers of people, fresh air might have been needed for comfort. The draft provided by the ventilators may have served to facilitate burning in the firepits. The activities carried out in the small rooms obviously did not require ventilation.

Although the special rooms (or kivas) were generally about the same size as those in the large-room category, their peculiar internal structural features leave no doubt that the activities performed in them were in some sense special. From their large size, it can be inferred that they were used by relatively large groups of people (or in several activities); the firepits suggest a need for heat and light; the ventilators indicate a need for fresh air or draft. The peculiar construction of these features, however, suggests that they were not used in the same way as those in any of the other rooms; and such features as wall niches, benches, and slab-lined floors support this idea.

In summary, it may be inferred that the large rooms were occupied by relatively large groups of people and that there might have been several different kinds of activities performed in them simultaneously; in any event, the activities evidently required more space than those carried out in the small rooms. Heat and/or light were also needed in these rooms, as well as fresh air and facilities for grinding food materials. All of these features would be expected to occur in living rooms, or the rooms in which most household activities were performed. The small rooms, on the other hand, were evidently not used for these activities but were used instead for activities that were suitably carried out in small, dark, un-

[6] There were eight large pit-ovens in the plaza, but these ovens would have been unsuitable for routine cooking; they were very deep (sometimes more than a meter deep), without draft, and contained large quantities of dense, fireburned volcanic rock. They were almost certainly used in roasting large game animals.

Figure 5. "*Special*" *rooms. Surface Room 6, top; subterranean room underlying Room 41, bottom.*

heated, and unventilated areas—a storage function seems most likely. The special rooms served an entirely different purpose, perhaps ceremonial.

Additional inferences about the three different kinds of rooms at Broken K Pueblo can also be made on the basis of the archeological data. The large and small rooms, for example, occur in an approximate ratio of 50:50, and they almost appear to occur in pairs throughout the site. It is thus logical to infer that each household (or social unit of some kind) occupied at least one pair of these rooms, and performed two different sets of activities in them. Further, each such social unit appears to have been a self-contained unit, each of which was carrying on the same general sets of activities.

The special rooms are also of interest here. Since only six of them were discovered in the random sample (four excavated), it can be predicted that not more than eight or nine of them existed at the site. Regardless of whether or not they were all used simultaneously, it is reasonable to infer that several of the units discussed above were participating in the activities performed in them. This ratio of special rooms to other kinds of rooms clearly indicates the possibility of some form of institutional linkages among the basic social segments of the population of Broken K.

Analogies to Modern Pueblos

At this point, it is useful to examine ethnographic data to find out whether or not the modern western Pueblo villages have analogous kinds of rooms. The attributes of the modern rooms that are relevant to such analogies are, of course, the same kinds of attributes that were found useful in measuring variability among the prehistoric rooms—namely, room-size and the presence or absence of firepits, mealing bins, and ventilators. If the functions of the modern rooms are in fact similar to the functions of the prehistoric rooms, they ought to have some of the same kinds of attributes.

This in fact proved to be the case; both the Hopi and Zuñi have large rooms, small rooms and special rooms (kivas) (Mindeleff, 1891, pp. 65, 102; Stevenson, 1904; Forde, 1931; E. Beaglehole, 1937; Titiev, 1944, p. 197). The large rooms contain a firepit (stove), mealing facilities, and ventilators or windows (Mindeleff, 1891, and personal observation). It is true, of course, that these features do not always look similar to their supposed prehistoric analogues, but they are certainly functionally similar.

The small rooms in the western Pueblo villages usually do not contain such features. Some of them do, however, have small holes excavated into their floors, and some contain bins or boxes of various sorts (Stevenson, 1904, pp. 292–93, 352; E. Beaglehole, 1937, pp. 43–45; Forde, 1931, pp. 393–94). I have myself observed such boxes in some of the smaller Hopi rooms, and there are occasionally mealing facilities in them as well. At

Zuñi, there are sometimes even firepits in these rooms, although they are a different style from those in the large rooms (Stevenson, 1904, pp. 292–93, 352). Nonetheless, the small rooms in western Pueblo villages contain fewer internal structural features than do the large rooms; they usually lack firepits and mealing bins, and they are usually poorly ventilated (Mindeleff, 1891; Donaldson, 1893). As I recall, they are less well lighted than the large rooms.

The third major type of pueblo room, the kiva, also appears in many ways similar to its suspected analogue at Broken K Pueblo. It is well known that among the Hopi, at least, these rooms contain such features as wall niches, a bench or platform along one side, and a host of other peculiarities including the construction of the firepits and ventilators (Mindeleff, 1891; Donaldson, 1893, p. 55; Parsons, 1936, pp. 719–22; Titiev, personal communication). Although the Zuñi do not, strictly speaking, have "kivas," they do have large living rooms that also serve as ceremonial rooms. In addition to being distinguished by their large size, they contain a special type of fireplace and a trap-door entrance (Mindeleff, 1891, p. 112).

There is one additional kind of room found in present-day pueblos that should be mentioned here. There are among the Hopi a few rooms in each village called "clanhouses." These rooms are distinguished primarily by being larger than other kinds of rooms (Eggan, 1950, pp. 62, 89–90, 178; Parsons, 1936, p. xxxii). Although the functions of these rooms will be considered later, it is important to note the possibility that they are analogous to the seven extra large rooms at Broken K Pueblo.

The evidence thus far indicates that the variations in rooms at Broken K are analogous to the variations in rooms found in modern pueblos—large rooms with firepits and mealing bins (including extra-large rooms), small rooms lacking certain features, and special rooms containing a set of peculiar features of their own. The fact that these detailed analogies can be established suggests that the analogous rooms had similar functions. Had there been a great deal of functional change between A.D. 1300 and the historic present, we would expect to find that there had also been changes in the kinds of rooms being utilized in performing the functions. The similarities between the suspected analogues are so great that they almost certainly cannot be coincidental.

There is an additional analogue that would appear to clinch the case. In addition to the fact that the formal properties of the prehistoric and historic rooms are similar, the relative proportions of the room-types are similar. The reader will recall that at Broken K Pueblo the ratio of large rooms to small rooms was almost 50:50, and there were very few special rooms or extra-large rooms. These proportions are evidently about the same in the modern Pueblo villages. While there are great numbers of large and small rooms, with a ratio close to 50:50, there are very few kivas or clanhouses (Mindeleff, 1891; Eggan, 1950; Parsons, 1936; and personal observation). With regard to kivas, Steward (1937, pp. 96–99) has observed that there is now only about one kiva for every hundred rooms in the pueblos; at Broken K the ratio was more like 1:20 (which corresponds nicely with Steward's Pueblo III ratio, 1:18). The general similarities in room-type ratios between Broken K Pueblo and the historic pueblos are again, too close to be coincidental. Further, the large and small rooms in the historic pueblos generally occur in pairs, just as appears to be the case at Broken K. If large-scale functional changes had occurred, the probability is very great that neither the ratios among room-types nor the paired nature of their distribution would have remained so nearly the same.

Given all of these analogies, it seems reasonable to state the proposition that the variability in rooms at the site has the same behavioral context as does the variability in modern pueblo rooms; the respective room-types are functional equivalents. It would not, however, be profitable to terminate the analysis at this point, as is so often done; the proposition must first be tested.

Testing the Proposition

The testing of this proposition requires additional data, and these data must be independent of those categories of data that have been used thus far in measuring formal variability among rooms. It would be neither logical nor useful to define rooms on the basis of size and internal features, and then use this same data in demonstrating that they were functionally similar to modern Hopi or Zuñi rooms; such a procedure would amount to testing the proposition with the same data used in generating it.

The procedure used here involved, first of all, an examination of the ethnographic literature to find out what kinds of activities are carried out in the different kinds of present-day pueblo rooms, and what kinds of artifacts and other materials might be expected to occur in the respective room-types as a result of these activities; and secondly, an examination of the archeological evidence to find out whether or not similar artifact clusters occurred in the supposedly analogous rooms at Broken K. If the proposition of functional equivalence is correct, the large, small, and special rooms at the site should contain similar cultural materials to the small, large, and special rooms in the modern pueblos (or materials useful in the same kinds of functions). Such a finding would, in fact, confirm the proposition.

ETHNOGRAPHIC DATA

The three major kinds of rooms found in modern Pueblo villages are habitation rooms (or living rooms), storage rooms, and ceremonial rooms. Each household or lineage segment occupies a group of rooms including at least one habitation room and one or more storage rooms (Mindeleff,

1891, pp. 65, 102; E. Beaglehole, 1937, p. 5; Titiev, 1944, p. 197). The habitation room corresponds to the large-room category mentioned above; in addition to being the largest, it is also the nucleus of the household (P. Beaglehole, 1935, p. 42). It is, in fact, the "general living room, where the entire household works, eats and sleeps, and where guests are entertained" (Stevenson, 1904, pp. 292–93). There is every indication that this room serves as the center of almost all the indoor activities that are of importance in maintaining a household, including a wide variety of crafts or manufacturing activities (although the specific kinds of manufacturing activities are apparently not reported).

One of the activities performed in these rooms is that of processing or preparing food prior to cooking. The mealing bin, in conjunction with the metate and mano, is used by the women for grinding corn, beans, squash, and other plant materials (including seeds) into flour for use in the diet (Mindeleff, 1891, pp. 211–12). There are often two or three metates in each habitation room, and they may vary in the coarseness of their grinding surfaces, depending on the stages of grinding for which they are used (Mindeleff, 1891, p. 212). In addition to preparing domestic crops for consumption, the Hopi and Zuñi are known to process the seeds, stems, flowers, and leaves of a variety of wild plants (Stevenson, 1909; Whiting, 1939). It also seems likely that the terminal phases of the butchering process are carried out in these rooms.

Cooking is also done in the habitation rooms; it is done on the fireplaces, and the task is usually performed by women (Eggan, personal communication). Although the Hopi occasionally cook in other kinds of rooms, and the Zuñi in special cooking rooms, most of it is done in habitation rooms (Cushing, 1920, pp. 295–96; Eggan, personal communication). The containers used in cooking are now nearly identical to our modern commercial hardware, but not many years ago the western Pueblos were using simple, undecorated ceramic vessels for this purpose (Donaldson, 1893, p. 127; Parsons, 1936, p. 1190).

There is also good evidence that the modern Pueblo peoples take their meals in the habitation rooms (Stevenson, 1904, pp. 292–93). Food is frequently served in bowls (Cushing, 1920, pp. 296, 313; Brainard, 1935, p. 267; E. Beaglehole, 1937, pp. 57–65; Roberts, 1956, p. 15), and these bowls often have smudged or darkened interiors (Alfonso Ortiz, San Juan Pueblo, personal communication).

Another function of these rooms is the storage and use of water. Water is, of course, important in preparing and cooking food, and it is necessary to have a supply for drinking as well. Both the Hopi and Zuñi use large decorated jars or "ollas" in the transportation and storage of water (Brainard, 1935, p. 72; Parsons, 1936, p. 614; E. Beaglehole, 1937, pp. 57, 72), and these are generally kept in the habitation rooms (Mindeleff, 1891, pp. 109–110).

The habitation rooms must certainly have a number of other functions, but evidence of them is not apparent in the literature. The functions of storage rooms are reported in somewhat more detail. The storage rooms are small, and their primary function is the storage of food crops (Mindeleff, 1891, pp. 143–44; Cushing, 1920, pp. 167, 171–73, 179). The most important crops stored are corn, squash, beans, fruit and cotton (E. Beaglehole, 1937, pp. 43–44). Among the Hopi, corn is usually dried, and the cobs are stored in stacks on the floor. Beans are stored in sacks (formerly pots), and sometimes in small holes dug into the floors of the rooms. Squash is cut into strips, dried, and hung from the rafters. Seed corn for the next season's planting is also hung from the rafters, while reserve squash seeds are kept in clay jars or boxes (E. Beaglehole, 1937, pp. 43–45; Forde, 1931, pp. 393–94). The Hopi also store jerked meat in their storage rooms.

The Zuñi use their storage rooms in much the same fashion (Stevenson, 1904, p. 352). In fact, the similarities between the Hopi and Zuñi, both in terms of the crops that are stored and the manner in which it is done, are striking. It is notable, also, that both groups are known to have made extensive use of large storage jars in these rooms (Bunzel, 1929, p. 41; Cushing, 1920, p. 208).

In addition to food, a great variety of other materials are also stored. The Zuñi, for example, store their ceremonial paraphernalia in these rooms. In fact, Stevenson reports that "A Zuñi storage room . . . contains a promiscuous mass of material ranging from objects of the most sacred character to those of little or no value" (1904, p. 352). A personal examination of several Hopi storage rooms indicates that this statement applies to them as well.

Although these small rooms are used primarily for storage among both groups, they are occasionally involved in other kinds of activities; they may serve as workrooms, kitchens and bedrooms (Roberts, 1956, pp. 11, 45–46, 80–81; Eggan, personal communication). While these usages may not be everyday occurrences, it is clear that the storerooms may be multi-functional. It is likely, in fact, that such rooms are at times involved in a number of activities that are more commonly carried out in the living rooms.

The activities carried on in the ceremonial rooms or kivas are largely different, of course, from those performed in other kinds of rooms. These rooms serve as the centers of ritual activity, and access to them is usually restricted to males (Mindeleff, 1891, pp. 130, 134; Titiev, 1944, p. 103). The ritual activities involve the use of artifacts and other materials that are usually not found in non-ceremonial rooms; these may include idols or fetishes, for example (Donaldson, 1893, p. 55). The Hopi have specific types of ceramic vessels (and perhaps other kinds of vessels) that are reserved for use in ritual activities (Titiev, 1944, p. 16), and the Zuñi have sacred vessels on which ritually important designs are painted (Bunzel, 1929, pp. 23–24). Presumably, such vessels are frequently used in ceremonial rooms.

Plant materials are also brought into the ceremonial rooms and used in ritual activity; the most important ones are the domesticates: corn, beans, and squash (Parsons, 1936, pp. 595, 608). Often, in fact, entire plants of these types are brought into the kivas, and they are even germinated in these rooms (Parsons, 1936, pp. 188, 287, 623, 690; Titiev, 1944, p. 166; Forde, 1931, p. 398). This is not surprising of course, since corn, beans, and squash are the economic mainstays of the Pueblos. In addition to these crops, however, a wide variety of wild plant materials are often introduced into the kivas (cf. Stevenson, 1909; Whiting, 1939).

Beyond their ritual functions, and probably just as important, is the fact that kivas also serve as male clubhouses and craft centers (Mindeleff, 1891, p. 130). The men do their weaving in these rooms (Mindeleff, 1891, p. 129; Parsons, 1936, pp. 33, 134, 188, 202), and they carry on a variety of leisure-time activities (Parsons, 1936, p. xliii). In addition to relaxation and manufacturing activities, the men sometimes eat and sleep in these rooms—although no cooking is done in them (Mindeleff, 1891, p. 130; Parsons, 1936, pp. 605, 607). Meetings of various kinds are also held in kivas, and decisions of public concern are made there.

While this concludes the discussion of the primary functional characteristics of the three major pueblo room-types, it will also be worthwhile to consider the functions of the clanhouses. As already mentioned, these are simply large habitation rooms. Although there are no recognized clanhouses at Zuñi (Kroeber, 1917, pp. 91, 118–19), the Hopi villages usually have several of them. Each clan in a village has one, and it is regarded as the "home" of that clan in the village. It is here that the headwoman of the clan usually lives, and where clan meetings are held. The ritual paraphernalia used in clan-controlled ceremonies are stored in the clanhouses, and sometimes certain rituals are carried out in these rooms (cf. Titiev, 1944, p. 103; Eggan, 1950, pp. 62, 89–90, 178).

It has already been pointed out that modern pueblo households are composed of pairs (or small groups) of rooms, each having at least one habitation room and one storage room. It is also important to note that this household unit is the basic economic unit in pueblo villages. Although households do indeed cooperate with one another on a large scale, they are basically self-contained units, and each of them carries on the same general kinds of activities in its respective rooms (E. Beaglehole, 1936, 1937). The kivas, however, are shared, and the membership of each kiva-group is drawn from a number of households, some of which belong to different lineages (Stevenson, 1904, pp. 413–21; Kroeber, 1917, pp. 151–54, 161; Hawley, 1937, p. 515; Eggan, 1950, pp. 52, 117, 203; 1964, pp. 181–82).

EXPECTATIONS

Given this discussion of the major activities that are carried out in different kinds of rooms among the Pueblos today, it is possible to make some specific statements concerning the kinds of artifacts and other cultural materials that can be expected to occur in the rooms at Broken K Pueblo—if indeed they were functionally similar to modern pueblo rooms. These expectations may be stated in the form of a series of limited propositions:

1. If the large rooms were all-purpose living rooms, they ought to contain larger numbers and higher densities of most categories of cultural remains than either the small rooms or the special rooms. If the small rooms were storage rooms, they should have the lowest densities of most materials, with the exception of food crops; and the special rooms should fall somewhere in between.
2. The large rooms should contain a wider variety of materials than are found in the other room-types, since the largest number of different kinds of activities were presumably performed in them.
3. The large rooms should contain evidence of the processing or preparing of food prior to cooking, independent of the mealing bins. They should contain most of the metates, manos, and other tools usable in food-processing; and they might be expected to contain some of the foodstuffs that had been processed, possibly including seeds or pollen in the basins of the mealing bins, and animal bones representing the remains of meat preparation (butchering). While the small rooms may also be expected to contain the remains of food materials, neither they nor the special rooms should contain evidence of food-processing.
4. The large rooms should contain evidence of cooking, in addition to the firepits. They might contain the burned or charred remains of various kinds of foods, and they might be expected to have the largest numbers of plain or textured (unpainted) utility vessels (some of which should exhibit evidence of having been placed on the fire). The other rooms, on the other hand, should contain little or no such evidence.
5. The large rooms should contain evidence that eating was done in them. In addition to having charred food remains (which may indicate cooking as well), they might be expected to contain the fragments of bowls that had been used in serving food—particularly bowls with smudged interiors.
6. The large rooms would be expected to contain evidence that water was stored in them. They should have more large, narrow-necked, decorated jars than the other rooms at the site.
7. The large rooms should contain evidence of manufacturing or craft activities; this should include the tools useful in such activities, as well as the debris that resulted.
8. The small rooms, in addition to containing only a small number and variety of artifacts and manufacturing debris, should contain reasonably large quantities of the remains of stored food crops—especially corn and squash (since beans do not preserve well). This evidence should be in the form of corn cobs, seeds, or pollen.

9. The small rooms can be expected to contain evidence of some of the ethnographically recorded storage techniques, although most of the traces of these techniques would almost certainly not have been preserved. These rooms can, however, be expected to contain more large undecorated jars than do the other rooms, since the ethnographic evidence indicates that such jars are often used in storing various kinds of materials.

10. The small rooms should contain evidence that materials other than food crops were stored in them—this might include ceremonial paraphernalia, tools, and even non-dietary plant remains (in the form of seeds or pollen).

11. The small rooms can be expected to contain the remains of manufacturing or other non-storage activites; but since they were probably not used frequently for such activities, they should not yield large quantities of such remains.

12. The special rooms should contain evidence of ritual activities, independent of the peculiar structural features noted. They might, for example, contain the remains of idols, fetishes, or other presumably ceremonially related materials. They might also be expected to contain special types of pottery, and they should contain large quantities of seeds or pollen of the domestic crops, corn and squash. They may even yield a variety of wild plants that are used for ritual purposes in the present-day pueblo kivas.

13. The special rooms should exhibit evidence of having been used in manufacturing or craft activities, and some of these activities could be expected to be different from those carried on in the large and small rooms. There should be evidence of weaving in these rooms, for example, and perhaps the remains of manufacturing chert hunting implements.

14. The special rooms ought to exhibit evidence that a certain amount of eating (but not cooking) had been done in them. This would be indicated by the presence of food remains, similar to those expected in the large rooms, but probably not in the same quantities. Serving bowls would also be expected.

15. If the seven extra-large rooms at the site were indeed clanhouses, one might expect to find some of the remains of ritual paraphernalia that had been stored in them.

16. It can be expected that the three major kinds of rooms at the site did not all have the same context with regard to the sexual division of labor. The special rooms should contain cultural items associated with male activities primarily, while the large and small rooms should contain both male- and female-associated items.

TESTING

In examining the archeological data to test the above propositions, I have dealt with them in the order of their presentation in the last section.

Table 2. Distribution of Artifact Types

Artifact Type	*Mean No. per Large Room*	*Mean No. per Small Room*	*Mean No. per Special Room*	*Total*	*Dominant Room-type*		
Projectile Points	.92	.08	.50	27	L		P
Arrowshaft Tools	.88	.11	.00	25	L		
Antler Flakers	.08	.08	.25	5			P
Saws	.28	.04	.00	8	L		
Graver-Burins	.20	.20	.00	10	L	S	
Flake Knives	1.70	.23	.00	48	L		
Bifacial Knives	.20	.07	.00	7	L		
Utilized Flakes	2.40	1.00	2.00	96	L	S	P
Blades	.16	.16	.00	8	L	S	
Cores	.92	.23	1.50*	35	L		P
Scrapers	3.00	.84	3.00*	108	L		P
Choppers	2.60	.44	4.70*	96	L		P
Axes	.32	.00	.00	8	L		
Mauls	.28	.11	.00	10	L		
Hammerstones	3.70	.69	2.00*	118	L		P
Metates	1.10	.15	.25	32	L		
Manos	6.60	1.00	.25	192	L		
Worked Slabs	.88	.15	.75	29	L		P
Worked Sherds	1.50	.15	.25	42	L		
Bone Awls	1.60	.27	.25	48	L		
Bone Rings and Ring Material	1.00	.11	.25	30	L		
"Ornamental" Items	.96	.19	.50	31	L		P

L = large room; S = small room; P = special room
*All from a single special room (room beneath Room 41)

There can be no doubt that the first two propositions are confirmed; the large rooms contained not only the largest numbers and highest densities of most cultural materials at the site, but also the widest variety of materials. The distribution of artifacts (Table 2) is a case in point. Notice that 21 out of 22 artifact types occurred in high frequencies in the large rooms, while only three types were associated with small rooms, and nine with the special rooms. Further, 11 out of the 22 types occurrred in the large rooms to the virtual exclusion of the other room-types, showing that the inhabitants of the village had discarded about 50 per cent of their non-perishable artifacts in these rooms. There were no types strongly dominant in the small rooms, and only one (antler-flakers) was of primary importance in the special rooms. There were eight types, however, which were common in both large and special rooms, and two types which were common in large rooms and small rooms. Only one type (utilized flakes) was clearly common in all three kinds of rooms.

These data demonstrate that the non-perishable tool kits used in each type of room were as follows:

Large Rooms: All types, except antler-flakers
Small Rooms: Utilized flakes, blades and graver-burins
Special Rooms: Projectile points, antler-flakers, utilized flakes, cores, choppers, scrapers, hammerstones, worked slabs, and ornamental items

It is thus clear that in addition to having the greatest numbers of artifacts, the large rooms had the greatest variety of them.

The large rooms also contained most of the lithic waste at the site (Table 3). A total of 5,868 unutilized chert chips were recovered during the excavation, representing all stages in the manufacture of chert tools. It was found that 17 out of 23 large rooms analyzed had an average of 127 chips per floor (13 per square meter), and an overall average of 98 chips per floor. The small rooms, on the other hand, averaged only 30 chips per floor, and 17 out of 24 of them had only 10 chips (2 per square meter). The special rooms generally had 8 to 14 chips each, although one of them (the room beneath Room 41) had 98. This evidence clearly demonstrates that lithic waste was primarily associated with large rooms, and it lends support to both proposition 1 and proposition 2.

Table 3. Distribution of Non-Artifact Materials

Item	*Mean No. per Large Room*	*Mean No. per Small Room*	*Mean No. per Special Room*
Lithic Waste	98.0	30.0	37.0
Animal Bone	120.0	26.0	29.0
Seeds	9.3	4.2	2.5
Pollen Grains (economic)	22.0	51.0	17.0

Further support is found in the differential distribution of pottery density; there were many more sherds in the large rooms and special rooms than in the small rooms. There were generally more than sixty sherds in the large rooms and special rooms, and many fewer than this in the small rooms. After the frequency of sherds in each of the rooms had been converted to a density figure, it was found that the large rooms and special rooms usually had more than three sherds per square meter of floor area, while the small rooms had fewer than this (Chi-square, .01 level).

While this supports proposition 1, the distribution of individual pottery-types lends support to the second proposition. The factor analysis of pottery types (which yielded non-random clusters of covarying types) revealed that there was a larger variety of different kinds of pottery in the large rooms than in either of the other two kinds of rooms. The pottery-type factors are given in Table 4. Four of these seven factors (factors 1, 2,

Table 4. Pottery-Type Factors

Factor Number	*Pottery Types*	*Vessel Forms*
1	Patterned Corrugated	Jars
	Pinto Polychrome	Bowls
	Brown Indented Corrugated	Jars
2	Brown Plain Corrugated (Smudged Interior)	Bowls
	Tularosa Black-on-White	Jars, Bowls
3	Snowflake Black-on-White (Snowflake Variety)	Jars, Bowls
4	Brown Plain Corrugated	Jars
	Brown Indented Corrugated	Jars
5	Brown Indented Corrugated (Smudged Interior)	Bowls
	McDonald Indented Corrugated	Bowls
	Snowflake Black-on-White (Hay Hollow Variety)	Bowls, Jars
6	McDonald Plain Corrugated	Bowls
	St. Johns Polychrome	Bowls
7	St. Johns Black-on-Red	Bowls

Bowl and jar forms are given in order of frequency.

3, and 5) occurred primarily in the large room category.[7] Table 5 shows that nine out of thirteen pottery-types represented in these factors were strongly associated with these rooms, while only two were associated strongly with the small rooms and six with the special rooms. These associations were tested by Chi-square (.05 level). There was clearly a wider variety of pottery types in the large rooms.

The distribution of animal bone at the site was also of interest with respect to the first two propositions (see Table 3). A total of 3,681 bones were found on the floors of rooms; of these, 2,895 were in large rooms, 671 were in small rooms, and 115 were in special rooms. The large rooms averaged 120 bones each, while the small rooms averaged only 26 each; the special rooms averaged 29 each. In fact, 77 per cent of the animal bones found on floors at the site came from large rooms, only 18.3 per cent from small rooms, and only 3.1 per cent from special rooms. A comparison of the rooms in terms of the density of bone revealed that the large rooms contained more than 2 bones per square meter (usually much more), and the small rooms and special rooms had less than this (Chi-square, .001).

Similar tests were performed to find out whether any individual species

[7] Using a multiple regression analysis, Freeman and Brown (1964) demonstrated that different clusters of pottery types occured in different rooms at Carter Ranch Site, a slightly earlier pueblo in the same valley.

or genus of animal bone distributed in some other way. That is, were there particular kinds of animals that were significantly represented in small rooms or special rooms? The result was negative. All of the animal bones followed the same pattern of distribution as did the lumped bone counts.[8]

Most of the plant remains in the form of seeds were also found in the large rooms (see Table 3). It was discovered that over twice as many seeds (including charred corn) were in the large rooms as in the small ones; most of these were found in the basins of mealing bins. Out of a total of 352 seeds (not including the seeds in a fecal sample from Room 31–33), there were 233 in large rooms, 109 in small rooms, and 10 in special rooms. The average numbers of seeds for these rooms were 9.3, 4.2, and 2.5, respectively. Furthermore, of the twenty rooms in which seeds were found, fourteen of them were large rooms, five were small rooms, and one was a special room (Room 6). The association of seeds with the large-room category was significant at the .01 level, and it may thus be considered culturally significant.

Having considered the major categories of cultural materials, it is clear that both propositions 1 and 2 are confirmed; the large rooms not only contained the largest quantities of most materials, but also the widest variety. They contained the largest numbers of different kinds of artifacts and pottery-types, as well as most of the lithic waste, animal bone, and seeds. They were living rooms par excellence.

The third proposition was that these rooms ought to exhibit evidence of food processing prior to cooking, while the other rooms should not. This, too, is confirmed. Food-processing activities are indicated by the fact that most of the metates and manos occurred in large rooms (see Table 2). There were, on the average, over seven times as many metates in large rooms as in small ones, and over four times as many as in the special rooms; there were six times as many manos in the large rooms as in the small ones, and twenty six times as many as in the special rooms. In terms of density (average number per square meter of floor area), these distributions are as follows:

	Large Rooms	*Small Rooms*	*Special Rooms*
Metates	.11	.03	.03
Manos	.86	.20	.03

Further, it was pointed out that most of the seeds found at the site were

[8] The animal bone found in the fills of rooms did not follow this pattern. It seems to have been distributed in a random manner with respect to the different kinds of rooms, and it was thus of no use to this analysis. This is a clear demonstration of the fact that the floors of rooms must be kept separate from the fills if we are to learn very much about the functions of rooms. Fill material may often reflect random distribution simply because it can be largely a result of indiscriminate trash dumping.

from the basins of mealing bins; this clearly indicates that seeds were being processed in the large rooms. Out of twelve different types of seeds found in mealing bins, seven of them are frequently eaten by the Hopi and Zuñi. These include *Amaranthus* (pigweed), *Chenopodium* (goosefoot family), *Cucurbita* (squash), *Cycloloma* (goosefoot family), *Opuntia* (prickly pear cactus), *Juniperus* (juniper), and *Zea* (corn) (Stevenson, 1909; Whiting, 1939).

Pollen samples collected from the basins of mealing bins yielded pollen from sixteen different kinds of plants, at least nine of which are eaten by the modern Pueblo peoples (Stevenson, 1909; Whiting, 1939). These include Cheno-ams (Chenopods and Amaranths), *Cleome* (bee weed), Compositae (two types, low-spine and high-spine, including *Artemisia*), *Cucurbita* (squash), Gramineae (grasses), *Juniperus* (juniper), *Opuntia* (prickly pear cactus), *Pinus* (probably *P. edulis,* pinyon pine), and *Zea* (corn).[9]

It is noteworthy in this connection that all of the above plants were present in a fecal sample from Room 31–33, so the evidence is even stronger that they were being prepared as food.

Vegetal foods were not the only foods prepared in the large rooms, however. Judging from the fact that 77 per cent of the animal bone was found in these rooms, it is clear that butchering, or particular stages in the butchering process, was being carried on in them. A large but unquantified number of these bones had butchering marks on them. And beyond this, the tools most reasonably associated with butchering were found primarily in large rooms (saws, flake knives, bifacial knives, and choppers; cf. Table 2). There can be no doubt that food processing prior to cooking was a major activity in these rooms and not in the others.

There is also good evidence that cooking was done in these rooms (proposition 4). This is not only indicated by the large amounts of animal bone and seeds present in these rooms, but also, and more importantly, by the fact that most of the burned bone and charrred corn cobs were found in the large rooms. Out of a total of 179 fragments of burned bone, nearly all were in these rooms (Chi-square, .001). And out of 37 charred corn cobs, 28 of them were in large rooms (Chi-square, .001).

Further, it was suggested that unpainted utility vessels could be expected to be found in these rooms; and this proved to be the case (Table 5). The large rooms contained two such vessel types, Indented Corrugated and Patterned Corrugated (factor 1). Both types were also represented in the special rooms, together with Brown Plain Corrugated (factor 4). Thus it is evident that the so-called utility wares were well represented in both large rooms and special rooms, but not in small rooms. Although no

[9] The reader will notice that five of these plants were not represented by seeds in the mealing bins. Why they should be represented by pollen alone is not clear, since it is usually the seeds of the plants that are ground today. It may be, of course, that flowers were ground for various non-dietary purposes, or that certain kinds of seeds were not preserved.

systematic record was kept concerning the distribution of sherds exhibiting evidence of exterior burning (and thus cooking), it was clear that most such sherds did occur in the large rooms. Considering all of this evidence, proposition 4 seems reasonably well confirmed.

Table 5. Distribution of Pottery Types

(Room Categories in Which Pottery Types Are Dominant, as Determined by Factor Analysis)

Pottery Type	*Large*	*Small*	*Special*
Brown Plain Corrugated (Smudged Interior) (B)	X		
Brown Indented Corrugated (Smudged Interior) (B)	X		
McDonald Indented Corrugated (B)	X		
Tularosa Black-on-White (J, B)	X		
Snowflake Black-on-White (Hay Hollow Variety) (B, J)	X		
Brown Indented Corrugated (J)	X		X
Patterned Corrugated (J)	X		X
Snowflake Black-on-White (Snowflake Variety) (J, B,)	X		X
Pinto Polychrome (B)	X		X
Brown Plain Corrugated (J)			X
St. Johns Black-on-Red (B)			X
McDonald Corrugated (B)		X	
St. Johns Polychrome (B)		X	

B = bowl; J = jar

The evidence expected under proposition 5 was also found. The idea that eating was being done in the large rooms is supported by the fact that most of the charred bone and corn cobs were found in these rooms, and by the fact that there was no evidence of dietary remains in the other rooms. It is also supported by the presence of ceramic vessels that would have been useful in serving food (that is, bowls; cf. Table 5). And, as expected, many of the bowls (three out of four types) had smudged interiors. These include Brown Plain Corrugated, smudged interior; Brown Indented Corrugated, smudged interior; and McDonald Indented Corrugated.

There was also good evidence of water storage in the large rooms (proposition 6). As mentioned, one would expect water to be stored in large, narrow-necked jars or ollas, and that these would be decorated or painted vessels (as among the historic pueblos). Such jars would be particularly necessary at Broken K Pueblo because the nearest source of water was probably not less than 300 yards from the village and some kind of transportation and storage vessel would have been required. An examination of the different kinds of large, painted olla-type jars at the site revealed that most of them were found in the large rooms. This was shown in the factor analysis of pottery-types (Table 5). Tularosa Black-on-white, Snowflake Black-on-white (Snowflake variety), and Snowflake black-on-white (Hay Hollow variety) were the only such types entering into the factors, and they belong in factors that were clearly associated with the large rooms. While it is true that Snowflake Black-on-white (Snowflake variety.) jars were also found in special rooms, this may simply mean that water was stored in these rooms too.

The large rooms also contained the expected evidence of manufacturing or craft activities (proposition 7). One of these activities was the manufacture of chert implements. Like so many of the materials recovered from the site, the implements which seem to be related to chert tool manufacture were far more common in the large rooms than anywhere else (except in one of the special rooms). These materials include hammerstones, cores, lithic waste, and antler-flakers (see Table 2). Some of this chert knapping activity probably involved the manufacture of hunting implements, since "arrowshaft tools" and projectile points also occurred predominantly in the large rooms (Table 2).

Certain stages in the process of pottery-making may also have been carried out in these rooms. The evidence for this is that most of the worked sherds were in large rooms (Table 2), and it is likely that they were used in scraping pottery prior to firing (Haury, 1940, p. 119). Out of a total of 42 worked sherds found on the floors of rooms, there were only four in the small rooms, and none in the special rooms.

Another manufacturing activity that may have been carried on in the large rooms is the making of ground and pecked stone implements such as metates and manos. The evidence for this is that most of the hammerstones were found in these rooms (Table 2). In addition to being used in chert knapping, hammerstones are also used in roughening the grinding surfaces of metates and manos (Rinaldo, 1964, p. 73).

The manufacture of ornamental items may also have been carried out in these rooms. Most ornamental items, including bone rings, occurred in the large rooms (Table 2). Further, it was found that the bone material from which the rings were cut was primarily in these rooms.

The fact that bone awls occurred almost exclusively in the large rooms (Table 2) also indicates that craft activities were being performed. Although bone awls may be multi-functional, it is reasonable to infer that they were being used in a manufacturing activity of some kind.

In short, there can be no doubt that proposition 7 is confirmed; in addition to the various manufacturing activities that are demonstrated to have occurred in the large rooms at the site, there must have been many others. This is indicated by the already established fact that almost all of the recovered artifacts were found in significant numbers in these rooms.

The small rooms also yielded a great deal of the expected evidence. In addition to having only small quantities of most materials, they yielded good evidence that they had been used for storing food crops (proposition 8); this evidence was largely palynological. The pollen of economic plants[10] was much more abundant on the floors of the small rooms than on those of either of the other room types (see Table 3). Most of the pollen samples from small rooms contained more than 43 grains of economic pollen each, while the large rooms generally had between 0 and 42 grains. A Fisher Exact Test revealed that there is less than one chance in a thousand that this distribution is in error (.001 level). A separate test was performed using the frequencies of *Zea* and *Cucurbita* alone, with exactly the same results. The special rooms had surprisingly small quantities of economic pollen.

This great density of economic pollen in the small rooms clearly indicates that crops were being stored in these rooms. It is difficult to imagine any alternative interpretation, because there is no evidence indicating that these crops were processed, cooked, or eaten in such rooms.

There is a logical argument in support of this, too. One would expect that when corn and squash were brought in from the fields for storage, a certain amount of pollen would have been carried in with them—either in the form of the flowers themselves, or simply by clinging to the produce. Then, as the crops were being stacked in these rooms, some of the pollen would fall onto the floor. And, finally, as the crops began to dry out, any flowers or pollen that had been introduced might also fall to the floor, depositing large amounts of pollen. By the time the crops were needed as food, much of the pollen would presumably have been deposited on storage room floors, and very little would find its way into the living rooms. Although this argument is speculative, it is certainly a reasonable explanation of the pollen distribution (Richard H. Hevly, Department of Botany, Northern Arizona University, personal communication). In any event, the fact that the small rooms contained most of the economic pollen is, in itself, sufficient evidence for inferring that they were used for the storage of food.

It was also expected that these rooms would yield some evidence of the storage techniques used (proposition 9). In this case, however, the unexpected occurred. The small rooms, instead of containing significant numbers of large textured storage jars, were characterized primarily by the presence of bowls. The only pottery-type factor of importance in the small rooms was factor 6 (McDonald Plain Corrugated and St. John Polychrome), and the vessel forms are both bowls (Table 4). This was so surprising that it was decided to ignore (temporarily) the results of the factor analysis, and reexamine the raw frequencies of the various pottery types by room. This exercise, however, yielded virtually the same results. While large unpainted jars (sherds) did occur in the small rooms, their frequencies were much lower than in either the large or special rooms.

[10] Economic plants are defined here as those for which there is evidence that they were introduced into the site by man rather than by natural agencies. They include *Zea, Cucurbita, Cleome, Opuntia,* and several others (Hevly, 1964.)

The average number of sherds per room-type of each of the three types of large undecorated jars is given as follows:

	Large Rooms	*Small Rooms*	*Special Rooms*
Brown Indented Corrugated	57.4	14.0	39.5
Brown Plain Corrugated	2.9	.9	3.0
Patterned Corrugated	2.8	.3	2.5

In terms of density (no. per sq. m.), the results are similar:

	Large Rooms	*Small Rooms*	*Special Rooms*
Brown Indented Corrugated	5.92	2.80	4.07
Brown Plain Corrugated	.30	.18	.22
Patterned Corrugated	.29	.06	.26

Thus, while the palynological evidence supports the idea that the small rooms were storage rooms, the pottery-type evidence does not. Proposition 9 is not confirmed.

Proposition 10 is also difficult to confirm. If materials other than food crops had been stored in the small rooms, there was little macroscopic evidence of it. To be sure, a number of different kinds of artifacts were represented in these rooms (Table 2), but it is unlikely that many of them were being stored (see below). Perhaps most important is the fact that of 29 different types of pollen found at the site, nearly all of them were found to some degree in the storage rooms (Hill and Hevly, 1968). Judging from the ethnobotanical evidence (Stevenson, 1909; Whiting, 1939), many of these pollen types do not represent plants that were eaten by the inhabitants of the site, and it is thus not likely that they were being stored as food crops. While this evidence tends to confirm proposition 10, it does not in any sense constitute proof.

There is good data, however, to support the idea that certain activities besides storage were carried out in small rooms; this is indicated by the artifact content of the rooms. It will be recalled that there were only three types of artifacts that were common in these rooms, relative to their frequencies of occurrence in the other rooms (graver-burins, blades and utilized flakes; cf. Table 2), and these occurred in small quantities. At the same time, however, almost *all* of the artifact types were present to some degree in at least a few of the small rooms, and some of them (for example, manos, hammerstones and scrapers) occurred in noticeable quantities. While these artifacts do not serve to distinguish the small rooms from the other rooms, they do permit the inference that activities other than storage were occasionally performed in these rooms. The possibility that these materials were all being stored is contradicted by the presence of an average of thirty pieces of lithic waste per small room. One would expect lithic waste to represent the by-product of chert tool manufacture.

Thus it is likely that the small rooms were multi-functional, as expected.

The archeological evidence, given the state of preservation at the site, indicates that food crops were being stored and that certain non-storage activities were being carried out; most of the latter, however, were probably activities that were more commonly carried out in the large rooms or special rooms.

The special rooms also conform to our expectations (proposition 12). Although there were no idols, fetishes, or other materials of that nature recovered, these rooms did contain a peculiar combination of pottery types. The dominant pottery-type factors in the special rooms were as follows (in order of importance; cf. Table 4):

Special Rooms	*Factors*
Room 6	7, 4
Room 29	1, 4
Room beneath Room 41	4, 3, 7
Room in N.W. corner of plaza	1, 3

Thus, out of a total of seven factors, four of them were commonly found in the special rooms (factors 1, 3 4, and 7). Although none of them were found in all of the special rooms, they clearly represent the major pottery types that were used in these rooms (Table 5). Factors 2 and 5, which were strongly represented in the large rooms, were not important in the special rooms; and factor 6, the small room factor, was also weakly represented.

Some interesting support for the idea that factors 1, 3, 4, and 7 were composed of ceremonial or ritual pottery types is found in an archeological context at another site in the same valley (Carter Ranch Site; cf. Longacre, 1963, 1964). Longacre discovered that at Carter Ranch Site there was a constellation of five pottery types that was largely peculiar to ceremonial-mortuary contexts, and he was able to make the following statement:

> Thus we can say with great probability, that these ceramic types were used together in ceremonial activities—the others were not. We can go one step further and suggest that when these types are found in non-random high frequency on the floor of a cultural unit, that particular unit must be classed as a ceremonial one (1963, p. 95).

Although his "ceremonial" types differ somewhat from the equivalent constellation at Broken K Pueblo, there are striking similarities. The two constellations are given in Table 6. The first three types listed were characteristic of kivas (special rooms) at both sites; the fourth type is also the same, except that it had a smudged interior and a different shape at Carter Ranch Site. The other types differ between the sites. The only major difference, however, is that the two smudged-interior types at Carter Ranch Site were not characteristic of the special rooms at Broken K; in their place we have a black-on-white and a polychrome type.

If these special rooms are in fact analogous to kivas, it is likely that the first three or four of these pottery types represent ceremonial types common to this area of the Southwest. They may be found in kivas (and perhaps cemeteries) at other pueblo sites in the area.

Table 6. Ceremonial-Mortuary Pottery Types

Broken K Pueblo	*Carter Ranch Site*
St. Johns Black-on-Red	St. Johns Black-on-Red
Patterned Corrugated	Patterned Corrugated
Brown Plain Corrugated	Brown Plain Corrugated
Brown Indented Corrugated	Brown Indented Corrugated (Smudged Interior)
Snowflake Black-on-White (Snowflake Variety)	Brown Plain Corrugated (Smudged Interior)
Pinto Polychrome	

There is some additional evidence, however, that the special rooms had a ceremonial function, and this evidence is palynological. The pollen content of the special rooms was in many ways similar to that of the habitation rooms (Hill and Hevly, 1968). A major difference, however, lay in the fact that the special rooms had greater concentrations of the pollen of *Ephedra* (Mormon tea) and *Eriogonum* (buckwheat). There was more pollen of these two types in the special rooms than the average amounts of these types in the other rooms at the site. Both of these plants have historically had ceremonial and medicinal uses among the Hopi and Zuñi Indians (Stevenson, 1909; Whiting, 1939). Their presence in the special rooms lends support to the idea that these rooms were indeed ceremonial rooms.

Perhaps most interesting is the fact that certain pollen types that were expected to occur in high amounts in the special rooms were present in extremely low amounts. These are the domesticates: corn and squash. Given the fact that the pollen of these plants (as well as whole plants) is extensively used in present-day Pueblo kivas, it is difficult to explain their small amounts in the special rooms at Broken K. It is possible, of course, that these domesticates were not as important ritually or economically in the past as they are today (cf. Hill, 1965, 1966).

Nonetheless, proposition 12 seems reasonably well confirmed. The special rooms did contain a special set of pottery types, and they contained significant quantities of two pollen types that may have been used ceremonially.

It was also expected, however, that these rooms would exhibit evidence of having been used in manufacturing or craft activities (proposition 13)—and there can be no doubt that this was the case. In the first place, two of these rooms had obvious loom-holes in their floors, indicating that weaving was being done in them. No such holes were found elsewhere in the site. And second, they contained significant quantities of chert-knapping tools, including hammerstones, cores, and antler-flakers (Table 2); and lithic waste was present.

It was also proposed that these rooms might be expected to yield evidence that eating (but not cooking) had occasionally been done in them. Evidence that eating was done is found in the fact that the special rooms had an average of 29 animal bones each, and this is slightly more than was found in the small rooms. In addition, three of the six pottery types found in these rooms were represented by bowl forms which would have been useful in serving food (Table 5). While this evidence tends to confirm the idea that eating was sometimes done in these rooms, there is a small amount of evidence indicating that cooking was *not* done. The fact that there were no charred corn cobs or seeds in these rooms, and only one of them had burned bones (two fragments), suggests that cooking could not have been a frequent occurrence. It should be noted, however, that there were three types of large, unpainted jars associated with these rooms that would have been usable for cooking; these include Brown Plain Corrugated, Brown Indented Corrugated and Patterned Corrugated; (cf. Table 5). Unfortunately, the pottery in the special rooms was not examined for evidence of exterior burning, which would be expected if any of it had been used in cooking.

Nonetheless, proposition 14 can be considered confirmed; there was evidence of eating in the special rooms, and the density of food remains indicates that this activity was not performed in such rooms very frequently.

Proposition 15, however, is definitely not confirmed. The extra-large rooms at the site yielded no evidence that they were in any way different from the other large rooms. If ceremonial paraphernalia had been kept in them, it was either removed upon abandonment, or simply not preserved. A closer study of present-day Pueblo clanhouses might suggest other kinds of data to look for in the larger prehistoric rooms, but this must remain a concern for the future.

The final proposition was that the special rooms at the site would contain cultural items associated primarily with male activities, while the large and small rooms would contain both male- and female-associated items. In attempting to confirm this proposition it has, of course, been necessary to deal only with those items that could reasonably be assigned a context with regard to the sexual division of labor. These include the following:

Male-Associated Artifacts	*Female-Associated Artifacts*
Projectile points	Metates
Arrowshaft tools	Manos
Antler-flakers	Worked Sherds
Cores	
Hammerstones	

An examination of Table 2 shows that the proposition is confirmed. The three female-associated items were found predominantly in the large rooms, and not in the special rooms; the male-associated items (except for arrowshaft tools) were strongly represented in both large and special rooms; both sets of items were found to some degree in the small rooms—although rarely in significant quantities. The important point, however, is that female-associated items were not significantly present in the special rooms; among all four of these rooms there was only one metate, one mano, and one worked sherd. This lends strong support to the idea that these rooms were generally restricted to males, as was seen to be the case among the present-day western Pueblos.

In summary, it is clear that twelve of the sixteen propositions are unequivocally confirmed (1–8, 11, 13, 14, and 16); two of them (10 and 12) are at least partially confirmed; and only two of them were not confirmed (9 and 15). It is thus demonstrated that the three major room types at Broken K Pueblo were the general functional equivalents of the three major kinds of rooms in present-day Pueblo villages; they may legitimately be called habitation, storage, and ceremonial rooms (or kivas). The primary functional characteristics of these rooms are summarized in Table 7. If the rooms were not functional equivalents of the modern room types, it is highly unlikely that so many of the expectations in terms of content would have been confirmed.

Table 7. Functions of the Room Types

Habitation	*Storage*	*Ceremonial*
Food Processing	Storage of Plant Foods	Ceremonies
Cooking		Manufacturing
Eating	Storage of Non-Food Materials (probably)	Eating (occasionally)
Water Storage		
Manufacturing	Manufacturing (occasionally)	

It has not been possible, however, to demonstrate that the seven extra-large rooms at the site were functionally equivalent to the modern clan-houses. It could not be shown by this analysis that they were different from the other habitation rooms, even in terms of floor area; they appear to have been nothing more than large living rooms. Nonetheless, they may have been clanhouses, and a more detailed study of present-day clanhouses may suggest other evidence that can be looked for in prehistoric pueblos to document the existence of such rooms.

Summary and Discussion

During the excavation of Broken K Pueblo, it was noticed that there were differences among the rooms, particularly with regard to size. To explain this variability in behavioral or functional terms, however, it was first necessary to describe the differences among the rooms more rigorously. In addition to discovering the attributes that would provide accurate measures of these differences, it was important to determine the extent to which clustering could be demonstrated among the attributes. Although seven different attributes were chosen for study, the ones that proved most useful included size (floor area) and the presence or absence of firepits, mealing bins, and ventilators. A series of simple but powerful statistical tests of association were employed in demonstrating that there were two clearly distinguishable kinds of rooms (large and small rooms), in addition to the already separated special rooms. The large rooms were distinguished by having more than 6.5 square meters of floor area (sometimes much more), and by the fact that they contained slab-lined firepits, mealing bins and ventilators; the small rooms had less than 6.5 square meters of floor area, and did not contain such features. The special rooms had a peculiar constellation of features all their own.

A series of logical explanations for this variability among rooms was then presented; it was obvious that this variability had resulted from the fact that the rooms had been built to house different kinds of activities. It was inferred that the large rooms had been designed for relatively large groups of people, or for activities that required a relatively large space for their performance. These activities must have required heat and/or light, as well as fresh air and facilities for grinding food materials; they gave every appearance of being living rooms. The small rooms, however, were dark, unheated, and unventilated, and it seemed likely that they had been storage rooms. The special rooms were inferred to have had an entirely different function than any of the other rooms, perhaps ceremonial. The scattered and paired nature of the spatial distribution of both large and small rooms permitted the inference that each household had occupied at least one pair of rooms (large and small), and that each such unit had performed similar sets of activities in their rooms. Because there were only a small number of special rooms, it was inferred that each of them had been shared by a number of family or household units.

An examination of the ethnographic evidence revealed a series of positive analogies between the nature of structural patterning at Broken K and that in the Hopi and Zuñi villages. It was found that the present-day villages also contain large, small, and special rooms, and the internal structural features of these rooms are generally the same as the features in their supposed analogues at the site. And further, the different kinds of rooms occurred in very similar relative proportions in both cases, and the large and small rooms tended to occur in pairs. The historic analogies were so good, in fact, that they could hardly have been coincidental; on this basis it was proposed that the three major kinds of rooms discovered at Broken K Pueblo were in fact the functional equivalents of their formal counterparts in present-day Pueblo villages. It also seemed possible that the extra-large rooms at the site were functionally equivalent to the large Hopi living rooms that serve as clanhouses.

The next step was to test this proposition of functional equivalence; and this required some additional (and independent) data. It was clear that if the proposition was in fact true, the same general kinds of artifacts and other cultural materials would be found in the three room types at Broken K as are found in their supposed historic counterparts—or at least it could be expected that evidence would be found at the site to document the existence of the same general kinds of activities in these respective rooms.

Upon examining the ethnographic evidence, it was found that the large rooms in Hopi and Zuñi villages are indeed living rooms, the small ones are storage rooms, and the special rooms serve as both ceremonial centers and as clubhouses or lounging areas for the men. Although there is some functional overlap among these kinds of rooms, it was found that they are each used in distinctive sets of activities; and distinctive sets of cultural materials occur in them as a result of these activities. The large rooms are used in the greatest number of indoor family activities, especially those of food processing, cooking, and eating. In addition, a great many manufacturing activities occur in these rooms, and water is stored and used in them. The most important function of the storage rooms, on the other hand, is the storage of food crops, especially corn, beans, and squash. They are also used to store a number of other things, and they are occasionally even involved in manufacturing activities, as well as some of the other activities that are usually carried out in the living rooms. The special rooms, in addition to being the centers of ritual activity, are used in a wide variety of manufacturing and other secular activities (including weaving). The extra-large rooms, or clanhouses, are occupied by the headwomen of the different clans in a village and, in addition to being ordinary living rooms, they serve as centers for clan meetings and the storage of ritual paraphernalia.

Given this discussion of the various kinds of activities that are commonly carried out in these different kinds of rooms, it was possible to point out some of the kinds of artifacts and other materials that could be expected to occur in the different rooms at Broken K Pueblo. This was presented in the form of a list of sixteen propositions or "expectations." An examination of the archeological data confirmed most of these propositions and, as was pointed out, we are justified in asserting that the three major room types at Broken K Pueblo really do represent habitation, storage, and ceremonial rooms. Whether or not the extra-large rooms were clanhouses is still not known.

There is no doubt, of course, that the activity-structure at Broken K remained stable during the 130 years in which the site was occupied. This is demonstrated by the fact that there were no major differences in either form or content among the rooms that had been constructed at different time periods.

Further, it is clear that the basic aspects of activity-organization have not been significantly altered since A.D. 1300; they are virtually the same among the modern Pueblos as they were then. In addition to the fact that both the prehistoric and historic rooms are similar in terms of form and function, the relative frequencies and spatial patterning among the rooms has remained remarkably stable. It is almost certain that Broken K Pueblo was composed of a number of households (perhaps about 25 of them), each occupying at least one habitation room and one storage room, and each carrying on the same fundamental sets of activities. This stability in activity-structure holds true even though villages have gotten larger in size, and have undergone changes in overall ground plan since A.D. 1300. Further, it is likely that this stability extends at least as far back in time as A.D. 800 or 900, the approximate period when surface masonry pueblos were first being constructed in the Southwest.

Nonetheless, while the general outlines of stability are evident, there may also have been a few minor changes in activity-structure since A.D. 1300. This is suggested by the fact that not all of the propositions that were tested were confirmed. Propositions 9 and 15 are particularly interesting in this respect. Under proposition 9, it was expected that the storage rooms at Broken K would contain great numbers of large undecorated storage jars; this was not the case, and we may infer that the inhabitants of the site were utilizing somewhat different storage techniques than are employed by historic western Pueblo peoples. Proposition 10, on the other hand, included the prediction that large quantities of the pollen or seeds of corn and squash would be found in the kivas; this, too, proved not to be the case; it may be that these domesticates were not as important ritually (or even economically) as they are among the present-day Pueblo peoples (Hill, 1964, 1966).

In any event, the propositions that were not confirmed are just as important as the ones that were (L R. Binford, 1967). In addition to providing evidence of culture-change, they provide new information that cannot be obtained from ethnographic materials. They raise new questions, and provide information which can serve as a basis for generating additional testable propositions. For example, one set of propositions, which can be generated solely on the basis of the archeological data, is suggested by the lack of pollen from domestic crops in the kivas:

1. There was a shift in the physical or biological environment during the time period in which the site was occupied.

2. This environmental shift created conditions inimical to agriculture, promoting reduced crop yields.

3. Reduced crop yields forced the inhabitants of the site to rely heavily on wild food crops, both economically and ritually.

While there are certainly other explanatory propositions that may pertain in this case, these particular ones are clearly testable. We can predict that if these propositions are correct, there ought to be independent evidence in the environmental and archeological records to confirm them. We can enumerate the kinds of evidence that could be expected under these conditions, and then proceed to collect the relevant data to test them—just as has been done in this paper with respect to the proposed functions of rooms. As a matter of fact, these propositions have already been tested, with marked success, using data derived from Broken K Pueblo and other sites in east-central Arizona (Hill, 1965).

In addition to the fact that new propositions can be generated on the basis of those propositions that were not confirmed, they can also be generated on the basis of information gained in the process of confirming the others. It was suggested, for example, that the apparently paired groups of rooms at the site probably represent the loci of individual household units. This proposition can be tested, of course, by examining the ethnographic evidence to discover the kinds of stylistic differences that distinguish present-day pueblo households and then examining the archeological data in an effort to confirm the presence of similar stylistic variation. One would not even think of gathering data relevant to such a problem unless the problem had been in mind prior to excavation. It is evident, however, that if residence units that are larger than households can be identified using stylistic variability in various kinds of materials (Longacre, 1963, 1964; Hill, 1965, 1966; Martin, Longacre, and Hill, 1967), then it ought to be possible to isolate the loci of individual households as well.

The number of testable propositions that can be generated with respect to past human behavior is virtually endless. The major conclusion to be drawn is that by using this approach of generating and testing propositions it should be possible to expand our knowledge of the past almost indefinitely. There is no need to rely solely on ethnographic data in making inferences about the past. Although ethnographic evidence can profitably be used to generate propositions, as has been done here, it is equally feasible to use archeological data in the same way. Actually, it matters little what kind of information is used; if the propositions are testable (and of some scientific importance), they are useful to the advancement of knowledge.

It cannot be stressed strongly enough, however, that our propositions must be tested with data that is independent of the data used in formulating them. The most common approach to making inferences about the past can be illustrated with an example of the way in which the functions of prehistoric pueblo rooms are usually inferred:

1. The premise is stated that certain rooms look like living rooms because they contain firepits and mealing bins.
2. Ethnographic data indicate that present-day pueblo living rooms also contain these features.
3. It is then proposed that since the prehistoric rooms have these features, they must in fact be functionally the same as the historically recorded living rooms.

This is reasonable, of course, as far as it goes; but the analysis frequently stops at this point, and the proposition (number 3 in this case) is represented as fact. In essence, the proposition is generated using both ethnographic and archeological evidence, but it is left untested; there is little attempt to find independent evidence that would either support or refute it. This situation is common in all of the social sciences, and the problem has been clearly stated by a noted philosopher of science:

> The most important feature about a hypothesis or proposition is that it is a mere trial idea. . . . Unfortunately, in many fields, especially on the border lines of science, hypotheses are often accepted without adequate tests. Plausibility is not a substitute for evidence, however great may be the emotional wish to believe. . . . The difficulty of testing hypotheses in the social sciences has led to an abbreviation of the scientific method in which this step is simply omitted. Plausible hypotheses are merely set down as facts without further ado (Wilson, 1952, pp. 26-27).

I have attempted to illustrate that we need not stop with the statement of propositions; it is nearly always possible to find independent data with which to test them.

It is of further importance to note in this connection that when propositions are properly tested we are provided with measures of the *degree* to which they are accurate. Such measures are not available when we simply use ethnographic data to interpret the past, and the reason for this is clear. If, for example, I had not tested the proposition of the functional equivalence of room types at Broken K Pueblo with those among the modern pueblos, there would have been no determination of the degree to which the prehistoric rooms actually differ from the historic ones. The discovery that the people of Broken K had different storage techniques would not have been made, nor would it have been seen that corn and squash were not frequently used in kiva rituals at the site. In applying ethnographic evidence directly, I would simply have been asserting that the prehistoric rooms (and activities) were the same as those that have been recorded ethnographically. In short, there would have been no expansion of our knowledge of the past; we would simply have demonstrated an ability to read the ethnographic literature.

The difference in storage technique between Broken K and the modern pueblos is probably the best illustration of this point. This incompatibility with the ethnographic evidence suggests not only that certain changes have occurred since A.D. 1300, but also that it is incorrect to assume that large undecorated jars are always storage jars; they apparently had a different function at Broken K Pueblo, and the same situation might be found in other Southwestern pueblos. Whether this is true or not remains to be seen, but it certainly warrants further investigation. Even as it stands, this discovery represents an advance in knowledge that would not have been forthcoming had the site been interpreted using ethnographic evidence alone.

It is evident, then, that archeology can contribute information of its own: propositions can be generated and tested, and a great many things can be learned that have not previously been known or speculated about before. In addition to making use of available ethnographic evidence, it is possible to discover new information that will be of use to ethnographers and social anthropologists. This general methodology of generating and testing propositions is, of course, not restricted to use in the American Southwest; it is universally applicable.

The substantive conclusions presented in this paper are not, of course, wholly new; investigators have frequently been able to identify different kinds of rooms in prehistoric pueblo sites. It is clear, however, that the functional equivalence of prehistoric and historic room types has *not* previously been demonstrated. Functional equivalence has been *proposed* (and believed), on the basis of the fact that there are obvious formal similarities; but the proposition has not been adequately tested.

Still, I do not pretend to have presented many substantive conclusions that have not already been believed for a number of years. I have used this particular Southwestern example as a vehicle to illustrate what I think is an important methodological approach in archeology. The substantive material was chosen because it is familiar to most archeologists and is not in itself controversial.

References

BEAGLEHOLE, ERNEST. 1936. *Hopi hunting and hunting ritual.* Yale University Publications in Anthropology, no. 4. New Haven: Yale University Press.

——. 1937. *Notes on Hopi economic life.* Yale University Publications in Anthropology, no. 15. New Haven: Yale University Press.

BEAGLEHOLE, PEARL. 1935. Census data from two Hopi villages. *American Anthropologist,* 37(1) Part 1: 41–54.

BINFORD, LEWIS R. 1967. Smudge pits and hide smoking: the use of analogy in archaeological reasoning. *American Antiquity,* 32(1): 1–12.

BRAINARD, MARGARET. 1935. *The Hopi Indian family: a study of the changes represented in its present structure and functions.* Unpublished Ph.D. dissertation, University of Chicago.

BUNZEL, RUTH L. 1929. *The Pueblo potter: a study of creative imagination in primitive art.* New York: Columbia University Press.

COCHRAN, WILLIAM G. 1952. The X^2 test of goodness of fit. *Annals of Mathematical Statistics,* 23: 315–45.

CUSHING, F. H. 1920. *Zuñi breadstuff.* Indian Notes and Monographs, vol. 8. New York: Museum of the American Indian.

DEETZ, JAMES D. F. 1960. *An archaeological approach to kinship change in eighteenth century Arikara culture.* Unpublished Ph.D. dissertation, Harvard University.

——. 1965. *The dynamics of stylistic change in Arikara ceramics.* Illinois Studies in Anthropology, no. 4. Urbana: University of Illinois.

DONALDSON, THOMAS. 1893. *Moqui Pueblo Indians of Arizona and New Mexico.* Eleventh census of the United States, extra census bulletin. Washington, D.C.: U. S. Government Printing Office.

EGGAN, FRED. 1950. *Social organization of the western Pueblos.* Chicago: University of Chicago Press.

——. 1964. Alliance and descent in western Pueblo society. In Robert A. Manners (Ed.), *Process and pattern in culture.* Chicago: Aldine Publishing Company.

FISHER, R. A. 1938. *Statistical methods for research workers.* Edinburgh and London: Oliver and Boyd.

FORDE, C. DARYELL. 1931. Hopi agriculture and land ownership. *Journal of the Royal Anthropological Institute of Great Britain and Ireland,* 61: 357–405.

FREEMAN, LESLIE G. JR., and JAMES A. BROWN. 1964. Statistical analysis of Carter Ranch pottery. In Paul S. Martin *et al.* (Eds.), Chapters in the prehistory of eastern Arizona, II. *Fieldiana: Anthropology,* 55: 126–54.

FRUCHTER, BENJAMIN. 1954. *Introduction to factor analysis.* Princeton, N.J.: D. van Nostrand.

HAURY, EMIL W. 1940. Excavations in the Forestdale Valley, east-central Arizona. *University of Arizona Bulletin,* 11(4) (Social Science Bulletin, no. 12).

HAWLEY, F. M. 1937. Pueblo social organization as a lead to Pueblo history. *American Anthropologist,* 39(3), Part 1: 504–22.

HEVLY, RICHARD HOLMES. 1964. *Pollen analysis of Quaternary achaeological and Lacustrine sediments from the Colorado Plateau.* Unpublished Ph.D. dissertation, University of Arizona.

HILL, JAMES N. 1965. *Broken K: a prehistoric society in eastern Arizona.* Unpublished Ph.D. dissertation, University of Chicago.

——. 1966. A prehistoric community in eastern Arizona. *Southwestern Journal of Anthropology,* 22(1): 9–30.

HILL, JAMES N., and RICHARD H. HEVLY. 1968. Pollen at Broken K Pueblo: some new interpretations. *American Antiquity* (In Press).

KROEBER, A. L. 1917. *Zuñi kin and clan.* Anthropological Papers of the American Museum of Natural History, vol. 28 (Part II). New York: American Museum of Natural History.

LONGACRE, WILLIAM A. 1963. *Archaeology as anthropology: a case study.* Unpublished Ph.D. dissertation, University of Chicago.

——. 1964. Archaeology as anthropology: a case study. *Science,* 144(3625) : 1454–55.

MARTIN, PAUL S., WILLIAM A. LONGACRE, and JAMES N. HILL. 1967. Chapters in the prehistory of eastern Arizona, III. *Fieldiana: Anthropology,* Vol. 57.

MINDELEFF, VICTOR. 1891. A Study of Pueblo architecture, Tusayan and Cibola. *Eighth Annual Report of the Bureau of American Ethnology, 1886–1887.* Washington, D.C.: U.S. Government Printing Office.

PARSONS, E. C. 1936. *Hopi journal of Alexander M. Stephen.* Columbia University Contributions to Anthropology, Vols. 23 and 24. New York: Columbia University Press.

RINALDO, JOHN B. 1964. Artifacts. In Paul S. Martin *et al.* (Eds.), Chapters in the prehistory of eastern Arizona, II. *Fieldiana: Anthropology,* 55: 63–109.

ROBERTS, JOHN M. 1956. *Zuñi daily life.* Monograph No. 2, Notebook No. 3, Lincoln: Laboratory of Anthropology, University of Nebraska.

SCHOENWETTER, JAMES. 1962. The pollen analysis of eighteen archaeological sites in Arizona and New Mexico. In Paul S. Martin *et al.* (Eds.). Chapters in the prehistory of eastern Arizona, I. *Fieldiana: Anthropology,* 53: 168–209.

SEARS, WILLIAM H. 1961. The study of social and religious systems in North American archaeology. *Current Anthropology,* 2(3): 223–46.

SIEGEL, SIDNEY. 1956. *Nonparametric statistics for the behavioral sciences.* New York: McGraw-Hill.

SPAULDING, ALBERT C. 1953. Statistical techniques for the discovery of artifact types. *American Antiquity,* 18(4): 305–13.

STEVENSON, MATILDA COXE. 1904. The Zuñi Indians: their mythology, esoteric fraternities, and ceremonies. *Twenty-Third Annual Report of the Bureau of American Ethnology.* Washington, D.C.: U.S. Government Printing Office.

——. 1909. Ethnobotany of the Zuñi Indians. *Thirtieth Annual Report of the Bureau of American Ethnology.* Washington, D.C.: U.S. Government Printing Office.

STEWARD, JULIAN H. 1937. Ecological aspects of Southwestern society. *Anthropos,* 32: 87–104.

TITIEV, MISCHA. 1944. Old Oraibi: a study of the Hopi Indians of Third Mesa. *Papers of the Peabody Museum of American Archaeology and Ethnology,* 22(1). Cambridge: Peabody Museum.

WHITING, ALFRED F. 1939. Ethnobotany of the Hopi. *Museum of Northern Arizona Bulletin,* No. 15. Flagstaff: Museum of Northern Arizona.

WILSON, E. BRIGHT, JR. 1952. *An introduction to scientific research.* New York: McGraw-Hill.

Computer Analysis of Archeological Data from Teotihuacan, Mexico

For the past several years, René Millon of the University of Rochester and his associates have been engaged in the detailed mapping and intensive archeological survey of the entire urban area of Teotihuacan, a great prehispanic city covering more than eight square miles in the Valley of Mexico (Millon, 1964). There have, of course, been many excavations and restorations of specific structures and localities at Teotihuacan during the past eighty years or so, but this is the first attempt to deal in a systematic and thorough way with the city as a whole. Records are being accumulated on all features detectable from the surface and on analyses of surface collections for each of some 5,000 separate tracts; leading to an enormous mass of detailed information.

The past few years have also seen rapidly growing use of computers for handling archeological data; especially in the use of multivariate statistical techniques which are too laborious to be feasible without computers. So far as I know, none of these computer studies have attempted to deal with a site as rich or as complex as Teotihuacan; they have all dealt with the much smaller settlements of food collectors or with towns or villages of food producers. This is not to say that studies of smaller sites have been any less important either for their contributions to anthropological theory or to computer technique; I merely wish to emphasize that the size and complexity of Teotihuacan present problems and opportunities somewhat different than those which characterized these earlier studies.

Since the spring of 1965, Millon and I have been collaborating in a pilot study of computer analysis of his Teotihuacan data, working with a few hundred tracts from those which have already been recorded.[1] We have received valuable assistance from other members of the mapping project, especially from Bruce Drewitt, James Bennyhoff, Matthew Wallrath, and James Dow.

One major aim of our computer work is to help us understand Teotihuacan better; in particular, to produce richer and better-substantiated reconstructions of the city as a going concern during each phase of its history. Here, instead of turning to the ethnographic literature on hunting and gathering or on horticultural people for enlightenment or hypotheses, one turns mainly to what is known of the broadly defined category of "pre-industrial cities" (Sjoberg, 1960; Kraeling and Adams, 1960; Braidwood and Willey, 1962). Topics that particularly interest us include the number and characteristics of the recognizable social classes in the city, the extent to which different classes were sharply or rigidly defined, and the kinds of craft specialties practiced. We would like to know the uses and social functions of various kinds of artifacts and structures. We would like to know what kinds of people lived in each district or neighborhood, and what kinds of activities were carried out where. How was the city organized and administered, and on what levels of centralization or decentralization were various ritual, political, and economic activities and services carried out? What kinds of changes and continuities through time can be seen during the six centuries or so (roughly A.D. 100 to 700) that the city flourished?

Clearly, much can be established about these topics without computer analysis of the survey data and, equally clearly, we do not expect that we can use a computer to answer every question we would like to ask about Teotihuacan. We do expect that we can establish some important findings which it would have been difficult or impossible to demonstrate without the aid of computer methods.

One ultimate objective, then, is to learn more about Teotihuacan per se, both for its own sake and as an important instance of an early urban society to be compared with other examples in the Old and New Worlds. At the same time, we find ourselves developing new concepts and techniques for computer analysis which will be quite generally useful for other bodies of archeological data. It is mainly some of these new concepts and techniques that I wish to discuss in this paper.

[1] Our computer work has been supported in part by the National Science Foundation (Grant GS916) and in part by the Wenner-Gren Foundation for Anthropological Research (Grant 1781). Brandeis University acted as the sponsoring institution and provided important facilities and services, including access to an IBM 1620 computer which, while too limited in capacity to handle many of our problems, has proved very useful for some preliminary operations. The data themselves have been provided by the Teotihuacan Mapping Project, directed by Millon, in part using University of Rochester facilities. We are most grateful to all these institutions for their support and assistance.

One of the most exciting archeological uses for computers is in the generation of better taxonomies and other systems of ordering and summarizing data on individual specimens and on assemblages of specimens; this is closely related to the field of storage and retrieval of data on specimens and assemblages. Each specimen is treated as a "case" characterized by some particular observed value or state for each of many variables or "dimensions" (the latter term was introduced and discussed by Spaulding [1953, 1960]; the terms are synonymous). We have not been pursuing this approach because an excellent classification and chronology of Teotihuacan material is already available, thanks largely to Bennyhoff; because fragmentary surface material is not nearly as good for this as would be more complete excavated specimens; and above all because we have more than enough to occupy us in working on other equally exciting problems.

Our conceptual framework is one in which tracts of the city, rather than specimens, are taken as units or "cases," and each tract is characterized by many variables, which include characteristics of features detectable from the surface and counts of artifacts of each category collected. It should be pointed out very plainly that it is not feasible to encode for machine processing everything recorded for every tract in the form of notes, drawings, and photographs, nor is it necessary—or even, in my opinion, desirable. Things which are unique to a single site or a very small number of sites are best apprehended and evaluated by more conventional methods; and the costs of a larger and more complicated data code that would attempt to provide for their description are not offset by any advantages of machine processing. We do, however, want to avoid leaving out anything which might later prove useful, and in this pilot study we have been following the rule "When in doubt, include." This has resulted in a set of variables which requires seven punch cards, of eighty columns each, to record the data from each tract. One of our objectives is to find out which variables seem too unprofitable to justify their inclusion in the final full analysis of the data. I should also mention that for any specific problem, not all variables will be relevant. In some cases the computer can be instructed to look at only some specified list of relevant variables, but in other cases, especially in using previously written programs with built-in limitations on the format of the input data, it will probably be easier to run our original data through a simple program which recodes it, deleting some variables, simplifying others, and sometimes creating new variables which are functions of two or more of the original variables. This recoded data can then be used as the input for other programs.

What we aim to create with our present seven-card code is essentially an "archival" record of all features which we think may be relevant for any problems we may want to investigate by machine. Building up the archive will be a relatively laborious job, but once it is done, a great many recodings and simplifications of this data for specific problems will be possible quickly and cheaply by machine, without need to return to further hand encoding of data.

Any two tracts can be compared by noting their similarity or dissimilarity for each variable considered relevant for any specific problem, and there are a number of different mathematical measures designed to summarize overall resemblance (many of which are reviewed by Sokal and Sneath, 1963). Once a matrix of similarity or correlation coefficients for all pairs of tracts has been obtained, multivariate techniques, including factor analysis and various clustering methods can be used to generate clusters and hierarchies of clusters of relatively similar tracts. This is a "Q-technique" approach (Tugby, 1965, p. 8). Alternatively, we can also evaluate the similarity in the distribution patterns of various pairs of artifact categories or other variables, which is "R-technique," and generate clusters and hierarchies of clusters of artifacts or other features with relatively similar patterns of distribution.

We aim to explore various methods of generating clusters and to compare their consistency, intelligibility, and economy. At least to begin with, we plan to make extensive use of computer programs contained in *The Multivariate Statistical Analyser*, a package of mulitvariate programs developed by Kenneth Jones of Harvard University for use on the IBM 7094 (Jones, 1964). These appear to be at least as good as any other programs of this kind available, and have the very great additional advantage that they are already in routine use on computers in the Boston area, and that Jones is readily available for assistance in using them.

The general idea, of course, is that tracts which turn out to be in the same cluster are importantly similar to one another, and presumably were used by much the same kind of people for much the same purposes. Artifact categories and other features which cluster together have highly similar patterns of distribution, and presumably these similarities are not accidental. Beyond this, it has to be stressed that clusters which emerge are important data, but their interpretation in cultural terms may not be self-evident. We see machine results as an aid to, not a substitute for, human judgments based on a combination of controlled intuition, thorough familiarity with the data, knowledge of relevant archeological and ethnographic literature, and respect for the nature and limitations of the evidence.

I should mention that we have several additional kinds of computer operations in mind; notably the production of quick but not too crude maps or visual displays of the distributions of artifact categories, architectural features, or clusters of any sort. We expect that such maps will be valuable in guiding hypotheses, and at times they may answer some questions quite directly.

Much of our work to date has been less concerned with these ultimate objectives than with some essential preliminaries, chiefly in assessment of the adequacy of the data and in some conceptual innovations we have developed for data coding.

At the outset I had some distinct misgivings about the reliability we could expect from surface collections, and I began by looking into the extent that different workers collecting at different times and different workers analyzing the collections at different times do in fact produce comparable results. For four sites near the eastern edge of the city, collections had been made and analyzed separately in 1962 and 1963. Five hundred and twenty sherds were collected in 1962, and 372 in 1963, which is 72 per cent of the 1962 total, a reduction which may be due wholly or partially to depletion from the previous collecting. Sherds had been classified into nine phases, running from late Preclassic to Aztec. A Chi-square analysis showed that for seven of the nine phases agreements between 1962 and 1963 were very good. In fact, for six phases the disagreement was considerably *less* than one might have expected from unavoidable sampling error. There was a greater discrepancy for one phase, Tlamimilolpa, and far less Mazapan phase material in 1963 than one would have expected. Nevertheless, excluding Mazapan and comparing the other eight phases, differences between 1962 and 1963 are not significant at the 5 per cent level. It seems probable that the Mazapan anomaly is due to shifting criteria for the recognition of that phase.

In the earlier work, less emphasis was placed on obsidian than later, and this is reflected by a pronounced increase in the 1963 proportion of obsidian. This complicates things but it does not mean that early collections cannot be compared with later ones. It means that date of collection must be taken into account as an important variable, and obsidian counts in early collections must be multiplied by a suitable factor, perhaps best determined by co-variance analysis.

Another check on our data was made by comparing the 126 Miccaotli phase sherds from these four sites at the eastern edge of the city with 586 sherds collected from 24 sites near the western edge of the city that were assigned to Miccaotli by a different analyst. The comparison was made on the basis of nine major ceramic categories. Here the agreements were all good, and mostly amazingly good.

Much more work remains to be done on checking the reliability and validity of collections; in particular we have to find out more about the effects of varying surface cover and varying degrees of site alteration. But, from what has been done so far, the variations due to different workers have been far smaller than I had expected. We also have at least a few indications that the effects of site alterations may also be unexpectedly small. Most important is that we have quite full data on present conditions of sites, and can do a great deal by way of assessment of these effects and correction for any that are large enough to warrant it.

The remarkably good agreement between proportions of Miccaotli ceramic categories at the eastern and western edges of the city calls for comment. It implies not only uniformity in collecting practices, but great similarity in what is actually in the sites, which in turn suggests considerable social similarity in these widely separated districts. This has to be qualified in several ways for the moment. First, this comparison takes no account of possible difference in non-ceramic features, nor of possible internal variability within each district. Second, it is not very conclusive for some rare categories in the smaller eastern sample. For example, six censer fragments were expected there, but only three were found. This discrepancy could easily be due to accidents in sampling. However, if the same proportions hold when a larger sample is studied, so that we find only thirty censer fragments where we would expect sixty, the difference would then be highly significant, and would point to real differences in the activities in the two districts. In other words, against a background of close similarity in the proportions of common ceramic categories, there may yet prove to be important contrasts between these two districts in the abundance of certain rare categories. Finally, it will be of great interest to see how both of these marginal districts compare with more central districts, which could prove to be very different indeed.

A somewhat different problem relating to adequacy of data derives from the fact that specimens of rare categories are quite likely to be collected from only a fraction of the sites in which they are really present. One might suppose that all that is needed to correct for this is to include a large number of sites in one's sample. Actually, our mathematical investigation shows that the expected absolute value of the correlation between any easily missed category and any other category becomes lower than the "true" value that would be found if the category were never missed, and increasing the number of sites only increases the reliability of this reduced correlation. This means that we can take individual sites as "cases" only when comparing common or not easily missed categories; while for scarcer categories we must pool sites and get a more "coarse-grained" picture of their associations. By experimenting with different criteria for pooling sites, a great deal of useful information can still be extracted from scarce categories, however. An important topic for further work will be improving criteria for deciding how "fine-grained" our treatment of any specific rare category can be before correlations are seriously reduced.

Possibly the knottiest conceptual problem we have had to solve in developing our data code concerns our units of analysis. I have so far spoken rather easily of tracts or sites as if what I meant were self-evident, but in fact it is not. Consider a case where four mounds are arranged around the sides of a plaza as part of a clearly interrelated complex. Certainly separate collections will have been made from each mound and from the plaza itself, and frequently there are separate collections from different parts of a single large mound or plaza. For some problems, we may want to compare collections from different parts of a single mound, treating each collection as a separate case. For other problems we want to treat each whole mound as a single case; while for yet other problems we want to compare the complex as a whole with other complexes, treating the entire complex as one case or unit. It can be seen that there is no single unit suitable for all problems.

After some effort, we have developed a scheme based on the concepts of collection tract, site, complex, macrocomplex, and neighborhood.

The elementary indivisible building block or atom of the scheme is the collection tract, which is whatever actual physical tract was collected from and described as a unit by the field workers. A site is a minimal distinguishable structural unit, such as a mound or an apparent residential unit. Often a collection tract corresponds to a single site, but often for various reasons one site was divided into two or more collection tracts. Many sites are not clearly linked to any others, but in other cases several sites form part of an interrelated architectural complex. Sometimes, in turn, several complexes appear to be interrelated as elements of a larger macrocomplex. If there are any meaningful macromacrocomplexes, they are too rare to be useful for computer work. A final concept is the neighborhood, which simply refers to the features that are physically close to a given collection tract, whether there is any obvious relationship between them or not. The neighborhood and the complex are quite different concepts, since there may be closely neighboring sites which are not part of the same complex, or sites belonging to one complex that are not especially close neighbors.

Each collection record pertains primarily to the specific collection tract from which the collection comes, and most of the data encoded for it are about precisely that tract—features observed on it and counts of material collected from it. But we also provide for data about the relationship of the collection tract to a site, about the site itself, about the complex (if any) that the site belongs to, about the macrocomplex (if any) that the complex belongs to, and about features in the neighborhood of the collection tract. Any or all of these kinds of data may be needed as relevant information about the context of a collection tract, and, starting with the record of any collection tract, they must be readily accessible, even when individual collection tracts are the units of analysis.

When sites, complexes, macrocomplexes, or neighborhoods are the units of analysis, we need a way for the computer to select all relevant collection tracts and summarize for itself the data from all of them. To do this for neighborhoods, we have encoded the position of the approximate center of each collection tract relative to the mapping project's central datum point, and this enables the machine to select all collection records within any specified radius of a given tract, or within any specified distance in any specified direction. To get data on all tracts of a given site, complex, or macrocomplex, we can construct a loop in which each tract record specifies the name of one other tract belonging to the same unit. That is, tract A lists tract B, tract B lists C, and C lists A, so that one can start at any given point in the loop and complete the whole circuit. Within any given loop all tracts belonging as well to the same complex or the same site can be identified, also. Once one has all tracts of a given site or complex or macrocomplex linked together in this fashion, it is really only necessary to encode data on the site as a whole for one collection tract of the site, or data on the complex as a whole for one collection tract of the whole complex, since we can get quickly from any collection tract record of the complex to any other.

Finally, even though the aim of our work is to enable us to make new interpretations of the data that would not otherwise be possible, it is extremely helpful to have available the various interpretations which suggest themselves in the field or in the course of encoding the data. We are calling all these interpretations "preliminary" in order to emphasize their distinctness from interpretations made after computer analysis. They range from some that strike us as inescapable conclusions, to others that are not much more than informed hunches. We have provided for ratings of our confidence in them and for alternative interpretations in ambiguous cases. One use to be made of these preliminary interpretations is in looking at all units interpreted as representing structures of a certain type or as having a certain function, and finding out all the ways in which they contrast as a group, with all other units. Or, we can see how much variation there is among units interpreted as belonging to some specific category. Also, clusters can be generated without regard to preliminary interpretations, and one can then observe the extent to which any resulting clusters coincide with any categories based on preliminary interpretations. In all these examples, of course, we must be constantly aware that insofar as some observed features point to specific preliminary interpretations, the logic involved is partly circular, and attention must be focused on *unexpected* associations or lacks of associations that turn up.

References

Braidwood, R. J., and G. R. Willey (Eds.). 1962. *Courses toward urban life.* Chicago: Aldine Publishing Company.

Jones, Kenneth. 1964. *The multivariate statistical analyser.* Cambridge: Harvard Computing Center, Harvard University.

Kraeling, C. H., and R. M. Adams (Eds.). 1960. *City invincible.* Chicago: University of Chicago Press.

Millon, René. 1964. The Teotihuacan mapping project. *American Antiquity,* 29(3): 345–52.

Sjoberg, Gideon. 1960. *The Preindustrial city.* Glencoe, Illinois: The Free Press.

Sokal, R. R., and Sneath, P. H. A. 1963. *Principles of numerical taxonomy.* San Francisco and London: W. H. Freeman.

Spaulding, A. C. 1953. Statistical techniques for the discovery of artifact types. *American Antiquity,* 18(4): 305–13.

——. 1960. The dimensions of archaeology. In Gertrude R. Dole and Robert L. Carneiro (Eds.), *Essays in the science of culture: in honor of Leslie A. White.* New York: Thomas Y. Crowell.

Tugby, Donald. 1965. Archaeological objectives and statistical methods: a frontier in archaeology. *American Antiquity,* 31(1): 1–16.

Archeological Lessons from an Apache Wickiup

During the summer of 1965, an abandoned Apache living site was investigated as a part of research undertaken by the University of Arizona Archaeological Field School.[1] The site appeared to have been deserted quite recently. The former occupants left behind a considerable quantity of cultural materials that seemed to have been only slightly disturbed. The patterned distribution of cultural items and features suggested that the site had a structure which might reflect aspects of the behavior and organization of the people who occupied it. To test this proposition, we tried to make deductions concerning the nature of activities carried out at the site. An Apache informant was used to check the validity of our interpretations.

Our first step in the investigation was to delimit the area of occupation and to describe the distribution and types of features and artifacts found. A general map of the site and a plan of the wickiup floor were drawn. Photos were taken of all features. While describing the features and artifacts, deductions were made concerning their use. Later, these interpretations were checked by consulting the female Apache informant. We made every effort to phrase our questions as objectively as possible so as not to

[1] Paper presented at the Annual Meeting, Society for American Archeology, Reno, Nevada, May, 1966. We thank Dr. Harry T. Getty, Department of Anthropology, University of Arizona, who made several valuable comments on this paper; Larry D. Agenbroad who made the site map; and Bev Lea Teasley and Lorraine Williams, field school students, who aided in the field work.

elicit answers she might have thought we wanted. We let her explain in her own words the use of the features and artifacts.

The living site is located in the northeast part of the Fort Apache Indian Reservation in the rugged, forested country south of the Mogollon Rim. It lies on the north side of the westernmost branch of Spring Creek, which follows a southerly course to join the Salt River. This area is included in the physiographic province known as the transition zone—transitional between the plateau to the north and the mountain region to the south.

The camp lies at an elevation of about 5750 feet on a structural terrace formed by differential erosion. Seventy feet below lies Spring Creek which flows only part of the year. A spring, located about 200 yards to the west of the site and slightly above Spring Creek, has a permanent flow. It occurs in an area where sandstone and shale are interbedded with the shale acting as a water-confining layer. The artesian spring is caused by a fracture which intersects an aquifer. The presence of this spring is probably the primary reason for the location of the Apache camp.

There is moderately dense vegetation, including shaggy-bark and alligator-bark juniper, piñon, and yellow pine, as well as live oak, yucca, bear grass and squaw bush.

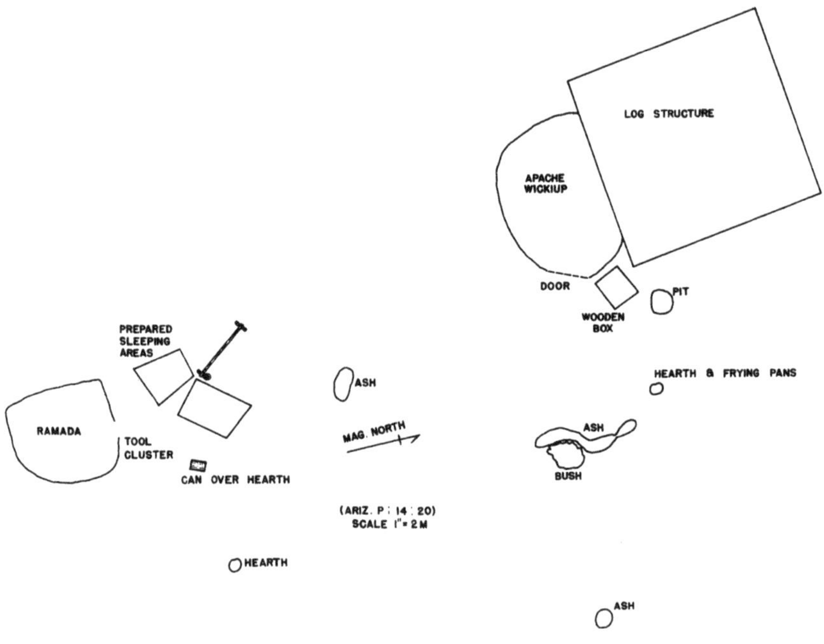

Figure 1. Site plan.

The immediate vicinity of the site revealed a long record of human occupation. The wickiup was constructed beside the remains of one of the buildings of a ranch built around the turn of the century. An older wickiup was discovered nearer the spring. The ranch was established on top of trash from a small thirteenth-century pueblo, which in turn was erected on a preceramic lithic site.

The campsite may be divided into three major units—the wickiup at the north end, a ramada at the south end about forty feet from the wickiup, and the space in between (Fig. 1). Many of the social and economic activities of the occupants appear to have taken place out-of-doors. Hearths, a tool cluster, and piles of ash, as well as other features attest to this fact.

A variety of tools and features appeared on the floor of the wickiup (Fig. 2). At the rear of the dwelling was a thick layer of pine needles placed in a shallow depression and surrounded by boards and poles. About one-third of the floor space was taken by this feature.

In the center of the floor we found a hearth covered by a small wash tub. On one side of the hearth lay a fan-shaped bundle of turkey feathers, and on the other side an enameled pail.

There were several tin cans of various sizes on the floor along the south wall, some of which showed unmistakable signs of having been used in a hearth. A denim sack containing pots and pans was hanging on a trimmed branch. A gallon-sized tin can with a homemade handle of wire, several cans full of nails, a wooden box, a piece of burlap sack, a one-hand mano, and a small slab metate were also found along the south wall.

Several pieces of wood, a piece of window screen, an enameled basin, a large milk can cover, a piece of plastic sheeting, and a bread wrapper were found in the northeast corner of the wickiup. Also, on the north side of the floor we found a wallet containing a paper on which was written a man's name. This was the only definitely male-associated item we discovered on the site.

Two plastic Clorox bottles were suspended by means of wire hooks from the walls.

At the south end of the site is a shade which was cut out of the center of a clump of juniper and pine. This forms a shelter that is the functional equivalent of a ramada and for which no formal construction was needed. The area was scraped clean of debris to form the floor. No tools and features were located in this structure. Other tools and features were located between the ramada and the wickiup; they clustered in two units, one around the ramada and one around the wickiup.

Just outside the ramada was a group of objects: the cover from a wooden Winchester cartridge case, a bundle of twigs, and a stick with a flattened tin can fastened to one end. North of the ramada, and in the same clump of trees, we found two scooped-out rectangular depressions filled with small pieces of juniper branches. We found a hearth covered

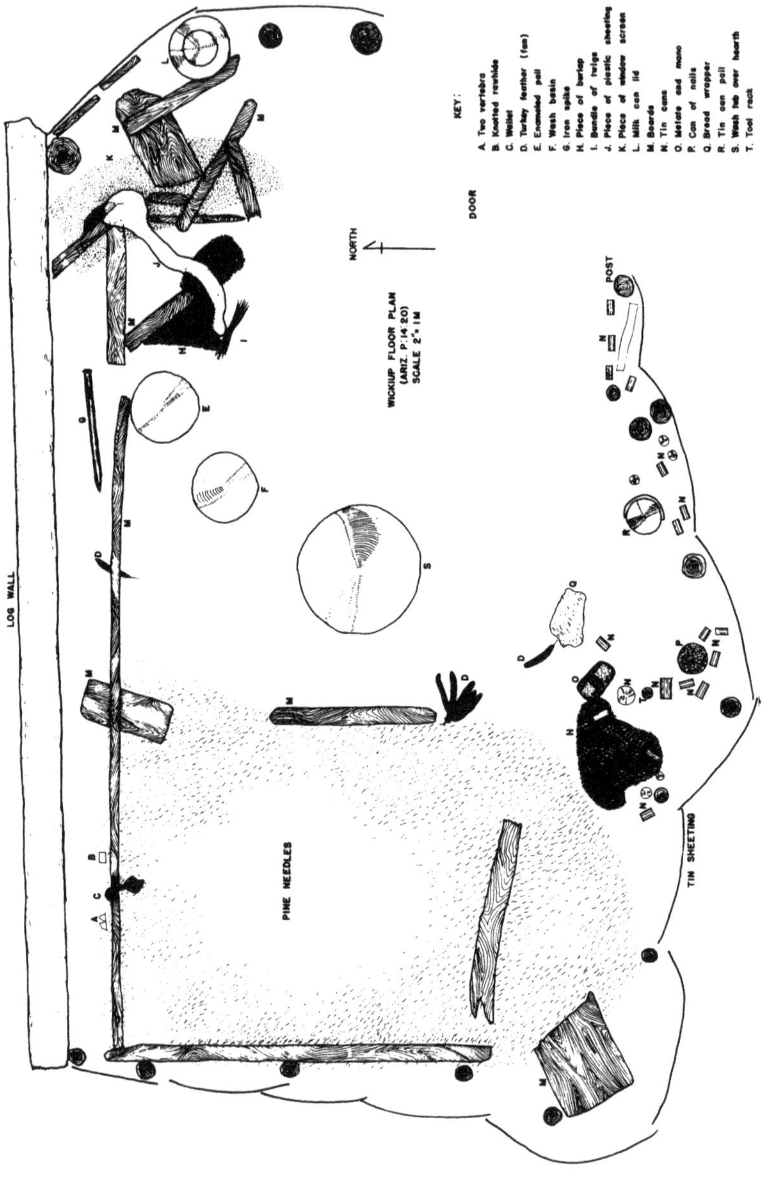

Figure 2. Wickiup floor plan.

by half a five-gallon can in the same area, and there was a small stick lying partially under it; to the east of this was another, larger hearth.

To the northwest of this area was a long pole supported on one end by a tree and on the other by a forked stick. Located northeast of the pole was a pile of ash.

At the entrance to the wickiup stood a large wooden-box open on one side, and behind the box was a small, shallow pit. To the east of the entrance lay a hearth with two frying pans and nearby was a large pile of ash. In a bush beside the ash pile, eight bundles of twigs were found.

The wickiup appears to be similar in size and shape to other wickiups in the area (Gerald, 1958; Shaeffer, 1958; Tuohy, 1960). The materials used in its construction are traditional except for the use of corrugated metal sheeting as an outside cover instead of bear grass (Shaeffer, 1958, pp. 17–18). The wickiup is built against one of the earlier ranch buildings and the wall of this structure forms one side of the wickiup. The remainder of the construction is similar to other Cibecue wickiups.

The size and nature of the site suggested that a small social unit had occupied it, probably a household consisting of a nuclear family. The well-built structure suggested that the occupation was not temporary, and the presence of the ramada indicated that at least part of the occupation was during warm weather.

The site is characterized by a series of discrete activity areas. The camp may be divided into three gross sections: (1) the wickiup itself, (2) the ramada, and (3) the spaces in front of the wickiup and near the ramada. The analysis of the features and the distribution of tools and other cultural items suggested that the nature of the activities and tasks carried out in these three areas was differentiated. The density of features and cultural items indicated that the wickiup and the outside activity area were used more intensively than was the featureless ramada where no cultural items were found.

A number of clues pointed to the specific nature of the activities carried out in these three sections of the site. The outside area contained three hearths, all of different types, as well as several ash dumps. In addition, there was a grouping of tools located near the ramada found in a cluster in an area about two feet in diameter. Also, near the ramada were two prepared sleeping areas adjacent to one another, but with different orientations. Near these sleeping areas were the pole and forked stick described above. The outside area lacked features and tools associated with storage and food preparation (for example, grinding tools).

The gross inferences from this array of tools and features suggested that the nature of out-of-doors activities included several forms of cookery, and a specific task associated with the cluster of tools. There was also an area for sleeping during pleasant weather. Except for the sleeping area, all these activity areas seemed to reflect female-task performance.

Three kinds of cookery were inferred from the different types of hearths and their associated artifacts. There was a fairly small circular hearth located in front of the wickiup with associated frying pans. We inferred that this specific area was used primarily for fry-pan cookery. Near the ramada was a larger hearth covered by half a metal can; this appeared to be either an oven or some sort of a grill. There was a stick in place in the ashes with a charred tip that apparently was used to adjust the coals. A larger irregular hearth was located more peripherally; there were no associated containers. We inferred a roasting or broiling function for this feature.

The cluster of tools near the ramada presented us with a problem. Because they were found together, we inferred that they were used in a single task, but we were unable to suggest the exact nature of the task. Had we been more familiar with Apache ethnography at the time of this investigation, the functional nature of this tool grouping would have been clear.

The two sleeping areas suggested that there was segregation in sleeping. The obvious division in a nuclear family unit would be between adults and children. We were unable to suggest the functional nature of the pole and forked stick adjacent to the sleeping area.

The absence of tools and features in the ramada indicated that certain types of activities were at least not carried out in this structure. Neither food preparation nor cookery was indicated. It probably was the scene of light tasks involving portable equipment and relaxation in the shade.

The wickiup itself reflected a much greater complexity of activities. The nature of features and equipment suggested the following: sleeping, storage, cookery, and food preparation. The location and nature of features and the associated tool clusters on the wickiup floor permitted some specific inferences regarding the nature of these activities.

The sleeping area was located at the rear of the structure and was well defined. The presence of the exterior sleeping areas suggested that the wickiup was used for sleeping when the weather was inclement.

The hearth in the wickiup was fairly large and was covered with an inverted wash tub. There was some sooting on the interior of the tub which we could not explain. The tub did not appear to be related to cookery of any sort.

There were several well-defined storage areas. One, near the doorway, was reserved for fuel. Along the south wall was a cluster of containers used in cookery. At another spot along the same wall was a wooden box which probably served as a storage facility. Pots and pans and plastic Clorox bottles, probably for water storage, were suspended from various hooks in the walls.

A cluster of tools occurring along the south wall was used in food preparation; these included grinding tools and an associated piece of burlap.

From this array we made the following inferences: (1) The range of activities carried out inside the wickiup was more varied than those undertaken elsewhere on the site. (2) The structure served as the primary storage facility for the social unit. (3) The wickiup was used for sleeping only in bad weather. (4) Some cookery and food preparation were carried out inside the structure. (5) The nature of the vessels inside the structure suggested a form of cooking involving boiling rather than frying, raising the possibility that this form of cookery may have been localized inside the wickiup. (6) There is also the possibility that activities of food preparation were localized inside the structure.

The spatial array of cultural items and features inside the wickiup was highly structured. This non-random distribution reflected a formal partitioning of space inside the wickiup in terms of specific activities. Tools and equipment used in specific tasks were segregated and occurred in clusters. There were well-defined use areas including storage, sleeping, cooking, and food preparation. The nature of task performance localized inside the wickiup appeared to be female-related, cookery and food preparation in particular.

Some summary remarks are in order at this point. The size and nature of the site suggested it was occupied by a single nuclear family: a husband, his wife, and unmarried children. The nature of activity areas and tools reflecting specific task performance appeared to be female-related. This indicated a strong sexual division of labor and that the primary activities carried out at the camp were female activities. The only tool noted at the site that might reflect male task performance was an axe head, but this is a tool used by females in firewood collection as well.

The nature of construction suggested a degree of permanence for the occupation, but the lack of any evidence for agriculture cast some doubt on this appraisal. There were no tools noted that might have functioned in farming; there were no indications of agricultural plots either near the site or down near the spring and creek. Also, single Apache families do not generally live in isolated camps (Goodwin, 1942, pp. 123–25). The common pattern among the Western Apache is family clusters. A great deal of sharing and cooperation necessitates spatial proximity of related families. There is a great deal of pooling of labor in agricultural endeavors; activities carried out by individuals are generally rare occurrences. The only exception to this is the temporary exploitation of seasonally available resources by family units (Goodwin, 1942, pp. 155–56). Historically, this included such activities as the exploitation of seasonally available wild plant resources.

All these factors suggested that although the camp was somewhat permanent in construction, it might have been seasonally occupied. The lack of male-related task performance reflected at the site suggests that the specific function of the site was as a temporary camp for logistic support of a nuclear family with the male member carrying out some sort of seasonal exploitative activity elsewhere.

To assess the validity of our inferences, we consulted an Apache informant, a female living at Grasshopper. She was most generous with her help and agreed to visit the site with us. As it turned out, this was fortunate as the women knew the family who had built and occupied the site and, in fact, had visited the family at the camp when it was in use. With her help, we were able to record a great deal of specific data regarding the localization of task performance and the specific function of areas, facilities and tools.

The site was occupied by a single Apache family from Cibecue, a husband and wife and two young children. The site was utilized from the fall of 1962 through the spring of 1963. Thus the site had been abandoned for more than two years before we began our investigation. The camp was established to serve as a base of operations while the husband cut and shaped juniper posts to sell during the following year.

Most of the general inferences we made were essentially correct, and the nature of the use of the sections of the camp was accurately inferred. Many of our specific inferences were also correct. Our suggestions concerning the localization of different forms of cookery as reflected in the feature analysis and the association of certain types of containers were accurate. The segregation of the exterior sleeping areas was in terms of the adults and their children. The primary storage facility was the wickiup.

Several problems were solved with the help of our informant. The pole and forked stick served as a framework on which to hang bedding to air. The cluster of tools located near the ramada was utilized in a single activity. The wife is well known for her pitch-lined water bottles which she makes during the winter, and the tools were used in the construction of water bottles. The wooden box top served as a platform, the spatulate tool was used to apply the pitch, and the bundle of shoots was simply a package of raw materials. The bottles are built from squawbush rods. The other tool clusters observed are also related to specific tasks. The mano, metate, and burlap form a single cluster; the burlap is used to catch the meal as it is ground. The can over the hearth near the ramada served as a grill on which the woman cooked tortillas. The tub inverted over the wickiup hearth was simply a safety device. The structure is not windproof and when it is left for any period of time the tub is used to cover the live coals to prevent them from spreading and causing a fire. The hearth in front of the wickiup was used primarily for fry-pan cooking of bread. The ash piles were dumps for disposal of ashes. No specific function could be determined for the large box outside the wickiup or for the pit.

The implications of this investigation are fairly obvious. What we have done is define the structure of a habitation site in some detail and relate this structure to the organization and behavior of the social group that produced it. We conclude that this experiment has been successful in that (1) we were able to define the material structure and (2) we were able to demonstrate the relations between this structure and the social unit and its behavior.

This suggests that the archeologist might well want to define and describe the material structure of an archeological site as a necessary step in inferring the structure and behavior of extinct social groups. It would seem to us that the material structure might be defined quantitatively, permitting the mutual variation among all types of data to be measured. Thus the archeologist might well attempt to assess the mutual variation among pottery styles and container types, stone and bone tools, types of features and structures to strengthen his inferences regarding behavior and organization of extinct social groups. We contrast this suggestion with the standard description of such archeological data in separate chapters of a monograph with little or no attempt at relating these different kinds of data in a systematic way.

It is the primary conclusion of this admittedly crude study that archeologists can go far beyond the statements contained in the standard summary chapters in reports, placing sites into a regional chronology and a general cultural context.

References

GERALD, REX E. 1958. Two wickiups on the San Carlos Indian Reservation, Arizona. *The Kiva,* 23(3): 5–11.

GOODWIN, GRENVILLE. 1942. *The social organization of the Western Apache.* Chicago: University of Chicago Press.

SHAEFFER, MARGARET W. M. 1958. The construction of a wickiup on the Fort Apache Indian Reservation. *The Kiva,* 24(2): 14–20.

TUOHY, DONALD R. 1960. Two more wickiups on the San Carlos Indian Reservation. *The Kiva,* 26(2): 27–30.

TEN

BOBBY JO WILLIAMS

Establishing Cultural Heterogeneities in Settlement Patterns: An Ethnographic Example

This paper began as a straightforward, brief ethnography of residence patterns among bands of a hunting-gathering group, the Birhor living on the Chota Nagpur plateau of southern Bihar, India. It was hoped that from the ethnographic data certain descriptive generalizations might be advanced which would be of use to the archeologist in making inferences about prehistoric cultures.

The possible generalizations entertained suffered, from the archeologist's point of view, from the fact that their confirmation on archeological data alone would require greater control in the observation and measurement of cultural variables than is presently provided in archeological method. On the other hand, the archeologist has at his disposal data which in some ways are a more direct reflection of the culture of a people than are those of the ethnographer. I suggest this because the ethnographer returns with data which are largely weighted in the direction of verbal behavior only; retrospective historical accounts, informants' descriptions, explanations and rationalizations concerning their way of life. Some of this verbal material is after-the-fact discussion of ecologically influenced cultural regularity and may obscure as well as reveal certain relationships.

The ability of the archeologist to test generalizations about culture depends to a large extent on his ability to detect minor cultural differences from this non-verbal data. The traditional approach to this problem has been that of distinguishing patterns—that is, setting up typologies of artifactual material, residence patterns, etc.—but the establishment of typologies, by its nature, obscures finer cultural differences. In this paper I would like to suggest a technique which will detect fairly fine or minor cultural differences prior to the establishment of typologies.

To make this thought less elliptical, let me cite a possible example. A current problem in theories on primitive society concerns the prevalence of the patrilocal exogamous band on Radcliffe-Brown's model of the Australian horde. The critics of the view that this form of organization was very widespread among hunters point to the many ethnographically known exceptions. Proponents of the model suggest that most of these exceptions are due, directly or indirectly, to European contact (cf. Service, 1962). Since discussion must usually stalemate at this point, I suggest that it is the archeologist who must provide the crucial data. Let us postulate, as I do, that pre-agricultural hunting society was in most circumstances a territorially localized, multi-family, unilineal descent group whose size variation was fairly closely bounded. If such bands are lineages, the recruitment or the ideological charter for membership involves reckoning of descent relationship. The latter can be carried out in either of two ways. First, this reckoning may be through kinship terminology without the use of proper names, as was found to be the case among the Birhor and has frequently been reported for hunting societies. On the other hand this reckoning may be true genealogical recitation.

The former system is much more rapidly adjustable to demographic realities than the latter, and lineage bands so chartered in ideology should be able to gain or lose account of membership so as to maintain optimum size more readily than the latter. The archeological hypothesis then might be that the coefficient of variation in household number per camp in Paleolithic society would be smaller than in ethnographically known, true genealogically based lineages.

Some of the difficulties in testing this are apparent as soon as the hypothesis is stated. An outstanding difficulty is in deciding whether house patterns which appear in the same horizon represent a single group, the same group occupying the site consecutively, or two or more groups occupying the site concurrently.

Solving such problems would be essential prior to dealing with the illustrative hypothesis posed above, just as it is essential to many other problems which archeologists hope to handle. The approach thus far to such problems is in the development of dating techniques for finer and finer control of the time variable. In this case it might be possible through palynology to establish that the houses were occupied at the same season. It might eventually be possible to show, through minor shifts in direction of magnetic flux detectable in the hearths, that a space of years separated certain houses. These and other dating improvements constitute possibilities but they will never answer the question which we shall address, was the site occupied concurrently by more than one band?

This is part of the general problem of detecting minor cultural heterogeneities within a site. I would like to suggest a method which can in some cases detect small cultural differences when no spatial or temporal heterogeneity is detectable. The method will be explicated, then illustrated with data of the kind easily recoverable by the archeologist on a single Birhor campsite occupied contemporaneously by four Birhor bands during the dry season and wet season of 1961.

The Method

Let us designate the nominal categories in two dichotomous variables in a population as A and $\hat{A}$
B and $\hat{B}$.

If A and $\hat{A}$ have relative frequencies in the population of p and q, respectively, and B and $\hat{B}$ have relative frequencies of r and s, respectively, then independence means that the joint distribution of the two variables will give cell frequencies

	A	$\hat{A}$
B	pr	qr
$\hat{B}$	sp	sq

If these dichotomies represent presence-absence, then the category "one present or the other present, but not both" (p/a) has the frequency $pr + sq$, the category "both present" (p/p) has frequency pr, and a/a has frquency sq.

Now assume we have M populations of equal size. If all M populations were identical with respect to these variables, we could treat the overall group as a single population and we would find

$$\text{Freq. } p/p = 1/M \sum_{i=1}^{M} p_i r_i = \bar{p}\,\bar{r}$$

$$\text{Freq. } p/a = 1/M \sum_{i=1}^{M} (s_i p_i + q_i r_i) = \bar{s}\,\bar{p} + \bar{q}\,\bar{r}$$

$$\text{Freq. } a/a = 1/M \sum_{i=1}^{M} s_i q_i = \bar{s}\,\bar{q}$$

Considering first the a/a category, it can be shown that

$$1/M \sum_{i=1}^{M} s_i q_i = \bar{s}\,\bar{q} = \left(\frac{\sum s_i}{M}\right) \left(\frac{\sum q_i}{M}\right)$$

$$\begin{array}{ll} \text{only when} & s_1 = s_2 = \cdots = s_M \\ \text{and} & q_1 = q_2 = \cdots = q_m \end{array} \quad \text{conditions of homogenity.}$$

If either of these conditions does not hold, then

$$\frac{\sum s_i q_i}{M} < \frac{\sum s_i \sum q_i}{M}.$$

We can specify the magnitude of the inequality in the following manner: By definition of co-variance,

$$\sigma_{sq} = 1/M \sum_{i=1}^{M} (s_i - \bar{s})\,(q_i - \bar{q})$$

$$= 1/M \sum_{i=1}^{M} s_i q_i - \bar{s}\,\bar{q}$$

therefore $1/M \sum s_i q_i = s\,q + \sigma_{sq}$.

This says that the frequency of the category a/a is $1/M\ \Sigma\ s_i q_i = sq$ when the overall sample is homogeneous.

When the overall sample is heterogeneous in the frequency of one or the other variable such that some $s_i \neq s_j$ or $p_i \neq p_j$, then the frequency of the category a/a is $1/M\ \Sigma s_i q_i = sq + \sigma_{sq}$. That is, heterogeneity inflates this category even though the variables are randomly distributed within the subpopulations.

Using the same line of reasoning, we can show that the category p/p has frequency

$= \bar{p}\,\bar{r}$ when homogeneous

$= \bar{p}\,\bar{r} + \sigma_{pr}$ when heterogeneous.

Further, it can be shown that $\sigma_{pr} = \sigma_{sq}$ as follows:

$$\sigma_{pr} = 1/M \sum pr - \bar{p}\,\bar{r} \qquad s = 1 - r$$

$$\sigma_{sq} = 1/M \sum sq - \bar{s}\,\bar{q} \qquad q = 1 - p$$

$$= 1/M \sum (1 - r)\,(1 - p) - (1 - \bar{r})\,(1 - \bar{p}),$$

which reduces to $\sigma_{sq} = 1/M \sum pr - \bar{p}\,\bar{r} = \sigma_{pr}$.

The above holds for the case where the M subpopulations are of unequal size but, in this case, the means $\bar{p}$, $\bar{q}$, $\bar{r}$, $\bar{s}$ must be weighted means.

To summarize, we have said that heterogeneity among the subpopulations with respect to one or more variables will inflate both the p/p and a/a classes by equal amounts. And since the relative frequencies

$$p/p + p/a + a/a = 1$$

$$\text{Freq. } p/p = \bar{p}\,\bar{r} + \sigma_{pr}$$

$$\text{Freq. } p/a = \bar{s}\,\bar{p} + \bar{p}\,\bar{r} - 2\,\sigma_{pr}$$

$$\text{Freq. } a/a = \bar{s}\,\bar{q} + \sigma_{pr}.$$

This means that when we have a priori knowledge or reason to believe that two variables are independently distributed we can test for cultural heterogeneity by means of a simple test of association such as χ^2.

An Ethnographic Example

Figure 1 illustrates an area known as Panch Pera (the five trees) which is a rise of ground near the Mohana River near the village of Kanosar, Hazaribagh District, Bihar. Four Birhor bands were camped at Panch Pera during the dry season and most of the following wet season of 1961. The location of the bands relative to one another is shown in Figure 1 as well as the placement of individual leaf huts.

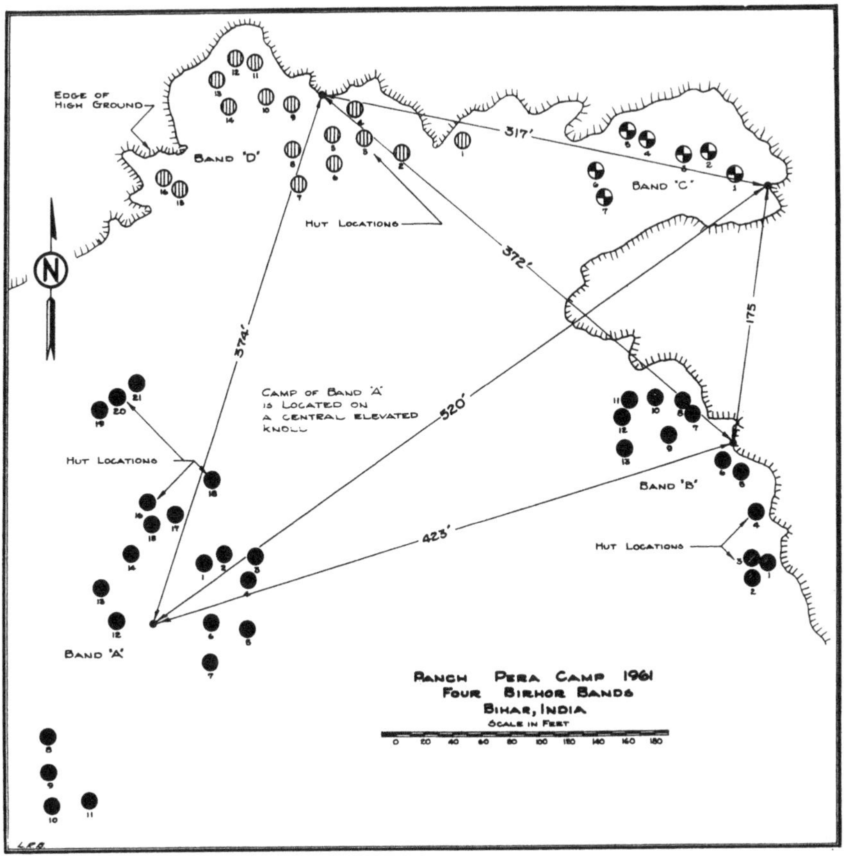

Figure 1.

The site is chosen as an illustration not because these bands were well known to the author—they were not—but because it is a case of four bands coming together at one site at one point in time. The four bands share the same general culture and in some detail. They are socially distant enough from one another, however, to be able to exchange daughters in marriage. A stated Birhor rule is that one does not marry relatives. In other words, these bands share the same culture but are more or less autonomous social units among whom we might expect minor differences in cultural practices.

In this case there is no problem in seeing that four bands were present as this is reflected in spatial aggregation; sociometric relations between families and between bands are always reflected in spacing of the houses among the Birhor. But for the sake of the argument being presented, we shall assume we cannot tell from house location whether one band or more than one band is present. The problem is to see if we can detect cultural heterogeneity, suggesting the presence of more than one group in the sample, on the basis of archeologically observable nominal-scale variables.

The most easily observable features which we can dichotomize and which refer to house patterns after the structure is no longer standing are: (a) whether the diameter of the floor was larger or smaller than some central figure; (b) whether or not a fire-pit was located inside the house;

Table 1. Houses in Birhor Camp Area A

House No.	*Diameter*	*Over-size*	*Fire-pit*	*Burned*
1	10′2″	−	−	+
2	12′0″	+	−	+
3	12′9″ (N-S), 10′0″ (E-W),	+	+	+
4	11′2″	+	−	+
5	9′4″	−	−	+
6	11′4″	+	−	+
7	10′0″	−	−	−
8	12′3″	+	+	+
9	10′5″	+	−	−
10	11′8″	+	−	−
11	8′2″	−	+	−
12	7′10″	−	−	−
13	10′6″	+	−	−
14	12′9″	+	−	−
15	9′6″	−	−	+
16	10′3″	+	−	+
17	9′2″	−	−	+
18	7′10″	−	−	−
19	9′7″	−	−	−
20	8′11″	−	−	−
21	9′10″	−	−	−

Table 2. Houses in Birhor Camp Area B

House No.	*Diameter*	*Over-size*	*Fire-pit*	*Burned*
1	10′9″	+	+	+
2	10′8″	+	−	+
3	9′10″	−	+	+
4	9′7″	−	−	+
5	6′10″	−	+	+
6	14′4″ (N-S), 9′2″ (E-W),	+	−	+
7	7′6″	−	−	+
8	10′4″	+	+	+
9	10′0″	−	−	+
10	10′10″	+	+	+
11	10′8″	+	+	+
12	7′4″	−	−	+
13	10′11″	−	+	+

Table 3. Houses in Birhor Camp Area C

House No.	*Diameter*	*Over-size*	*Fire-pit*	*Burned*
1	15′8″ (N-S), 10′3″ (E-W)	+	+	−
2	7′8″	−	−	−
3	12′3″	+	+	−
4	10′2″	−	−	−
5	12′0″	+	−	−
6	17′0″ (N-S), 8′6″ (E-W)	+	+	−
7	7′1″	−	−	−

Table 4. Houses in Birhor Camp Area D

House No.	*Diameter*	*Over-size*	*Fire-pit*	*Burned*
1	12′10″	+	−	−
2	9′1″	−	−	−
3	10′4″	+	−	−
4	9′5″	−	−	−
5	10′6″	+	−	−
6	12′3″ (N-S), 7′6″ (E-W)	−	−	−
7	9′9″	−	−	−
8	9′7″	−	+	−
9	11′5″	+	−	−
10	9′7″	−	−	−
11	10′8″	+	−	−
12	9′5″	−	−	−
13	10′8″	+	−	−
14	9′10″	−	−	−
15	8′7″	−	−	−
16	12′0″	+	+	−

(c) whether or not the house was burned by the occupants on their departure. A number of other features could have been recorded and used but these will be sufficient.

The observations on individual houses in the separate bands are given as Tables 1 through 4. Some Birhor now use a "new" house form which is rectangular in outline but the Panch Pera bands, being conservative in a number of ways, stick to the older, beehive-shaped hut which has a circular floor plan and can, therefore, be characterized by a single diameter. Five houses, however, were pronouncedly oblong and the mean of the maximum and minimum diameters was used for comparability to other houses. Since these houses were occupied in the wet season, some had an outer drainage trench and all had an inner bank of dirt at the wall. Diameters were taken from the outer edge of this inner bank.

Let us now make the assumption that the three variables tabulated are distributed independently within bands. In this case, being an ethnographic example, we can test to see if the assumption was justified. Below are listed 2 × 2 matrices, one set for each band, which show the distribution of the variables, taken two at a time, within that band. Figures are too small to utilize a Chi-square approximation. Therefore Fisher's Exact Test was applied and the value of P underneath each matrix represents the probability that the least frequent cell could be that small or smaller due to chance alone.

Band A

oversize	*burned* +	*burned* −	
+	6	4	10
−	4	7	11
	10	11	21

$P = .34$

burned	*firepit* +	*firepit* −	
+	2	8	10
−	1	10	11
	3	18	21

$P = .46$

oversize	*firepit* +	*firepit* −	
+	2	8	10
−	1	10	11
	3	18	21

$P = .46$

Band B

oversize	*burned* +	*burned* −	
+	6	0	6
−	7	0	7
	13	0	13

$P = 1$

burned	*firepit* +	*firepit* −	
+	7	6	13
−	0	0	0
	7	6	13

$P = 1$

oversize	*firepit* +	*firepit* −	
+	4	2	6
−	3	4	7
	7	6	13

$P = .38$

Band C

oversize	*burned* +	*burned* −	
+	0	4	4
−	0	3	3
	0	7	7

$P = 1$

burned	*firepit* +	*firepit* −	
+	0	0	0
−	3	4	7
	3	4	7

$P = 1$

oversize	*firepit* +	*firepit* −	
+	3	1	4
−	0	3	3
	3	4	7

$P = .11$

Band D

oversize	*burned* +	*burned* −	
+	0	7	7
−	0	9	9
	0	16	16

$P = 1$

burned	*firepit* +	*firepit* −	
+	0	0	0
−	2	14	16
	2	14	16

$P = 1$

oversize	*firepit* +	*firepit* −	
+	1	6	7
−	1	8	9
	2	14	16

$P = .82$

If we set a level of significance at $\alpha = .05$, this level is hardly approached in any of the above. Upon inspection of the above matrices, we can find some hint of directionality only in Band A. In this band we find a non-significant, but consistent in all three comparisons, excess of p/p and a/a. Considering all three variables simultaneously for Band A, we find $P = .35$. This is the only band which shows consistent deviations from randomness and the effect is insufficient to account for any significant deviation in the overall sample.

Now let us consider what happens when we merge bands. This will first be done for two variables at a time as shown below.

Merged Frequencies

oversize \ *burned*	+	−	
+	12	15	27
−	11	19	30
	23	34	57

$\chi^2 = 0.36$

$.50 < P < .70$

burned \ *firepit*	+	−	
+	9	14	23
−	6	28	34
	15	42	57

$\chi^2 = 3.3$

$.05 < P < .10$

oversize \ *firepit*	+	−	
+	10	17	27
−	5	25	30
	15	42	57

$\chi^2 = 3.1$

$.05 < P < .10$

These three 2×2 matrices represent the situation as it would be tabulated by the archeologist. The minor differences that clearly differentiate bands as shown in Tables A–D are not discernable as there is, in the situation supposed, no *a priori* way to assign houses to particular bands. In the first comparison, oversize versus burned, there is no evidence of association and therefore no evidence of between-group heterogeneity. In the remaining two comparisons there is an obvious effect of heterogeneity. By combining the latter two χ^2 values we find

$$\chi^2 = 6.4 \qquad \text{p.} < .05 \qquad \text{for} \qquad \text{d.f.} = 2.$$

In other words, on the basis of the last two comparisons, we can reject the null hypothesis of homogeneity. The house floors present do not represent the variability within a single social unit but reflect at least minor cultural differentiation among units. It must be noted that this method does not distinguish social units and, therefore, does not give an indication of the number of such units present. It does say that more than one unit was present.

In résumé, a method has been presented for a simple test of minor cultural heterogeneities in archeological material. The method involves the assumption of the independent distribution of two or more variables within units. The finding of an excess of cases in the *p*/*p* and *a*/*a* categories, tested by χ^2, is an indication of the presence of heterogeneity. This method was tested against a known ethnographic situation among hunters. The existence of small cultural differences (that is, band identity) is confirmed by this method using house-pattern data even when data on spatial heterogeneities in the settlement pattern are suppressed.

Discussion

Although the test data used in the foregoing concern settlement patterns only, it must be stressed that the method has quite general applications. Indeed there is no reason that the method can not be applied to skeletal material. It could be possible to detect the presence of more than one breeding population within a region by the use of traits known to be uncorrelated in living populations—for example, the frequency of shovelling in I^1 and size progression between M^1 and M^2.

For cultural data, the method's primary weakness will be found to be the necessary assumption of independence of the variables within social units, within tool traditions, or within any unit of postulated homogeneity. The case used to illustrate the point is trivial only in the sense that the differences utilized are so minor as to be assignable no social significance and of a nature such as is not normally noticed by the ethnographer. But this can also be argued as a strength of the method—to be able to pick up cultural heterogeneities of fairly fine scale in archeological data.

References

Service, E. R. 1962. *Primitive social organization*. New York: Random House.

PART III

Investigating Variability in the Archeological Record: Variability among Occupational Units

In the previous section we emphasized the study of variability within a single occupation unit. In this section we shift to a different comparative framework, one in which a number of archeological components (or their attributes) are studied, and explanations are sought for observed differences and similarities. The assumption underlying the discussion of single-site variability was that the occupational episodes were of sufficiently short duration to allow for systemic stability for the period represented by the archeological remains. If the remains suggested occupations of considerable duration, or showed internal variability which contradicted the assumption of stability, then the examples would be more appropriately discussed in this section.

The assumption underlying the analyses in this section is that observed differences between occupation units are to be attributed either to change within a system or to systemic independence for the units under study. Where we can justify this assumption, our explanations for observed differences take the form of arguments regarding processes which operated in the past to determine changes and to promote diversification among cultural systems.

In formulating explanations, we are constantly faced with a dual problem. On the one hand, archeological observations must be shown to be relevant to conditions which existed in the past; this is a problem of archeological theory. On the other hand, once we have documented the operation of cultural or ecological processes in the past, we seek to develop arguments regarding the relevance of certain variables to these processes; the concern here is with general anthropological or ecological theory.

An example of the first problem—the relevance of archeological observations to past conditions—can be seen when we note that much of the variability among occupation units (between-site variability) may derive from spatial differentiation in activities which may have varied seasonally or with respect to other periodic events within a stable system of adaptation (see Winters, 1963; Binford and Binford, 1966; Thompson, 1939). There is also the possibility that directional changes through time may not always indicate systematic cultural change or replacements; they may well be due to successional phenomena—that is, to changes produced in the site itself by an earlier occupation which then limits the nature of succeeding occupations (for example, see Binford, Binford, Whallon, and Hardin, 1966). Other sources of variability can be simple sampling error (L. R. Binford, 1965), cultural drift (L. R. Binford, 1963), or from a particular form of sampling bias produced by data collection techniques (Deetz and Dethlefsen, 1965). These different sources and kinds of variation between occupation units make it absolutely essential that we develop significant arguments of relevance and means for verification.

The papers in this section range along a scale from an almost exclusive concern with explaining archeological observations per se to an equally exclusive theoretical concern. The papers by Whallon and Winters attempt to develop techniques for measurement and arguments of relevance for archeological observations. Winters proceeds to tests of confidence for his propositions by recourse to ethnohistorical data, a procedure we have seen used in the previous section by Williams and Longacre and Ayres.

The papers by Hole, Flannery and Coe, Struever, and L. R. Binford exemplify archeological concern with documenting and trying to explain change in or diversification among cultural systems. Here the appropriate analytical framework is ecological, and interest centers on the recognition, isolation, and measurement of variables external to the cultural system under study. The ecological relationships between components of the cultural system and the biophysical or sociocultural variables of the system's environment become the focus of investigation. In these presentations the emphasis has shifted from arguments of relevance for archeological observations among variables of the extinct systems to an emphasis on arguments of relevance for ecological or sociocultural relationships in explaining culture change. The papers have a secondary concern with operationalizing the measurement of variables using archeological data.

The four papers in question (Hole, Flannery and Coe, Struever, and L. R. Binford) are themselves arranged in a general progression from lesser to greater theoretical concern. Hole asks a question of the archeological record from the Near East which has not been thoroughly explored previously. The only available information consists of observations made with very different problems in mind. At such an initial stage of investigation, Hole proceeded by perusing the data on the culture history of the period under study. He then offers a substantive inventory of observations he considers relevant to what is known of forms of ethnographically documented social organization for societies analogous to those represented archeologically. His principal concern is with the relevance of the record insofar as it can document certain variables he considers significant in the past organizations and relevant to discussions of change.

Flannery and Coe are more explicitly involved with theoretical arguments which elucidate the relevance of the variable of "microenvironmental heterogeneity" to observed differences in socioeconomic organization of a number of independent cultural systems. They explore the problem of how to operationalize measurement of this critical variable as well as others postulated to co-vary with it.

Struever documents a series of marked changes in human adaptations to a particular geographical zone. He is particularly concerned with documenting the nature of the ecological relationships between the local environment and the occupants of the habitat. He justifies this emphasis by arguing that culture is man's extrasomatic means of adaptation and that changes in culture must be viewed as changes in the adaptive niche occupied by a cultural system. This is another example of archeological investigation of variables justified as relevant through a theoretical argument on the nature of culture. Struever concludes by stating that he has not explained the observed adaptive change; he has, however, been highly successful in explicating the nature of the successive niches occupied by populations in the region. The next step in this intellectual feedback system will undoubtedly be the construction of explanatory models for the documented changes of niche; such explanatory models and the design for testing them are based on evolutionary theory—the framework for understanding structural changes through time.

The final paper (L. R. Binford) is almost exclusively concerned with the nature of cultural systems of adaptation and the conditions under which such systems might be disrupted, producing a situation in which evolutionary change would occur. This paper discusses at the theoretical level the problem which Struever's analysis introduced—under what conditions do "maximizing adaptations" occur.

References

Binford, Lewis R. 1963. Red ocher caches from the Michigan area: a possible case of cultural drift. *Southwestern Journal of Anthropology,* 19(1): 89–108.

——. 1964. Considerations of archaeological research design. *American Antiquity*, 29(4): 425–41.

Binford, Lewis R., and Sally R. Binford. 1966. A preliminary analysis of functional variability in the Mousterian of Levallois facies. *American Anthropologist*, 68(2) Part 2: 238–95.

Binford, Lewis R., Sally R. Binford, Robert Whallon, and Margaret Hardin. 1966. *Archaeology at Hatchery West*. Southern Illinois University Museum, Archaeological Salvage Report no. 25.

Deetz, James, and Edwin Dethlefsen. 1965. The Doppler effect and archaeology: a consideration of the spatial aspects of seriation. *Southwestern Journal of Anthropology*, 21(3): 196–206.

Thompson, Donald F. 1939. The seasonal factor in human culture, illustrated from the life of a contemporary nomadic group. *Proceedings of the Prehistoric Society* (London), no. 10, pp. 209–221.

Winters, Howard D. 1963. *An archaeological survey of the Wabash Valley in Illinois*. Illinois State Museum Reports of Investigations, No. 19.

ELEVEN HOWARD D. WINTERS

Value Systems and Trade Cycles of the Late Archaic in the Midwest

This paper is a composite of two papers delivered at the 1964 and 1965 meetings of the Society for American Archaeology at the University of North Carolina and the University of Illinois. It represents an attempt to develop the techniques for interpreting economic data from the analysis of the artifactual material of prehistoric societies. The data used are derived from published reports on sites of the Indian Knoll Culture, namely Indian Knoll (Webb, 1946), Carlson Annis (Webb, 1950a), Read (Webb, 1950b), Ward and Kirkland (Webb and Haag, 1940), Chiggerville (Webb and Haag, 1939), and Barrett and Butterfield (Webb and Haag, 1947).

I should like to acknowledge my indebtedness to Professor Webb for the help that the foregoing monographs have provided both in present and past research efforts. Although in many respects, the publications may prove frustrating when attempts are made to use them for current problems, the vast quantities of information contained in them remain invaluable and stand as a monument to Professor Webb's genius. It is perhaps overly easy today to see how a more adequate presentation might have been accomplished, but we should all ponder whether our own efforts will have the same utility after two or three decades as his have.

Although ten carbon-14 dates are available for Carlson Annis (six dates) and Indian Knoll (four dates)–(Johnson, 1951; Libby, 1952), the

Indian Knoll Culture can hardly be said to be dated adequately. Dating was by the solid carbon method, with its potential sources of error, and shell was used for two of the Carlson Annis samples. Furthermore, at Carlson Annis there is a case of dates that are the direct reverse of the stratigraphic position of the samples dated. But a number of dates on antler suggest a temporal position for the two sites within the third millennium B.C. Our own guess based upon the rate of accumulation for similar shell middens in the Wabash Valley (Winters, 1968) would be that the time span of the Indian Knoll Culture should be on the order of *ca.* 2500 to *ca.* 2000 B.C.

It should be remembered also that the sites are not single component middens. Earlier Archaic, and even Paleo-Indian, materials are present, as well as Woodland and Mississippian artifacts. But quantitatively, the other components are minor in the massive concentration of artifacts assignable to the Indian Knoll Culture. Most of the Woodland and Mississippian manifestations are superficial and suggest little more than utilization of the sites as camps or farmsteads. And only at Butterfield is there earlier Archaic material present in sufficient quantity to pose a serious statistical problem. (Our data for the latter site should be treated with considerable circumspection since it has not been possible to sort many of the earlier Archaic artifacts from the Indian Knoll artifacts in the published report.)

The origins of the study go back to an earlier analysis undertaken by the author to secure comparative material from the Green River sites on the nature of the settlement systems in that area. Tentatively it was concluded that a settlement system of the Riverton type (Winters, 1963, 1968) was also operative in the Green River area. Thus, the sites are no longer viewed as discrete units by the author, but as elements in three settlement system units of the Indian Knoll Culture. The first of these, termed the Ward Unit, is known from a settlement, the Ward Site, a base camp, the Barrett Site, a specialized collecting camp, and Kirkland, a hunting camp; the second, termed the Read Unit, is known from Read, a settlement, and Carlson Annis, a base camp; the third, termed the Chiggerville Unit, from Chiggerville, a settlement, and Indian Knoll, a base camp.

It was noted during the quantification of data for the interpretation of the settlement system of the Indian Knoll Culture that conch shell seemed to follow a cyclical pattern of appearance and disappearance at Carlson Annis, Read, and Indian Knoll, the three sites for which adequate quantitative data were available for these artifacts. Subsequently, it was decided to investigate this regularity of patterning somewhat further to see how it correlated with variations in population and utilitarian items. These various units of raw data will be introduced as we develop the major themes of this paper: difference in "value" of categories of artifacts, variations in sex and age association of certain artifacts of "special value," preliminary conclusions about the meaning of differentials in the distribution of wealth, cyclical fluctuations in imported raw materials, and observations on the possibilities of a trade network within which the Indian Knoll Culture was an element.

Utilizing burial tables and summary artifact tables, we were able to assemble data basic to our analyses on the following subjects:

1. Sex linkage of artifacts, derived by listing associations with only those burials definitely identified as to sex.
2. The vertical distribution patterns of artifacts that were associated only with burials, or artifacts that had only insignificant quantitative expression apart from the latter context.
3. Proportions of each artifact in burial or midden association.
4. Association of artifacts by age groups.
5. A rough estimate of population fluctuation through plotting of burials by 6-in. levels, a procedure that will be discussed in greater detail later.

First of all, we shall consider the contexts of particular functional categories of artifacts, as they relate to burial or midden association (Table 1). One group consisting of general utility implements, weapons, fabricating and processing tools, domestic implements, and woodworking tools was present with burials only in low percentages of the total recovered at the site, often being only 1 to 2 per cent of the total and rarely exceeding 10 per cent of the total.

A few anomalies exist within the group, of course. As a general rule, one can say that the earlier the excavation and reporting of the site, the grosser the level of the anomalies. There seems to have been an improvement in excavation techniques as time went on, and there were certainly greatly improved standards of reporting. In defense of any implication of inadequacy within the foregoing, it should be realized that the rather curious figures for hammerstones at Barrett, Butterfield, and Kirkland might well be duplicated in excavations and publications in 1966. There are any number of archeologists, including a sprinkling of eminent figures, who are still unable to distinguish a mano from a hammerstone unless the shaping and wear are too obvious to be ignored, and who solve their laboratory storage problems by returning from the field with the few selected hammerstones or manos that have struck their fancy.

As examples of the anomalies, the following are noted: At Barrett 50 per cent of the total sample of two grooved mauls was in burial association, a not very impressive statistical determination when we compare the data for Carlson Annis and Indian Knoll where none of the respective samples of 129 mauls and 11 mauls were found in burial context. And similar observations pertain where other high percentages of 50 per cent or more occur for items such as hammerstones (Kirkland–two specimens), abrading stones (Barrett–two; Butterfield–one), whetstones (Ward–one; Indian Knoll–three); reamers (Carlson Annis–one).

Table 1. Percentage of Artifacts in Burial Association

	Ward	Barrett	Butterfield	Kirkland	Read	Carlson Annis	Chiggerville	Indian Knoll
General Utility								
1. Knives	7.4	2.4	12.3	16.7	0	1.2	0	3.0
2. Scrapers	2.8	1.7	2.1	0	0.7	0.4	0	0.8
3. Grooved Mauls	NP	50.0	NP	NP	NP	0	NP	0
4. Hammerstones*	3.8	25.0	20.0	50.0	0	0	0	0.9
Weapons								
1. Proj. Pts., Chert	0	6.7	9.6	2.9	5.6	0.8	1.0	0.9
2. Proj. Pts., Bone	0	33.3	X	X	0	0.9	0	0
3. Proj. Pts., Ant.	18.8	20.0	X	X	0	1.9	0	1.3
4. Atlatl Wt's, Stone	27.3	57.1	?	0	35.9	11.1	16.7	11.0
5. Atlatl Wt's, Shell	NP	NP	X	X	NP	100.0	100.0	100.0
6. Atlatl Hooks	72.7	100.0	X	X	77.8	11.8	25.0	45.5
7. Atlatl Handles	?	100.0	X	X	100.0	22.2	NP	21.4
8. Fishooks	0	14.3	X	X	1.7	0	0	1.2
9. Cylindroids	NP?	0	0	NP	NP	0	0	?
Fabricating and Processing								
1. Drills	0	1.6	2.6	0	2.2	0.9	0	0.2
2. Abrading Stones	NP	50.0	100.0	NP	NP	0	NP	0
3. Whetstones	100.0	0	0	NP	20.0	6.7	NP	100.0
4. Gouges+	NP	NP	NP	NP	0	0	NP	1.0
5. Copper Pins and Needles	NP	100.0	NP	NP	NP	0	NP	100.0
6. Awls	0	39.1	X	X	3.8	0.8	0.3	0.9
7. Flakers	0	?	X	X	1.1	2.9	0	NP
8. Drifts	0	0	X	X	0	2.7	0	4.1
9. Antler Chisels	NP	0	X	X	NP	0	NP	0
10. Beaver Incisors	NP	NP	X	X	100.0	0	NP	100.0
11. Rodent Incisors	NP	NP	X	X	NP	NP	NP	100.0
12. Reamers	NP	0	NP	NP	NP	100.0	NP	0

	Ward	Barrett	Butterfield	Kirkland	Read	Carlson Annis	Chiggerville	Indian Knoll
Domestic								
1. Pestles	0	10.3	3.6	4.8	2.3	1.1	0	1.6
2. Nutstones	NP	0	0	NP	0	0	NP	1.8
3. "Lapstones"	0	0	NP	0	0	0	0	5.3
Woodworking								
1. Axes	7.8	12.5	0	NP	2.5	4.2	0	1.7
Ceremonial								
1. Flutes	NP	?	X	X	0	66.7	NP	100.0
2. Rattles	NP	100.0	X	X	75.0	75.0	?	100.0
3. Conch Cups	NP	100.0	X	X	NP	100.0	NP	100.0
4. Pipes	NP	NP	NP	NP	NP	33.3	NP	X
ORNAMENTS								
Stone:								
1. Beads	NP	85.7	100.0?	NP	100.0	70.8	66.7	81.0
2. Beads, Cannel Coal	NP	?	?	NP	100.0	100.0	NP	96.7
3. Beads, Crinoid	NP	0	33.3	NP	NP	88.0	NP	NP
4. Pendants	NP	100.0	0	NP	100.0	0	NP	40.0
Bone:								
1. Beads, Tubular	?	37.5	X	X	100.0	14.3	NP	0
2. Beads, Disc	NP	33.3	X	X	0	NP	?	0
3. Canines, Perf.	100.0	100.0	X	X	100.0	93.7	100.0	100.0
4. Pendants	?	NP	X	X	NP	50.0	?	0
5. Hairpins	NP	0	X	X	28.6	13.2	NP	27.6
Shell:								
1. Beads, Disc	100.0	98.8	X	X	100.0	100.0	93.5	99.8
2. Beads, Anculosa	61.1	100.0	X	X	NP	?	100.0	98.4
3. Beads, Marginella	NP	NP	X	X	NP	100.0	NP	100.0
4. Beads, Olivella	NP	NP	X	X	NP	100.0	NP	100.0

(*Continued overleaf*)

(Table 1.—Continued)

(Shells, cont'd.)	*Ward*	*Barrett*	*Butterfield*	*Kirkland*	*Read*	*Carlson Annis*	*Chiggerville*	*Indian Knoll*
5. Beads, Pearl	NP	NP	X	X	NP	NP	NP	100.0
6. Beads, Tubular Conch	40.0	100.0	X	X	100.0	100.0	100.0	98.5
7. Beads, Spherical Conch	NP	NP	X	X	NP	NP	NP	100.0
8. Pendants, Conch	NP	87.5	X	X	NP	100.0	100.0	100.0
9. Gorgets, Conch	100.0	100.0	X	X	100.0	NP	100.0	100.0
10. Earplugs, Conch	NP	NP	X	X	NP	100.0	100.0	100.0
11. Columella, Conch	NP	100.0	X	X	NP	NP	NP	100.0
12. Discs, Conch?	?	NP	X	X	NP	100.0	NP	100.0
13. Rings, Conch?	NP	NP	X	X	NP	NP	NP	100.0
Antler:								
1. Beads	NP	NP	X	X	NP	0	NP	50.0
Copper:								
1. Bars	NP	100.0	NP	NP	NP	NP	NP	100.0
2. Pendants	NP	100.0	NP	NP	NP	NP	NP	100.0
3. Beads	NP	NP	NP	NP	NP	0	NP	NP

NP = Not present
X = Adequacy of preservation uncertain
? = Ambiguous data
*Undoubtedly includes many manos
+Correspond to Webb's chipped rectangles, and may actually be woodworking tools

These may be compared to such sites as Carlson Annis with 222 hammerstones, and Indian Knoll with 316 abrading stones and 78 reamers, none of which were in burial association.

There are curiously high percentages for beaver and rodent incisors at Read and Indian Knoll, and an equally curious dearth of such items at the other sites, with the data for Barrett and Ward inadequate for reliable interpretation of the occurrence of incisors. Of course, there were only three such items at Read, in contrast to the 28 recovered from Indian Knoll. But Webb (1946, p. 298) points out that "except for having a sharp cutting edge [these artifacts] show no evidence of having been worked." Only very careful checking would have identified the incisors as artifacts if they had occurred in the midden. A check of the faunal analysis for Indian Knoll by Skaggs (in Webb, 1946, pp. 334–39) failed to disclose any mention of beaver incisors in the midden, although beaver mandibles are mentioned. But there is a remarkable lacuna in the reporting of teeth in the list, for that matter, with the sole exception being two cottontail rabbit teeth. In the light of our own experience with Midwestern shell middens, the bone sample seems to be rather unusual.

Stone atlatl weights, prized by collectors for their workmanship and often exotic materials, seem to display extreme variability, with percentages ranging from zero for the two at Kirkland to 57.1 per cent for the fourteen at Barrett. Other components of atlatls also show similar wide swings in their proportional representation in burial association, with ataltl hooks, for example, having a range from 11.8 to 100 per cent, and atlatl handles, from 21.4 to 100 per cent. But again, the very high percentages correlate with the rarity of the item at the site, with those sites having atlatl components in abundance consistently showing much lower percentages.

We cannot even begin to explain the variability of the items pertaining to the atlatl. Utilization of exotic raw materials does not seem to be involved, since the limestones, sandstones, and various igneous rocks are common to the Midwest. A few examples may have been manufactured from materials not immediately available in the lower Ohio Valley area, but these are in a decided minority. At this point, it can only be suggested that atlatl components vary sufficiently from other items in the first category to consider the possibility that they might better be considered as a special subcategory.

Finally, there are two categories, shell atlatl weights and copper pins, awls and needles, which, with the exception of a copper awl at Carlson Annis, are never found outside of burial association. We suspect that the important variable here is the raw material involved, not the basic function of the artifact. In both cases, the imported copper and conch shell may have added an intrinsic value to these items beyond their basic utilitarian properties. If this be the case, these exceptional items within the functional categories of general utility tools, weapons, and fabricating and processing tools should be considered for our present purposes with the Class III artifacts to be discussed below, not with the Class I artifacts where their functional counterparts appear.

A second group consisted of items which we have argued elsewhere (Winters, 1968) to be of the sort properly included in the category of ceremonial equipment, that is, flutes, rattles, and pipes, all of which, with the exception of conch shell cups, were made from local raw materials and in the pattern of localized Midwestern styles. To these may be added cups made from imported conch shell, which we consider ceremonial items because of the special contexts in which they occur in late Archaic, Woodland, and even historic times. (We have excluded computations for medicine bags since those not in burial association are represented by animal bones which would in all likelihood have simply been included with the faunal sample recovered from the midden.) Items in this category generally occur only in burial association, and rarely fall below 75 per cent of the specimens recovered at any site.

A third group consisted of items which have been termed ornaments. In terms of proportional representation with burials, there are at least two subdivisions, one consisting of ornaments manufactured from bone and the other of items manufactured from imported raw materials such as copper and conch shell. A third subdivision might be created for stone ornaments, but the data on raw materials are inadequate for analyzing the types or sources of raw materials. In other respects, these stone items show much the same percentage as that of the subdivision for ornaments of imported raw materials, although the former tend to be somewhat lower.

While ornaments in general occur in rather higher frequencies in burial association than the artifacts of the first group, antler and bone ornaments such as tubular beads, disc beads, pendants, and hairpins tend to occur more frequently in the midden than in burial association. An unexplained exception to this observation is found in the case of perforated canine pendants.

Both conch shell and copper stand in marked contrast to the preceding subdivision. Normally, burial association is 100 per cent with only 13 per cent of the 52 recorded observations (Table 1) falling below 98 per cent. There would seem to be decided differential in the mode of disposition of ornaments. There may be many factors leading to differences in disposition of tubular bone beads and tubular shell beads, or bone disc beads and shell disc beads, but there still remains the simple fact that beads made of local raw materials tend to be disposed of rather casually, while those that are made of imported raw materials tend to occur in special context and only rarely in the midden debris.

Furthermore, to emphasize the point, with the exception of atlatl weights there was no diversion of imported marine shell for the manufacture of utilitarian artifacts, quite unlike sites of the Florida area adjacent to the sources of much of the marine shell. Rouse (1951) in his publication on the survey of the Indian River in Florida, an area which he notes has less variety of shell artifacts than southern Florida, records chopping tools, which constitute the majority of shell artifacts, including celts, gouges, chisels, and picks. The use of *Busycon* as a hammer is also recorded. Along with these, of course, there occurs an assortment of cups, dippers, beads, and pendants.

One obvious objection to the previous observations is that sampling error may be a significant factor. The sites in question are shell middens, and they were not excavated with the best recovery techniques. While admitting that the sample does not conform to present-day standards, we do not feel that it is necessarily unrepresentative, for the following reasons:

1. Our own experience with Midwestern shell middens has been that such middens consist only in small part of actual shell accumulations, which occur as lenses in the conglomeration of black soil, rock, and other midden debris. In this respect, some observations of Webb are pertinent: Of Indian Knoll itself he says, "While the site here is a shell 'mound,' shell is by no means the major constituent in the accumulation" (1946). Or again, "It will be remembered that, at Indian Knoll, there was a very considerable midden deposit, but relatively a small amount of shell in the midden" (Webb and Haag, 1940). Of Kirkland, "Mussell shells were extremely rare and only noted by occasional fragments" (Webb and Haag, 1940). Of Chiggerville, "Near the bottom of the heap there was quite uniformly a stratum of concentrated shell. Between the shell lenses there was black earth mixed with shell, which contained the usual refuse material of a shell midden" (Webb and Haag, 1939). In connection with Ward and Kirkland, "in Kentucky some shell-mound people lived on shell mounds but others having the same or similar cultural status lived in villages [Ward and Kirkland] quite removed from any shell accumulation" (Webb and Haag, 1940). Of Barrett, "The midden material consisted of many stones, scattered mussel shells, and worked and unworked flint, and polished stone material" (Webb and Haag, 1947). And finally, Butterfield, although classed as a shell midden, is described in these terms: "A result of this condition of extreme porosity and acid soil was the poor preservation of human skeletons and other bone material." But a few lines later is the notation that "the presence of large quantities of mussel shells in the midden suggest that there must have been a shoals here prior to the damming of the river" (Webb and Haag, 1947). We do not know quite how to reconcile these two statements, since if there were large quantities of mussel shell present, the soil should not have been very acid.

But one is left with the total impression that, while the quantity of shell varied in the middens, at no site was there simply a dense homogeneous mass of river mussels in which other shell artifacts might well disappear, particularly since the material was double shoveled for at least some of the sites in checking for artifacts. We should grant that small shell artifacts might be overlooked with such techniques, but we doubt very much that the larger items would have been missed so consistently if they were actually present in the middens.

Nor can we invoke differential preservation from soil factors to account for the distribution pattern. With the exception of Butterfield, the statement on which is ambiguous, soil conditions should have been ideal for the preservation of both bone and shell, and the sites are indeed notable for the quantities of bone artifacts which have been recovered from them. While the sites vary considerably in the number and types of shell artifacts, such variability is perhaps best explained by the function of the site within the settlement system, and hence quantitative and qualitative differences in the activities associated therewith, than to preservation factors per se.

We feel that there is some reason, then, for postulating that the preceding categories, with modifications, represent sets of artifacts that express broad differences in their values based in part upon the functions to which they were related in the Indian Knoll society, and in part upon the raw materials from which they were manufactured.

Using ethnographic parallels, we might then restate the categories in terms of a value system for the Indian Knoll Culture:

Class I. Items of personal equipment with value expressible only in terms of the functional worth to the owner. This would include most items classifiable as general utility tools, weapons, fabricating and processing tools, and domestic implements, and ornaments manufactured from locally available raw materials.

Class II. Items of personal equipment but of a ceremonial nature. These items would generally have had no direct exchange value but would possess an intrinsic value stemming mainly from their symbolic nature. This would include artifacts generally classified as ceremonial equipment, and any other artifacts which by context should be separated from their normal class affiliations and considered as ceremonial equipment.

Class III. Items of equipment with special value. This would include those items occurring in special, segregated context that are manufactured from rare and/or imported raw materials; consists primarily of certain classes of ornaments, but in the Indian Knoll Culture can also include ceremonial and utilitarian artifacts manufactured from imported marine shells and copper. A contemporary analogy for the latter case might be found in gift shops that provide for the man who has everything items such as gold toothpicks, gem-studded can openers, and a host of other impedimenta the prices of which obscure the lowly, utilitarian function of the artifact itself. The foregoing observation should not be taken as meaning that the utilitarian function of the item was of no consequence. Copper awls, for example, might be desirable because of their superiority over their counterparts manufactured from other raw materials.

It might be germane at this point to pause and consider the question of why marine shell and copper have rarely been considered in archeological reporting in any systematic way as items that may well have been associated with special value. An immediate factor has been the rather casual, and probably ethnocentric, manner in which some archeologists tend to regard items such as shell beads and other small "trinkets." For example, in respect to the Indian Knoll sites themselves, the following revealing comments were made in the discussion of burial associations:

> Relatively few [burials at Indian Knoll] had artifacts placed with them at burial (275 out of 879), and if one excludes burials having only beads (88 burials), which are worn as body decorations and in part attached to clothing, there remain only 187 burials having artifacts which might be considered as having been placed in the graves intentionally, from a desire to make a burial offering (Webb, 1946).

In respect to Carlson Annis:

> Of the 390 burials only 215 had any artifacts of any kind in association. Of these, 158 had only shell beads, gorgets, awls, clothes pins, or hairpins, or other artifacts which were worn as personal adornments, and which may be regarded as part of the ordinary clothing of the deceased. These were worn buried with the dead as a matter of course and with no intention to make a burial offering (Webb, 1950).

There would seem to be an a priori assumption that ornaments are inevitably some sort of equivalent of ten-cent-store baubles. In respect to disc and tubular shell beads, most archeologists have tended to follow the position taken by Speck (1919) and others that wampum as a limited medium of exchange can be explained by European influence.

Speck assumes an evolution in both function and form for shell beads. Of form he states, "the Indians . . . were not capable of drilling the finest tubular beads until they had acquired metal drills from Europeans" (1919, p. 6). He concludes that the disc shaped beads must have been the earlier type. Of function, "Deducing from the material presented a possibility or two concerning the state of development through which wampum must have passed, it seems reasonable to suppose that wampum of the disc type was originally used in simple lengths or strings functioning primarily as a means of ornamentation, then as instruments of ceremony, negotiation, and as mnemonic documents. The substitution of cylindrical beads assuredly came later as an improvement" (1919, p. 22). There is a certain ambivalence, however, in Speck's discussions of disc beads throughout his monograph, and at times he seems to imply that these beads may have been items of special value prior to the historic period, as one might gather from the preceding quotation.

If such an interpretation were tenable, one might well view skeptically any claims that prehistoric tubular and disc shell beads, or other artifacts of exotic shell, could be interpreted as having any sort of special value attached thereto. But Slotkin and Schmitt (1949) in their reexamination of the evidence relevant to wampum have demonstrated that stylistically wampum can be traced from the late Archaic of some three to four millennia ago through subsequent Woodland and Mississippian manifestations into historic times, and that the evidence from early documentary sources points to wampum's having been used in eastern north America at the time of European contact as a limited medium of exchange for such diverse purposes as bride price, remuneration for special services, compensation for injury, and in ritual gift exchange.

Having established that there is substantial basis for postulating autocthonous systems of limited media of exchange in eastern North America in early historic times, and the fact that in late Archaic times there were classes of artifacts that sort contextually according to their functions, the raw materials from which they were made, and the remoteness of the sources of those materials, it would be interesting to compare the contexts of artifacts from sites pertaining to the cultures cited by Slotkin and Schmitt in their wampum study with those of the Indian Knoll Culture to see to what extent the contexts of historic artifact categories and raw materials correspond to or differ from those of the Archaic sites. Unfortunately, historic sites with both large midden excavations and burial samples are unavailable in the literature for the critical areas of the Northeast and the Atlantic coastal areas, and we shall turn instead to the Hardin Site (Hanson, 1966), an early historic component of the Fort Ancient Culture located on the Ohio River in Kentucky. The bulk of the midden materials at the Hardin Site can be assigned to the aforementioned culture, although the presence of eighteen sherds of Watson cordmarked and Watson plain, which tended to be concentrated in a small area of the site (Hanson, 1966, p. 109), along with some fifty stemmed and notched projectile points (Hanson, 1966, Fig. 50) indicate minor utilization of the area by earlier Woodland and Archaic groups. Both the paucity of the earlier artifacts and the diversity of their types point to little more than utilization of the area for small and temporary encampments over a period of several thousand years. Hence, we doubt that debris from the earlier occupations could appreciably affect the reliability of our sample and, of course, none of the material specifically assignable to the earlier components has been included in the calculation of percentages. Moreover, unless special preservation factors were present, we should be very surprised if any of the burials or artifacts made from organic materials could pertain to the Archaic occupations of this open site, particularly since there seems to be no indication of shell midden zones or lenses assignable to an Archaic occupation.

Hanson assigns the site to the Shawnee and estimates the dates of occupancy as ranging from 1500 to 1675 A.D. Limited contact with a distribution network involving European trade goods is shown by the presence of brass artifacts, but Hanson (1966, p. 175) argues convincingly that "The European brass fragments and artifacts found at the Hardin Village Site were probably the result of trade with other Indians, who acted as intermediaries, rather than directly with Europeans." Thus we assume that the traditional precontact values of the Fort Ancient people still prevailed during the period of occupancy of the Hardin Site, since little evidence exists for any profound change in the way of life of the village inhabitants during their residence at the Hardin Site, with their indirect contacts with the outer world of the European settlers being expressed only in the appearance of a few ornaments of brass.

When the contexts of the artifacts from midden and burial association at the Hardin Site are listed (Table 2), the parallels between the historic site and the prehistoric Archaic sites are remarkable. But again we must note that there is some ambiguity as to the source of the raw materials for the shell artifacts. Some are clearly of marine origin as specified in the text (*Marginella* beads, large barrel-shaped beads, rectangular gorgets, engraved shell gorgets, pear-shaped gorgets, conch columella pendants), others appear from the illustrations to be local riverine mollusks ("hoes," spoons, and possibly the shell scrapers), while still a third group cannot be identified specifically as to source from either the text or the illustrations (disc beads, small barrel-shaped beads, circular gorgets, diamond-shaped gorgets, three-holed gorgets, imitation claw pendants, tear-shaped pendants, rectangular pendants, and an engraved mollusk). Many, or most, of the last group may well be marine shell, however, since we have rarely seen examples of such ornaments in the Midwest that were manufactured from local mollusks, and we shall assume for the present that the Hardin Site artifacts correspond to the Midwestern norms.

Table 2. Context of Artifacts at the Hardin Site

General Utility Tools	*Quantity*	*Percentage Midden*	*Percentage Pits, etc.*	*Percentage Burials*
Chert Scrapers	297	89	4	7
Scrapers, Shell	3	67	—	33
Leaf-shaped Knives	19	74	5	21
Trianguloid Knives	9	56	11	33
Circular Knives	3	100	—	—
Lunate Knives	3	100	—	—
Hammerstones	15	60	13	27
Disc Choppers	6	100	—	—
Weapons				
Projectile points:				
Fine Triangular	702	83	6	11
Crude Triangular	228	87	6	7
"Tear-shaped"	8	100	—	—
Antler	42	81	12	7
Bone Fishhooks	8	62	13	25
Fabricating and Processing Equipment				
Bipointed Drills	42	88	5	7
Flaring Based Drills	17	83	6	11
Stone Picks	1	100	—	—
Sandstone Saw	1	100	—	—
Whetstones	29	87	10	3
Splinter Awls	64	75	11	14
Turkey Bone Awls	32	78	9	13

(*Continued overleaf*)

(*Table 2.—Continued*)

Fabricating and Processing Equipment	*Quantity*	*Percentage Midden*	*Percentage Pits, etc.*	*Percentage Burials*
Deer Bone Awls	18	83	17	—
Antler Chisels	19	90	5	5
Antler Punches	22	77	5	18
Bone Punches and Needles	12	92	—	8
Racoon Penis Bone Punches	5	40	20	40
Bone Flakers	6	67	—	33
Gouges or Beamers	143	90	6	4
Antler Scrapers	8	62	13	25
Pottery Spindle Whorls?	196	100	—	—
Sherd Pottery Smoothers	145	100	—	—
Pottery Anvil	1	100	—	—
Domestic Equipment				
"Anvils" (pitted manos)	11	64	18	18
Grinding Stones	5	40	40	20
Shell Spoons	25	—	88	12
Pottery Pestles	42	100	—	—
Pottery Spoon	1	100	—	—
Pottery Cup	1	100	—	—
Woodworking Equipment				
Celts	65	86	5	9
Beaver Incisor Chisels	3	100	—	—
Digging Equipment				
Stone Hoes	4	25	25	50
Shell Hoes	2	50	—	50
ORNAMENTS				
Bone:				
Pendants	6	50	—	50
Drilled Dog or Wolf Teeth	66	36	14	50
Drilled Bear Teeth	11	82	18	—
Drilled Elk Teeth	1	—	—	100
Beads (tubular, bone)	211	74	10	16
Beads (barrel-shaped)	147	30	1	69
Collar	1	100	—	—
Pins	9	22	22	56
Pottery:				
Pendants	1	100	—	—
Ear Plug	1	—	100	—
Ground Stone:				
Pendants	9	78	22	—
Gorgets	2	50	—	50
Shell:				
Pendants (claw)	54	7	—	93
Pendants (geometric)	3	100	—	—
Conch Columella Pendant	1	—	—	100
Gorgets (plain, mask, and engraved)	60	3	—	97
Beads (barrel shaped)	214	—	—	100
Disk Beads	765	x	—	99.6
Marginella Beads	336	x	—	99.7
Engraved Mollusk	1	100	—	—

(*Table 2.—Continued*)

Copper:	*Quantity*	*Percentage Midden*	*Percentage Pits, etc.*	*Percentage Burials*
Pendants	1	—	—	100
Beads (rolled)	120	2	—	98
Beads (flattened)	5	20	—	80
Bracelets	2	—	—	100
Tubes	9	22	—	78
Brass:				
Beads (rolled)	28	—	—	100
Beads (flattened)	22	—	—	100
Bracelets	1	—	—	100
Tubes	4	—	—	100
Coils	9	—	x	x
Wire Fragments	2	100	—	—
Ceremonial Equipment				
Stone Pipes	22	77	—	23
Pottery Pipes	5	100	—	—
Bone Rasps	2	50	50	—
Whistles or Flutes	1	89	11	—
Pottery Rattles	1	100	—	—
Pottery Effigies	3	100	—	—
Skull Cap Ladle	1	—	100	—
Recreational Equipment				
Discoidals	4	75	—	25
Drilled Deer Toes	2	100	—	—
Bone Gaming Pieces	113	71	12	17
Miscellaneous				
Stone Balls	1	100	—	—
Altered Concretions	2	100	—	—
Drilled Terrapin Carapace	1	100	—	—
Unworked Copper Scrap	1	100	—	—
Pottery Balls	1	100	—	—
Pottery Rings	1	100	—	—

x = Quantities not specifically assigned

As Table 2 shows, items that correspond to our previously defined Class I artifacts rarely occur in any numbers outside of the general midden, while Class III artifacts, which are limited at this particular Fort Ancient site entirely to ornaments, rarely appear in other than burial context. Hanson is led to remark of shell artifacts in general that "Of a total of 1,464 shell artifacts, 35.1 percent of the nonceramic artifacts, only sixteen came from the general midden. Significantly, nearly all were for decorative purposes" (1966, pp. 155–56). Once more, a remarkable dichotomy in context can be shown to exist between artifacts of imported marine shell and more obviously utilitarian objects such as the 702 fine triangular points (83 per cent in the midden, 11 per cent with burial), the 297 chert scrapers (89 per cent in the midden, 7 per cent with burials), and the 145 pottery smoothers (100 per cent in the midden). And, as in the Indian Knoll Culture sites, a considerable contrast also exists within the category of ornaments between those of local raw materials such as bone, pottery, and stone and those made from exotic raw materials, whether they be marine shell, copper, or brass. Or one might note the contrast between the contexts of mussel shell spoons (12 per cent in burial association) and those of marine shell pendants, gorgets, and beads, which for most types range from 93 per cent to 100 per cent in burial association.

There are, as one might anticipate, anomalies and inconsistencies within some of the categories of raw materials. For example, one should note the high frequency of the 147 barrel-shaped bone beads in burial association (69 per cent) and the midden linkage of the three geometric shell pendants (100 per cent) or the two pieces of brass wire (100 per cent). Notably, as with the geometric shell pendants and the brass wire, many of the anomalies involve artifacts that are rare or unique at the site, thus making it difficult to assess whether we are dealing with chance or accidental disposition of the artifacts rather than with the patterned social behavior inferrable from the artifacts represented both by large numbers and wide distribution within the site.

While the contextual patterns of Class I and Class III artifacts are very similar for both the Indian Knoll Culture and Hardin sites, there is a considerable divergence in respect to Class II artifacts. Consistently at the Hardin Site, pipes, rasps, flutes, rattles, etc., appear predominantly in the midden, although among these items, only pipes could be considered as anything other than exceedingly rare. We shall not even attempt to decide whether the disparities arise from a faulty assignment of artifacts to the category of ceremonial in this site of the Fort Ancient Culture, a shift from ceremonial to more secular associations of such items, or sampling errors that might arise from special disposition of ceremonial equipment beyond the village peripheries or, even, the possibility that such equipment might be associated only with the larger and more specialized Fort Ancient towns and villages. (At this point, one might raise the question as to where such known items of historic Shawnee ceremonial equipment as turtle shell rattles are in this putatively Shawnee site. Was this musical instrument with its millennia-old record in eastern North America [Winter, 1968] an innovation among the Shawnee within the historic period, or is sampling error a factor, or should the evidence be reviewed for the assignment of the Fort Ancient Culture village to the Shawnee?) The problems raised by the contextual disparities between the two cultures in respect to Class II (ceremonial) artifacts go far beyond the purposes of the present analysis, however. Suffice it to say that for the categories that do concern us the parallels between the proveniences of artifacts manufactured from local raw materials and from exotic, imported raw materials are such that they suggest similar attitudes towards these commodities on the part of the late Archaic Indian Knoll Culture and the proto-historic and historic Fort Ancient Culture, although we cannot infer any direct continuity in such attitudes during the intervening centuries of Woodland occupations in the Kentucky area of the Ohio Valley.

Obviously, though, the interpretations of Slotkin and Schmitt on the context of marine shell, copper, and brass in sites of the Fort Ancient Culture cannot be used to verify our own conclusions about the value of marine shell and copper in the Indian Knoll Culture. All that can be said is that our interpretations do not conflict with data from the early historic period prior to the time that acculturation had seriously modified the use of wampum as a limited medium of exchange, or with historic records that report marine shell as an item of considerable value.

Nor do we go so far as to propose that assignment of special value to marine shell in the Indian Knoll Culture carries with it an implication of usage as a medium of exchange, although we should not be particularly surprised had it served such a function. All too frequently, the Archaic peoples, who were greatly diversified culturally through space and time, are treated as though they were a homogeneous array of hunters and gatherers, and as though they were *idiots savants* capable only of changing styles of artifacts, producing an occasional nicely ground piece of stone, continuously foraging for a precarious and uncertain subsistence, and in general doing little beyond surviving as noble and unspoiled primitives. The complex technology and way of life of both the Indian Knoll and Riverton Cultures belie such an interpretation, and we should be very much surprised if the level of complexity was not close to that of succeeding eastern cultures prior to the advent of cultures of the Mississippian Pattern.

But to move from pejorative declamation to more productive considerations, if we are correct in our assumptions about the special value of marine shell imported from Florida and coastal areas of the Southeast and copper from the Great Lakes area, there remains the problem of establishing techniques for estimating the comparative values of the various categories of artifacts. One way would be to construct a rough scale of values for shell and copper artifacts in terms of the amounts of raw material contained therein. Such a scale is defective, of course, in that we have no way at present of estimating the accretion of value that may result from the expenditure of labor in the manufacturing process or of ascertaining the value that may accrue through such factors as the associations and ownership of the specimen. And in historic exchange systems, such as the kula ring, the value of a particular shell item depended in no small part on the history and associations of the shell item in its exchange circuit. Nor have we worked out experimentally the precise quantities of various artifacts that could be manufactured from shells of different size, so that our ranking will be rather more subjective than it should be.

Another problem has been adequate identification of the raw materials used in the manufacture of the many shell artifacts listed in Table 3. For example, Webb states in his discussion of small disc beads that

"Seemingly large conchs were cut into strips of the desired width. These in turn were cut into squares, and then these squares were drilled, centrally. From these, the disc beads were formed" (1946, p. 137). But there is no way of ascertaining whether all such beads were manufactured from conch, or whether local mussel shell was used for some. Webb's statement on composite shell atlatl wieghts also leads to difficulties in the interpretation: "composite shell weights made of bivalve shells, or sections of conch shells, were worked into prismoidal forms having straight edges, or convex edges like the varied stone forms" (1950a, p. 89). But actual identification for individual composite weights is rare. For better or worse, we shall treat disc-shell beads as derivative from conch, and shall drop composite shell weights from our analysis as an item too surrounded by ambiguity.

For some items, such as shell discs and rings there is rarely any information one way or the other, and these will also be omitted from the analysis.

Table 3. Large Shell Artifacts in Sites of the Indian Knoll Culture

Artifact	*Depth in Feet*	*Context*
Barrett:		
Marine gastropod gorgets (4)	1.5	YA, Male burial 1
Marine gastropod gorgets (4)	1.5	YA, Male burial 44
Drilled conch rectangle	3.1	YA, Male burial 47
Tubular shell beads (3)	3.9	YA, Male burial 77
Marine gastropod gorgets (4)	1.8	YA, Male burial 100
Marine gastropod gorgets (4)	1.6	YA, Male burial 116
Tubular conch columella beads (6)	2.2	C, Female? burial 136
Conch columella (32)	2.3	Ad., Male burial 156
Conch shell pendant [a]	2.3	I, ? burial 157
Tubular shell beads (2)	1.7	YA, Male burial 215
Broken conch shell (cup?)	1.6	I, ? burial 372
Conch shell cup	2.1	YA, Male burial 381
Shell (unident.) pendants (2)	2.3	YA, Female burial 216
Ward:		
Shell atlatl weight [b] *	?	A, Male burial 118
Tubular shell beads [b] (2)	?	A, Female burial 163
Conch gorget	?	A, Female burial 188
Shell (unident.) disc *	?	A, Female burial 234
Conch gorget	?	C, ? burial 383
Kirkland:		
Conch gorgets (2) [c]	?	A, Female burial 12
Conch pendant	?	A, Female burial 12
Carlson Annis:		
Triangular conch pendants (3)	2.4	Ad., ? burial 44
Tubular shell beads [d] (X)	6.3	I, ? burial 59
Tubular shell beads (X)	2.1	C, ? burial 131
Conch pendants (5)	3.0	YA, Male burial 146
Tubular shell beads (2)	5.5	C, Male? burial 177
Perforated shell (unident.) disc [d] *	5.5	C, Male? burial 177

(*Table* 3.—*Continued*)

Artifact	*Depth in Feet*	*Context*
Shell (unident.) pendant	5.5	C, Male? burial 177
Tubular shell beads (X)	2.3	Ad., ? burial 190
Tubular shell beads (X)	6.5	I, Male burial 220
Conch disc (2)	7.6	I, Male? burial 229
Shell (unident.) pendants (2)	7.6	I, Male? burial 229
Conch ear plugs (2)	7.6	I, Male? burial 229
Tubular shell beads (X)	7.0	C, Female? burial 230
Conch pendants (X)	5.4	Ad., ? burial 236
Conch disc pendant	5.4	Ad., ? burial 236
Tubular conch bead	1.5	YA, Male burial 256
Shell ear plugs (2)	6.1	Ad., ? burial 274
Conch ear plugs (2)	6.0	I, ? burial 290
Shell (unident.) discs (2) *	6.0	I, ? burial 290
Shell (unident.) atlatl weight *	6.0	I, ? burial 290
Conch pendants (5)	5.6	I, ? burial 309
Conch shell (bead?)	5.6	I, ? burial 309
Conch (*Fasciolaria gigantea*) cup	6.8	Ad., ? burial 335
Conch ear plugs (2)	6.0	C, ? burial 341
Shell (unident.) pendant	4.4	AD., ? burial 350
Shell (unident.) pendants (2)	6.9	C, Female burial 360
Conch ear plug (1)	5.0	Ad., ? burial 385
Conch pendant	5.0	Ad., ? burial 385
Read:		
Tubular shell beads [e] (6)	3.0	YA, Male burial 1
Conch section (gorget?)	2.0	J, ? burial 24
Conch gorgets (3)	2.9	SA, Male burial 66
Conch gorget	3.5	J, ? burial 70
Chiggerville:		
Conch ear plugs (2)	?	I, ? burial 58
Conch gorget	?	I, ? burial 60
Conch composite atlatl weight *	?	I, ? burial 60
Conch gorget	?	I, ? burial 61
Shell (unident.) pendant [f]	?	I, ? burial 76
Tubular shell beads (9)	?	C, Male? burial 30
Conch gorgets (2)	?	J, Male burial 25
Shell (unident.) pendants (6)	?	A, Female burial 43
Shell (unident.) rings (11)	5.7	Ad., Female burial 47
Conch gorget	?	A, Male burial 63
Tubular shell beads (80)	?	A, Female burial 79
Shell (unident.) pendant	?	A, Female burial 73
Indian Knoll:		
Shell (unident.) pendant	4.8	I, Male? burial 33
Conch pendants (2)	6.3	YA, Male burial 55
Shell (unident.) atlatl weight *	6.3	Y, Female burial 56
Shell (unident.) atlatl weight *	6.4	Y, Male burial 58
Shell (unident.) pendant	6.1	SA, Male burial 123
Marine shell atlatl weight *	7.2	MA, Male burial 218
Shell (unident.) pendants (4)	3.2	Ad., Male burial 236
Conch (*Busycon perversum*) container	3.2	Ad., Male burial 236

(*Continued overleaf*)

(*Table* 3.—*Continued*)

Artifact	*Depth in Feet*	*Context*
Tubular shell beads (38)	3.0	YA, Female burial 237
Conch cup	3.0	YA, Female burial 237
Fasciolaria gigantea (Kiener) shell	3.0	YA, Female burial 237
Curved shell (unident.) pendants	4.1	I, Female? burial 257
Conch (*Busycon perversum*) cup	8.3	YA, Male burial 310
Tubular shell beads (14)	2.0	Ad., Female burial 315
Conch pendants (3)	2.0	Ad., Female burial 315
Conch pendant	2.1	I, Male? burial 337
Shell (unident.) pendants (4)	3.5	I, Male? burial 339
Conch shell	7.1	C, Female? burial 354
Conch pendants (4)	2.1	Ad., Male burial 395
Curved shell (unident.) ornament	1.9	Nb, Male? burial 434
Conch shells (cups?) (2)	2.9	C, Male burial 439
Shell (unident.) pendants (2)	6.8	I, Female? burial 445
Tubular shell beads (2)	6.8	I, Female? burial 445
Shell (unident.) rings (3) *	6.8	I, Female? burial 445
Tubular conch beads (2)	3.2	C, Male? burial 503
Conch pendant	5.1	I, Female? burial 512
Conch pendant	4.6	C, Female burial 515
Conch earplugs (2)	4.6	C, Female burial 515
Tubular shell beads (4)	4.7	I, Male? burial 517
Composite shell (unident.) atlatl weight *	6.0	YA, Female burial 560
Composite shell (unident.) atlatl weight *	6.7	YA, Male burial 561
Shell (unident.) ornaments (gorgets?) (2)	7.7	YA, Male burial 561
Tubular shell beads (51)	3.7	C, Female? burial 571
Shell (unident.) rings (12) *	3.7	C, Female? burial 571
Tusk shaped shell (unident.) ornaments (2)	5.6	YA, Male burial 575
Shell (unident.) strip pendants (2)	4.9	I, Female? burial 579
Conch strips (2)	5.0	I, Male burial, 610
Conch shell squares (33)	5.0	I, Male burial, 610
Large conch sections (2)	5.0	I, Male burial, 610
Curved shell (unident.) pendants (2)	3.5	YA, Male burial 661
Conch pendants (3)	4.3	YA, Male burial 687
Shell (unident.) pendants (2)	6.0	YA, Female burial 696
End whorl (conch?) pendant	1.5	YA, Male burial 697
Tubular shell beads (3)	3.7	YA, Female burial 708
Tubular shell beads (6)	3.2	Nb, Female? burial 721
Shell (unident.) pendants (2)	3.5	Nb, Male? burial 729
Tubular shell beads (7)	2.9	Nb, Male? burial 734
Curved shell (unident.) pendants (2)	4.3	YA, Male burial 744
Shell (unident.) disc, perforated *	2.1	YA, Female burial 761
Conch gorgets (4)	2.2	I, Female? burial 767
Conch gorgets (4)	3.4	Ad., Male burial 769
Tusk shaped shell (unident.) pendants (1)	2.2	YA, Male burial 827
Composite shell (unident.) shell atlatl weight *	7.6	YA, Male burial 853

* Used only as specified in text.

a. The list on p. 20 (Webb and Haag, 1947) notes five pendants from five burials and a pair of tooth-like shell pendants from a single burial. Their trait list on p. 42 lists six long, slender conch pendants. One pendant is listed for Burial 157, and apparently the pair of tooth-like pendants are the pair listed for Burial 216. This leaves four conch pendants from four burials unaccounted for, and the possibility that a sixth was found in the midden.

b. Tabulation of burial artifacts on p. 84 (Webb and Haag, 1940) also lists shell atlatl weight for Burial 438. No mention is made of this item in the description of the burial on p. 438, and only one shell atlatl weight is listed in the trait list on p. 104. Note also that the same trait list gives five tubular shell beads, but no tubular bone beads. Two tubular shell beads are noted in the burial list, along with two tubular bone beads (Burial 406). It is possible that these should have been shell beads.

c. Three conch gorgets are mentioned in the trait list on p. 104 (Webb and Haag, 1940), so there may be an additional gorget from the midden or some other context.

d. As usual, there are inconsistencies in counts of artifacts with burials at the site. The trait list on p. 305 (Webb, 1950a) lists two large conch shell discs and one perforated conch shell disc. The burial list has a conch disc pendant (Burial 236), a perforated shell disc (Burial 177), two conch discs (Burial 229), and two shell discs (Burial 290). And the same trait list on p. 304 mentions 16 strings of short tubular shell beads and three strings of long tubular shell beads. Of these, only seven could be located in the burial listings. Probably the others were recorded simply as shell beads in the burial tabulations.

e. Twenty-one tubular shell beads are listed in burial association in the trait list on p. 383 (Webb, 1950b), but only the six with Burial 1 can be identified as such on the burial tabulation sheets.

f. All eight of the pendants from the site were in burial association. The three triangular pendants and three tusk shaped pendants illustrated in Fig. 15 (Webb and Haag, 1939) are marine shell (*ibid.*, p. 25). So, at least six of the eight pendants with the burials must be of marine shell.

g. As with the other sites, there are many discrepancies in the tabulations and descriptions of artifacts for the Indian Knoll Site. They are too numerous to record here. Wherever possible, we have corrected errors in the burial description. For example, the description of Burial 721 (Webb, 1946, p. 196) does not include the six tubular beads that are illustrated in Fig. 23C and mentioned in the description of the illustration on p. 207. In the case of Burial 237, the description mentions only cut conch shell, but illustrated in Fig. 25B is a conch shell cup and in Fig. 30 a *Fasciolaria gigantea* (Kiener) shell, both of which are mentioned on p. 213 in the discussion of the illustrated artifacts from Burial 237. Many similar corrections were made by checking all references that we could find to a particular burial.

In the case of other items, where adequate identification is not provided in the trait lists or burial tabulations, internal textual evidence is sufficient to warrant the assumption of marine shell as the raw material. For example, tubular shell beads are very rarely given adequate classification. But Webb (1946) states that, "these were made from the columella of large conch shells." Similar statements pertaining to perforated or notched strip pendants, curved pendants, and tooth-shaped pendants both in the Indian Knoll (Webb, 1946) and Chiggerville (Webb and Haag, 1939) reports permit a similar assumption about the use of marine shells as raw material. In the latter report, Webb and Haag comment that, "The shell artifacts are, with very few exceptions, made from sections of marine conchs." There are also supplementary indentifications in figure descriptions, artifact analyses, and discussions of individual burials.

Other difficulties have arisen from discrepancies in quantitative data and the use of two or more referrents for a single type of artifact in various reports. For "conch" shell, we have tried to resolve some of the quantitative discrepancies by internal analysis of the textual material, where illustrations, detailed discussions of features, or of particular categories of artifacts have permitted resolution of the problem in one way or another. Insofar as possible, we have also tried to standardize terminology after having checked illustrations and descriptions of the artifacts in question. Hence, in Table 3 the reader will not always find an item designated by the term given to it in the original burial description. There remains a residue of conflicting quantitative statements that could not be resolved, and many of these are noted in notes appended to Table 3. Some items in the table could not be used simply because of vague description or fragmentary condition of the artifacts; for example, Burials 354 and 439 at Indian Knoll simply have the notation "conch shell." It is impossible to decide whether these are whole shells, cups, or smaller artifacts.

Nor has it been possible to use marine shells such as *Marginella* and *Olivella*, which are rare in sites of the Indian Knoll Culture, being reported only for Carlson Annis and Indian Knoll. Of the fourteen strings of *Marginella* reported for Carlson Annis (Webb, 1950a, p. 304), it has been possible to identify only ten strings in burial association (Burials 59, 77, 103, 130, 155, 230, 233, 234, 266, and 362), and for none of these is the quantity given. Of the four groups reported for Indian Knoll (Webb, 1946, p. 235), only the one group of *Marginella apicina* (*Menke*) in association with Burial 571 is mentioned. While data are provided for the one string of *Olivella* beads at Indian Knoll (Burial 1), no indication is given in the Carlson Annis report as to which burials were associated with the three strings of *Olivella* mentioned.

One item of interest that was noted during the checking of the data on the associations of *Marginella* and *Olivella* is that none of them has been reported with adults. At Carlson Annis, *Marginella* beads were found with one newborn, two infants, three children, three juveniles, and one adolescent, while at Indian Knoll, the association is with a child. The one record for *Olivella* at Indian Knoll is with a newborn. It would be interesting to see if this pattern is borne out by the other unreported strings in burial context. (In passing, another shell item, not of marine origin, should be mentioned as a possible item of trade and special value at the Indian Knoll site. This was a group of beads made from *Lithasia obovata* [Say], riverine snail species having as its present-day habitat rivers of the Tennessee region. The necklace was in association with an infant—an interesting parallel to our previous observations on *Olivella* and *Marginella*.)

But at best, the following attempt at interpreting the distribution of items of special value in the Indian Knoll Culture must be understood as an exercise in method, rather than any definitive statement on the subject of the context and quantitative occurrence of imported marine shell within the culture. Such can be accomplished only with thorough reanalysis of the original collections made by Webb and his associates.

Our attention will perforce be centered upon the shells loosely designated as conchs by archeologists, including whelks such as *Busycon perversum* and band shells such as *Fasciolaria gigantea* (Kiener), for which abundant specific identification or good presumptive evidence is available. For such shells and their derivatives, the following rough scale of ranking by arbitrary points is proposed:

150 points–Whole shells
100 points–Shell cups and atlatl weights
50 points–Shell gorgets and rectangles
25 points–Shell pendants, earplugs, tusk-shaped ornaments, discs
10 points–Tubular shell beads and shell rings
5 points–Unmodified columella
? points–Disc shell beads

Of course some items such as gorgets vary from examples that are simply cut to shape, the edges ground off, and perforated for suspension, to rare examples that are engraved with geometric motifs. The latter might have greater value than the former, but we are unable to allow for variables of this type. And, ultimately, we are unable to decide upon a relative point-ranking for disc shell beads, since these have a range from small to large, and are not usually so distinguished in the burial tabulations. Consideration of the ranking of disc beads in our arbitrary scale must await clarification of the size range and quantitative disposition of these beads.

One might also question the appropriateness of assigning the same values to derivatives of both *Busycon perversum* and *Fasciolaria gigantea,* in view of the disparities in size. This issue will be avoided for the present on the pragmatic grounds that the application of our value scale will not be affected to a significant degree by such a potential variable, there being only two examples of *Fasciolaria,* one with an adult female at Indian Knoll, the other with an adolescent of unknown sex at Carlson Annis.

Our first application of the scale will be to an analysis of burials which have been definitely identified as to sex, with the results as given in Table 4.

The range for males was from 10 to 200 units of shell, with an average of 98 units. For females, from 20 to 800 units, with an average of 185 units. The average for females is distorted, however, by the two burials with extraordinary value ratings; if these were not included, the average would be only 79 for females. Thus, while females could be associated with quantities of marine shell far in excess of any male, as a rule they were less frequently provided with marine shell and, in terms of the arbitrary value units, on a scale somewhat less than that of males. For example, of the 503 burials definitely identifiable as to sex (children and adults) at Indian Knoll, 14 of the 283 males (4.9 per cent) had large marine shell items in association, while 5 of the 220 females (2.3 per cent) were so accompanied. (If one were to assume that all the items from Indian Knoll were marine shell in Table 3, the respective figures would be 17 [6.0 per cent] for males and 8 [3.6 per cent] for females.) Or in respect to disc shell beads which have not been used in our previous

Table 4. Distribution of Shell Items, Value-scaled

MALES				FEMALES			
Site	*Burial No.*	*Age Group*	*Value Units*	*Site*	*Burial No.*	*Age Group*	*Value Units*
Barrett	1	YA	200	Ward	163	A	20
Barrett	44	YA	200	Ward	188	A	50
Barrett	47	YA	50	Kirkland	12	A	125
Barrett	100	YA	200	Carlson Annis	360	C	50
Barrett	116	YA	200	Chiggerville	43	A	150
Barrett	156	Ad.	160	Chiggerville	79	A	800
Barrett	381	YA	100	Chiggerville	73	A	25
Barrett	77	YA	30	Indian Knoll	237	YA	630
Barrett	215	YA	20	Indian Knoll	315	Ad.	215
Carlson Annis	146	YA	125	Indian Knoll	515	C	75
Carlson Annis	256	YA	10	Indian Knoll	696	YA	50
Read	1	YA	60	Indian Knoll	708	YA	30
Read	66	SA	150			*Total*	2,220
Chiggerville	25	J	100				
Chiggerville	63	A	50				
Indian Knoll	55	YA	50				
Indian Knoll	123	SA	25				
Indian Knoll	236	Ad.	200				
Indian Knoll	310	YA	100				
Indian Knoll	395	Ad.	100				
Indian Knoll	439	C	200?				
Indian Knoll	561	YA	100?				
Indian Knoll	575	YA	50				
Indian Knoll	661	YA	50				
Indian Knoll	687	YA	75				
Indian Knoll	697	YA	25				
Indian Knoll	744	YA	50				
Indian Knoll	769	Ad.	200				
Indian Knoll	827	YA	25				
		Total	2,855				

computations, at Indian Knoll 48 of the 283 males (16.6 per cent) were associated with these artifacts, contrasting with the 26 females out of 229 (11.8 per cent).

There are also distinctions between the sexes (children and adults) in other respects. Again using only burials definitely identified as to sex, males tend to be associated with the largest items such as gorgets (27 of the 30) and cups (3+ of the 4+). Males are also exclusively linked to items such as conch columella and tusk-shaped pendants, while the items unique to older females include conch earplugs and shell discs. A preponderance of the tubular shell beads (137 of the 149) also occurred with female burials. The only items divided about equally between the sexes were the triangular and strip pendants, with 19 of the 35 associated with males.

Similar procedures can be adopted for creating an arbitrary value scale for copper artifacts. However, since there is no way of correlating the marine shell and copper scales, the ranking units for copper will be designated as C-units.

200 C-units—Expanded-center gorgets
100 C-units—Small ornaments
50 C-units—Awls, pins, and needles
25 C-units—Large copper beads
10 C-units—Small copper beads

The arbitrariness of the scale must again be emphasized, since the necessary research for determining actual quantities of copper in the artifacts and the amount of labor involved in their manufacture has not been performed.

Before continuing our discussion of copper artifacts from the sites of the Indian Knoll Culture, we must pause to examine problems recently raised by Rolingson and Schwartz (1966) in their discussion of copper in Kentucky sites. First of all, let us mark the notable differences between the types of copper artifacts associated with the Indian Knoll sites and those of northern cultures such as Old Copper and Frontenac. At the latter sites, utilitarian implements predominate, while at the former, ornaments constitute 69 per cent of the thirteen copper artifacts from sites along the Green River. (The percentage may be even higher if the two pins from Barrett are actually ornaments rather than items of utilitarian function.) Even in the nearby drainage of the Tradewater River, where sites such as Morris (Rolingson and Schwartz, 1966) and Parrish (Rolingson and Schwartz, 1966; Webb, 1951) produce copper, the emphasis on ornaments is noticeable, with three copper gorgets and three sheet copper fragments having been reported from Morris and a copper pin from Parrish. Although the relationship of these latter very multi-component sites to the Indian Knoll Culture is obscure, the occurrence of the expanded-center copper gorgets at the Morris Site on the Tradewater River and the Barrett and Indian Knoll sites on the Green River is interesting, since to the best of our knowledge this copper artifact is unknown outside of the lower Ohio Valley and its environs. In addition to these and other examples reported by Rolingson and Schwartz (1966) for that area, another gorget of the same style is present in the Peithmann Collection in The Museum of Southern Illinois University. Little is known about the provenience of this specimen, a surface find, but it is from the drainage of the Big Muddy River, a tributary of the Mississippi, which joins that river not far above its confluence with the Ohio. Thus, the copper artifacts that we are discussing consist of items that relate primarily to the supra-subsistence sphere and include a gorget type that is very limited spatially in its distribution.

Rolingson and Schwartz remark on the restricted distribution pattern, but conclude that a local origin for the gorgets is doubtful. The objects suggest sufficient leisure for their manufacture, leisure time which should also be evident in other ways at the sites. The context in which ceremonial copper objects are found in Middle Woodland also suggests differentiations in social rank, again not otherwise manifest in the Green River region. Copper, in an unworked state, available through trade, has not been found in western Kentucky sites. These factors, then, suggest that the copper gorgets were trade items (1966, p. 90).

The final conclusion does not necessarily follow. First of all, there is no anthropological principle which permits the interpretation of the type and degree of cultural productivity as a direct function of leisure time. A successful Tiwi elder may produce elaborate grave posts and intricately crafted songs and dances, but these and the remaining assignments of his leisure time will produce little and leave less to mark the choices that he has made in such expenditures for supra-subsistence activities. Within the statement of the authors there is a reflection of the myth current among archeologists that leisure time is not available in quantity to primitive hunters and gatherers, and the corollary that once leisure time is available to human groups, an inexorable advance toward the complex behavior of the urbanized elements of the Old World *oikoumene* is inevitable. The essential difference between hunters and gatherers and sedentary cultivators is in the pattern of availability of the leisure time, not its presence or absence. Thus, hunters and gatherers may have their leisure available in smaller, less predictable, discontinuous units than would be the case in sedentary societies, but we suspect that there would have been quite a sufficiency of leisure time to the Indian Knoll craftsmen in their richly endowed environment for producing some dozen or so copper artifacts, without, however, expecting them to use their leisure time in a much more extravagant fashion than the craftsmen of the Old Copper Culture, who may be lauded for their industriousness in hammering copper, but who seem to have lacked any spectacular initiative in other areas of cultural florescence.

In respect to the second proposition in the argument of the authors, both the relevance and the documentation are obscure. That is, the positing of differences of social rank for individuals in Middle Woodland societies elsewhere, and the lack thereof for individuals in the Archaic Green River societies in general upon the basis of artifact associations depends upon gratuitous assumptions. Both Woodland burials in the Midwest and late Archaic burials in the Green River Valley differ widely in the quantity and quality of grave goods (including copper artifacts) that are associated with individual burials. If the assumption is to be made that copious quantities and/or particular types of grave goods indicate social ranking in Woodland cultures, then the same assumption must be extended to Archaic cultures. But since no rigorous criteria have been defined for evaluating from archeological data the significance of differentials deriving from statuses within an egalitarian system and differentials deriving from statuses within a ranked system, it would be best to drop the entire subject until archeologists are prepared to cope with it effectively and objectively.

Anent the third proposition in the statement, if raw copper is a valued and rare import, it is not particularly surprising that it is missing as an element of the Kentucky middens. The quantity of raw diamonds in the New York City dumps probably does not warrant the screening of these cultural residues.

Finally, we must comment on the context of copper at both the Morris and Parrish sites, since the artifacts were recovered from general midden situations rather than special contexts, and assignment to a specific culture is difficult. Does the variation in context at these sites invalidate our conclusions about the special context of copper in sites of the Indian Knoll Culture? First of all we shall observe that neither site is particularly notable for the number of burials removed, there being 28 at Morris and 133 at Parrish, and preservation of burials and artifacts made from organic materials was not at all good at Parrish. In view of the very considerable inventory of lithic Archaic artifacts at each site, there would seem to be a deficiency of burials if the numbers present in sites of the Indian Knoll Culture, where preservation of bone and other organic materials is good, are any indication. Nor is it possible to tell how many of the twenty-eight burials at Morris belong with the sizeable Woodland and Mississippian occupations. We conclude that the evidence is such that the context of copper in the Tradewater River sites neither confirms nor denies our assignment of special value to copper, since the chances for inadequate preservation and later disturbance of Archaic burials at Morris and Parrish are such that it is impossible to reach any conclusion as to whether the copper was or was not originally present in special context.

Of considerable importance is the observation by Rolingson and Schwartz (1966) that the Archaic associations of at least the expanded-center copper gorget with Burial 1 at the Barrett Site are clear. We shall add that the depths of other burials with copper artifacts at Barrett (for example, Burial 43) and Indian Knoll (for example, Burial 248) and the sparseness of later components at these sites would also point to the probability that these burials pertain to one of the Archaic components at these sites. However, Rolingson and Schwartz conclude from the similarities of the Archaic copper gorgets to counterparts in stone in Early and Middle Woodland cultures, the absence of similar ornaments in other Archaic sites in eastern North America, and the lack of experimental prototypes in the sites of the Green River Valley, that the gorgets are "potentially Woodland objects in Archaic burials . . . [and that] . . . an Archaic economy may have continued to live in the Green River region of Kentucky after the development of a Woodland subsistence in surrounding areas" (1966, p. 91). For a number of reasons, we are disinclined to accept the content of this analysis. First of all, we are not particularly impressed with the similarity of the copper gorgets to the expanded-center stone gorgets of the Adena or Scioto Traditions. As a second point, it is questionable that experimental prototypes would be necessary. That is, precisely how much skill is needed to hammer and anneal copper into a simple geometric shape once the basic technique is known, particularly given both the possibility of infinite re-hammering on initially unsatisfactory attempts and the fact that Indian Knoll craftsmen were accustomed to handling reasonably sophisticated geometric shapes in stone and shell? (Or, for that matter, one might ask where are the prototypes of the stone-expanded center gorgets of the Adena Tradition, if prototypes are an important consideration—or the prototypes of most prehistoric styles in eastern North America, Archaic or Woodland?) As a third point, while the association of the expanded-center copper gorget can be demonstrated for the Archaic Indian Knoll Culture, no such association can be shown for any Early or Middle Woodland culture in the Midwest or any other part of eastern North America. We should be forced to conclude that if they were being manufactured by Woodland groups, they were being produced as export items to satisfy the tastes in copper artifacts of their still culturally "Archaic" neighbors. And, finally, no matter how poor the dating of the Indian Knoll sites may be, there are certainly no carbon-14 dates from high or low in the middens that point to contemporaneity of the Indian Knoll Culture with the advent or subsequent duration of any of the known Woodland cultures of the Midwest. Our conclusions are that the expanded-center gorgets (and possibly the other copper artifacts as well) were made by the Archaic craftsmen of the second or third millennium B.C. for the use of their Archaic contemporaries, and that they were produced in the environs of the lower Ohio Valley.

To return to our basic theme, it must be observed that the dearth of copper artifacts in the Indian Knoll sites (see Table 10) precludes the formation of any very definite conclusions about the context of copper within the Indian Knoll population. Only three individuals are identified as to sex, all from Barrett, where males are associated with copper ornaments having a total rating of 300 C-units and a single female with a needle rating at 50 C-units. Men *may* have had control of the bulk of the copper, particularly ornaments, while women *may* have been limited to lesser quantities and utilitarian implements, but the foregoing data are definitely inadequate for reaching a firm conclusion.

Another type of data can be treated somewhat more extensively, namely the age groups with which copper appeared (see Table 5). Fifty per cent of all copper artifacts are seen to belong with the non-productive, pre-adolescent portion of the population, as well as 45 per cent of the value units. It seems unlikely that the association with the former group can be on the basis of personal activities or contributions to the welfare of the group through economic endeavors on an adequate

Table 5. Copper Artifact Appearance

Age Group	*No. of Items*	*C-units*	*Type*
New born (0)	0	0	—
Infants (2)	3	300	Ornaments
Children (2)	2	200	Ornaments
Adolescents (1)	1	50	Utility tools
Adults (5)	4	550	Ornaments and Utility tools

scale. A more likely explanation would be that the association reflects ascribed status, whether that status be engendered by psychological factors, sociological factors or a combination of the two.

A similar examination of age groups for large marine shell artifacts gives the results shown in Table 6.

Table 6. Shell Appearance

Age Group	*No. of Items*	*Value Units*	*Types*
Newborn (4)	16	205	Pendants, tubular beads
Infants (21)	80+	1410+	Pendants, tubular beads, discs, earplugs, gorgets, atlatl weights, cups?
Children (13)	89+	1420+	Pendants, tubular beads, gorgets, earplugs, cups?
Adolescents (12)	76+	1270+	Pendants, tubular beads, gorgets, earplugs, discs, columella, cups
Adults (34)	195	3975	Pendants, tubular beads, gorgets, atlatl weights, whole shells, cups

Again, the pre-adolescent group is seen to be associated with a very sizeable quantity of marine shell, having had placed with them some 40.6 per cent of the total items, or 36.6 per cent of the value units attributed to the shell items. Actually, the percentages are low, since minimal counts and value units are used for four infants, one child, and two adolescents, the exact counts not being given, and three juveniles associated with four items and 150-point value units are not included because of the inadequacy of age-group assignment.

The types of artifacts associated with the various age groups tend to be very similar, although earplugs tend to occur predominantly with infants and children, ten of the thirteen examples being with this latter group, the remaining three with adolescents. No examples are known with adults. On the other hand, conch shell cups may be entirely an adult item, with the two specimens designated by the inadequate description "conch shell" as possibilities reflecting the association of cups with infants and children.

Data on disc-shell beads at Indian Knoll, the only site with adequate counts for age groups, differ somewhat from the preceding pattern, but again show that pre-adolescents were also receiving their share of these artifacts.

Table 7. Disc-shell Bead Appearance

Age Group		*Age Group in Population (Percentage)*	*Age Group with Beads (Percentage)*	*Total Beads (Percentage)*	*Bead Count**
Newborn	(12)	6.5	21.8	1.6	296
Infants	(46)	24.7	22.0	22.9	4223
Children	(13)	8.9	17.3	6.8	1252
Adolescents	(14)	6.1	26.9	33.9	6241
Adults	(58)	53.4	12.7	34.6	6366
Total	(143)	99.6	100.7	99.8	18378

*Note the gross disparity between totals derived here from burial associations and the summary tabulations of artifacts, for Indian Knoll in Webb's (1946) report.

While only a relatively small proportion of each age group was provided with disc-shell beads, adolescents and pre-adolescents were more frequently so equipped than adults, and about a third of all beads (31.3 per cent) were with the pre-adolescents.

All of the quantitative data on copper, large shell artifacts, and disc-shell beads point to the same obvious fact. Wealth as expressed in these items was being removed constantly from the society through placement with members of age groups who during their life span could not have contributed effectively to its procurement, hence producing a constant deficit that would have to be met through the activities of productive members of the society above and beyond their own personal requirements. This point will become more significant when we examine the cyclical patterns of shell accumulation and diminution in the last section of this paper.

For comparative purposes, one might examine the roughly contemporaneous Frontenac Culture of New York (Ritchie, 1945). Conch shell is not particularly plentiful at Frontenac, but some fourteen items of conch are recorded with burials at this site, all of which are the burials of children, adolescents, or adult females, with shell being conspicuously absent from adult male burials. Six of the fourteen shell artifacts (a container, a piece of worked shell, and four circular, perforated pendants) are associated with adult females, one with an adolescent (pendant), and seven with children (all pendants). In terms of the rating system which we have been using, adult females are associated with 215 of the 415 units at the site, or 51.8 per cent; adolescents with 25 units, or 6 per cent; and children with 175 units, or 42.2 per cent. (There is also an infant with an oyster shell pendant which has not been included in the calculations.) Frontenac and Indian Knoll are alike in the proportion of imported marine shell that is provided for the pre-adolescent burials, but are quite different in the apparent exclusion of males from association with such *Beigaben* at Frontenac. Of course, such an exclusion does not mean that males played no role in the control of the resource, since the public display of the ornaments often may be linked to females, the procurement and distribution to males, who apparently receive their satisfactions from the control of wealth, with females serving as the observable symbols of that wealth—a procedure not without parallels in contemporary American society.

Before attempting a final assessment of the significance of the preceding data, it might be well to consider for the Indian Knoll Culture other types of artifacts in burial context to see if further light can be thrown on possible similarities and differences in status and role of the respective sexes.

To summarize—and disregarding unique artifacts—the only artifacts solely associated with males definitely identified as to sex were axes, cannon bone awls, fish hooks, groundhog incisors, antler drifts, flakers, antler chisels, and animal bones and jaws of several species (raccoon, weasel, wolf, deer, squirrel, groundhog, fishes, snake, drumfish, etc.). Such a list indicates the association of woodworking with males (axes and, possibly, groundhog incisors); at least one type of fishing (fishhooks); certain manufacturing operations (cannon bone awls); flint working (flakers and antler drifts); and the possession of certain types of medicine bag contents (animal bones and jaws) assuming that Webb (1950) was correct in his interpretation of these items.

Predominantly in male association, but also found with females, were weapons or components thereof (projectile points, atlatl weights, atlatl hooks and handles); general utility artifacts (knives, scrapers); fabricating and processing tools (drills, various types of bone awls); certain ornaments (bone hairpins); and items of uncertain function such as bone pins. Generally speaking, men had a greater variety of artifacts in association, with particular concentrations of fabricating and processing tools.

For females, the only definitely linked items were domestic equipment (nutting stones), certain ornaments (bone beads), and an item of fabricating and processing equipment (gravers). Pestles (domestic equipment) were predominantly associated with females.

It should be noted that the overlap in sex association, barring faulty sexual identification, may be the result of inadequate functional identification or misinterpretation of context. All too often all stemmed objects with pointed blades are classified as projectile points, without distinguishing through preparation and use characteristics those stemmed objects that are either prepared as knives or have been used as knives. Or, again, the significance of a pestle may be ambiguous. That is, this item might be included with a male without implying that the association indicates the grinding of seeds or other foods on his part. The inclusion of a "mint" copy might just as well indicate that the association was based upon his role in the manufacture of these items, or in the instance of a heavily battered specimen, his utilization of an artifact that has many of the necessary characteristics of a hammerstone for the latter purpose, rather than as a grinding implement. In short, our observations on context and functional characteristics must be far more precise than they have generally been in the past if we are to use individual classes of artifacts for the analysis of variation of status and role between the two sexes.

But even with such possible defects in the data, the preceding differences point to little more than expectable differences in roles between the sexes in a hunting and gathering society.

Another and rather curious associational pattern involves the atlatl. As Webb (1946, p. 330) points out, a very considerable number of females are found with atlatl parts. Even using only adults, and those definitely identified as to sex, ten (seven at Indian Knoll, one at Chiggerville, one at Ward, and one at Barrett) of the 54 burials so identified with atlatl parts were those of females. A figure of 18 per cent is rather surprising for an item of equipment that one would expect to be basically an item of male equipment in a hunting and gathering society.

Webb (1946, p. 331) rejects the contention that the atlatl is a purely ceremonial implement, hence sometimes associated with females because of their role in ceremonial activities, on the grounds that there are too many examples showing extensive wear from use, numerous repaired atlatl components, and far too many fragmentary remains in the middens. Of course establishing that the atlatl is a utility implement does not prove that all atlatls were functionally so identified within the culture, and the earlier analysis in this paper of the association patterns of the atlatl indicated that there are some peculiarities about the distribution of the atlatl when contrasted with other utilitarian items. It would be interesting to learn what the use characteristics of the atlatl parts with females may have been, and if there are significant differences in respect to those with males.

But we join Webb in lacking enthusiasm for the interpretation of the atlatl as a ceremonial item associated with females. Nor are we quite willing to evoke a platoon of Amazons, or a succession of Boadiceas defending the Green River mussel beds against the onslaught of intruders, although history is legion with militant females who acquitted themselves well in combat.

Possibly the association relates to the transfer of the contents of a corporate estate, and has nothing directly to do with the sex of the individual per se. Or perhaps the answer is simply that some women were hunters of one type of game or another.

But none of these speculations can be seen as having any particular merit, there being no evidence permitting substantiation one way or the other. Of course, re-analysis of the Indian Knoll sites might provide data suitable for eliminating some possibilities, and favoring others. But at the moment, all that can be concluded is that the roles of females overlapped those of males in some way, leading to occasional association with the former of a weapon that one would expect a priori to be a symbol of male activities.

On the other hand, females do show rather high percentages in respect to certain types of ceremonial equipment and burial practices. For example at Indian Knoll, the percentages given in Table 8 were noted, including in the samples all individuals definitely or tentatively identified as to sex.

Table 8. Ceremonial Equipment Appearance and Burial Practices

	Males (*Percentage*)	*Females* (*Percentage*)
*Ceremonial Equipment:**		
Medicine bags	60	40
Turtle shell rattles	50	50
Flutes	50	50
Burial Practices:		
With grave goods	25.7	30.3
Per cent of all burials with red ocher	37	63
Per cent of all burials with dog burials	67	33

*The rationale for assigning these items to ceremonial equipment has been discussed at length in Winters, 1968.

It seems obvious that females were receiving equal, or even greater attention than males with respect to certain aspects of burial customs, and that for some reason they were often associated with just as much ceremonial equipment as males, with the equipment being identical for each sex. We refuse to derive any very specific conclusions from such data, our only purpose at the moment being to furnish some basis for speculating that the females of the Indian Knoll culture were more than chattels, since they shared access with males to certain types of equipment best related to roles connected with the supernatural, and were accorded at least as much attention in death as the males, even though an individual male might surpass any female in total quantity of grave goods.

The point might be further emphasized by noting in Table 9 the percentages of total burials with grave goods for each site, correcting where possible for intrusive burials. (We are unable to compute percentages of males and females for this item for the other sites because of lack of data.)

Table 9. Burials with Grave Goods as Percentage of Total Burials

Sites	*Percentage*
Ward	12.7
Barrett	25.1
Butterfield	10.5
Kirkland	5.7
Chiggerville	30.7
Indian Knoll	30.8
Read	30.8
Carlson Annis	44.6

The reasons for the variability are undoubtedly complex but may relate in part to function in the settlement system. The highest percentage are from settlements and base camps, the lowest, from Kirkland, a hunting camp. One can speculate that there might have been differential treatment of the dead, depending upon the circumstance and place of death. That is, if the Indian Knoll sample is at all representative, both males and females with grave goods represent some small, specially selected segment of the population, whatever the basis for selection may have been. Hence, we conclude that *some* females occupied special statuses of one sort or another, as did *some* males, and that there was a considerable sharing of the artifacts symbolic of those statuses. (A psychological explanation of differentials in grief and the outward expression of that grief hardly seems adequate to explain the consistently low selection rate for either sex.)

Throughout the preceding discussion, the term *association* has been used without any implication that the placement of artifacts necessarily means ownership by the deceased. Ethnohistoric examples point out the perils attendant upon any such assumption. Lescarbot (in Slotkin and Schmitt, 1949), states that "after they have laid the dead to rest, every one makes him a present of the best thing he has. Some cover him with skins of beavers, of otters, and other beasts: others present him with bows, arrows, quivers, knives, matachias, and other things."

But we do assume that grave goods represent appropriate equipment for the deceased in terms of the norms of the culture, and thus in general reflect concepts of a society as they pertain to the statuses and roles of the two sexes and the various age groups, regardless of the idiosyncratic behavior of any individual member of the society. And it is with this interpretation of the significance of grave goods that we now summarize our conclusions about the distribution patterns of Class III artifacts from the preceding data, granting that such "conclusions" in the present formulation are very tentative, or even very nebulous, at best: (1) Males are associated with the largest conch artifacts and, hence, may have controlled the essential raw materials that constituted the "capital" for the manufacture of the various categories of conch artifacts. (2) There was a continuous flow of such tranformed capital to both females, who as individuals could possess more wealth than males, and to non-productive, preadolescent members of the society. (Conjectures as to the mechanisms of such transfers can run the gamut of psychological and sociological explanations, there being no clear indication from the archeological data of how such distribution was effected.) (3) There was a constant drain of wealth from the society through burial practices, with a continuing need for replacement of the items in question, and this drain was accelerated by the assignment of the special Class III artifacts to the newborn, infants, and children, who were certainly unable to contribute towards a replenishment of the supply, and probably by the assignment of the same items to females, whose productivity was along lines other than the procurement and transformation of such basic raw materials as marine shell and copper. (4) Only a very small proportion of the population was tangibly associated with the special artifacts, perhaps implying differentials within the society in respect to the distribution of wealth among the living. Such a statement carries with it no implication that the society was ranked in rigid divisions, since in other respects the archeological data suggest that the population was socially homogeneous and without great differentials in the basic way of life of the individuals composing the population.

Moreover, there is a subsidiary observation that may be derived from the data. Prior to the appearance of cultures such as Indian Knoll, there is little indication, if any, of specialized craft activities in the Midwest. But in view of the concentration of shell in the hands of a small segment of the Indian Knoll population, we might assume that the working of shell was also concentrated within the same population segment, and that we have during late Archaic times the beginnings of craft specialization that apparently became important during Woodland times. The association of a shell-working kit with burial 610, an infant, indicates that the working of at least some of the shell was taking place within the Indian Knoll Culture, no matter how much may have been imported as finished products.

Up to this point, a synchronic approach has been followed, with the intention of interpreting general patterns within the Indian Knoll Culture, rather than variations within the individual settlement system units or through time. The inadequacies of the published data prohibit the consideration of inter-unit variation on any adequate level, but it is possible to consider the problem of change through time within individual sites with the aid of burial records and the limited reporting of stratigraphic units from Carlson Annis and Read.

On the graphs shown as Figures 1 through 3, the following information was plotted:

1. A curve designed to represent population trends based upon the

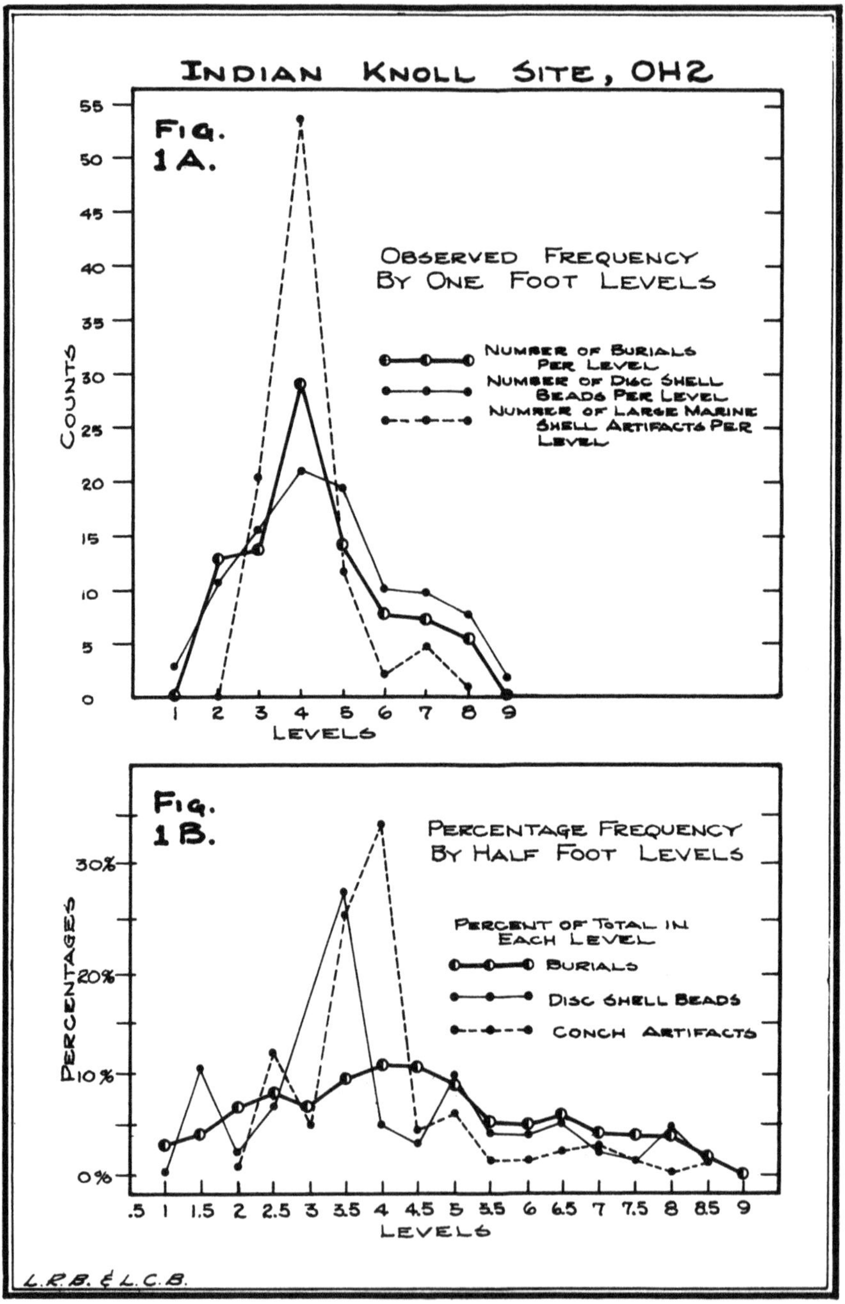

Figure 1. Indian Knoll Site Burials.

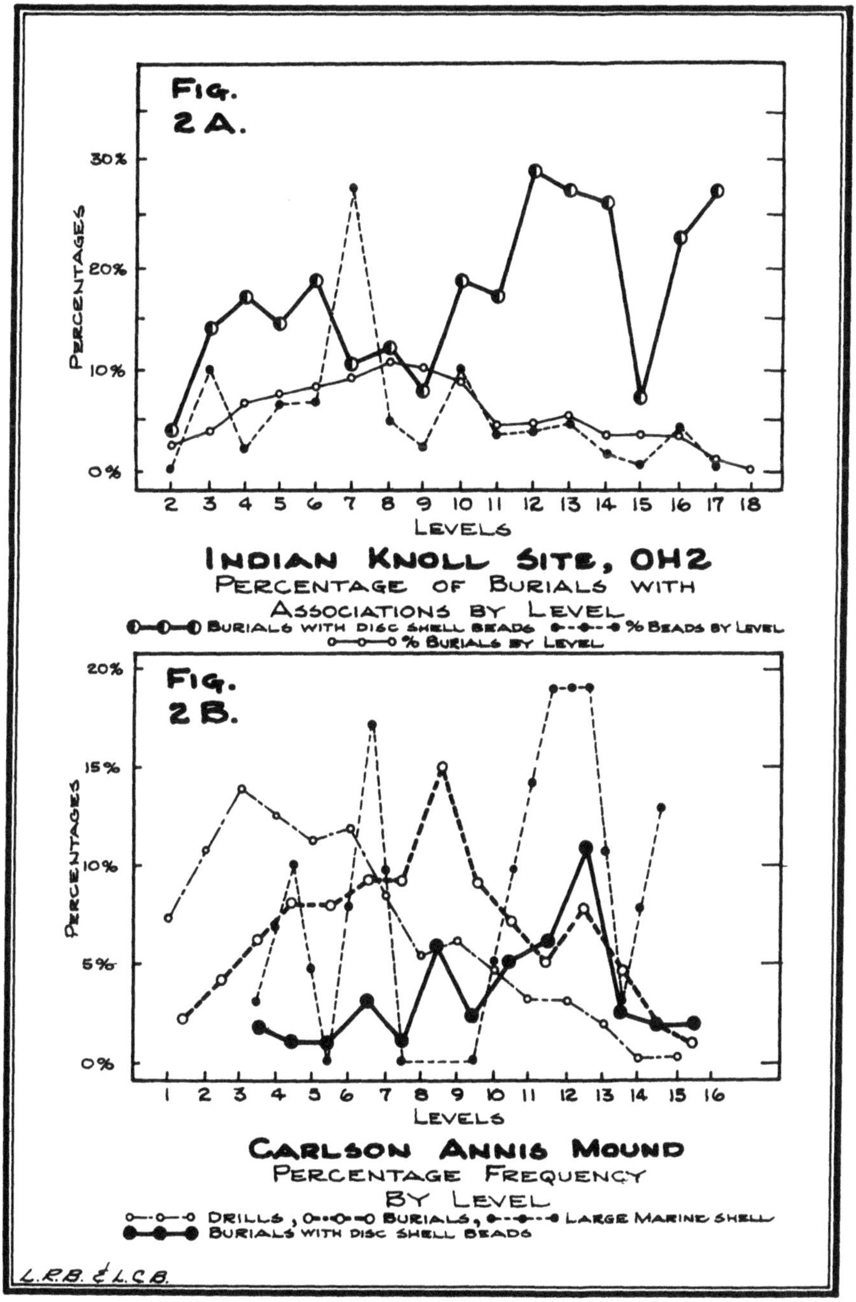

Figure 2. Graphs of studied grave goods.

numbers of burials per 0.5-ft. level. The rationale here was simply that, other things being equal, the number of burials should be a function of the population size at any given time. It might be argued that the use of half-foot levels would lead to a distortion of population figures through variation in the depth of the burial pits themselves, the actual point of pit origin not being stated in the reports, only the depth below surface of the bottom of the pit. We do not consider the foregoing a particularly crucial problem. Middens of the Midwestern shell mound type tend to build up through fairly uniform accretion over their expanse, although there may be more rapid accretion on the marginal slopes where trash seems to have accumulated in considerable bulk. And Archaic burial pits tend to be both small and quite shallow. While Webb does not give detailed information on dimensions of burial pits in his publications, those reported for Indian Knoll (1946, p. 137) range from 0.5 to 1.2 feet in depth, with diameters from 2.1 to 3.1 feet. At Ward (1940, p. 89) the depth of only one pit is mentioned, the figure given being 0.5 ft. The overwhelming predominance of tightly flexed burials, as opposed to extended burials, is also commented on by Webb several times. Our own experience with such burials in shell middens of the Wabash Valley has been that the burial pits are quite small both in diameter and depth, rarely being larger than the absolutely minimal cavity needed for jamming the tightly flexed remains into the ground. The illustrations in the various Indian Knoll reports indicate similarly minimal pits. Hence, we doubt that there was any great variation in pit depths, and shall assume that depths ranging from 0.5 to 1.2 ft. would be quite representative of the pits in general, with most of them being nearer the latter figure. While the results shown on the graphs from the plotting of depths of the bottoms of pits cannot be as satisfactory as curves based upon the depth of pit origin, the amount of error is probably not sufficient to vitiate the purposes of the graph.

2. Percentages of total large shell artifacts (Table 3) by 0.5-ft. levels.

3. The percentages of total disc shell beads, or entire units of beads for those sites where individual counts are not available, by 0.5-ft. levels.

4. Percentages of individuals associated with disc shell beads at Carlson Annis and Indian Knoll per 0.5-ft. level.

5. As a control device for Carlson Annis and Read, the only sites for which the necessary information is available, the percentages of the total of a midden-associated utility artifact by 0.5-ft. levels.

Initially, we attempted to use one-foot levels, as shown in Fig. 1A. The resulting graph simply showed normal curves for all items plotted for Indian Knoll. But, assuming a 500-year span for the accumulation of the larger Indian Knoll Culture middens, such units would be equivalent to an approximate time span of a hundred years, an interval that might be much too great to show more than the grosser types of variation in cultural activities as manifested in artifactual remains, or events of a catastrophic nature with long-enduring results. Subsequent graphs using half-foot levels seem to indicate that the foregoing misgivings were correct. While the curves for population continued to approach normal curves, the graphs for shell artifacts showed wide swings above and below the population curves. Utility artifacts, on the other hand, tended to conform to the population curve, as in the case of bone awls at Read, or to show a constant and continuous rise, as in the case of drills at Carlson Annis. Thus, although the quantitative data used in plotting the frequencies of shell artifacts are derived from the quantities of shell in association with the burials used for the population curve, there is a pattern of variation that does not conform closely to the population curve itself or to the occurrence of utility artifacts in the middens. In other words, the curves derived for shell artifacts are not solely the function of fluctuations in the population occupying the site, but instead appear as a cyclical series of maxima and minima that may vary in a fashion often directly opposite to the trend of the population curve.

The interpretation of the significance of the shell curves is difficult. Barring the imposition of external factors that would lead to a regularly recurring reduction in the procurement of shell in the society, a phenomenon for which we are at present unable to provide even conjectures, the source of the fluctuations might best be sought within the society itself. One possibility might be the occurrence of special activities at century intervals, with an accompanying demand for imported marine shell. But such a conjecture would demand that two out of three, or three out of four, generations concern themselves with the preparations or the aftermath of an event carried to its fulfillment by a third or fourth. Within a semi-sedentary society, operating presumably only on oral tradition, such repetitive long-range planning does not seem to provide a very satisfactory basis even for conjectural explanation.

Perhaps a more satisfactory answer can be found in generational patterning. Assuming a range of constantly present activities with which marine shell is associated, either in connection with the realms of the living or of the dead, we might assume a two-generation span of intensive accumulation of sufficient quantities of marine shell to serve the general needs of the society, followed by the gradual depletion of the reserves over a two-generation period to the point that renewed intensive accumulation must begin again. We assume, of course, that some shell was being procured at all times from foreign sources, whatever the procurement mechanisms may have been, but that the variation indicated by the shell curves reflects the rate of accumulation, not discrete phases of acquisition and non-acquisition. A complete breaking off of procurement for protracted intervals would hardly permit a relatively even pattern of continuous variation.

Another consistent pattern is found in the relative positions of the crests of the curves for large shell and disc-shell beads, the crest for the latter tending to lag behind that of the former. Here the explanation may be

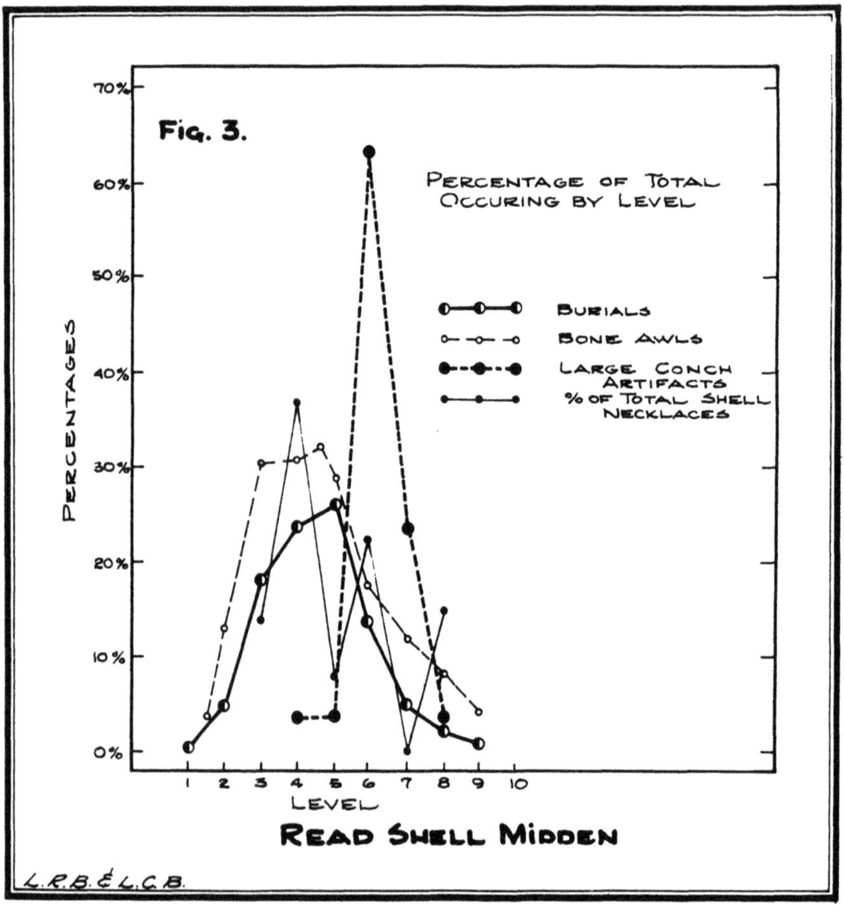

Figure 3. Read Shell Midden, graph of studied materials.

simply that the large shell items were manufactured rather quickly after the importation of the basic raw materials, there probably being rather little labor connected with the completion of the finished product, while the shell beads, the production of which would have necessitated the expenditure of a considerable amount of labor in their shaping, perforating, and grinding, were being manufactured over a somewhat longer time from basic raw materials and perhaps from broken examples of the larger conch artifacts as these became available.

A final point to be made about the charts is that as Figures 2A and 2B show, albeit Figure 2A less clearly, there seems to have been a noticeable decrease through time in the number of burials associated with disc-shell beads, primarily necklaces, as the proportional quantities of the beads themselves rose. In other words, fewer and fewer people seem to have controlled more and more of the shell beads through time. Control of this form of wealth may well have been increasingly concentrated in the hands of a smaller segment of the population—perhaps a prehistoric example of the "rich get richer, the poor get poorer" or "he who has gets" pattern of economic behavior.

But returning to the problem of the fluctuations in shell procurement, it might be well to examine how such a system might relate to the world beyond the narrow confines of the Indian Knoll Culture in the Green River and Ohio valleys.

First of all, what are the actual sources of the imported shell? They are all concentrated in the southeastern coastal areas of the United States, with distribution patterns and other pertinent data as follows according to Abbott (1954) and other authors:

Pleuroploca gigantea Kiener[1] (*Fasciolaria gigantea* Kiener)—North Carolina to both sides of Florida. Found in shallow water. Normally about a foot in length, but may be as large as two feet.

Prunum apicinum Menke (*Marginella apicinum Menke*)—North Carolina to Florida, the Gulf States and the West Indies. A shallow water species.

Busycon perversum Linne—Both sides of central Florida. Four to eight inches in length. Occur in four to ten fathoms of water. Hence are difficult to obtain, although they may be washed onto beaches by storms.

Olivella spp. Species not reported for Indian Knoll sites. Excluding the West Coast species, the range of the several species in the genus is from North Carolina to the West Indies, with two species localized to lower Florida and adjacent islands.

It is not possible to pinpoint the locus from which the shells derived, although if they were being obtained from a single source, central Florida

[1] Taxonomic designation in current usage given first, with obsolete form used in the reports on the Indian Knoll Culture following in parentheses.

would have to have been the area, *Busycon perversum* being obtainable only within that limited range. But even granting that each species was obtained from its nearest possible source, none of the species could have come from locations closer than six hundred miles by the most direct overland route, and some would have had to have been derived from sources as far away as 750 miles. Actual transportation routes, whether by land or water, or both, must have been much longer.

How then could the shells have been introduced into the sites of the Indian Knoll Culture? Three major alternatives (and combinations thereof) present themselves:

1. The Indian Knoll peoples (or portions of the population) regularly left the Green River Valley and moved to coastal areas in the manner of known historic tribes in their seasonal rounds. The main objection to this proposal is that so far no sites attributable to the Indian Knoll Culture are known from the coastal areas, and one might well expect fairly sizeable middens to have accumulated during the some 500-year span that we think must be assigned to the Kentucky sites. Furthermore, one might also expect a rather more abundant range of marine species and other exotic materials in the Kentucky middens had this pattern of "transhumance" been a characteristic feature of the Indian Knoll cycle.

2. Trading relationships were maintained with neighboring groups who in turn received marine shells from their neighbors in a system that ultimately linked the Indian Knoll area with the coastal sources of supply. There are no basic theoretical objections to such a postulated exchange system, the minimal requirements being only a supply of items acceptable between groups for exchange and a basis for continuing reciprocity between trading partners so that the flow of goods is uninterrupted.

The existence of such trading systems is very well documented for other parts of the world. For example, the nomadic tribes of Australia maintain trade networks that distribute a number of commodities over large areas. The exchange of goods takes many forms, includes a wide variety of commodities and finished products, and is accompanied by short-term and long-term balancing of accounts between the participants in the exchange system. Movement of goods is not random, but follows well defined paths, usually along waterhole routes (Berndt and Berndt, 1964). The system is so effective that Kimberley pearl shell is distributed from one end of the continent to the other. Notably, in a ceremonial exchange system such as the *merbok*, trading partners in maintaining reciprocity with each other may have to accept things for which they have no use in order to keep the orderly flow of goods unimpeded.

Even in somewhat more sedentary societies, elaborate exchange systems are maintained in a similar fashion. Uberoi (1962) in his brilliant reanalysis of the kula ring has this to say, quoting in part from Fortes and Evans-Pritchard (1940);

> The islands of the kula ring are all "societies which lack centralized authority, administrative machinery, and constituted judicial institutions—in short which lack government—and in which there are no sharp differences of rank, status, or wealth," . . . The kula islands are all inhabited by small groups of people who make their living by use of simple tools. Technically expressed, the Massim have a rudimentary technology and a subsistence economy (p. 214).

That the Indian Knoll peoples possessed a settlement system, a subsistence base, and a level of technology sufficient for maintaining an exchange system in the fashion of the *merbok* or the kula ring seems beyond question. Whether they did so, and how they did so are other questions. The basic problem seems to be the nature of the commodities available to the Indian Knoll people for exchange. The Green River area is not particularly well endowed with natural resources that would lend themselves to a viable exchange system with their neighbors. Chert is present, but neighboring areas are well supplied with this raw material and the Indian Knoll cherts do not seem to have any special characteristics that would place them in the class of "luxury" cherts. Nor do the various sandstones, limestones, shells, and animal bones available to the Indian Knoll people seem to be likely raw materials for exchange.

A remote possibility is that in the manner of Australian trading partners, the neighbors of the Green River peoples were willing to accept items such as chert until they could be passed on to other groups in the trading network. But these latter people in the Midwest and Midsouth would also have had access to the same raw materials, so that there would have had to have been a prolonged series of exchanges of relatively worthless commodities for items of high value. And in the Australian system, acceptance of an inutile item seems to be based on the knowledge that it could be rapidly disposed of for some desired and useful item.

Possibly copper was being passed on by Indian Knoll traders. But the insignificant quantities in the Green River sites themselves (see Table 10) hardly support the suggestion that copper could have furnished a basis for the several centuries during which marine shell was being procured in considerable quantity. It is possible, of course, that copper was such a valuable item that a small amount would procure a large amount of shell.

A final conjecture is that the actual exchange system was based upon raw materials (pitch might be suggested as one commodity available to the Indian Knoll peoples from local sources) or upon finished products that have either gone unrecognized or have not been preserved in the archeological record.

Ultimately we reject this second method of procurement as an important factor in the importation of shell by the Indian Knoll peoples, although such an arrangement for an exchange involving marine shell from the Indian Knoll area and copper from the north seems a fairly good possibility. Our reasons for rejecting it in the case of neighbors to the south lie in the considerable and repetitive fluctuations in sites of the Indian Knoll Culture of the imported marine items. The very essence of a system based upon trading partners is the maintenance of regular and continuous exchange, and we doubt that satisfactory and regular relationships could have survived over several centuries of widely fluctuating shifts in demand so evident within the Indian Knoll Culture itelf.

A third possibility is that there were ties with a redistribution center which provided raw materials or finished products for a number of inland groups. Here the assumption would be that Indian Knollers were engaged in regular trading expeditions, with the intensity of the trading varying with the current demand. The significant flaw in such a proposal is that no such centers have as yet been identified for the third millennium B.C., although the Indian Knoll sites may in themselves have functioned as such centers for the Midwest.

Table 10. Copper Artifacts in Sites of the Indian Knoll Culture

Site	*Artifact*	*Depth in Ft.*	*Context*
Barrett	Expanded-center gorget	1.5	YA, Male burial 1
Barrett	Broken ornament	1.5	YA, Male burial 44
Barrett	Needle	1.2	YA, Female burial 6
Barrett	Pin	2.8	Ad, Female? burial 43
Barrett	Pin*	?	?
Carlson Annis	Bead	?	Midden
Carlson Annis	Double pointed awl	?	Midden
Indian Knoll	Oval pendants (2)	0.8	I, Male? burial 632
Indian Knoll	Spiraled end ornament	4.4	I, Male? burial 248
Indian Knoll	Ornament	?	C ? burial 64
Indian Knoll	Expanded center gorget	?	YA ? burial 103
Indian Knoll	Ornament	?	C ? burial 185

*In Webb and Haag (1947, p. 5), five burials with copper artifacts are reported, but burial tabulations record only four with copper.

As a conjecture, since we tend to favor this last proposal, we shall predict that such focal trading centers did exist, and that when they are discovered, they will share many characteristics with the Poverty Point site of the first millennium B.C. (Ford and Webb, 1956). Poverty Point has an array of imported raw materials, including copper (Great Lakes area?), cherts (Midwest, Arkansas, Missouri), steatite and chlorite schists (North Carolina), crystal quartz, novaculite, magnetite, and hematite (Arkansas), and sandstone (Mississippi). The various minerals that are so abundant in the Midwest apparently had a very different sort of value in the lower Mississippi Valley and the Gulf coastal plains where these resources are lacking.

Perhaps similar minerals were important in the chertless areas of the deep South long before Poverty Point became an important focus of exchange activities. (We doubt that the Poverty Point people could have obtained their raw materials over any length of time by actual mining operations in distant areas not under their control, and at least in the Midwest the areas from which their imported commodities were obtained were under the control of well-established groups long before the first millennium B.C.) If a number of groups were involved with such centers, the cyclical fluctuations of demand for any one trading group would not necessarily impair the functioning of the system itself.

Although we cannot go beyond the level of conjecture in analyzing how the Indian Knoll procurement system might have functioned, we can be sure that elements of a trading system existed, having rejected extensive and continuous population movements as an adequate explanation, and that marine shell and copper were being distributed over vast distances within eastern North America by the third millennium B.C. It remains to be demonstrated that cherts were an important commodity at that time, and that they were being distributed to the chertless areas of the South. But if such movement is demonstrable through future reconnaissance and excavation, a very important contribution will have been made to archeological theory, for from the Early Woodland cultures of the first millennium to Mississippian times, the basic triumvirate of trade items in the Midwest and adjacent areas consisted of chert, copper, and marine shells, particular types of the first item even being imported into areas abundantly supplied with chert. (For example, in early sites of the Havana Tradition such as Dickson and Pond in Fulton County, Illinois, 25 to 30 per cent of the cherts were imported from southern Illinois in spite of the fact that there were abundant supplies at the nearby Avon quarries.)

But regardless of the nebulous and conjectural nature of the previous arguments, we wish to emphasize here that there is good evidence that the vast trade network that links the various regional traditions of the Hopewellian Interaction Sphere (Caldwell, 1964) has its roots in the simpler exchange systems of late Archaic cultures such as Indian Knoll, regardless of whether chert was a component of the system at that early time or not.

Let it be emphasized in conclusion that we do not feel that we have *proved* anything in the present paper. Our objective has been in the nature of an exploratory operation in a search of techniques for the simplest sort of interpretation of the economic sphere of prehistoric societies and to indicate some hypotheses that suggest themselves. Only future work with data collected *specifically* for studies with such emphases over a wide geographic range of contemporaneous cultures can permit analyses refined to the point that they have a reasonably high degree of probability as to their conclusions.

References

ABBOTT, R. TUCKER. 1954. *American seashells.* New York: D. Van Nostrand.

BERNDT, ROLAND M., and CATHERINE H. BERNDT. 1964. *The world of the first Australians.* Chicago: University of Chicago Press.

CALDWELL, JOSEPH R. 1964. Interaction spheres in prehistory. In Joseph R. Caldwell and Robert R. Hall (Eds.), *Hopewellian studies;* Scientific Papers, Vol. 12. Springfield: Illinois State Museum.

FORD, JAMES A., and CLARENCE WEBB. 1956. Poverty point. *Archaeological Papers,* 46, Part I: New York: American Museum of Natural History.

FORTES, M., and E. E. EVANS-PRITCHARD. 1940. *African political systems.* London, New York: Oxford University Press.

HANSON, LEE H., JR. 1966. The Hardin Village site. *Studies in Anthropology,* No. 4. Lexington: University of Kentucky Press.

JOHNSON, FREDERICK (Assembler). 1951. *Radiocarbon dating.* Memoir no. 8. Salt Lake City: Society for American Archaeology.

LIBBY, WILLARD F. 1952. Chicago radiocarbon dates III. *Science,* 116(3025): 673–681.

MORGAN, LEWIS H. 1851. *League of the Ho-De-No-Sau-Nee or Iroquois.* Rochester, N.Y.: Sage and Bros.

RITCHIE, WILLIAM A. 1945. An early site in Cayuga County, New York. *Research Records,* no. 7, Rochester. Rochester: Museum of Arts and Sciences.

ROLINGSON, MARTHA ANN, and DOUGLAS W. SCHWARTZ. 1966. Late Paleo-Indian and Early Archaic manifestations in western Kentucky *Studies in Anthropology,* No. 3. Lexington: University of Kentucky Press.

ROUSE, IRVING. 1951. A survey of Indian River archaeology. *Florida Publications in Anthropology,* No. 44. New Haven: Yale University.

SLOTKIN, J. S., and KARL SCHMITT. 1949. Studies of wampum. *American Anthropologist,* 51(2): 223–236.

SPECK, FRANK G. 1919. The functions of wampum among the eastern Algonkian. Memoirs, Vol. 6, American Anthropological Association.

UBEROI, J. P. SINGH. 1962. *Politics of the Kula Ring.* Manchester: Manchester University Press.

WEBB, W. S. 1946. Indian Knoll. *Reports in Anthropology,* 4(3) Part 1: Lexington: University of Kentucky.

——. 1950a. The Carlson Annis Mound. *Reports in Anthropology,* 7(4): Lexington: University of Kentucky.

——. 1950b. The Read shell midden. *Reports in Anthropology,* 7(5): Lexington: University of Kentucky.

WEBB, W. S., and W. G. HAAG. 1939. The Chiggerville Site. *Reports in Anthropology,* 4(1): Lexington: University of Kentucky.

——. 1940. Cypress Creek villages. *Reports in Anthropology,* 4(2): Lexington: University of Kentucky.

——. 1947. Archaic sites in McLean County, Kentucky. *Reports in Anthropology,* 7(1): Lexington: University of Kentucky.

WINTERS, H. D. 1963. An archaeological survey of the Wabash Valley in Illinois. Reports of Investigations, No. 10. Springfield: Illinois State Museum.

——. 1968. *The Riverton culture*. Springfield: Illinois State Museum.

TWELVE

ROBERT WHALLON, JR.

Investigations of Late Prehistoric Social Organization in New York State

One of the important problems of archeology today is the understanding of the interrelationships between the stylistic behavior of material items and the structure of the sociocultural systems within which these items were produced and in which they found their function. Although this should be a problem of general anthropological interest, it is of particular concern to archeology, which is dependent for much of its interpretation on the analysis of style.

The hypothesis that measurable relationships exist between style and social organization is founded upon two basic assumptions. The first of these is that style has many aspects and levels of behavior which may be analytically distinguished and measured. Many of these aspects of style are not intuitively obvious, and each aspect of stylistic behavior may demand a separate and different method of analysis. The second assumption basic to this hypothesis is that the nature of the diffusion of stylistic ideas and practices, both within and between communities, will be determined by the nature of interaction among artisans. The aspect of style concerned, the rate of diffusion, and the directions and limits of diffusion will be conditioned by the kind, frequency, and channeling of interaction among the producers of the stylistic material. These patterns of interaction either define, or are the result of, the social organization of the community or region, depending on the theoretical view of social organization adopted.

The validity of the first assumption was demonstrated in a series of rigorous analyses by Kroeber and Richardson (1940). Realizing, thus, the complex and numerous aspects of behavior of even seemingly simple stylistic features, Kroeber later discussed the impossibility of giving a precise and simple definition of style (Kroeber, 1963, chap. 1). The meaning of style has so many ramifications that an attempt at a comprehensive definition must either arrive at a vague, theoretical statement or become involved in an extensive review of specific usages.

In developing methods for the analysis of style in archeological materials, therefore, it has generally proved useful and efficient to adopt a simple rule of thumb rather than to establish any rigorous definition. Initial selection of attributes for analysis is made largely intuitively, though often with consideration of experiences in previous analyses. If these attributes then exhibit systematic patterns of behavior which can be related to the influence of social, cultural, or individual factors rather than to factors of function or of the physical environment, both the attributes and their behavior are considered "stylistic."

The second basic assumption behind the hypothesis was first explicitly developed by Deetz in his study of stylistic behavior in Arikara ceramics (1965). It was hypothetically predicted that mutual associations among stylistic attributes would tend to be particularly developed on items produced by women in a community with a high rate of matrilocal residence. This pattern of stylistic behavior was theoretically attributed to the channeling of interaction among the female artisans within the lines of these matrilocal residence groups. Later, Longacre and then Hill utilized practically the same basic assumptions and hypothesis to predict and interpret another aspect of stylistic behavior which they demonstrated for the ceramics from two pueblo sites (Longacre, 1964; Longacre and Hill, this volume).

Data from New York

To further develop this approach to the analysis of archeological materials, and to extend the examination of its general validity, several aspects of stylistic behavior were studied in the ceramics from a series of late prehistoric sites in New York State.[1] The two latest sites in this series

[1] I would like to thank the many people who allowed me access to the collections and data on which these analyses are based. Dr. William A. Ritchie and Robert Funk of the New York State Museum and Science Service were most generous in permitting me to study materials both from previously published excavations, and from their current investigations. Charles F. Hayes, III, and Daniel Barber of the Rochester Museum of Arts and Sciences were very helpful in providing access to data and collections stored in the museum. Charles F. Wray of West Rush, New York, very kindly loaned his personal collection of pottery from the Factory Hollow site for the purposes of this study.

were fully developed Iroquois, which allowed an ethnographic control of interpretation at one end of the series.

The chronological sequence of these sites is presented in Figure 1. It will be seen that the majority of the sites fall within the Late Woodland Owasco period or culture. This is the best-known archeological period in New York. The documentation of most of these sites is extensive and is amply discussed and illustrated in several of Ritchie's general publications (1944, 1951, 1965) in addition to specific site reports. The materials from these sites have been preserved virtually intact in the Rochester Museum

FIGURE 1: Sites and Chronology

PERIOD	PHASE				
IROQUOIS		Factory Hollow			
		Garoga			
TRANSITIONAL	OAK HILL	Kelso	1390	100	(Y-1380)
	LATE or CASTLE CREEK	Bainbridge			
		Castle Creek	1435	100	(M-179)
			1196	200	(M-493)
OWASCO	MIDDLE or CANANDAIGUA	Bates	1298	200	(M-762)
			1190	100	(Y-1174)
			1125	100	(I-425)
		Canandaigua	1140	150	
		Morrow			
	EARLY or CARPENTER BROOK	Levanna			
		Maxon-Derby	1100	100	(Y-1173)
			1100	150	(M-1077)
		Round Top			
		Wickham			
		Carpenter Brook			

of Arts and Sciences and the New York State Museum. The quality and quantity of information on these sites provide an indispensable foundation for the types of analysis which we have undertaken.

This chronological sequence is not based on stratigraphic evidence, but is built on the seriation of pottery types. The Owasco pottery types and the basis of most of this seriation were established by Ritchie and MacNeish (1949) after long experience on the part of Ritchie in handling materials of this period. Transitional and Iroquois types were defined by MacNeish (1952). Some sites have since been added by Ritchie (1965), and two sites (Morrow and Round Top) have been here inserted from our analysis of the unpublished materials.

Chronologies built on seriation may sometimes be deceptive if functional or areal variations are confused with temporal change (cf. Brown and Freeman, 1964, pp. 166–67; Deetz and Dethlefsen, 1965), but the rapid typologic change in this roughly 400-year period and the general agreement of the radiocarbon dates with the seriation lend support to the argument that temporal change is the primary basis for this arrangement of sites. It is not our intention to reexamine these previous analyses which rely heavily on long and detailed experience, and we have accepted this chronology as a reliable and adequate background for other investigations of stylistic behavior.

The discrete stylistic elements exhibited by each well-preserved rim sherd were recorded for each site in terms of a consistent attribute list. Actually, two attribute lists were used. One was applicable to all of the Owasco and transitional ceramics, and although this list could have been modified for use with the Iroquois pottery, also, it was quicker and easier to devise a separate list. The use of two unconnected attribute lists was not inconsistent with our approach, since we were concerned at every step with stylistic behavior on a within-site level, and not with the tracing of style elements through time.

A number of different classes of attributes composed these lists. Certain morphologically variable features of the sherds were included, such as lip profile and collar shape. Vessel morphology was represented by lip orientation and neck form. Technique of design execution was maintained separate from the actual motifs present, and both technique and motif were recorded in terms of their location on the vessel.

As mentioned, the different aspects of the behavior of style are not yet well enough understood to allow us to say in detail what classes of attributes or what particular manner of structuring an attribute list will be most relevant and appropriate for any given problem and analysis. The best course therefore seemed to be to base our lists partly on previous models (for example, Deetz, 1965, pp. 46–49; McPherron, 1963) and partly on our own a priori judgments as to the significance and usefulness of various classes of "stylistic" attributes. In subsequent analyses it was occasionally apparent that these judgments had been mistaken.

A Stylistic Correlate of Between-Community Interaction

Our analyses began with a reevaluation of Deetz's (1965) hypotheses and analytic methods in terms of our data from New York. In the course of this reevaluation a technique was discovered for exposing an aspect of stylistic variation, not originally considered by Deetz, which seems to be a reflection of the intensity of intercommunity contacts.

The development, through relative isolation, of stylistic variations more characteristic of individual villages than of a total style horizon or ceramic type has previously been demonstrated (Cronin, 1962). These findings, however, were based on the comparative analysis of assemblages from several villages. The method we present here derives separate measures of interaction rate from the analysis of individual assemblages, expresses this measure as a single coefficient, and uses this coefficient for comparative purposes. Comparisons between any number of sites are thus greatly facilitated.

Deetz predicted that if women made the pottery, there would be a greater tendency for attribute associations within an assemblage from a matrilocal community than within one from a community with any other rule of residence (Deetz, 1965, p. 2). His demonstration of patterns of attribute association was based on the use of row and column percentages from cross-tabulations of selected sets of stylistic attributes. The appropriate technique for the demonstration of non-random associations in a cross-tabulation table, however, is the use of the statistic of Chi-square or one of its several functions (DuBois, 1965, pp. 52–72, 312–21; Siegel, 1956, pp. 104–111).

In an ideal, perfectly random case, the row and column percentages in such a table are exactly the same as the percentages of the column and row marginal totals. This is the basis on which expected values and probabilities are calculated for these tables. The use of row and column percentages of co-occurrence for the analysis of attribute association therefore results in an ambiguous situation. Relative numbers of high and low percentages do not necessarily demonstrate different degrees of non-random attribute association.

In fact, a comparison of Deetz's results with the results which were predictable from his own data on the assumption of purely random associations among attributes showed an uncomfortably close correspondence and indicated that there was a strong possibility that another type of stylistic variation was also being reflected in the analysis.

It should be noted that these considerations do not disprove Deetz's hypotheses or models of stylistic behavior. As will be discussed below, they proved to be valid and useful in the interpretation of certain of the analyses of our materials from New York.

If Deetz's results, then, can be so closely approximated on the assumption of perfect random association of attributes in his data, we may ask what other type of stylistic variation might also be reflected in his analysis. There seems to be a real difference between the behavior of materials from a matrilocal community and that of materials from a non-matrilocal group. It can readily be seen from the above discussion of the relationships between percentages within cross-tabulation tables and the percentages of the marginal totals that at least one source of this difference may be in different patterns of marginal percentages. It was necessary to analyze these patterns separately from other aspects of style to see if they formed a real and meaningful component of stylistic variation.

The two contrasting patterns of marginal percentages which might have accounted for some of the difference between these two situations may be briefly characterized. The results obtained for the matrilocal situation indicated that in any class of attributes there was a tendency for a few individual attributes of that class to be present in high frequencies and for the other attributes to be relatively few. In contrast, the materials of the non-matrilocal group tended to have a more equal representation of all possible attributes within each class. If we imagine a class of attributes in which only three different categories occur, the first situation might be represented by a percentage distribution of 90 per cent–8 per cent–2 per cent, and the second pattern by precentages of 45 per cent–35 per cent–20 per cent.

This difference has been termed here a difference in stylistic variability or homogeneity. Complete homogeneity or lack of variability is easily recognized in any class of attributes as the existence of only one possible attribute which represents that class on all artifacts; for example, a single, uniform motif which occurs on the lip surface of all sherds in an assemblage. Greater degrees of heterogeneity or variability depend, first, on the number of attributes present in each class and, second, on the degree to which all of these alternatives are represented in equal proportions in the assemblage. The final measure which was devised for this aspect of stylistic behavior takes both of these factors into account.

Changing stylistic variability was not, however, the type of style behavior hypothetically predicted to coincide with changing patterns of residence. Reasoning inductively from the nature of this type of stylistic behavior and from the kinds of other changes correlated with variation of this aspect of style, in Deetz's analysis, and in this data from New York, we would here hypothesize that changes in the degree of stylistic variability are primarily related to changes in the rate of interaction between communities in a region.

Rate of interaction as reflected in this aspect of artifact style is detectable only insofar as the inferred interaction affects the persons producing the artifacts studied. When the artifact class under consideration was certainly, or very probably, manufactured by members of one sex only, two components of "interaction" may be distinguished. First, the rate of actual movement of individuals of that sex between communities, as determined by the rules or customs of post-marital residence, will be a primary component. This concern with post-marital residence in terms of the movement of individuals from one village to another is not necessarily related to the structure of within-village residence groups, which will be considered later. This primary component would hypothetically be the factor determining a basically high or low level of stylistic variability. Superimposed on this basic level of variability will be relatively minor trends and fluctuations which may be related to differential rates of simple intercommunication between villages.

The process by which interaction rate affects the level of stylistic variability is diffusion, or, perhaps more closely defined, a process of regional distribution of stylistic elements similar to the distribution of genetic traits by gene flow. The greater the rates of "flow" within a region, the greater will be the stylistic variability within individual communities. Stylistic ideas, motifs, and techniques are all spread within a region by this mechanism.

If residence is generally not in the village of the bride, women will move about among several villages, bringing with them all their characteristic techniques and styles of pottery manufacture. Under this hypothesis, the presence in a community of women who have come from several different villages at marriage should create a situation of relative heterogeneity of style. Conversely, a high rate of village matrilocality should be characterized by a greater stylistic homogeneity within each village.

Similarly, greater or lesser rates of simple intercommunication between villages should hypothetically allow greater or lesser rates of exchange of ideas, or diffusion by copying. Stylistic variability should be affected much less strongly by this type of diffusion than by the actual movements of artisans.

A central point in this conception of stylistic variability is the relationship between the substantive content of a style and the degree of variability. We have tried to form a measure of simple variability irrespective of any consideration of the actual substance of the style. As will be clear in the course of the description of the results of our analyses, therefore, there is no relationship at all between the attributes considered in any case and the measure of variability derived from that case. For this reason, the final coefficients of variability have been termed coefficients of "basic" stylistic variability. We are able to compare such distinct styles as early Owasco and Iroquois on the same basis. Considerations of the differential frequencies of specific stylistic attributes are important in certain problems of inferring the nature of regional interaction patterns (Cronin, 1962; Longacre, 1963, p. 83), but are not relevant to the analysis of rates of interaction.

In the analyses and interpretations presented below it is assumed that the pottery from these sites in New York was made entirely by women.

The ethnography of the Iroquois and neighboring groups shows a uniform pattern of female manufacture of pottery, and the continuity of stylistic development from Owasco through Iroquois periods (cf. MacNeish, 1952; Ritchie, 1961, pp. 32–33; 1965, p. 303) supports the supposition that this pattern existed prehistorically also.

After some preliminary analysis of the Owasco and Iroquois materials, a satisfactory method of graphically determining the degree of stylistic variability in any class of attributes was developed. Cumulative percentage graphs provided a good representation of this variability. In a cumulative percentage graph, a maximum degree of variability produces a straight, diagonal line across the graph. Complete homogeneity is indicated by a single, almost vertical line rising to one hundred per cent at the first attribute. The spacing of other lines between these two extremes, then, provides a relative measure of variability.

Five sites, two late Owasco and three post-Owasco, in our sample had enough collared sherds that percentages of different collar shapes were meaningful. The range of stylistic variability exhibited for this one attribute class by these five sites is represented by the use of cumulative graphing in Figure 2. In this figure it can be seen that the order of these sites from more to less variability in collar shape is the approximate chronological order. In a number of such cumulative percentage graphs, a similar trend was noted.

Several difficulties, however, appeared in the utilization of these graphs for the definition of the changing degrees of stylistic variability between sites. It was impossible to make decisions on constant and accurate criteria as to greater or lesser variability between sites when the numbers of attributes in the class being considered varied to any great extent between these sites. In other words, degree of slope could not be handled simultaneously with a consideration of number of attributes when making subjective comparisons between graphs. Where slopes varied slightly at different points along closely spaced lines it was again impossible to rank the different lines according to relative variability by inspection alone. These problems were greatly compounded when more than a very few sites were compared on the same graph. The most serious difficulty with the use of cumulative graphs, however, was the inability to consider more than one class of attributes at a time. No form of summary measure for total assemblages or categories of attribute classes was possible. All of these difficulties were removed by the use of a coefficient-type measure.

The use of cumulative graphs provided the foundation for the calculation of a coefficient of variability. As we have mentioned, maximum homogeneity and maximum heterogeneity of style form definite limits in a cumulative graph. All intermediate degrees of variability fall somewhere between these two limits on the graph. Since these graph lines are not continuous curves, but consist of straight-line segments between points, the surface area of the graph can be divided into geometric fig-

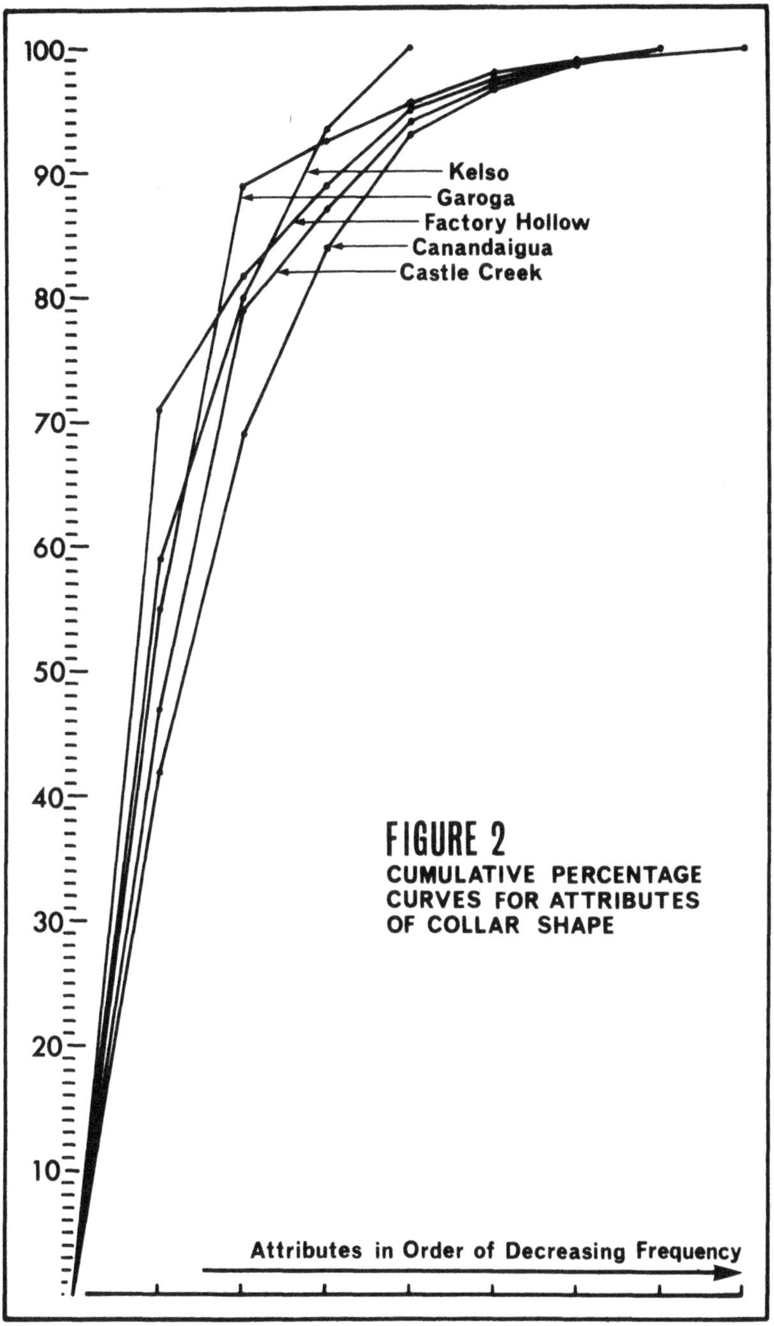

FIGURE 2
CUMULATIVE PERCENTAGE CURVES FOR ATTRIBUTES OF COLLAR SHAPE

ures, that is, right triangles and rectangles. The area which would be included underneath a line representing maximum stylistic variability can easily be calculated in this manner, and the ratio of this area to the area included under any intermediate line may thus be used as a convenient and accurate coefficient measure of the degree of variability represented by such an intermediate line.

The methods of deriving coefficients from cumulative percentage curves have been considerably developed in the field of geography. A series of applications of these techniques to the study of degrees of population concentration is discussed by Wright (1937), who also explains in detail the mathematical background for the derivation of various types of coefficients. In our analysis we have used a modification of one of the geographers coefficients (Wright, 1937, pp. 181–83).

We have changed the direction of the coefficient so that higher values of the coefficient represent greater degrees of homogeneity, and we have utilized a constant maximum area to represent complete heterogeneity of style. Normally, the degree of variability within an attribute class is calculated with reference to the maximum area of the graph that would be covered in a situation of maximum variability for that class. This maximum area is obviously dependent on the number of attributes included within that class. In other words, slope of the line, alone, is considered. To eliminate this dependency on the numbers of attributes present in each class, and to utilize this information at the same time, we used an arbitrary constant of twenty possible attributes per class. This had the effect of somewhat increasing the coefficient in cases where few attributes were represented and gradually decreasing it as the number of attributes in a given line increased. As implied by our previous definitions of heterogeneity *vs.* homogeneity, this was the desired result, and it was incorporated in the value of the coefficient simultaneously with the measurement of the relative slope of the line.[2]

Coefficients of basic stylistic variability were calculated for each class of ceramic attributes in the assemblages from every site. A single, total

[2] The formula actually used was:

$$C = 1 - \frac{2\,(n_0 p - \Sigma\, c)}{p\,(N-1)}$$

C = coefficient of homogeneity

c = the distance from the x axis to the graph line at each successive point

p = the total height of the cumulative graph (here = 100.00)

n_0 = the number of observed nominal categories represented in the cumulative graph

N = the total number of nominal categories in the set making up the scale, (here a constant of 20 was used for comparison *vs.* less attributes).

The value of the coefficient varies between 1.00, representing perfect stylistic homogenity, and .00, indicating the greatest possible degree of heterogeneity.

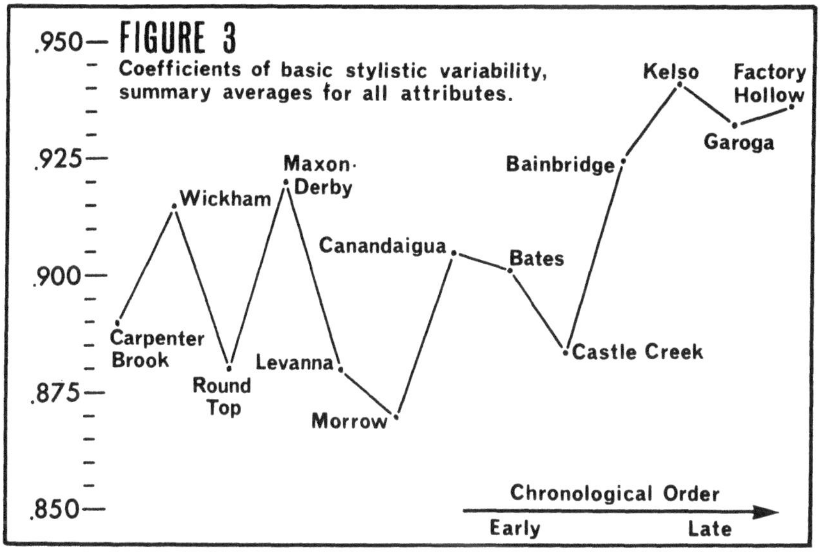

FIGURE 3
Coefficients of basic stylistic variability, summary averages for all attributes.

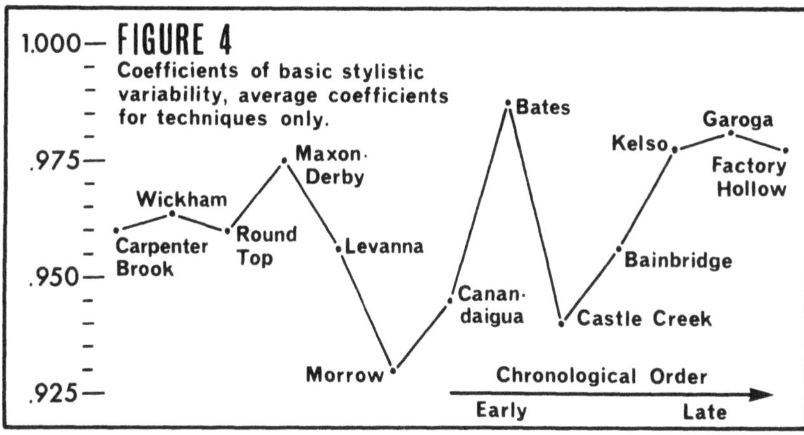

FIGURE 4
Coefficients of basic stylistic variability, average coefficients for techniques only.

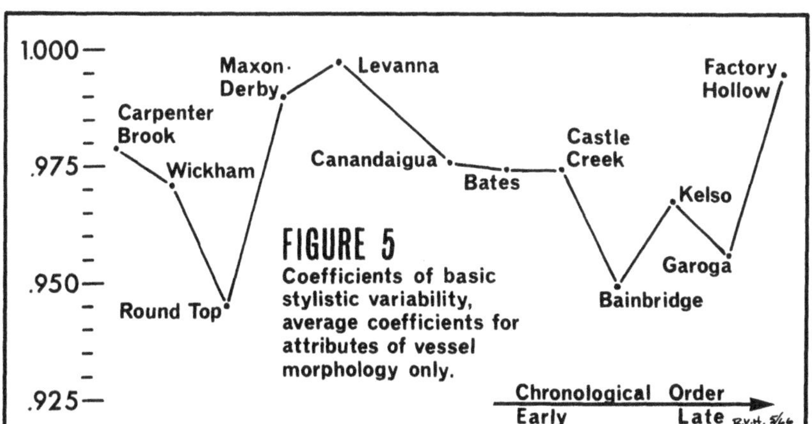

FIGURE 5
Coefficients of basic stylistic variability, average coefficients for attributes of vessel morphology only.

coefficient was obtained for whole assemblages by averaging all of the separate coefficients for the different attribute classes. This total coefficient could be broken down into component parts by similarly finding the average coefficients for various categories of attribute classes. The change through time of levels of "basic stylistic variability" could then be analyzed with simple, clear graphs. These graphs are presented as Figures 3 through 8.

Brief inspection of these several graphs reveals that there are often indications of a temporal trend in the level of stylistic variability. This is true of the graph for total coefficients and for most of the graphs of the components of this total coefficient. The significance of these apparent trends can be evaluated by determining the correlation between an ordering of sites in terms of the calculated levels of stylistic variability and the independently established chronological order. The statistic used for this purpose was Spearman's rank correlation coefficient, to which a level of statistical significance may be assigned (Siegel, 1956, pp. 202–213; DuBois, 1965, pp. 90–92, 228–29). We have used this method to determine whether the indicated trends are more meaningful than the many fluctuations observed (Table 1).

Table 1. Correlations between Chronological Order of Sites and Site Order Established by Basic Variability of Various Categories of Attributes

Category of Attributes	*Correlation*	*Significance*[a]
Total Assemblage	.600	.05
Decorative Techniques	.345	N.S.[b]
Vessel Morphology	.125	N.S.[b]
Decorative Motifs	.638	.05
Collar Shape	.772	N.S.[c]
Lip Profiles	.731	.01

[a] From Siegel, 1956, Appendix, Table p. 284
[b] N.S. = Does not reach a .05 level of significance.
[c] Too few sites could be included in this category to apply this test of significance really meaningfully.

The results of these evaluations show that there is a definite trend towards increasing stylistic homogeneity through time. This trend is imposed on a generally high level of stylistic homogeneity throughout. The total coefficients for whole assemblages (Fig. 3) exhibit this trend to a significant degree. Attributes of decorative technique (Fig. 4) also have a positive trend in this direction, but it is too weak to be put forward as significant. In contrast, our attributes of vessel morphology show only a random temporal fluctuation in variability (Fig. 5 and Table 1). Freed from these levelling influences, decorative motifs (Fig. 6) and the two

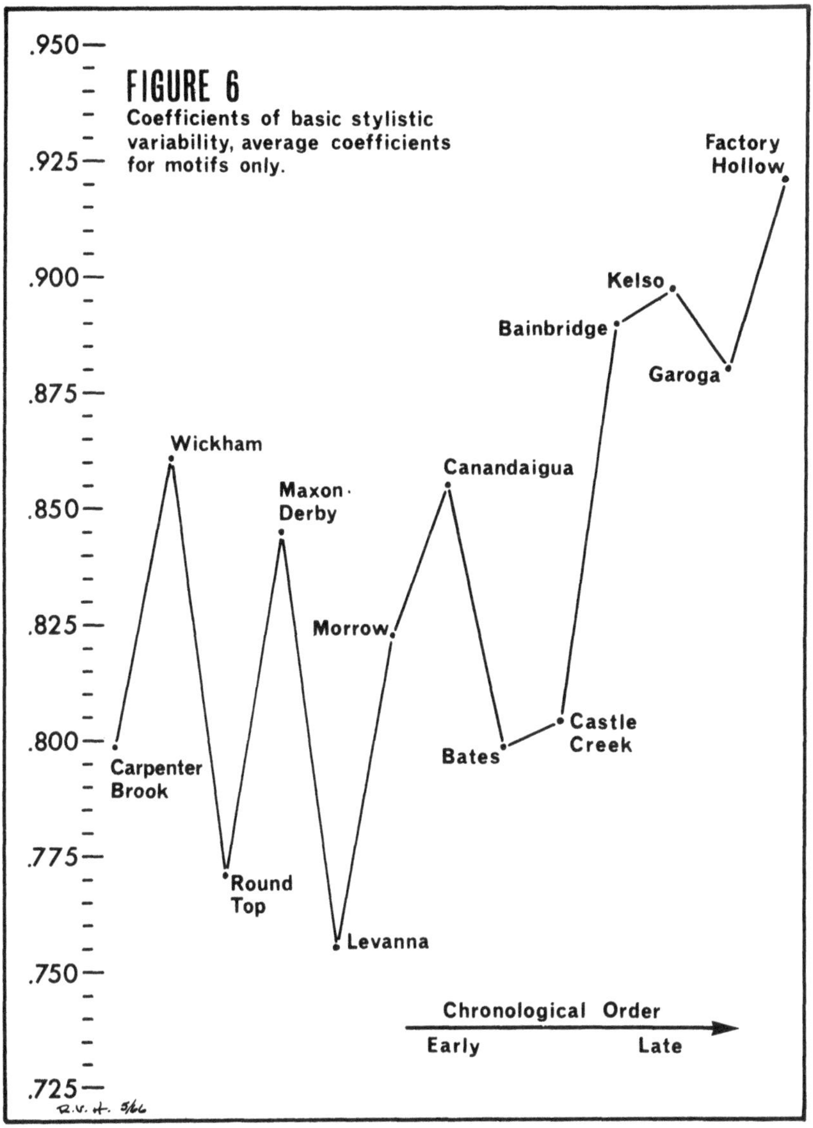

FIGURE 6
Coefficients of basic stylistic variability, average coefficients for motifs only.

morphological features which show stylistic variation, that is, lip profile and collar shape (Fig. 7 and 8), have a marked and significant trend towards increasing homogeneity of style through time.

Following the hypothesis we have established as to the meaning of variation in stylistic variability, the generally high level of homogeneity of style in all of these sites would seem indicative of a high rate, at least, of village matrilocality. Even those attributes which show no temporal trend have high coefficient values. This interpretation is congruent with the known social organization of the Iroquois and with inferences of basic Owasco social organization. The existence of female work groups engaged in horticulture has been interpreted generally (Aberle, 1961, pp. 660–61, 676), and specifically for the Owasco (Ritchie, 1965, p. 296), as a causative factor in the development of matrilocal residence. The existence of a basic pattern of matrilocal residence in Owasco times is further supported by the Owasco-Iroquois continuity of large, multi-family houses (Ritchie, 1961, p. 35; 1965, p. 296) and by our analysis below of the degrees of attribute associations in the ceramics of this series of sites.

The general trend towards a slight increase in stylistic homogeneity from early Owasco to Iroquois is interpreted as a reflection of a gradually decreasing rate of social contact between villages. As discussed hypothetically above, rates of intercommunication are believed to be manifested in stylistic variability through a process similar to that of "flow" in a genetic sense. Decreasing variability is thus thought to reflect decreasing communication.

This interpretation of the trend observed in style behavior is again congruent with other archeological facts. There are no known fortifications associated with early Owasco villages. Several sites, such as Levanna, Round Top, and Maxon Derby, were directly open to attack. In middle Owasco times, fortifications appear. There are surrounding ditches at Canandaigua and Morrow and a single palisade at Bates. The only excavated Owasco cemeteries, those at Canadaigua, contained six males with projectile points embedded in their bones, and the similarity between the points imbedded in these bodies and the points found in the village debris suggests death at the hands of culturally similar enemies. In late Owasco sites, fortification was increased as evidenced in double and triple palisade lines at Castle Creek. Kelso, too, has double palisade lines, and in late prehistoric Iroquois times multiple stockades were constructed, at least at Garoga, from much larger, heavy posts sunk deeply into the ground (cf. discussion by Ritchie, 1965, pp. 280, 293).

There was certainly a relatively large increase in aboriginal population during the Owasco period. Ritchie's observations (1965, p. 280) indicate a progressive development of larger and more numerous villages. It may be possible to relate the inferred decline in peaceful relations between villages to the pressure on resources caused by this population expansion. At some point in the Iroquois period, the formation of the league must have brought about a reversal in this trend, but this probably post-dates the latest site in our sample. The probably concomitant movement of Iroquois towns from their previous defensible positions to lowland, open sites has been noted (Parker, 1922, p. 128), but in the Seneca area, at least, this shift did not occur until approximately 1630 (Wray and Schoff, 1953, p. 57).

We have left some fluctuations in the coefficients of basic stylistic variability unexplained, but it is quite probable that with fuller data they

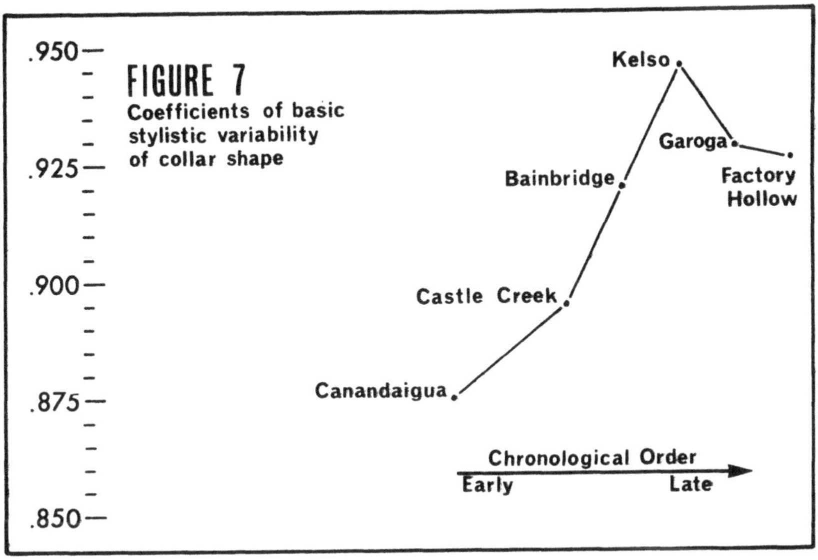
.950
.925
.900
.875
.850
FIGURE 7
Coefficients of basic stylistic variability of collar shape
Kelso
Garoga
Factory Hollow
Bainbridge
Castle Creek
Canandaigua
Chronological Order
Early
Late

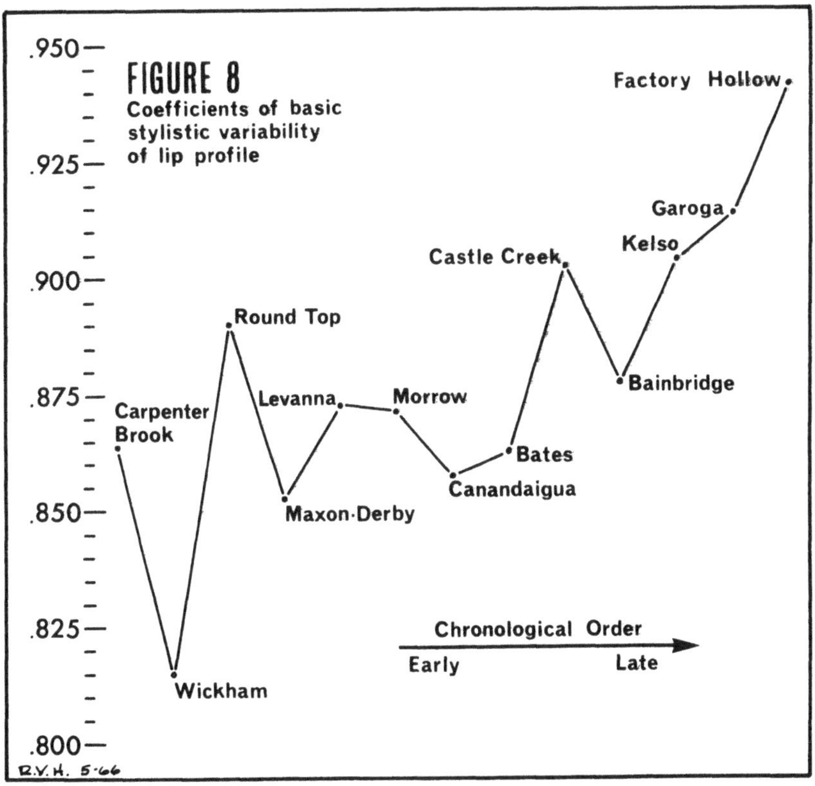
.950
.925
.900
.875
.850
.825
.800
FIGURE 8
Coefficients of basic stylistic variability of lip profile
Factory Hollow
Garoga
Kelso
Castle Creek
Round Top
Bainbridge
Carpenter Brook
Levanna
Morrow
Bates
Canandaigua
Maxon-Derby
Wickham
Chronological Order
Early
Late
R.V.H. 5-66

might be related to such factors of regional interaction as relative isolation from, or proximity to major routes of trade or communication. At this point, however, we turn to another level of social interaction and another aspect of stylistic behavior.

A Stylistic Correlate of Within-Village Residence Pattern

Up to this point the validity of Deetz's original hypothesis has remained untested. His statistical methods were noted to be ambiguous in the demonstration of his prediction that a greater degee of patterned attribute association in ceramic material made by women would be characteristic of style in a highly matrilocal group as compared to groups with any other pattern of residence. A relevant statistical technique for the analysis of attribute associations within an assemblage was mentioned, however. We have applied this technique to our data.

The statistic is Chi-square, a common and familiar one throughout the social sciences (Siegel, 1956, pp. 104–111; DuBois, 1965, pp. 52–72). Chi-square is calculated from cross-tabulation tables similar to those used by Deetz. Cross-tabulations were prepared, therefore, for all possible combinations of attribute classes within each assemblage used for this analysis. Each and every possible pair of individual attributes was thus represented once in the total set of tables. The amount of tabulations and computations involved in such an analysis is very large, and could not have been done at all by hand in the amount of time at our disposal. Even using a computer for all statistical manipulations as we were, it was necessary to restrict the sample of sites for this part of the analysis to seven. These seven were chosen, however, so that the full temporal range of our original sample was represented, and at least one site was included from every major archeological phase currently recognized.

The value of Chi-square with the number of degrees of freedom (based on the number of attributes in the tabulation) was calculated for each table. We were not interested here, however, in the associations between specific attributes. A summary value indicating the total tendency within the whole assemblage for mutual associations between attributes was desired.

It was not possible to consider each table separately and then make an accurate, summary judgment of the total degree to which attributes tended to associate within an assemblage. We therefore took advantage of the additive properties of Chi-square (DuBois, 1965, pp. 69, 319). Chi-square and its degrees of freedom are additive if the observations added are independent. Since, for any site, every pair of attribute classes tabulated produced a series of unique attribute combinations in the table, and since all of the tables prepared were necessary to provide a complete cross-tabulaion of all attributes recorded from the ceramics, we may say that each table provides an independent indication of the total degree of attribute association within the whole assemblage.

Adding in this manner, total values for Chi-square and its degrees of freedom were determined for each site. These total values, of course, became very large. A function of Chi-square was therefore used. This function is normally distributed, and has a calculable mean and standard deviation (DuBois, 1965, p. 317). The degree of total attribute association could thus be expressed in terms of standard deviations from an expected mean value.

These summary values for total tendency of attribute association are plotted in temporal sequence in Figure 9. A very clear trend is apparent in this aspect of stylistic behavior. Already in Carpenter Brook, the ear-

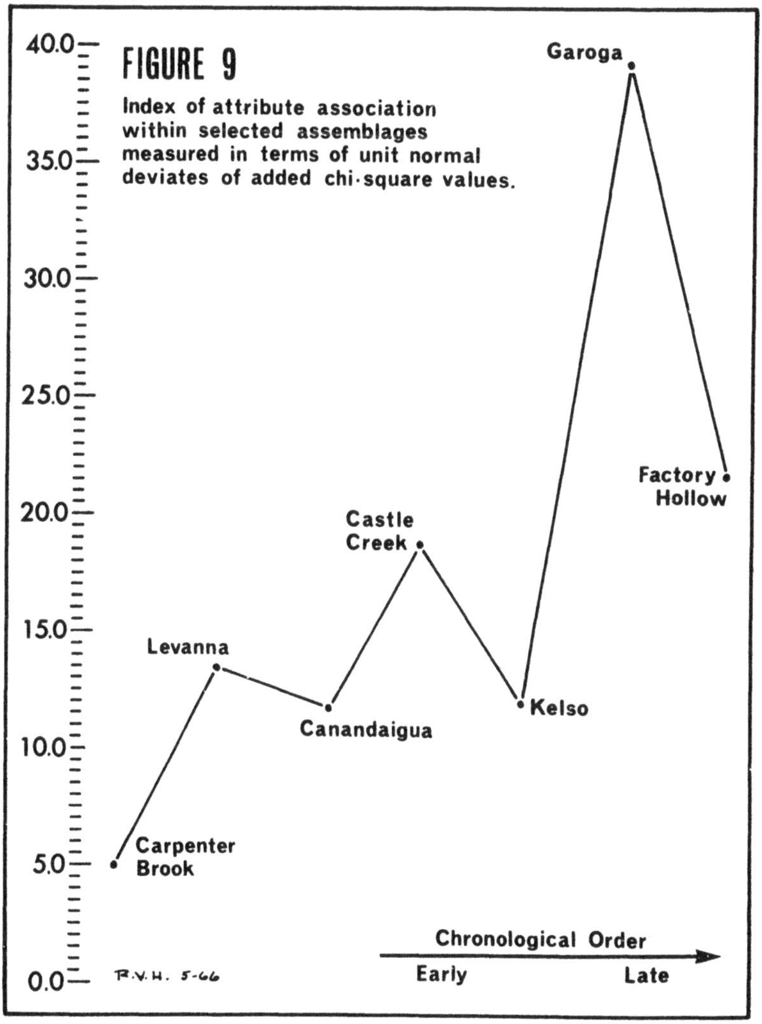

FIGURE 9

Index of attribute association within selected assemblages measured in terms of unit normal deviates of added chi-square values.

liest Owasco site, we obtain a value of five standard deviations from the expected value. This clearly represents a significant degree of association. The amount of attribute clustering slowly rises throughout all the pre-Iroquois assemblages. Then, there is a sharp rise in the value of this measurement with Garoga, the first Iroquois site. Factory Hollow is not as high as Garoga, but is higher than any of the non-Iroquois sites.

This analysis seems to confirm the basic hypothesis behind Deetz's predictions of stylistic behavior. We believe that it further adds a refinement in method and interpretation which Deetz was not able to consider. With the support of other archeological and ethnographic evidence, we have interpreted the behavior disclosed in Figure 9 as demonstrative of changes in size and in degree of integration of within-village matrilocal residence groups.

The high degrees of attribute association present in the Iroquois assemblages are congruent with Deetz's hypothesis in that matrilineages, residing together in one or more longhouses, were the basic social units in an Iroquois village (Goldenweiser, 1913, p. 468; Fenton, 1951, pp. 45–46). The long, oval houses of the Owasco period and the Oak Hill phase have also been interpreted as the possible residences of matrilocal, multi-family social groups, perhaps ancestral to those of the Iroquois (Ritchie, 1961, p. 35; 1965, p. 296). Our results would indicate that, in contrast to the Iroquois matrilineages, the Owasco residence groups were not as strongly integrated and probably were simple extended families.

The minor trends in the level of stylistic attribute association seem, on the other hand, to be possibly related to the size of the residence groups. In this analysis we selected the largest and best preserved assemblages from our sample of sites. Unfortunately, these assemblages are not always from sites for which good settlement pattern data are available, and a direct comparison between house size and degrees of attribute association was not possible. The gradual increase in this degree through Owasco times, nevertheless, is roughly paralleled by a gradual increase for the same period in the average size of house. The difference in the values obtained for the two Iroquois sites also parallels a difference in the sizes of the longhouses at these two sites.

This aspect of stylistic behavior, like the measurement of basic variability, shows both major differences in level, and minor trends within these levels. The former seems related to the degree of integration and importance of co-resident groups; the latter seems to reflect the average size of such groups.

Summary: Causes for Social Change

In discussing the changes in intergroup relations inferred from the analysis of stylistic variability, population expansion was mentioned as a possible causative factor. This in turn appears to be the result of certain changes in the subsistence base. By considering, also, the probable form of late prehistoric subsistence economy, the data of Iroquois ethnography, and the changes in regional interaction indicated by our first analysis, some possible causes for the social changes inferred from the analysis of attribute association may be found, and we may hypothesize in more detail the exact nature of these changes.

The form of subsistence seems to have been remarkably stable throughout the period with which we are concerned. A consideration of the different types of Owasco sites and of their total artifact assemblages allows the inference that the organization of economic activities characteristic of the historic Iroquois was present in all essential details in the early Owasco period (Ritchie, 1961, p. 31; 1965, pp. 275, 296, 300–301). There seems to have been a slight shift in emphasis from hunting to agricultural activities between the early and middle Owasco periods, but the present evidence indicates that the relative emphasis on different aspects of the economy remained stable from then on. There was, however, a gradual diversification in the crops raised. Corn appears first, followed by beans in middle Owasco, and finally by squash in the Oak Hill phase.

It seems reasonable to interpret this gradual intensification and diversification of the agricultural base as the primary cause of the increase in population mentioned above.

From our second analysis of stylistic behavior, a shift in the size and importance of the residentially localized segments of the Owasco and Iroquois villages has been inferred for the Oak Hill–Iroquois period. The ethnographic sources indicate that one of the important cooperative functions of these segments was agriculture (Stites, 1905, p. 31), and land was communally owned by these or larger segments (Fenton, 1951, pp. 42–43; Goldenweiser, 1913, p. 467). It might be argued that these social units in the villages increased in size and integration in response to the increasing importance of agriculture in the economy. Such an explanation might not be unreasonable for the increasing size of these groups, but it does not seem adequate to account for the inferred change in their degree of integration. If we look at other functions of these groups, we find that they are most important politically, in terms of the inheritance of sachemships (Fenton, 1951, p. 45; Goldenweiser, 1913, p. 408). They also held certain religious and ceremonial prerogatives of a minor nature (Goldenweiser, 1913, p. 467; 1914, p. 368), and they were apparently the important social units in the functioning of blood feuds (Snyderman, 1948, p. 11).

Working backwards from these ethnographic facts, two possible explanations for the Owasco-Iroquois change in the nature of these social segments are readily apparent. There is, first, the importance of these groups in blood-feuding. Blood feuds seem to have been one of the common reasons for entering the warpath, and the importance of the social units involved in blood-feuding may have grown in response to the general increase in warfare in the region. This may be a partial reason for the inferred changes, but a second possible explanation is more convincing.

This second explanation also sees the changes in these subunits of local communities as part of the social adaptation to the regional demographic situation, but interprets the function of more rigidly structured descent groups in terms of status ascription and the provision for specific and permanent governmental functionaries. In proposing this possibility, we are making an analogy between this pattern of change in social organization and the process of development of "statehood" as outlined by Gearing (1962). The differences between these two cases lie in the level of complexity attained and the way in which power to control war-making was institutionalized.

In the development of the Cherokee "state" under intense pressure from the whites, a leader arose who eventually obtained autocratic authority largely through his importance in the direction of war and control over the warriors. It is probable that this position of autocratic authority could never have developed in the Cherokee case except under the heavy pressure of white attack.

In New York, under aboriginal conditions, the pressure of war was probably not so intense. Yet, as warfare increased, an institutionalized method of control very likely became more and more desirable. The posession of titles by the descent groups in Iroquois society provided a method whereby the governing officials formed a relatively permanent council which was not under the control of the strongest and most active men of the group, but was composed of older men with reputations for judgment whose selection was controlled by the women (Goldenweiser, 1913, p. 468). When a title was vacant, a nomination was made by the women of the appropriate lineage, and this nomination submitted to the other chiefs for approval. Control of the council over warfare was generally only advisory (Snyderman, 1948, p. 13), but a final recourse to check a war party was available to the women in the form of a direct order and warning against the expedition (Snyderman, 1948, p. 19).

Considering the above facts of Iroquois ethnography, we are inclined to propose the hypothesis that the developments in size and apparent rigidity of structure and integration of the matrilocal (and matrilineal, at least in the Iroquois sites) segments of local groups to two factors. Their gradual growth in size seems primarily related to the growing importance of agriculture. The apparently rapid increase in the importance and internal integration of these groups, between the Oak Hill phase and Iroquois phases, seems the result of a change in internal organization which is possibly related to the development of a local governing council composed of men with permanent, titled positions pertaining to the various matrilineages of the village.

The adaptive advantages of this form of government were numerous, but it did not function at all importantly in agricultural activities. Its important function lay in the making of decisions regarding the policy of the group in questions of inter-group relations. Subsumed under this general area of responsibility of course, was some degree of regulation of warfare, which had been becoming a more prominent feature of inter-group contact. These governments of village councils composed of permanent, titled "chiefs" opened the way for formal contact between groups to negotiate and reduce the likelihood of wholesale warfare. Ultimately, they formed the local basis for the organization of the Iroquois League.

References

ABERLE, DAVID F. 1961. Matrilineal descent in cross-cultural perspective. In David M. Schneider and Kathleen Gough (Eds.), *Matrilineal kinship*. Berkeley: University of California Press.

BROWN, J. A., and L. G. FREEMAN, JR. 1964. A Univac analysis of sherd frequencies from the Carter Ranch Pueblo, eastern Arizona. *American Antiquity*, 30: 162–67.

CRONIN, CONSTANCE. 1962. An analysis of pottery design elements, indicating possible relationships between three decorated types. In Paul S. Martin *et al.* (Eds.), Chapters in the prehistory of eastern Arizona, I. Chicago Natural History Museum, *Fieldiana, Anthropology*, 53: 105–14.

DEETZ, JAMES. 1965. The dynamics of stylistic change in Arikara ceramics. Illinois Studies in Anthropology, No. 4. Urbana: University of Illinois Press.

DEETZ, JAMES, and EDWIN DETHLEFSEN. 1965. The Doppler effect and archaeology: a consideration of the spatial aspects of seriation. *Southwestern Journal of Anthropology*, 21: 196–206.

DUBOIS, PHILLIP H. 1965. *An introduction to psychological statistics.* New York: Harper and Row.

FENTON, WILLIAM N. 1951. Locality as a basic factor in the development of Iroquois social structure. In William N. Fenton (Ed.), Symposium on local diversity in Iroquois culture. Bureau of American Ethnology, *Bulletin*, 149: 39–54.

GEARING, FRED. 1962. Priests and warriors, social structures for Cherokee politics in the 18th century. Memoirs of the American Anthropological Association, No. 93. Menasha.

GOLDENWEISER, ALEXANDER A. 1913. On Iroquois work, 1912. *Canada geological survey, summary report for 1912*: 464–75.

——. 1914. On Iroquois work, 1913–14. *Canada geological survey, summary report for 1913*: 365–72.

KROEBER, A. L. 1963. *Style and civilizations.* Berkeley: University of California Press.

KROEBER, A. L., and JANE RICHARDSON. 1940. Three centuries of women's dress fashions: a quantitative analysis. University of California Publications, *Anthropological Records* 5, No. 2.

LONGACRE, WILLIAM A. 1963. Archaeology as anthropology: a case study. Unpublished Ph.D. dissertation, University of Chicago.

——. 1964. Sociological implications of the ceramic analysis. In Paul S. Martin *et al.* (Eds.), Chapters in the prehistory of eastern Arizona, II. Chicago Natural History Museum, *Fieldiana, Anthropology*, 22: 155–70.

MacNeish, Richard S. 1952. Iroquois pottery types, a technique for the study of Iroquois prehistory. National Museum of Canada, Bulletin 124.

McPherron, Alan. 1963. Programming the IBM 7090 for optimizing taxonomy in archeology. Paper presented at the 62nd annual meeting of the American Anthropological Association, Chicago.

Parker, A. C. 1922. The archaeological history of New York, Part I. New York State Museum, *Bulletins*: 235–36.

Ritchie, William A. 1944. *The pre-Iroquoian occupations of New York State.* Rochester, N.Y.: Rochester Museum of Arts and Sciences.

——. 1951. Their mouths are stopped with dust. *Archaelogy*, 4: 136–44.

——. 1961. Iroquois archaeology and settlement patterns. In William N. Fenton and John Gulick (Eds.), Symposium on Cherokee and Iroquois culture. Bureau of American Ethnology, *Bulletin*, 180: 27–38.

——. 1965. *The archaeology of New York State.* New York: Natural History Press.

Ritchie, William A., and Richard S. MacNeish. 1949. The pre-Iroquoian pottery of New York State. *American Antiquity*, 15: 97–124.

Siegel, Sidney. 1956. *Nonparametric statistics for the behavioral sciences.* New York: McGraw-Hill.

Smith, Watson. 1962. Schools, pots, and potters. *American Anthropologist*, 64: 1165–78.

Snyderman, George S. 1948. *Behind the tree of peace: a sociological analysis of Iroquois warfare.* Philadelphia: University of Pennsylvania Press.

Stites, Sara Henry. 1905. *Economics of the Iroquois.* Lancaster, Pa.: New Era.

Wray, Charles F , and Harry L. Schoff. 1953. A preliminary report on the Seneca sequence in western New York, 1550–1685. *Pennsylvania Archaeologist,* 23: 53–63.

Wright, J. K. 1937. Some measures of distributions. *Annals of the Association of American Geographers,* 27: 177–211.

Evidence of Social Organization from Western Iran, 8000-4000 B.C.

This paper is a trial essay designed to illustrate how archeologists can make inferences about social organization, rather than a source of basic data on the prehistory of Iran.[1] I have selectively drawn from a great deal of unpublished data from recent excavations in the Deh Luran region of Southwest Iran (Hole and Flannery, 1962; Hole, Flannery, and Neely, 1965) and supplemented this with information derived from surface surveys and published reports concerning sites in southern and eastern Mesopotamia and the flanking Zagros mountains. Nevertheless the general picture is so spotty that I can say relatively little about the particulars of social organization in western Iran during the later phases of prehistory. What I can do is to show what lines of evidence are available, the general nature and extent of the data, and finally the inferences that can be made about social organization in Deh Luran at three "moments" (liberally interpreted) in time: 8000, 6000, and 4000 B.C.

There are three principal lines of evidence on which we can draw for

[1] I should like to acknowledge help by Barbara Stark in the preparation of the manuscript. Leo L. Anderson, Development and Resources Corporation, kindly made facilities available to me in Iran and subsequently furnished me with copies of unpublished reports that were made for Development and Resources Corporation and the Khuzistan Water and Power Authority. Much of the success of the excavations in Deh Luran depended on the hard work of Kent V. Flannery, James A. Neely, all of our wives, and Hans Helbaek. For permission to work in Iran and for timely help I should like to acknowledge the services of personnel in the Antiquities Services, Musée Bastan, Tehran. The field work was supported by a grant from the National Science Foundation.

inferences. First, knowledge of the paleoenvironment and the opportunities and limitations it afforded, given certain technologies and subsistence activities; second, the actual or inferred settlement patterns and population size; and third, inferences about division of labor, status and sex differentiation, craft specialization, and trade that can be made from a study of artifacts.

In making inferences about the archeological data, I depend largely on ethnographic analogy, and very little on historical sources. We should bear in mind, however, that the prehistoric context is that of a historically unique situation which does not correspond in all particulars to any modern community that we might wish to use in analogy.

The Cultural Setting

It is sound practice in reconstructing culture history to treat each area in its own right; for this reason I deal specifically with sites near Deh Luran. On the other hand, Deh Luran did not exist in a cultural vacuum. During each of the three periods under study the people in Deh Luran shared in technological and social developments that affected a wider area. At a minimum, the cultural setting during each period included people living in upper Khuzistan, southwest Iran, the mountain valleys of the Zagros mountains, and the central plateau of Iran (See Fig. 1). By 4000 B.C. the cultural context had expanded to include southern Mesopotamia and even the western fringes of northern Mesopotamia and Anatolia.

Considering Southwest Asia as a whole, at 8000 B.C. most of the people were nomadic hunters; in a few places people settled in permanent villages and began to produce their food by planting crops and herding animals. By 6000 B.C. there were perhaps hundreds of small villages of agriculturalists and probably relatively few people who subsisted solely by hunting. Shortly after 6000 B.C., when simple techniques of irrigation had been mastered, people began to settle southern Mesopotamia as agriculturalists. After this time, the population increased dramatically, new areas were colonized, and some villages grew to towns or even cities as the thresholds of civilization were approached.

Looking back from the perspective of history, there was a development of society from simple bands of hunters to class-stratified urbanites. In view of this, a charting of history in Southwest Asia requires both a definition of the changing techniques of subsistence and demographic forms, and a recognition of the emergence of more complex forms of society. It is to this latter task, as it pertains to a relatively small area of Southwest Asia, that I address myself in this essay.

The Geographic Setting

From all that we have learned so far, the climate during the period in question was essentially the same as today (Butzer, 1965; Van Zeist and

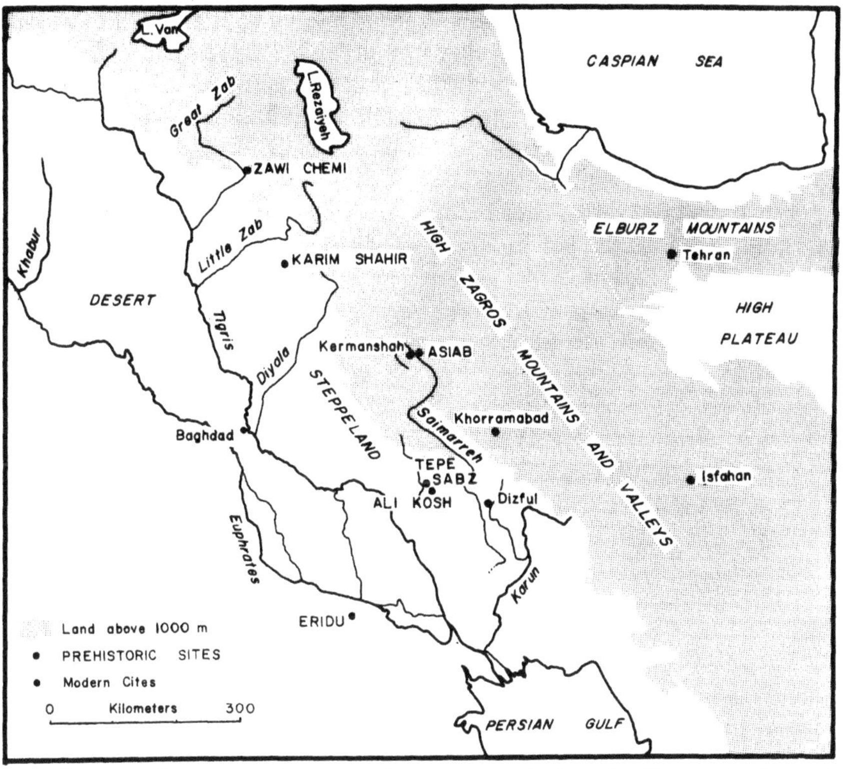

Figure 1. Location of geographic areas and sites in Mesopotamia and western Iran.

Wright, 1963). This does not rule out minor fluctuations nor does it mean that the environment was the same. In fact, we know full well that the landscape has suffered severe changes for the worse in the 10,000 years since our reconstruction begins. Ten thousand years of intensive exploitation of the natural resources through farming, grazing and cutting of timber have reduced much of the area to commercially worthless desert or rocky, thorn-studded waste lands, but the potential ecological diversity and wealth of resources is apparent to the practiced eye even today (Flannery, 1965).

Deh Luran is part of the upper Khuzistan steppe, a natural grassland at the verge of the desert and the Zagros mountains (see Fig. 1). Although the summer climate ranks with the hottest and driest on earth, this steppe land is important both for grazing and for dry farming. During the mild winters up to 15 inches of rain fall, and the formerly parched earth turns green with vegetation. With irrigation, crop yields can be increased by up to one-third. Moreover, as long as fresh water can be brought to the earth, even the desert that stretches south from the steppe land is extraordinarily productive. In Khuzistan, permanent and seasonal rivers provide water for domestic and agricultural use and feed the swamps that alternate with sand dunes and hard-packed desert. Available to hunters on the steppe were deer, gazelle, onagers, and cattle and in the rivers and swamps pigs, fish, clams, and migratory birds. Important even in prehistory were the fabulous reserves of petroleum which oozed to the surface at many places to provide natural asphalt.

The mountain slopes and valleys to the north of Khuzistan were an essential part of the environment of the Deh Luran steppe dwellers. These upland regions were summer grazing lands for the animals that wintered in Khuzistan, and throughout history they have served as pastures for the flocks of the transhumant natives. Farming was seldom as important as grazing in these areas, although at various times settlements flourished. The mountains were also the source of oak, pistachio, and almonds, as well as the wild ancestors of wheat, barley, sheep, and goats.

Farther north and east, on the high central plateau of Iran is another steppe-land and desert system that was not especially suitable for early villagers but which was the source of readily available and easily worked native copper.

Lines of Evidence

In this section I shall treat each of the three lines of evidence separately, period by period. This is a useful way to approach the problem of inferring social organization because it enables us to comprehend relatively simple factors and to make interpretations from them; we see both the evidence and the method of arriving at inferences in this way. Recognizing that this approach fragments the data, I shall synthesize the material by period in the Summary.

ENVIRONMENT AND SUBSISTENCE

The bare facts of environment must be seen in light of subsistence patterns and technology. At 8000 B.C. the natural environment had scarcely been altered by man. We reconstruct a grassy Deh Luran valley with a swamp in its lower portion covering about one-fifth of the available land surface. It was not far from the edge of this swamp that people settled during Bus Mordeh times, perhaps as the first permanent residents in the area.

Our reconstruction of the subsistence (based on studies by Dr. Hans Helbaek) shows that the villagers were principally engaged in collecting wild plant foods such as wild alfalfa, spring milk vetch (*Trigonella*, a small pea), canary grass, oat grass, goosefoot, and the fruit of the wild caper. In addition, the Bus Mordeh folk planted small amounts of emmer wheat and two-row hulled barley, both early forms of the modern hybrid grains. Except for sickles, we see no evidence of special agricultural tools. If the land was prepared for seed at all it was probably done with a digging stick, but even without preparation, the mud flats at swamp's edge could have received seeds.

Meat was obtained in two ways, by herding of goats and by hunting. The former activity probably took at least some of the people seasonally into the nearby mountains when the summer's heat had desiccated the grassy vegetation. Since Deh Luran is situated within a few hour's walk of the high mountains, transhumance could have been accomplished easily. Saimarreh, a large, fertile, but isolated river valley, ideal for seasonal grazing, lies just 59 km. north of Deh Luran.

Hunting was probably as important for food as stockbreeding, and it is just possible that most of the goats were kept for their hair or milk rather than for meat. Gazelle, onager, wild ox, and pig were the most commonly hunted beasts, but fish, mussels, and turtles, along with migratory water fowl, were also taken from the swamp (faunal studies made by Kent V. Flannery).

In short, during the Bus Mordeh we are dealing with people who were exploiting a broad spectrum of their environment for subsistence, and the domesticates were only one aspect of a diversified subsistence economy. Although the pattern suggests "incipient agriculture," we should imagine the activities were not greatly different from those practiced by hunters in the same area for tens of thousands of years.

If we pay attention only to subsistence, I think we would argue that only a simple social organization is called for. Since flocks were probably property, however, it is likely that some device of inheritance, perhaps lineages, was used to keep them "in the family." The amount of farming does not suggest a need for ownership of land, and there is no activity that I can imagine that would have required much central direction. At most, I can imagine simple bands composed of lineages which, by analogy with hunters today, were probably patrilineal.

At 6000 B.C. the people of the Mohammad Jaffar Phase occupied an area that had been in use for some 2,000 years by farmers and herders. During this time patterns of cropping, fallowing, and grazing had probably developed and we see the beginnings of the use of crude stone hoes to break the soil. Emmer wheat and two-row barley were still virtually the only crops grown, but the sheer acreage under cultivation had probably increased. The patterns of exploitation are seen indirectly in the vegetation. We infer that a great deal of the natural vegetation had already been removed because we find pasture plants like plantain, mallow, vetch, oat grass, and canary grass in its place. In particular we find great amounts of the mesquite-like, woody, perennial legume, *Prosopis*, whose fleshy pods are edible. Intensive grazing alone would probably have led to these botanical changes, but habits of cropping were also contributory factors. To supplement agricultural crops, villagers still collected wild rye-grass, goat-face grass, vetchling, and caper.

Herding was probably more important economically than in the Bus Mordeh, for now we find both sheep and goats that show in their skeletons clear signs of domestication. Nevertheless, hunting was still important. In fact, the percentages of bones of domesticates to wild animals shows that there are relatively twice as many wild animal bones in the Mohammad Jaffar as there were in the Bus Mordeh. What this may suggest is that sheep and goats were being kept for their wool, hair, and milk rather than for their meat. The same wild animals as before were hunted and the pattern of exploitation cannot have been much different.

In summary, we cannot infer very much about social organization just on the basis of subsistence practices. The patterns must have been much as they were during the Bus Mordeh Phase: relatively undifferentiated communities organized into lineages. Men probably did the hunting and women were responsible for gathering wild plants; the women may also have done the farming as an extension to their usual food-gathering activities. Shepherds may have gathered *Prosopis* pods.

By 4000 B.C. we see quite different patterns of subsistence. The most important change was the establishment of simple but systematic irrigation, even in places like Deh Luran where rainfall is usually sufficient to support crops. Helping to increase the agricultural profits was a fully modern complex of grains and animals. These included free-threshing hexaploid wheat, emmer, six-row barley, and a variety of plants of lesser importance such as peas and lentils. This complex of plants is significant because it comprises even today the most important crops in the area, a sign that the Bayat people had attained an optimum adaptation to their environment. Flax, another commercially important crop in later times was being grown, perhaps more for its oil than for its fibers. Important additions to the livestock were cattle, soon (if not already) to be used as draft animals, and dogs skeletally similar to the familiar guard dogs of the area today. Skeletally modern sheep and goats were present and we infer from finding evidence of textiles that they may have been kept partly for their wool and hair.

In spite of the balanced agricultural complex, hunting continued to be important, as did the gathering of wild food from the swamp. Perhaps in subsistence the people were never better off than during the Bayat Phase when they had fully effective agriculture and stock breeding, and they could supplement their diet with a variety of wild foods.

With the new agricultural practices, there was possibly a revision of the division of labor. As irrigation proved valuable, some men probably labored at making the small canals and tending them (at least seasonally) instead of spending the bulk of their time in hunting. If more land were under cultivation, men were probably also pressed into duty at harvest time. If draft animals were used to pull plows, we should be even more confident that man's role as hunter was beginning to lessen in importance relative to farming.

Unfortunately we have no evidence for either beer-making or the use of milk for yoghurt or cheese, but all of these products could have been developed by this time. One supposes that women, as today, were responsible for the dairy products. This also goes for bread, which had probably replaced gruel as a staple when bread wheat became available.

Although our data suggest prosperity, we have not found any signs in Deh Luran that the people stored food. On the other hand, given the environment, one should be very much surprised to find that sufficient resources existed for year-round maintenance on a hand-to-mouth basis. If nothing else, the potential of irrigation farming suggests that there must have been seasonal surpluses.

Assuming agricultural surpluses, we can go farther with our inferences by following the arguments made by Sahlins in his study of social stratification in Polynesia (Sahlins, 1958). There, where social stratification is related to production, the greater the surpluses the greater the degree of stratification. Sahlins maintains this will be true *so long as there is a redistributional system.*

Still assuming surpluses, the question is, how were they depleted? In Polynesia they were eaten and distributed at feasts or displayed until they rotted. But there are other ways of disposing of them. The Indians of the Northwest Coast destroyed their property, and we know from both archeology and historical sources that food was used as offerings in temples in Mesopotamia. The destruction of surpluses seems especially appropriate where they are annual and predictable, but where annual surpluses may be more doubtful, perhaps sacrifices or offerings are the more reasonable disposition. Looking at southern Mesopotamia, we know that temples were centers for redistributing the economy's surpluses (Hole, 1966). After they were received in the temple warehouses, the surpluses were partly distributed to support craft specialists, some of whom made goods for use by the upper stratum of society.

Before this chain of inferences goes too far, let me say that if we look only at Deh Luran, there is no evidence for actual redistribution, but if the Deh Luranis were keeping pace with neighboring areas, by 4000 B.C. they were channeling some of their surpluses into temple centers. In fact, the available evidence suggests that Deh Luran was not as far advanced in social organization as southern Mesopotamia. This leaves us with the probability that, as a minimum, in all three periods dissemination of surpluses took the form of periodic slaughter of livestock for feasts on ceremonial occasions.

In summary, during the Bayat Phase, subsistence patterns allow us to infer a social organization of only the same complexity as earlier: a lineage organization and perhaps landholding bands. On the other hand, there are hints that the division of labor may have changed, principally to draw men more actively into food production. There is no reason to believe that much central authority was required to manage the simple irrigation for which we have evidence.

SETTLEMENT PATTERNS

Our second line of evidence is settlement patterns and population size. Our data here are woefully meager in some respects and fairly rich in others. They consist of a handful of test excavations coupled with extensive surface surveys in west Iran and adjacent Iraq. We are particularly short in excavations. Archeologists working in the American Southwest or the Great Plains are accustomed to digging whole villages or at least significant portions of them; in the Near East where mounds may be tens of meters high and acres in extent containing remains of houses built of sun-dried mud, one seldom digs a site extensively. And even in sites where large areas have been exposed, the subtle traces of architecture have often gone unrecognized.

Archeologists often base inferences about social organization on settlement patterns (Wauchope, 1956, pp. 129–57; Willey, 1956). This is true both where whole settlements can be stripped to show the layout of a village and the relationship of different structures within it, and where areas have been surveyed extensively enough to show the distribution of sites. No site in west Iran has been entirely laid bare; therefore, I can only make inference about the size of population in particular villages. However, since survey data are relatively fuller, I can make inferences about the sizes and types of sites in each period and also—from the location of villages—some inferences about subsistence practices.

Inferring social organization directly from the size of a population is a little known and relatively untested procedure but it is suggestive and should not be ignored when we are grasping at inferential straws anyway. Some years ago Raoul Naroll (1956) published a paper in which he related population size to social organization and craft specialization. His reasoning was based on sociological studies which suggested that the administrative component of a society will increase in proportion to the size of the society. In other words, as the number of people increases and therefore also the potential relationships among them inevitably increase, the structures for supervising these additional relationships will also increase. By structures I refer to families, lineages, clans, sodalities, councils, and the like. When Naroll tested this proposition with a sample of primitive societies he found it to be true. For example, he found that authoritative officials are necessary when the size of the group exceeds 500; 1,000 people require policing. I think most of us would also intuitively recognize the validity of the proposition for our modern society (cf. Parkinson's Law). At the present time, even though we cannot test the hypothesis with our own data, we shall consider it true and see where its implications lead.

The method I use to arrive at an estimate of the population of a village requires some explanation. My data on the sizes of villages are derived mainly from surface survey, admittedly a risky procedure when sites were occupied for more than one period, but at least a maximum size is thereby established. I then use an index to arrive at a possible range in the size of the population. The index is based on the area of the village and the estimated number of people who would have lived there. I use demographic data from two sources, a survey by Frankfort (1950) of modern Mesopotamian towns and a survey by Gremliza (1962) of villages in Khuzistan. Frankfort found roughly twenty houses per acre and between six and ten persons per house. From this he deduced that there are between 120 and 200 persons per acre in a modern town. Gremliza found twelve houses per acre and about four or five persons per room, about 55 people per acre, less than half Frankfort's findings. Frankfort's data are derived from cities where non-agricultural people live densely packed into crowded quarters, a situation not to be expected in rural areas or in prehistoric villages. For this reason, I shall use an index of twelve to fifteen houses per acre and four to six persons per room in calculating my estimates of population.

In this section I shall depart somewhat from my previous presentation and include data from areas outside Deh Luran so as to get a notion of orders of magnitude.

The Bus Mordeh settlement in Deh Luran is unique in the immediate vicinity and we know of no others in Southwest Iran. This may be due to the nature of the surveys and the fact that the small settlements of this age are likely buried under subsequent accumulations of silt. The nearest possibly comparable site is in the Kermanshah Valley, well into the mountains at an elevation of about 4,500 feet. The preliminary report on work in this valley suggests that Asiab was a camp of hunters (Braidwood, 1960; Braidwood, Howe, and Reed, 1961). In this same valley system was also found a handful of preceramic open sites that are probably comparable to Asiab. Zawi Chemi Shanidar (Solecki, 1964) in the mountains of northeast Iraq at an elevation of about 2200 feet seems to have been a camp of herders, and Karim Shahir (Braidwood and Howe, 1960, pp. 52–54), also in northeast Iraq, may have been a hunters' or herders' camp. The latter two sites showed only the most tenuous evidence of architecture, but Asiab had a large ovoid depression that may have been some form of pit house.

When we take later periods into consideration, the evidence seems to show a relatively small population throughout the Zagros. All of the sites are themselves small and they are widely scattered with respect to one another. The Bus Mordeh settlement was probably not much larger than an acre, from which we would infer a population of between 50 and 100 persons.

Basing our reconstruction of social organization on the distribution of sites, each settlement must have been a separate band, perhaps holding rights to certain territories. Since the Bus Mordeh village was relatively permanent, even though it may have been used only seasonally, we should expect that houses were regarded as forms of property to be inherited in the family line. The size of the population would not suggest any organizational groups beyond the family or lineage.

Architectural evidence from various sites shows a variety of types of dwellings; in the Bus Mordeh itself, there are very small rooms constructed of slabs of clay, laid like bricks. The rooms, measuring some 2 by 2½ meters, may have been for storage or pens rather than dwellings, but of this we have no direct evidence. At the moment, the most we can say is that we have absolutely no evidence for the differentiation of functions or status on the basis of architecture.

For the Mohammad Jaffar Phase, we can draw on substantial data from surrounding areas. In Deh Luran itself there may be one more site of this age although this cannot be certain from our survey data alone. As we noted before, negative demographic data must be used with caution. It appears, however, that for Deh Luran, the population was not greatly larger than previously. We do have better information for the excavated Mohammad Jaffar village's size, however; it could have been as large as three acres in extent and may have contained 145 to 270 people.

Additionally, we can bring to bear survey data from a nearby area of Khuzistan, where Adams (1962) found some 34 sites of an age immediately successive to the Mohammad Jaffar. Perhaps of greater interest than the number of sites is the fact that they were all between two and five acres in extent. This suggests a maximum size to allow for villages of Mohammad Jaffar age, and accords well with our estimate of the Mohammad Jaffar settlement in Deh Luran. Neither do these inferences contradict data we have from other Mohammad Jaffar age sites (Jarmo, Sarab, and Guran) excavated in the Zagros mountains.

Using my index, a typical settlement contained between 100 and 450 persons. Although the absolute size of the population in Deh Luran is still not very large, there may well have been more organizational units than previously. Using Naroll's results for what they are worth, we calculate about five organizational types in a typical village. Translating this into actual offices, there may have been a village council, made up of heads of lineages, administering the largest of the villages.

To supplement these data we have two other excavations in west Iran. Guran in the Hulilan mountain valley is a fully settled village, apparently with substantial houses and year-round occupation (Mortensen, 1963). The picture here is very much like what we find in the Mohammad Jaffar settlement. The site of Sarab, not far from Guran, is another case, however (Braidwood, 1960). There we did not find evidence for substantial architecture nor for prolonged settlement. It appears to have been a summer camp used by herders whose parent village, if any, might well have been like Guran or Mohammad Jaffar.

Some years ago, Braidwood's teams surveyed the large Mahi-Dasht and Kermanshah valleys and found about sixteen sites of Mohammad Jaffar age (Braidwood, 1960). The distribution of these sites can only be described as scattered, from which I infer that each village retained the surrounding lands for farming and grazing. In other words, I suspect some sort of corporate ownership of a territory large enough to support the major subsistence activities. The major problem with this reconstruction is that we do not really know which of the settlements may have been permanent and which were camps like Sarab. In view of the height of many of the sites, I find it hard to believe that at least some of them were not permanent villages with substantial structures suitable for year-round occupation.

It is probably significant that we did not find settlements of this age in many valleys as we surveyed western Iran (Hole, 1962). We only found them where there was a complex of good soil, sufficient rainfall for dry farming, and plenty of surface water. In many areas the earliest sites pertain to the final period of our interest. From this we infer that during Mohammad Jaffar times the population was not very great, and that transhumant herding was more important in many areas than farming.

With regard to the internal differentiation of villages, we are again troubled by lack of architectural details. We have no evidence for buildings that show unusual function and certainly none that would indicate differentiation of status.

Settlement data thus lead us to the conclusion that the Mohammad Jaffar people were living in autonomous villages composed of self-sufficient, socially equal people.

If we include data from outside Deh Luran, evidence for the Bayat Phase, around 4000 B.C., is fuller. For this period we can use data from Khuzistan and the Diyala plain where surface surveys (Adams, 1962, 1965) have yielded extensive information about settlement patterns and land use. Our work in Deh Luran shows similar results but on a much smaller scale. In brief, we find a large increase in the number of sites; three-fold would not be out of order for Khuzistan generally. In the Diyala region east of Baghdad, where no earlier settlements were found, there were 22 sites of this period. According to Adams, the Diyala was settled by farmers moving out of southern Mesopotamia, a fact suggesting that the density of settlement in the south was becoming uncomfortable (cf. Buringh, 1957). That the people settled where rainfall could still be used to advantage when supplemented with limited irrigation may indicate that irrigation techniques had not yet developed very far, or that population pressure was not severe.

Such clustering of sites as we can discern is around shallow basins where water would have stood, or along the edges of braided, meandering streams. There is very little evidence in the distribution of sites that cooperative irrigation projects were undertaken. In fact, Adams says that the typical sites in the Diyala region are 10 to 20 km. apart, a distribution that hardly suggests political or economic integration.

We can hardly deny a large population increase between 6000 B.C. and 4000 B.C., but we see a curious thing; most of the additional population settled in uniformly small villages. It looks as if there were an upper limit to the size of a village that people preferred and when it was reached, a group of people budded off to settle a new village on virgin lands.

According to Adams' Khuzistan data (Adams, 1962), most of the villages were two to five acres, but by 4000 B.C. a few settlements approached the size of towns—nine to twelve acres. In these we should expect to find a population up to 800 persons, a sufficient concentration to require some organized authority—at least a village council. From settlement alone we can infer little more, for in west Iran we do not have excavations that reveal buildings of sacred or public function nor buildings that might have housed an elite class. Unfortunately where we do have towns with temples and presumably a priestly organization to run them, we do not know the size of the population, the details of subsistence, or the range of crafts that were practiced. Eridu in southern Mesopotamia is said to have been about twenty acres in extent, but a large part of that was taken up by the temples and subsequent settlements (Lloyd, 1948). Eridu may have been the largest settlement in the world for its time, and we know of nothing in west Iran comparable to it.

In the Deh Luran valley for this period we are still faced with a lack of evidence in architecture or settlement patterns for status differentiation and occupational specialization. The increased size of the population still does not suggest any particular pressure on the land. We should be surprised as a consequence if we have anything more than self-sufficient, autonomous villages in the economic sense, although surely marriage ties must have linked the settlements with reciprocal obligations between families.

ARTIFACTS

Our third line of evidence is inference drawn from the occurrence of artifacts in archeological sites. Study of these artifacts can reveal trade items and their sources, evidence of craft specialization, perhaps sex or status symbols, and ceremonial objects.

During the Bus Mordeh Phase we have, in the presence of obsidian and cowrie shells, limited but positive evidence of trade. The obsidian, amounting to less than 1 per cent of the total chipped stone, probably came from eastern Turkey, and the cowrie shells, used for beads, came from the Persian Gulf. In the case of shells we should imagine that they were passed on during sporadic and unpredictable times of contact between the Deh Luranis and peoples to the south. But obsidian may be a different case. In view of the fact that this material occurs in all sites of Mohammad Jaffar Phase agriculturalists in the Zagros, in some cases in amounts up to 40 per cent of the total flint, I should think some sort of regular trade must have been carried out. Deh Luran on the lowland steppe appears to be out of the main stream of this trade, however. If we seek a mechanism for ensuring continuous trade, we can probably find it in the seasonal gathering of shepherds in mountain valleys along the route where most of the obsidian seems to have been distributed. No merchants or markets are implied by this trade.

Other hints of similar interaction with peoples of the mountains can be found in the presence in Deh Luran of emmer wheat and two-row barley, both native to the mountains and therefore imports to Deh Luran. Although I see no reason to think that the Bus Mordeh villagers were not themselves cultivating these grains, the possibility remains that they could have traded for them with the mountain folk.

The artifacts give us no reason to think that the division of labor was not that commonly found among hunting peoples: men hunt and women gather and prepare wild plant food. Herding was probably done by men and boys, farming by women. Proficiency in crafts, but not necessarily much specialization, is seen in the flint chipping and manufacture of stone bowls, matting and basketry, and ornaments.

Some clues to the ritual or ceremonial activities of these people are given by the presence of phallic objects and animal figurines. Both classes of object could well have had magical significance, and I think it is noteworthy that the figurines were of goats, the only domesticated animals kept by the villagers.There is no hint that there were notions of formal religion or that there were even special religious practitioners. Rather, I am inclined to see in these data a do-it-yourself magic of the sort commonly found among primitive people today. This, of course, would not necessarily preclude the presence of part-time shamans or magicians.

There are no artifacts that would contradict the impression that the Bus Mordeh society was egalitarian. We find beads, pendants, and labrets scattered throughout the deposits, but unfortunately we found no burials. In view of what we find in the Bayat Phase, perhaps the mere presence of ornaments is significant—an indication that they were available to anyone who chose to wear them.

Taking into consideration the artifacts we have mentioned, the overriding impression is that the Bus Mordeh society was relatively undifferentiated and egalitarian.

There is slighty fuller evidence for the Mohammad Jaffar Phase. Obsidian was still being obtained, but at this time it comprised about 2 per cent of the total chipped stone, perhaps an indication that the line of supply had become more dependable. In addition to obsidian, there are beads of turquoise whose source seems to have been the northeast part of Iran and, again, cowrie shells from the Persian Gulf. Also present is a small amount of native copper hammered, cut, and rolled into shape (Smith, 1965). This material came from the Iranian plateau, probably near the site of Sialk. A single seed of a lentil is the only evidence for new mountain plants appearing in this phase.

Perhaps significant in regard to trade and/or transhumance is the fact that during our surveys in the Khorramabad Valley, we found sherds of a type made by the Mohammad Jaffar villagers. These sherds were found in caves, sites that had been used as shepherds' camps. There were no contemporary villages in the Khorramabad Valley. Along with the indigenous sherds in Deh Luran, we also turned up a few pieces of pottery that seem to be imports, but we are at a loss to specify their origin. We should imagine that they came from the south which is archeological terra incognita at this period.

Trade items thus show somewhat wider contacts at this period, although the amount of this evidence is not overwhelming. There is no reason to think that any of these artifacts could not have been procured through exchange by shepherds coming in contact seasonally with other peoples.

The division of labor was probably essentially as before, since the major activities had not changed greatly. The only additional craft that would require any new skills was pottery making and that, as Matson (1965) has pointed out, can easily be viewed as a simple extension of the housewife's chores.

Turning to the ritual or ceremonial practices, we have the continued use of figurines and phallic symbols, but now, rather than animals, we find crude human figurines and a great many stylized "figurines" that might have been humans. Significantly, perhaps, we do not continue to find goat figurines although goat herding was at least as important as earlier. Still, nothing in these data suggests a basically different ceremonial orientation from what we found in the Bus Mordeh.

Some burials show an elaboration of personal ornamentation but no unequivocal signs of rank or status. All the skeletons that we have found were wearing beads and some of them had labrets and bell-shaped pubic coverings. About all I would hazard at the present time is that there was some sexual differentiation in apparel. The fact that turquoise beads occurred with the burials suggests that the material was not overly expensive and that rights to property of this sort were personal. From the artifacts I infer that the Mohammad Jaffar people could indulge small luxuries and cater to their individual whims in matters of dress, but I cannot see any signs of rank or status differentiation.

In some ways the Bayat people look colorless compared with the Mohammad Jaffar folk, for there are many fewer types of artifacts and virtually no ornaments.

The making of flint tools was much less important and less than 1 per cent of the total chipped stone was obsidian. A recent analysis of some of this obsidian indicates that it may have an Anatolian origin (Renfrew, personal communication; Cann and Renfrew, 1964). Interestingly enough, however, there is some evidence—in the type of stone and in the technique of chipping—that finished flint blades were also imported, perhaps a sign that the local craftsmen had given up the art of fine flint chipping. A few copper pins from the Iranian plateau occur in these contexts but not in sufficient numbers to suggest regular trade. Rare sherds turn up that look as if they were derived from northwest Iraq or Turkey, but the bulk of the "foreign" sherds seem to have their closest links with southern Mesopotamia and Khuzistan. What we see, generally speaking, is the opening up for the first time of contacts with the west as well as with the Zagros mountain region. Unfortunately, we cannot specify the mechanics of exchange between these regions.

When new methods for using the land had been invented, farming became much more important economically and men were probably drawn more and more into agricultural labor. The few burials we found had grinding stones in association, probably a sign that the women looked forward to an eternity of labor preparing food. Craft specialization is best seen in the making of pottery, which, by this time, was done largely with the wheel and fired to high temperatures. The wares are well-made, standardized in style and design, and show considerable functional differentiation. Storage vessels, drinking cups, cooking pots, and dishes are well represented. However, there is no evidence that pottery was manufactured for trade or export; I should think that women continued to produce it largely for their own families.

The burials were remarkable for their lack of ornamentation, considering what we had found in the earlier phase. Perhaps this negative evidence is significant in the sense either that ornaments could not be obtained or, as seems more likely, that decoration was reserved for special persons. Unfortunately, except for a few labrets scattered through the deposits, we find no evidence that anyone was decorated. On the other hand, we did find seals, which are usually interpreted as signs of individual ownership and this could be taken as a sign of burgeoning status differentiation. What I refer to here is a difference between the producers and those who organized and directed production and distributed the surpluses.

When we turn to evidence for ritual or ceremonial activities, curiously enough, we find none; there are no figurines or phallic symbols. Considering data from other regions, I wonder if we are not justified in assuming that religious practices have taken a different bent. I wonder whether the personal, do-it-yourself magic of earlier times had not been replaced by a less personal, more formal ritual presided over by trained attendants.

Since we know, for example at Eridu, that contemporary peoples were making offerings and sacrifices at temples, it does not seem wholly out of the question that the Bayat folk may have been doing likewise. Obviously we need far more data than we have, preferably positive rather than negative.

A study of the artifacts found in the Bayat Phase leads me to wonder if there are not some status differences among persons and perhaps even special offices. Otherwise I see a community of prosperous farmers most of whom are equal to one another, although perhaps not as rich in artifacts or ornaments as in earlier times.

Summary

BUS MORDEH PHASE, ABOUT 8000 B.C.

The Bus Mordeh villagers exploited a wide spectrum of their environment as they practiced their diversified subsistence activities. In terms of economic importance it would be hard to decide which activity contributed the most, but we do know that they herded goats, planted emmer wheat and two-row barley, engaged in extensive collecting of wild plant food, hunted the wild ungulates of the plain—ox, onager, gazelle, and deer—and obtained fish, clams, turtles, and migratory birds from the swamps. We know that the people resided in Deh Luran during the winter but we infer that they moved seasonally into the mountains with their herds when the hot dry summer began and the crops were harvested. We cannot imagine a much better example of what one might call "incipient agriculture."

The subsistence activities suggest that the people probably divided their labor much as modern hunting peoples do—the men hunted and the women collected and prepared plant food. Children and old people might have been employed in herding or collecting.

The Bus Mordeh folk lived in a small village, of no more than 200 persons and probably half that many. Their small houses were of mud. There is no indication from our excavation in this settlement of rooms of diversified function or that any persons enjoyed larger or better built dwellings.

Sites of this age are rare in the Near East and we can only conclude that the population was fairly small. It seems likely, in view of the permanence of the settlement, that the Bus Mordeh people held traditional rights to the land surrounding the site but there is no reason to suspect that individuals held rights to certain fields. In fact, the agriculture was probably so rudimentary and land so relatively available that ownership of fields would not have been an issue.

On the other hand, in the fact that there were houses of some permanence and flocks of goats, I wonder if there might not have been some corporate ownership of these tangible assets. One could easily imagine that a lineage organization would be sufficient to keep such property in the family. If there were lineages, I should expect them to have been patrilineal by analogy with most hunting peoples today.

The people engaged in a minor amount of trade for obsidian and cowrie shells but this was not of an amount or economic consequence to suggest that markets or commerce might have been a factor.

Figurines of goats and phallic symbols suggest some sort of magical practices but not the sort that would require any professional practitioners. Neither are there crafts that we should think complex enough to have required full-time craftsmen.

In all, I should think that family units were essentially self-sufficient and that the most embracive social organization was the lineage. The people were probably egalitarian with the major subdivisions of labor based on sex and age.

MOHAMMAD JAFFAR PHASE, 6000 B.C.

At 6000 B.C. the people exploited the same broad spectrum of their environment as before, but there is some evidence that their system of cropping, fallowing, and grazing was beginning to have deleterious effects on the landscape. We see this especially in the occurrence of the edible *Prosopis* plant, a woody legume that favors a landscape from which the natural vegetation has been removed either by repeated cropping or extended grazing. The agricultural techniques show some signs of innovation; crude hoes were used to break up clods and more land was probably under cultivation. Along with the farming, however, was the continuation of herding, now of both sheep and goats. The probable pattern of transhumance into the mountains during the summer is underscored by our finding Deh Luran type pottery in Khorramabad. These sherds were found in caves that had been used by shepherds before people settled down there as farmers.

Hunting was at least as important as before and men must have spent a large portion of their time in this pursuit. If this is the case, women were probably doing most of the farming along with their other activities in collecting wild foods.

From our surveys we see some increase in population generally, although we are not sure there was more than one village in the Deh Luran Valley. At a maximum, the Mohammad Jaffar village covered three acres and contained 270 people. This size of settlement seems to be typical of the times and was not greatly surpassed until later. There is no evidence that population pressure was a factor in social relations. In fact, where we have good survey data, as for instance in the Kermanshah Valley, we find that the sites are scattered. From this I infer that each village retained rights to enough land surrounding it to ensure a comfortable subsistence. Mountainous terrain for grazing was probably open to whomever wished to use it, although traditional territories must have been recognized.

It would be interesting in this regard to know what became of the hunters that used to live in the mountains. Did they give up the chase and become farmers, or were they exterminated by herders whose flocks were subjected to depredations by human hunters?

Trade in obsidian and cowrie shells continued and, at least in the former commodity, increased. Perhaps this reflects the additional links in the chain that would have resulted from a larger population. Interestingly enough, during this period we find both copper and turquoise, products of the Iranian plateau. Although this suggests wider contacts, we are still not dealing with regular trade, and certainly not with commerce.

Excavations have not revealed any unusual building that would indicate either public functions or status differentiation. The adornment of burials shows that people wore many kinds of ornaments, but since all the burials show this, we cannot see ornamentation as anything special. In a few cases it looks as if we can distinguish men by their ornaments, but the data are still too scarce to push very far.

The only new craft is the making of pottery, a not very difficult recombination of arts that had long been practiced by women. We do not see any specialization here.

A slightly different focus of magic or religion is suggested by figurines. We still find phallic pieces, but instead of goats we now have human figurines, some of them highly stylized. Although perhaps the focus has changed, the essentially non-specialized nature of these practices is still indicated.

Viewing the phase generally, I see population being added in small-village increments, none of which is large enough to require much government. I should think that each village was probably composed of several lineages and, when necessary, group activities were presided over by elders. The picture is that of the self-sufficient egalitarian community.

BAYAT PHASE, ABOUT 4000 B.C.

By 4000 B.C. subsistence patterns had changed considerably and with them the general productivity had risen. Free-threshing hexaploid wheat and six-row barley were the principal crops, and these were grown with the aid of a simple system of irrigation on land that was prepared with stone hoes. Along with sheep and goats, we also find the Bayat people keeping cattle and using guard dogs. Some hunting and gathering was also practiced, although wild cattle had evidently disappeared by this time.

Considering the more effective subsistence practices, I wonder whether men were not drawn into agriculture much more than in earlier phases. Setting up the irrigated plots, breaking the soil and harvesting the larger areas under cultivation may have required the services of men. Women's tasks probably increased. They were no doubt engaged in preparing the food and in gathering wild plants, but with the coming of bread wheats, they would also have had to grind flour and make bread and perhaps beer. Moreover, once the Deh Luranis had cattle, I should be surprised if cheese and yoghurt were not being used. Textiles and spindle whorls attest to the art of weaving, and sheep were probably being kept more for their wool than for their meat. By this time women may have had enough to do around the house without going out to till the soil.

Although we do not find evidence of storage, the potential for producing considerable agricultural surpluses existed. Wherever there are surpluses it is usual to dispose of them in a way that will enhance the prestige of the giver or the good of the community. In early historic times in Mesopotamia the preferred method of disposing of surplus was to redistribute it through the temple both in the form of offerings and as a means of supporting the temple and its officials. Since we have no evidence yet of contemporary temples in Deh Luran, the specific disposition of any possible surpluses will have to remain a question.

I judge from surveys that at least a three-fold increase in population, added in small-village increments, occurred in the 2,000 years following the Mohammad Jaffar Phase. Most of the settlements were between two and five acres but a few were between nine and twelve acres. These latter, found in Khuzistan, were towns in which up to 800 people lived. The size of these groups is certainly sufficient to allow, if not absolutely require, additional governmental or regulatory groups on the order of sodalities and councils. In Deh Luran itself we find only a few other relatively small villages that may have been linked by marriage ties, but I see no reason why they should have been linked governmentally.

During the Bayat Phase, for the first time, there is contact with lands to the west. Some of the sherds and obsidian look as if they had come from Anatolia, other sherds as if from Mesopotamia. Continued contacts with the mountain and interior portions of Iran is indicated by the presence of obsidian, and flint blades were probably being imported. If this is true, the people were resorting to trade to supply a necessary tool.

A greater degree of craft specialization than earlier is seen in the making of pottery which by now was well-fired, wheeled, standardized, and displayed a wide range of functions. Although the pots were well made, I see no reason to think that they were imported; indeed they display locally specific designs.

A curious fact is the lack of ornaments in the Bayat deposits. Although there were scattered occurrences of labrets and "studs," there were no beads and pendants. The few burials were interred without equipment, except for grinding stones, a fact that gives us some idea about the peoples' notions of the role of women in the after-life. On the other hand, although "jewelry" is not present, we do find seals, engraved stones that were used to make individual signs of ownership when pressed into wet clay. This suggests that some notion of property existed and that there may have been persons who had accumulated more than others. In connection with this, I wonder if ornaments were not reserved for persons of status.

Finally, we can consider religious or magical beliefs. We found no phallic objects, and only one fragment of a figurine, in this or any of the phases intervening betwween the Mohammad Jaffar and Bayat Phases. This suggests a different focus of expression and I wonder, by analogy with other areas, if religion had become less personal and directed mainly by semi-professional priests toward the pantheon of gods who controlled natural events and, ultimately, agricultural productivity.

In summary, from the evidence in Deh Luran, I see little more complexity of society than in the previous phase, but I should think that the former divisions of labor between the sexes may have changed somewhat. Each community was certainly self-sufficient economically and there is no indication of any inter-village cooperation. The larger communities of this time were likely directed by a council of elders and, to judge from certain negative evidence, sumptuary goods may have been reserved for persons of unusual status, a cut above the typical villager.

It should be apparent from this brief summary that our data from Deh Luran and surrounding areas are far too skimpy to allow many detailed inferences about social organization. Still, I think we can see avenues to pursue in future seasons of excavation that will lead to much more precise insights into the nature of the society that for the first time in culture history was called upon to adapt itself to agriculture and then to urbanism and finally to civilization.

References

ADAMS, R. M., JR. 1962. Agriculture and urban life in early southwestern Iran. *Science*, 136: 109–122.

——. 1965. *Land behind Baghdad*. Chicago: University of Chicago Press.

BRAIDWOOD, R. J. 1960. Seeking the world's first farmers in Persian Kurdistan. *Illustrated London News*, 237: 695–97.

BRAIDWOOD, R. J., and B. HOWE. 1960. *Prehistoric investigations in Iraqi Kurdistan*. Studies in Ancient Oriental Civilization, No. 31. Chicago: University of Chicago Press.

BRAIDWOOD, R. J., B. HOWE, and C. A. REED. 1961. The Iranian prehistoric project. *Science*, 133: 2008–2010.

BURINGH, P. 1957. Living conditions in the lower Mesopotamian plain in ancient times. *Sumer*, 13: 30–46.

BUTZER, KARL W. 1965. Physical conditions in eastern Europe, western Asia and Egypt. In *Cambridge Ancient History*, vol. 1, chap. 2. Cambridge: Cambridge University Press.

CANN, J. R., and COLIN RENFREW. 1964. The characterization of obsidian and its application to the Mediterranean region. *Proceedings of the Prehistoric Society*, 30: 111–33. (This gives an example of the method, although data from Deh Luran are not included.)

FLANNERY, K. V. 1965. The ecology of early food production in Mesopotamia. *Science,* 147: 1247–56.

FRANKFORT, HENRI. 1950 Town planning in ancient Mesopotamia. *Town Planning Review,* 21: 98–115.

GREMLIZA, F. G. L. 1962. Ecology of endemic diseases in the Dez irrigation pilot area. (A report to the Khuzistan Water and Power Authority and Plan Organization, Government of Iran.) New York: Development and Resources Corporation. (Unpublished.)

HOLE, FRANK. 1962. Archeological survey and excavation in Iran, 1961. *Science,* 137: 524–26.

——. 1966 Investigating the origins of Mesopotamian civilization. *Science,* 153 (3736): 605–611.

HOLE, FRANK, and K. V. FLANNERY. 1962. Excavations at Ali Kosh, Iran, 1961. *Iranica Antiqua,* 2: 97–148.

HOLE, FRANK, K. V. FLANNERY, and J. A. NEELY. 1965. Early agriculture and animal husbandry in Deh Luran, Iran. *Current Anthropology,* 6: 105–106

LLOYD, SETON. 1948. The oldest city of Sumeria: Establishing the origins of Eridu. *Illustrated London News,* 213: 303–305.

MATSON, F. R. 1965. Ceramic ecology: An approach to the study of the early cultures of the Near East. In F. R. Matson (Ed.), *Ceramics and man.* Chicago: Aldine Publishing Company.

MORTENSEN, PEDER. 1963. Excavations at Tepe Guran, Luristan. *Acta Archeologica,* 34: 110–21.

NARROLL, RAOUL. 1956. A preliminary index of social development. *American Anthropologist,* 58: 687–715.

SAHLINS, M. D. 1958. *Social stratification in Polynesia.* Seattle: University of Washington Press.

SMITH, C. S. 1965. Metallographic study of early artifacts made from native copper. Paper presented at XI International Congress of the History of Science, Poland (mimeographed).

SOLECKI, R. L. 1964. Zawi Chemi Shanidar, a post-Pleistocene village site in northern Iraq. Report of the Sixth International Congress on the Quaternary, Warsaw, 1961, 4: 405–412.

VAN ZEIST, W., and H. E. WRIGHT, JR. 1963. Preliminary pollen studies at Lake Zeribar, Zagros mountains, southwestern Iran. *Science,* 140: 65–67.

WAUCHOPE, ROBERT (Ed.). 1956. Functional and evolutionary implications of community patterning. In Seminars in Archaelogy: 1955, Memoir No. 11, Society for American Archaeology.

WILLEY, G. R. (Ed.). 1956. *Prehistoric settlement patterns in the New World.* New York: Wenner-Gren Foundation for Anthropological Research.

FOURTEEN

KENT V. FLANNERY AND MICHAEL D. COE

Social and Economic Systems in Formative Mesoamerica

Between 1500 and 800 B.C., Mesoamerica made the transition from semi-sedentary food-collecting and primitive cultivation to the threshold of early state formation. From central Mexico to northern Honduras, this half-millennium was characterized by stable villages of pole-and-thatch or wattle-and-daub houses, sometimes accompanied (by the end of the period) by mounds which enclosed high-status burials or served as platforms for temples. At the start of this period, known as the Early Formative, a social type previously unrecorded for North America came into being: the sedentary village farming community.[1]

A number of authors have already speculated on the social organization which may have characterized the Formative village. All see it as being on a "tribal" level of complexity, with some principal of clanship, presumably based on descent, as the organizing factor in society. Piña Chán (1955, p. 39), Wolf (1959, p. 57), and MacNeish (1964, p. 536) have all tentatively suggested that descent may have been matrilineal.[2] From the comments by Willey, Ekholm, and Millon (1964, p. 456), we suspect they

[1] Although we accept full responsibility for the content of this paper, we wish to thank Robert McC. Adams, Marshall D. Sahlins, Saul H. Reisenberg, and Stephen F. Borhegyi for constructive criticism and suggestions. Nancy H. Flannery prepared all the accompanying illustrations.

[2] Matrilineality seems extremely unlikely to us, as it is practically unknown anywhere in Mesoamerica, least of all among the marginal groups like the Cora-Huichol, Tarahumara, etc. who might conceivably have maintained some vestiges of the pre-civilized sociopolitical institutions of the region. So far as we know, all unilateral clan systems in the area are patrilineal.

would reconstruct it as bilateral or patrilineal. The bases for these previous speculations have been certain aspects of material culture (like female figurines), or ethnographic data taken from codices or colonial documents, or ethnographic analogies drawn from cultures believed to be on the same level of development as the Formative cultures of Mesoamerica. We agree that ethnographic analogy is a useful tool, but that, as Clark (1952) suggests, it must not be done indiscriminately: some reasonable methodology must be applied.

An excellent discussion of such methodology was presented by Sapir (1916) half a century ago. Sapir was attempting to derive chronology from the available ethnographic data on the American Indian. It is our hope eventually to be able to put some ethnography into the available chronology of the prehistoric American Indian.

There are a number of methodologies through which one could approach a reconstruction of social organization in Formative Mesoamerica. It could be attempted through studying the social systems of contemporary or near-contemporary peoples on the margins of Mesoamerica, whose way of life may bear some resemblance to that of the Formative. The Cora-Huichol, Tepehuan, Lenca, Jicaque, and Tarahumara come to mind, but with the exception of the latter group, they are poorly documented. Alternatively, one could study the "internal marginals" in Mesoamerica, like the Huave or Sierra Mixe, who may have participated only to a limited extent in the "Classic" or "Post-Classic" civilizations of that region. One problem is that it is extremely difficult, in the case of all these "marginal" peoples, to sort out the cultural elements which diffused to them at a late time level. Nor do we know to what degree they actually represent "survivals" of a Formative way of life; though their technology may in some ways hark back to that period, there is little guarantee that their social organization has remained the same.

Still another method has been applied in recent years with increasing frequency. This is to examine the sociopolitical system of an area in the ethnographic present in an attempt to isolate the ecological and economic systems with which it is interrelated. This approach argues that sociopolitical systems can be seen to function as *adaptive mechanisms,* and that certain forms of society may be seen to occur repeatedly with certain types of economy or exploitive production. This being the case, tentative analogies can be drawn between peoples in like ecological situations using like means of production. As pointed out by Clark (1952, p. 3), this can be a dangerous game if the cultures involved are "far removed in time and space" and with "no continuity of tradition" between them. It is made correspondingly safer the closer the two societies lie in time and space, and the closer their cultural relationship.

One way of reconstructing the exploitive systems of Formative cultures in various ecological areas is through a study of settlement patterns, combined with examination of the plant and animal remains from archeological sites. We attempted this in a paper (Coe and Flannery, 1964a), at the close of which we advanced some theories about the possible conditions under which the settled communities characteristic of the Mesoamerican Formative first appeared. These theories had to do with the number and spacing of the resource areas (or "microenvironments") exploited by communities which were either sedentary or well on their way to sedentism. Since the publication of that paper, a number of colleagues have drawn to our attention some interesting parallels between our comments on the exploitation of different resource areas in Mesoamerica, and Sahlins' comments on the exploitation of different resource areas in Polynesia (Sahlins, 1958). In this paper we would like to examine those parallels a bit further, and to suggest how Sahlins' approach enables us, using our 1964 paper as a take-off point, to present two models for consideration with regard to the social organization of Formative communities. That these models have at least a degree of historical reality will be shown by their applicability to documented Classic and Post-Classic cultures in Mesoamerica.

The "Microenvironment Reduction" Process

In our 1964 paper we compared and contrasted the economies of the Early Formative period in the arid highland valley of Tehuacán, Mexico (MacNeish, 1964), and the wet tropical Pacific coast of Guatemala where we had excavated in 1962. Both areas had Formative villages in the second millennium B.C., but we inferred from archeological data that the Guatemalan coast had a higher density of stable villages with a larger and more sedentary population. It was our suspicion that this had come about (at least partially) because the early farmers of the Guatemalan coast had supplemented their highly productive maize crop mainly with the products of a single resource area: the lagoon and estuary system. Our excavations produced mineralized corn cobs of Nal-Tel/Chapalote type as well as cultivated avocados, but these domesticates were heavily supplemented with marine catfish, red snapper, gar, snook, crabs, oysters, mussels, marsh clams, and other products of the estuary system. Products of other resource areas were lacking; the Early Formative villagers of the Guatemalan coast seemed to have remained stable and sedentary year-round in a single "microenvironment" out of the eight we defined for that part of the coast.

In contrast to this, the early villagers at Tehuacán exploited a whole range of different resource areas, no one of which could be counted on for sustenance throughout the year. There were mountain woodlands, whose acorns and wild avocados ripened in September; cactus forests on the lower mountain talus, whose fruits (like prickly pear) were available in April; alluvial valley floors, where the rainy-season corn farming was done, and where the mesquite trees bore edible pods in July; and so on through several environmental zones. Long after villages of wattle-and-daub houses appeared, MacNeish's data (1964) showed extensive forays into distant resource areas to supplement agriculture with wild products; and these forays mitigated against fully sedentary life. Our 1964 article concluded that a "reduction in the number and spacing of the microenvironments needed for exploitation by a given community" was one factor, at least, in early settled life.

Unfortunately, we presented this in somewhat oversimplified form, a situation we hope partially to correct here. First of all, there are *many* methods of "microenvironment reduction" other than the one chosen by the farmer-fishers of the coastal lowlands. Second (and here is where Sahlins' data may be relevant), the method chosen can have quite profound effects on both the basic economy and the sociopolitical organization of the Formative group in question. We would like to begin by distinguishing *two* basic means by which "microenvironment reduction" can be accomplished, and two different kinds of societies which can result. Later we will refer to the ethnographic literature to see if there is any indication that such societies ever existed in Mesoamerica.

Figure 1 gives our first theoretical model. Let us suppose, for example, that a pioneer band of Mesoamerican Indians arrives for the first time in an ecological zone which contains four clear-cut microenvironments: a tidewater lagoon, an oak woodland, a talus area of maguey and prickly pear, and an alluvial plain. The band plants its corn on the alluvial plain and supplements its harvest with wild resources gathered in the various resource areas (Fig. 1a). At least two possibilities for settled life are open to them.

The first (Fig. 1b) results in what animal ecologists call a "contagious distribution." This term is used, among other things, to describe "aggregations on suitable but limited substrate" (Allee *et al.*, 1949, p. 393). Here the choice made by the band is to concentrate all its exploitive effort on the one resource area which it deems most productive, largely ignoring the others. In the case of our hypothetical band, let us suppose that they settle on the edge of the tidewater lagoon, farming the surrounding flats while developing a highly productive fishing technology. Villages begin to appear along the shore of the lagoon; settlement is permanent there, with the oak woodland and maguey/prickly-pear habitats left vacant. As daughter communities segment or "bud off," they stay within the same resource area, simply moving a convenient distance downshore from the parent community. When the number of villages has reached, let us say, eight, all eight will be concentrated in the lagoon microenvironment.

The second type of "microenvironment reduction" involves a more balanced distribution of settlement through all habitats—even those which, taken alone, could not support a self-sufficient village. The point is that self-sufficiency is not achieved (or even desired), because permanent settlement is possible through cooperative specialization. A single village

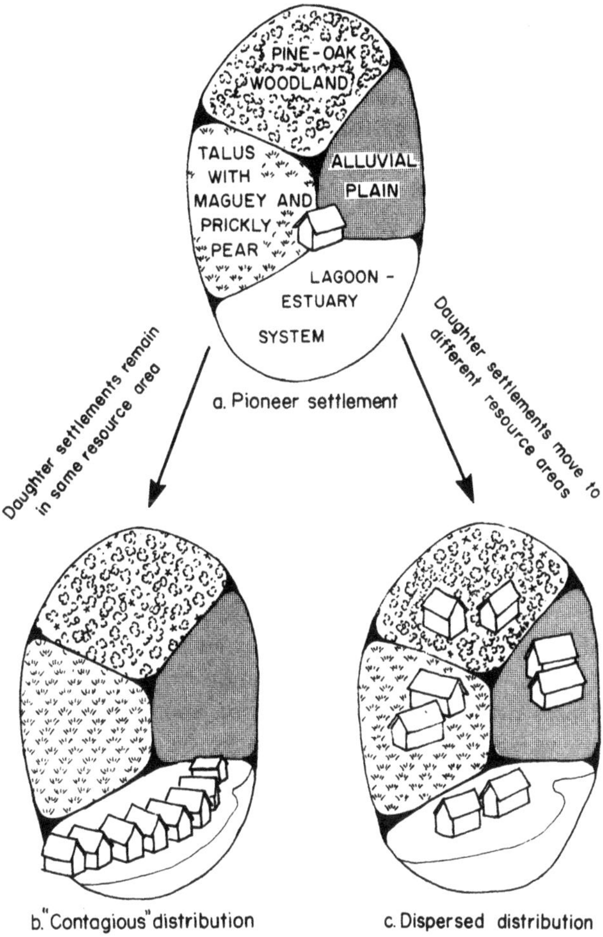

Figure 1. Theoretical models.

does not attempt to exploit all resource areas; each exploits the habitat in which it is settled, and exchanges its products for those of other habitats. To modify our hypothetical case, let us now imagine our eight villages distributed two-to-a-resource-area (as in Fig. 1c). The villagers in the oak woodland zone hunt deer and collect acorns, trading nuts and dried meat to the lagoon-side villages in exchange for fish and maize, or to the talus slope area in exchange for cactus fruits, maguey fiber and pulque, and so forth. Each village has reduced the number of microenvironments *it* must exploit to *one*, yet it shares in the products of all zones. This is the kind of situation which Sanders (1956) has already called "symbiosis."

What are the evidences that such choices were actually made in Formative Mesoamerica? We offer Figure 2 as a sample. These are not theoretical models, but actual settlement pattern maps showing Formative sites known for identical time periods (1500 to 200 B.C.) on the Guatemalan coast (Fig. 2a) and in the Tehuacán Valley (Fig. 2b). The Guatemalan coastal map is probably as close as anyone will come to finding truly "contagious" distribution of sites; although future survey will undoubtedly recover additional villages upstream in the tropical forest, nearly all sites we found (especially in the Early Formative) cluster along the estuary system. In the Tehuacán Valley, MacNeish's survey showed a complex settlement system involving villages with temples, villages without temples, and seasonal camps (MacNeish, 1964, Fig. 6). These were distributed through a number of resource areas, with temple villages mainly on the central alluvial plain.

Economic Systems

Certain obvious economic differences go hand in hand with these two distinct modes of microenvironment reduction. In the case of the "contagiously distributed" villages on the Guatemalan coast, each household had access to all means of production utilized in the area, and the exploitive tasks performed by any one community were probably "carbon copies" of the tasks performed by every other community. Probably there was little movement of products from house to house or from village to village; at least, faunal remains suggest little dependence on resources which would not have been available to all villages (Coe and Flannery, 1964a). Nor would there have been seasonal differences in surpluses between villages. When the fish are running, all villages have fish; when the corn is ripe, all villages have corn. Under such conditions, any "trade" is usually limited to balanced reciprocity.

In the "symbiotic" situation, the reverse is true. There are great differences between communities regarding access to specific resources and performance of specific tasks, as can be imagined in the Tehuacán situation. When acorns are ripe, cactus fruits are not. When cactus fruits are ripe, maize is not. Products move between households and between villages, and members of the same kin group may perform drastically different exploitive tasks should they happen to live in different resource areas. We know for a fact that basic subsistence products and raw materials were on the move all over the highlands of Mexico in the Formative: examples that come to mind include obsidian, as well as tropical products traded into temperate parts of the Tehuacán Valley, like cotton and zapotes (MacNeish, 1964, and personal communication). Obsidian reached the Early Formative villages of the Guatemalan coast in very tiny amounts despite the presence of extensive natural deposits in the adjacent highlands (Coe and Flannery, 1964b).

Reciprocal exchanges between villages soon cease to be the most ef-

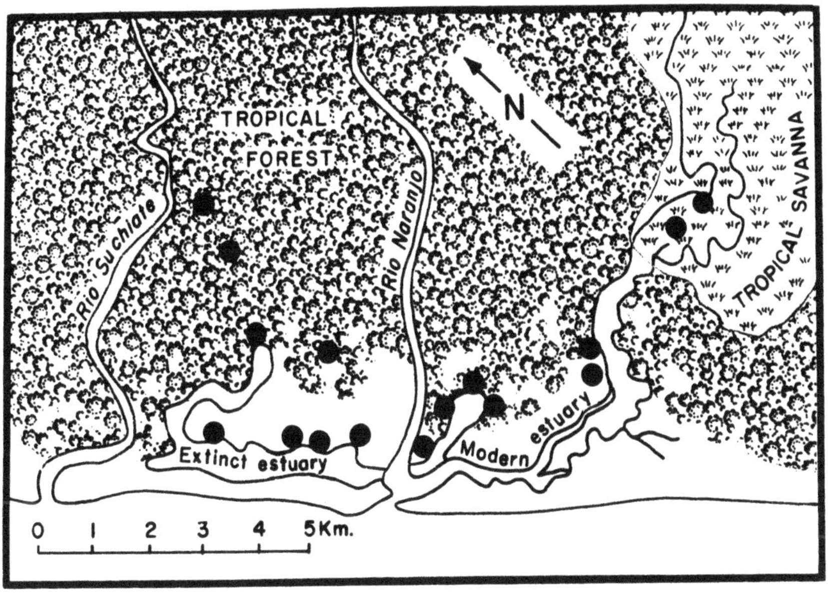

a.

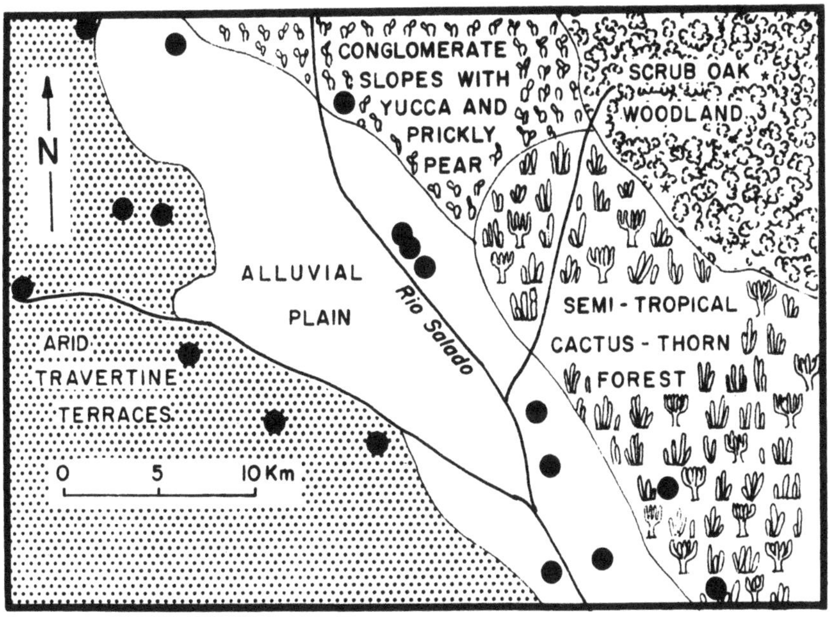

b.

Figure 2. Settlement patterns.

ficient method of exchange under the conditions described for the Mexican highlands. Under a reciprocal system, the villages farthest from the obsidian fields would have to wait until handfuls of obsidian had slowly been traded from village to village along the route; perishable products like zapotes would not last out such a trip. One solution to this was the famous market system of the Mexican highlands. Still another, with an even greater potential for the support of an *aristoi* and full-time religious functionaries, is what Polanyi (1957) calls a "redistributive" system. Through such a system, all resource areas channel their products direct to a single local accumulative center from which goods can then be redistributed to the scattered network of surrounding villages. The surpluses accumulated in this local center support civic activities not seen in the satellite villages; compare the pattern MacNeish (1964, Fig. 6) gives for "temple towns" and their surrounding villages during the Santa Maria Phase in the Tehuacán Valley.

Social Systems

Now, one might legitimately ask, so what? What difference could these alternative settlement and economic systems make in the social organization of Formative Mesoamerica? It is here that we feel Sahlins' Polynesian data can usefully be called into play.

In his study of social stratification in Polynesia, Sahlins (1958) distinguished two basic types of sociopolitical organization, and these seem to be associated with differences in resource exploitation very like those we have just finished describing. The first type of social organization was the "descent line," or simple "unilateral exogamous clan" of Kirchhoff (1959). These we might describe as corporate groups united by actual (or fictionalized) common descent through the male or female line; all members of a given lineage being regarded as equals. The second type of social organization was the ramified system, "ramage," or "conical clan" of Kirchhoff (1959), which is not really a clan at all. The basic difference between this and the preceding type of organization is that it is based not on unilateral descent but on primogeniture; individuals are ranked in status according to their distance from the direct line of descent from an ancestor at the apex of the ramified system. (For a more detailed description of these systems, see Kirchhoff, 1959; Sahlins, 1958).

The distribution of these two social types in Polynesia was such that Sahlins concluded that "the two systems, the ramified and the descent-line, may represent differing adaptations related to variations in ecological conditions. In particular, the distribution of natural resources, i.e., of the zones of exploitation, may have been a factor prejudicing the development of ramified or descent-line systems" (Sahlins, 1958, p. 201).

Inspection of Sahlins' data shows that unilateral exogamous clans were almost inevitably associated with a settlement pattern of our "contagious" type and an exploitive economy aimed at a relatively small number of resource zones; that is, in situations analogous to our Guatemalan coastal example. Ramified systems, on the other hand, occurred in areas where the settlement pattern more closely resembled the Mexican highland type, with balanced distribution through a number of strategic resource areas and an economy involving redistribution. According to Sahlins, these differences were related to the segmentation process, the "budding off" of new villages, which (in Polynesia as in Mesoamerica) differed greatly depending on the exploitive pattern. Stated in simplest terms:

> connection between segmented households would tend to be maintained if, in the process of segmentation, the new household was apt to move into a new resource area and thus specialize in a particular type of strategic production. Maintenance of ties would result in the growth of interconnected ramages and a hierarchy for purposes of effecting equitable distribution of goods, by both reciprocal and redistributive methods. If, on the other hand, a new household moved into an area identical in exploitable opportunities to that in which the parent household was situated, connection between the two would weaken and dissolve and descent-line systems result (Sahlins, 1958, p. 215).

Let us compare for a moment the highland Mexican settlement pattern and that of the analogous "high island" peoples examined by Sahlins. If exploitive and segmentary factors do indeed prejudice the development of sociopolitical systems, the most effective type of organization for the redistributive economy of the highland "symbiotic" areas would have been a ramified system. Our Formative highland peoples should have had an organization based not on participation in an equalitarian descent group, but on a great branching network of individuals of varying rank. Such a system would perhaps involve a paramount chief responsible for the main centers of accumulation and redistribution, and a carefully-kept system of genealogies designed to establish at all times the complex levels of rank within the society. Based on the functioning of such a system elsewhere, we might tentatively construct a hypothetical model for its function in highland Formative Mesoamerica (see Fig. 3).

Here the branches of the ramified system serve as channels or "conveyor belts" along which goods flow to and from the redistributive center: the head of each ramage is responsible for all the goods produced by all households whose status derives from their relationship with him; he in turn deals with the persons from whom he derives his inherited status. Groups producing products of the oak woodland channel them to their subchief, who relays them to the redistributive center; the same is done with the products of the lagoon-side villages and the maguey-producing areas. The paramount chief insures redistribution of all products in an equitable manner down the same chain of command. The system can be expanded indefinitely into any number of environmental zones, even ones which would not support individual communities on a basis of self-sufficiency. Near-total exploitation of a diverse environmental area results, maintaining the system as well as producing surpluses which can be used in ways which ritually reinforce the status of the chiefs and sub-chiefs. Elaborate genealogies controlled the ranking system in Polynesia and reified the paramount chief by tracing his direct ancestors back to mythical culture heroes or dieties.

Ethnographic Data

The model given in Figure 3 is admittedly no more than hypothetical with regard to the Formative symbiotic areas of highland Mesoamerica. It worked in regions far removed in time and space; but, as Clark has stressed, we must demonstrate its presence in Mesoamerica itself before it attains the status of an acceptable hypothesis. Actually, although the details are not identical, one can find in the ethnographic literature of the southern Mexican highlands, evidence of social systems analogous to those of Sahlins' ramified, status-conscious Polynesians. And interestingly

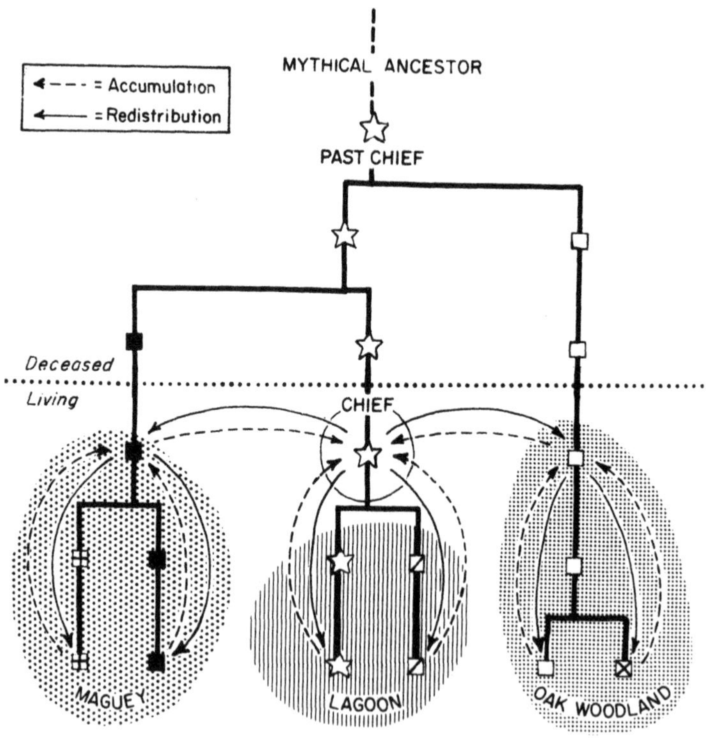

Figure 3. Hypothetical model for symbiotic areas.

enough, these peoples occur in the very areas where we assume a "symbiotic" economy, with redistribution and regional market systems.

One reference which comes immediately to mind is the study by Dahlgren de Jordan (1954) on the Mixtecs of Oaxaca, based on colonial documents and on Alfonso Caso's studies of the Pre-Columbian codices of the Mixteca. After a few abortive attempts to fit the Mixtecs into one or another category of unilateral clan, Dahlgren (1954, p. 150) concluded that the codices, at least, "excluded the existence of exogamous unilateral clans, patrilineal as well as matrilineal." None of the ancient sources suggest unilateral descent or inheritance of property. The term Dahlgren eventually settled on was "ambilateral clans with endogamous tendencies" (1954, p. 151). In point of fact, her description is one of a ramified system with status based on primogeniture.

The Mixtecs could have been lifted, with slight modification, directly out of Sahlins' study. They kept elaborate genealogies of their royal lineages—like those of Tilantongo and Teozacualco—many of which have come down to us in the form of codices. The same term was used for paternal and maternal uncles, and for paternal and maternal aunts. There were marriages between cross-cousins, parallel-cousins, and even (among the *aristoi*) between brother and sister. Marriage was not rigorously exogamic, but rather rigorously "*cacique con cacica y principal con principala*", according to rank within the system. The caciques of Tilantongo, Tlaxiaco, Achiutla, and Teposcolula are described as having been "*hermanos*," and among the direct descendants of the Mixtec ruler "Eight Deer" alone there were four cases of brother-sister marriage. In the empire of the Mixteca the distinctions of rank were inherited and extreme: those of high birth were civil and spiritual leaders and below them spread a complex hierarchy of caciques, principales, macehuales, and even slaves—slaves who did not form a separate caste, but were ultimately related to the rest of Mixtec society (Dahlgren, 1954, pp. 145–62).

That the Mixtecs were hardly unique is suggested by codices from other parts of the Mexican highlands which show genealogies distinguishing direct-line descent *versus* collateral relatives. We in no way claim that these social systems were identical to those of the highly stratified Polynesians. We conclude, however, that there is in highland Mexico (south of the Aztec area) a suggestion of ramified systems rather than unilateral exogamous clans—and, moreover, that such organization occurs in areas which had (so far as we can infer from archeological data) a balanced, "symbiotic" settlement pattern dispersed through a number of different strategic resource areas. It therefore seems to us reasonable to postulate that the Formative villagers of highland regions like the Tehuacán Valley (Fig. 2b) had a ramified type of organization, albeit in a somewhat less elaborately developed form.

What about the lowland Formative villagers, with their "contagious" settlement pattern, their reciprocal economy, and their essentially "one-resource-zone" economy? Theoretically, they should have had a unilateral exogamous clan system in the Formative, with equalitarian lineages and little status differentiation. This seems to us a not unreasonable picture to paint for the Guatemalan Pacific coast, and perhaps much of the Maya lowlands, at 1500 B.C. However, by Late Formative times the Guatemalan coast was the scene of the highly complex Izapa-style ceremonial centers (Stirling, 1943; Coe, 1963, p. 34), and the Maya region had emerged as a nuclear area. This poses certain theoretical problems which we will now discuss.

According to Kirchhoff, the distinction between the exogamous unilateral clan and the ramified system of organization is not merely typological: the ramified system is a *virtual prerequisite for all higher forms of social organization.* "The form of kinship organization which the unilateral-exogamous principal of clanship creates appears definitely as a blind alley, and more than that; at a certain stage of economic and general cultural evolution as an obstacle to further development" (Kirchhoff, 1959, p. 265). This is because the corporate, equalitarian nature of the unilateral lineage, while it creates solidarity, does not provide the distinctions of *inequality* which are a necessary precursor of stratified society. The ramified system, whose very principle is rooted in differences of rank, provides the basis out of which social classes can emerge. And the individual ramages which are its building blocks can proliferate indefinitely, while the gulf between slave and paramount chief continues to widen. According to the Kirchhoff hypothesis, it is no surprise that highland Mesoamerica, with its ramified system, reached a level of civilization. But the Maya empire comes as a great surprise, and it is here that we would like to suggest a slight modification in theory. We propose that the lowland civilizations of Mesoamerica could, and did, arise out of an Early Formative unilateral-exogamous clan system.

One of us (Coe, 1961) has already argued that the Petén Maya did in fact exploit one relatively homogeneous environmental zone, with no regional differences in crop cycles or exploitive techniques, and a segmentation pattern which presumably resembled that of our "contagious" Formative villages: new communities remained in the same resource area. And in fact, the Maya did have unilateral exogamous clans—patrilineal ones—or "double unilineal descent," with the patrilineage being the most important in terms of land inheritance, governmental position, and exogamic marriage (Coe, 1965, p. 104; Roys, 1940, p. 38). But far from being in a "blind alley," the Maya reached a level of civilization, with carefully kept royal genealogies and enormous status differences, accumulation and redistribution of surpluses, and a truly pyramidal society. This suggests some rethinking of the potential of the unilateral exogamous clan system.

For one possible explanation of what happened in lowland Mesoamerica, two quotations from Fried may be relevant. "In all egalitarian economies . . . there is also a germ of redistribution. It receives its simplest expression in the family but can grow no more complex than the pooling and redisbursing of stored food for an extended family . . ." (1960, p. 716). This is the situation we picture along the lagoon and estuary systems of the coastal lowlands in the Early Formative.

> The move from egalitarian to rank society is essentially the shift from an economy dominated by reciprocity to one having redistribution as a major device. That being the case, one must look for the causes of ranking . . . in the conditions which enable the redistributive economy to emerge from its position of latency . . . to dominate a network of kin groups which extend beyond the boundaries of anything known on the reciprocal level (Fried, 1960, p. 719).

Our settlement pattern surveys indicate that this had indeed happened by Late Formative times on the Guatemalan coast: major agricultural activity had shifted inland to the piedmont in the vicinity of the Izapan ceremonial centers, leaving specialized salt-making communities behind to exploit the lagoon-estuary area (Coe and Flannery, 1967). Moreover, there is clear evidence that our coastal farmer-fishers were now linked into the diversified economic network of the adjacent highland area, with its specialized exploitive communities (like obsidian knapperies: see Shook and Proskouriakoff, 1956, p. 96).

However, we would like to suggest that the lowland Maya provide one example of the way in which a redistributive economy and a stratified society can grow out of patrilineal exogamous clans, even in a region where only one "resource area" is exploited, if *services* are substituted for *products*. Our model for this situation is indicated in Figure 4. The maize produced by the patrilineages engaged in farming is channeled into the regional center not for redistribution to food-producing lineages in other resource areas, but to lineages dealing in services: stone-masons, architects, lapidaries, priests, bureaucrats, and all the craft specialists who went into the making of the Maya empire. These lineages reciprocated by channeling into the redistributive center not products, but services. A kind of stratified society can be built up by ranking the patrilineages involved in these various activities (Fig. 5). The patrilineage directing all this, from whom the caciques were recruited, as pointed out by Roys (1957, p. 4), became reified to the point where it justified its lofty position by claiming descent from the gods. So stratified was the society that although individual patrilineages practiced exogamy, they married only with members of equally highly-ranked patrilineages. Four classes—nobles, commoners, serfs, and slaves—could be recognized at the time of European contact (Roys, 1940). Proskouriakoff (1961) has indicated that many inscriptions of the Classic Maya were the genealogies of ruling patrilineages; Kelley (1962) believes he has detected such a royal patrilineage in the monuments of Quiriguá and Copan. It seems not unreasonable to suppose that this stratified society grew out of a Formative pattern of patrilineal exogamous clans, a supposition which is lent support by the fact that the historic Maya did continue to practice strict patrilineal exogamy—in contrast to the ramified Mixtecs, with their brother-sister marriages.

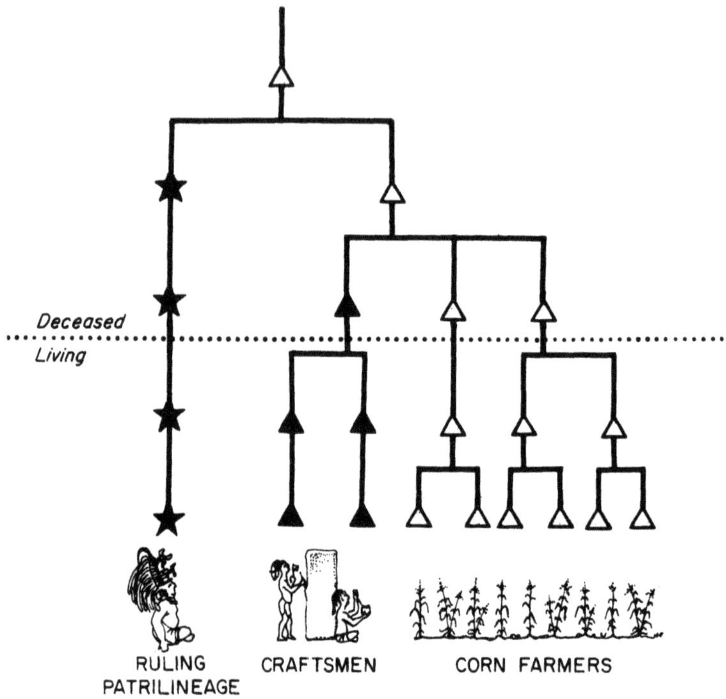

Figure 4. Lowland Mayan model.

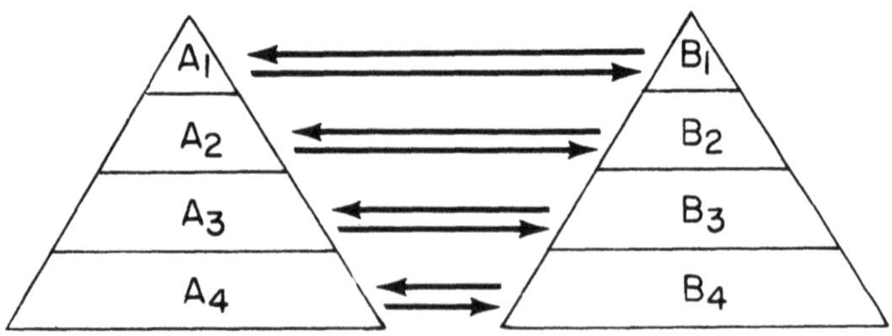

Figure 5. Patrilineage ranking.

Conclusions

Since we cannot step into a time-machine, there is much we can never know about the social organization of Formative Mesoamerica. We believe that on the basis of settlement patterns we can detect two basic types of exploitive systems: the "contagious" of the coastal lowlands and the "symbiotic" of the highlands. There is ethnographic evidence that the lowland area had exogamous patrilineal clans at time of European contact, while the southern highlands had a ramified type of organization. This would tend to support Sahlins' theories of a functional correlation between, on the one hand, the "contagious" segmentation process and unilateral-exogamous organization and, on the other hand, between ramified organization and a symbiotic economic pattern with redistribution. We would therefore like to suggest a tentative methodology for Mesoamerican archeologists who are interested in reconstructions of Pre-Columbian social organization.

1. Settlement pattern surveys aimed at showing whether the distribution of sites is "contagious" or a "balanced dispersal" with regard to resource areas.
2. The recovery of plant and animal foods in an effort to define specifically the products relied on, and the resource areas from which they come, with such a study's implications for the nature of the economy: whether balanced reciprocity or redistribution dominates.
3. The investigation of house and even room patterns within villages where possible, searching for clues such as Longacre (1964) and Hill (1965) have found, regarding the residence of corporate groups within the community itself.
4. Excavation of cemeteries such as reported by Longacre (1964) in an effort to determine degree of ranking, whether inherited or acquired, and the degree of status between members of adjacent dwellings and adjacent communities.
5. Utilization of ethnographic data from areas closely associated in time and space, where possible, with the prehistoric community.
6. Last, a search for correlations such as Sahlins attempted between residence patterns, economy, and social systems. This is the most difficult step, and the one which leaves us most open to error. But it is only through taking this step that we may enable ourselves, some day, to reconstruct in detail the processes that shaped early Mesoamerican civilization.

Postscript, 1968

This article was written in 1965. In the intervening years, further research by Flannery, Coe, and Sahlins (independently), plus cogent criticisms by Roy A. Rappaport and Ben Finney, render untenable part of the scheme presented here. Redistribution is indeed an efficient means of exploiting a varied environment, but it now seems unlikely that it is functionally related to stratification or "ranking" of the kind seen in rampages. Our new data suggest that stratification is more closely linked to preferential access to the most highly productive of the local resource areas. In the case of the Valley of Oaxaca (where Flannery is now working), the critical area is a narrow belt of river land which can produce two to three crops a year if irrigated. On the Gulf Coast (where Coe is now working), the key zone is the natural levee of the Coatzacoalcos River. Hereditary control of these zones by caciques (today) or high-status lineages (prehistorically) seems more important in the origins of stratification than redistribution. It is hoped that future research in Mesoamerica will clarify the extent to which redistribution is a tangentially related or a completely independent variable.

References

ALLEE, W. C., ALFRED E. EMERSON, ORLANDO PARK, THOMAS PARK and KARL P. SCHMIDT. 1949. *Principles of animal ecology*. Philadelphia: W. B. Saunders.

COE, MICHAEL D. 1961. Social typology and the tropical forest civilizations. *Comparative Studies in Society and History*, vol. 4, No. 1.

——. 1963. Cultural development in Southeastern Mesoamerica In Betty J. Meggers and Clifford Evans (Eds.), Aboriginal cultural development in Latin America: an interpretative review. *Smithsonian Miscellaneous Collections*, 146(1): 27–44.

——. 1965. A model of ancient community structure in the Maya lowlands. *Southwestern Journal of Anthropology*, 21(2): 27–114.

COE, MICHAEL D., and KENT V. FLANNERY. 1964a. Microenvironments and Mesoamerican prehistory. *Science*, 143(3607): 650–54.

——. 1964b. The Pre-Columbian obsidian industry of El Chayal, Guatemala. *American Antiquity*, 30(1): 43–49.

——. Early cultures and human ecology in South Coastal Guatemala. *Smithsonian Contributions to Anthropology*, Vol. 3. Washington, D.C.: *Smithsonian* Press.

CLARK, J. G. D. 1952. *Prehistoric Europe: the economic basis*. New York: Philosophical Library.

DAHLGREN DE JORDAN, BARBRO. 1954. La Mixteca: Su cultura e historia prehispánicas. *Colección cultura Mexicana*, No. 11. Mexico, D.F.: Imprenta Universitaria.

FRIED, MORTON H. 1960. On the evolution of social stratification and the state. In Stanley Diamond (Ed.), *Culture in history: essays in honor of Paul Radin*. New York: Columbia University Press.

HILL, JAMES N. 1965. The Broken K Site. Unpublished Ph.D. dissertation, University of Chicago.

KELLEY, DAVID H. 1963. Glyphic evidence for a dynastic sequence at Quiriqúa, Guatemala. *American Antiquity*, 27(3): 323–35.

KIRCHHOFF, PAUL. 1959. The principle of clanship in human society. Reprinted in Morton H. Fried (Ed.), *Readings in anthropology*, Vol. 2. New York: Thomas Y. Crowell. (Originally published in *Davidson Journal of Anthropology*, Vol. 1, 1955.)

LONGACRE, WILLIAM A. 1964. Archaelogy as anthropology: a case study. *Science*, 144(3625): 1454–55.

MACNEISH, RICHARD S. 1964. Ancient Mesoamerican civilization. *Science*, 143 (3606): 531–37.

PIÑA CHÁN, ROMAN. 1955. *Las culturas preclásicas de la cuenca de Mexico.* Mexico, D. F.: Fondo de Cultura Economica.

POLANYI, KARL. 1957. The economy as instituted process. In Karl Polanyi, Conrad M. Arensberg, and Harry W. Pearson (Eds.), *Trade and market in the early empires: economies in history and theory.* Glencoe, Ill.: The Free Press.

PROSKOURIAKOFF, TATIANA. 1961. The lords of the Maya realm. *Expedition,* 4: 14–21.

ROYS, RALPH L. 1940. Personal names of the Maya of Yucatán. *Contributions to American Anthropology and History,* No. 31. Washington, D.C.: Carnegie Institution of Washington.

——. 1957. The political geography of the Yucatán Maya. *Publications,* No. 613. Washington, D.C.: Carnegie Institution of Washington.

SAHLINS, MARSHALL D. 1958. *Social stratification in Polynesia.* Seattle: University of Washington Press.

SANDERS, WILLIAM T. 1956. The central Mexican symbiotic region: a study in prehistoric settlement patterns. In Gordon R. Willey (Ed.), *Prehistoric settlement patterns in the New World.* New York: Wenner-Gren Foundation for Anthropological Research.

SAPIR, EDWARD. 1916. Time perspective in aboriginal American culture, a study in method. Geological Survey, *Memoir* No. 90, *Anthropological Series,* No. 13. Ottawa: Canada Dept. Of Mines.

SHOOK, EDWIN M., and TATIANA PROSKOURIAKOFF. 1956. Settlement patterns in Meso-America and the sequence in the Guatemalan highlands. In Gordon R. Willey (Ed.), *Prehistoric settlement patterns in the New World.* New York: Wenner-Gren Foundation for Anthropological Research.

STIRLING, MATTHEW W. 1943. Stone monuments of southern Mexico. Bureau of American Ethnology, *Bulletin,* No. 138. Washington, D.C.: Smithsonian Institution.

WILLEY, GORDON R., GORDON F. EKHOLM, and RENÉ F. MILLON. 1964. The patterns of farming life and civilization. In Robert C. West (Ed.), *Natural environment and early cultures. Handbook of Middle American Indians,* Vol. 1 (Robert Wauchope, Gen. Ed.). Austin: University of Texas Press.

WOLF, ERIC R. 1959. *Sons of the shaking earth.* Chicago: University of Chicago Press.

Woodland Subsistence-Settlement Systems in the Lower Illinois Valley

This paper analyzes material remains to arrive at an interpretation of the *structure of segmentation* of two prehistoric cultural systems; that is, it investigates how the structure of material remains reflects the manner in which a social unit segments to exploit its biophysical environment. It is not a study of social organization in the sense that it analyzes material remains to arrive at the *behavioral attributes* of a social system (that is, the mechanisms for maintaining social integration, such as descent rules, post-marital residence patterns, etc.), but rather it is an attempt to sketch the morphology of two subsistence-settlement systems—to point up the kinds, quantities, and spatial configurations of material items that represent the skeleton of an extinct system for exploiting, processing, and storing food and other resources. This paper also attempts to compare these two sequentially related systems, to describe the important differences between them, and at least to broach the problem of explaining the observable changes between the earlier and later systems.

Premises: Archeological Research Objectives and the Nature of Culture

Archeology as conceived here attempts to describe and, more particularly, *to explain* the total range of cultural similarities and cultural differences observable in space and through time (L. R. Binford, 1962, p. 217). An evolutionary perspective is appropriate to the explanation of these similarities and differences. More efficient, therefore more differentiated, cultural forms replace less efficient ones, and higher levels of integration replace lower ones in the history of culture change. Structural diversity of cultures is expected consistent with widely varying social and natural environments, and culture history bespeaks of increasing diversity through time. The latter reflects higher levels of adaptive specificity as cultures become more closely geared to differing environments. Rates of cultural evolution are not uniform: they change with shifting selective pressures and vary with the adaptive requirements of diverse environments.

Culture is viewed as a system of functionally interdependent parts in which change in one aspect is related in specifiable ways to changes in others. Explanations for change in a cultural system require understanding of these linkages. Cultural variations in space are seen in terms of the differing adaptive requirements of specific environments; accordingly, varying ecological potentialities are linked to different exploitative economies and the latter, in turn, to differing integrative requirements and therefore to different forms of social structure, etc.

The job of archeology is to demonstrate correlations of structural elements within, and co-variation of elements between, cultural units through time and space. Archeology seeks, first, to reconstruct historical sequences of cultural systems with focus on the linkages between variables involved in the structural modification of these systems through time. And secondly, through controlled comparative studies between sequences it seeks to elucidate the functional relationships pertaining between these variables.

L. R. Binford (1962) suggests that material culture and the material by-products of living relate in a systematic way to the structure of the total culture. Archeology—and social anthropology alike—are faced with the task of correlating the structure of material elements of a cultural system with the structure of behavioral attributes of that same system. The structure of material remains is observable in terms of the qualitative and quantitative representation and spatial configurations of all classes of debris.

Recently, there have been several efforts to excavate and analyze prehistoric sites with the express purpose of describing this structure of material remains (for example, Binford and Binford, 1966). Winters (1966) has given us a detailed description of the structure of a Late Archaic subsistence-settlement system in the Wabash Valley. However, there still does not exist a sequence of structurally defined cultural systems for any region. Only when such information becomes available can hypotheses be developed that elucidate the functional relationships between variables in the history of systemic change.

Many archeologists who accept these premises and the research aims stemming from them, consider subsistence and settlement the most accessible aspects of the extinct culture.[1] The literature is replete with intuitive assessments of archeological complexes with respect to the problem of subsistence and settlement, but descriptions based on the qualitive-quantitative–spatial relationships pertaining within and between classes of artifacts, features, food debris, and other material remains are scarce.

Once the archeologist accepts the premise that the material culture of the extinct system will reveal a structured set of relationships, just as social anthropology has demonstrated these relationships in the behavioral aspects of cultural systems, he then takes as his problem the analysis of this structure within the universe of the site, the region, and so on. Within the site this structure might manifest itself in the definition of *activity areas* (for example, cooking locality) and *areas of social distinction* (for example, locus of a kin-defined residence unit). Each of these will have a formal definition based on the correlations of material cultural elements. A cooking locality might be defined in terms of one or more *tool kits* or *activity sets,* themselves defined on the basis of the spatial clustering of certain artifact types (for example, pestles and slab grinding stones), kinds of life-maintenance by-products (for example, fire residues and plant remains), and structural feature types (for example, hearths and earth ovens). In addition, each activity area can be expected to have spatial extension, since activities tend to be localized and to a degree spatially segregated within the area of a community. The analysis of kind, number, and distribution of material elements recovered from an archeological site, therefore, enables the archeologist to define tool kits, activity sets, and—it is hoped—activity areas. These, in turn, are the building blocks upon which *settlement types* are defined. All sites in which a particular configuration of exploitative and maintenance activities were carried out will disclose a similar structure of material elements and thus become examples of a single settlement type.

If focus shifts to a regional universe, the structure of an extinct settlement system should be reflected in the kind, number, and distribution of settlement types, each defined as indicated above. Since the biophysical environment is itself structured, and since culture is an *adaptive* system, its articulation with the environment should be reflected in the differential geographic distribution of settlement types.

The applicability of the foregoing concepts (1) for developing hypotheses to explain observed cultural variations in time and space, (2) for planning an archeological research design appropriate to testing these hypotheses, and (3) for devising effective methods of excavation and

[1] Many of the ideas presented here are the outgrowth of continuous discussion over the past five years involving James Brown, Lewis and Sally Binford, Joseph Caldwell, Melvin Fowler, Robert Whallon, Howard Winters, myself, and others. To Lewis Binford's work in sharpening the concepts of culture and culture change as these pertain to archeological objectives, I am particularly indebted. This paper was presented at the 1965 American Anthropological Association Meetings, Denver.

approaches to analysis that maximize the interpretive potential of the recovered data is best illustrated by describing them in the context of a specific archeological program.

Middle Woodland Period Culture Change in the Great Lakes-Riverine Area: Problem and Explanatory Model

Archeological work in the major river valleys south of the western Great Lakes highlights a period of extensive cultural change during the final centuries before Christ. These events, indicating a shift to higher levels of cultural complexity, mark the advent of what has been described as Hopewell Culture. (See Caldwell and Hall [1964] for recent statements on Hopewell).

The nature of the recognized culture change is threefold: (1) a rapid and marked increase in population; (2) development of complex ceremonial-mortuary activity reflecting increased status differentiation; and (3) an extension and intensification of "interaction" between cultural groups scattered over much of eastern United States. This interaction involved movement of exotic raw materials (for example, obsidian) and selected artifact styles (for example, zoomorphic effigy pipes) often between widely separated localities. Importantly, this synchronous emergence of style-sharing and raw material exchange over a wide area, of mortuary practices which reflect increasing status differentiation, and of rapid population expansion *was confined to certain localities within the Illinois, Mississippi, and a few other major valleys* within the Great Lakes –Riverine area. Contemporary cultural groups located outside these valleys apparently participated little or not at all in this interaction, and—more importantly—lack of evidence for both a population increase and the distinctive Hopewellian mortuary forms suggests they remained on a lower level of complexity (cf. Struever, 1965a).

In short, the archeological record for the Hopewellian manifestation during the Middle Woodland period suggests that the three developments in the culture change were interrelated aspects of a single phenomenon largely restricted to a few river valleys. The problem poses itself: are these in fact interdependent phenomena? If so, what model of systemic change best explains the available evidence for this episode of cultural development?

I began an attempt to answer these questions by assuming that economic change was an initiating factor; this inference was based upon the apparent correlation of known Hopewellian mound groups in the western Great Lakes with several important ecological variables, including temperature clines, major waterfowl migration routes, and variants of a particular river valley ecosystem (Struever, 1964, pp. 98–99). It was further hypothesized that the degree to which Woodland groups in different locales underwent a shift to a higher level of complexity was closley related to whether or not (and if so, to what degree) they experienced these still unknown adaptive changes.

The Illinois Valley Archeological Program

In 1959 I began a continuing program of site survey and excavation in the lower Illinois Valley, a region in which Hopewellian development was particularly marked. The first phase of this program sought to learn what changes, if any, had occurred in the exploitative economy and the structure of settlement and social organization between the terminal, or Black Sand, phase of the Early Woodland period (*ca.* 450 to 200 B.C.) and Middle Woodland times (200 B.C. to A.D. 400).

To date, three multi-component Woodland habitation sites have been excavated and surface survey has yielded cultural debris from about thirty additional sites with occupations falling into this time range. Effort was made to maximize recovery of materials relating to the exploitative economy of the resident Woodland groups.

No matter how detailed the collection and analysis of Early and Middle Woodland cultural remains, subsistence-settlement systems cannot be inferred without knowing something of the environmental context within which these systems evolved. If, for example, Middle Woodland communities in the lower Illinois Valley were situated partly in terms of the distribution of certain natural food resources, correlation between sites and these resources should provide valuable clues for understanding their subsistence-settlement system.

Vegetation is pivotal to understanding natural food resource distribution. Not only are the plants themselves a potential food source, but adaptation of animal species is in part dependent on the kind and distribution of plants. Accordingly, Allison (1966) has attempted a reconstruction of the floral make-up of the lower Illinois Valley based on the kind, quantity and spatial relationships of potential vegetal foods. This reconstruction is based on data from the original land surveyor's logs and maps, together with Turner's (1931) ecological studies of the 1920's. The results can be regarded as a valid picture of the vegetation during the early nineteenth century.[2] To what degree this early nineteenth-century floral makeup is similar to that of Woodland times remains to be learned; in this discussion the reconstructed nineteenth-century vegetation is treated as comparable to that of the centuries immediately before and after Christ. Allison was able to define ten microvegetation zones. Each is based upon a complex of natural food plants which, because of similar adaptive requirements, have a localized distribution within the lower Illinois Valley

[2] The early nineteenth century was chosen "because it is the earliest period for which there is good documentary evidence on the vegetation . . . and because this period preceded major changes in the flora . . . due to the influx of settlers, bringing modern technology and large scale agriculture into the area" (Allison, 1966, p. 3).

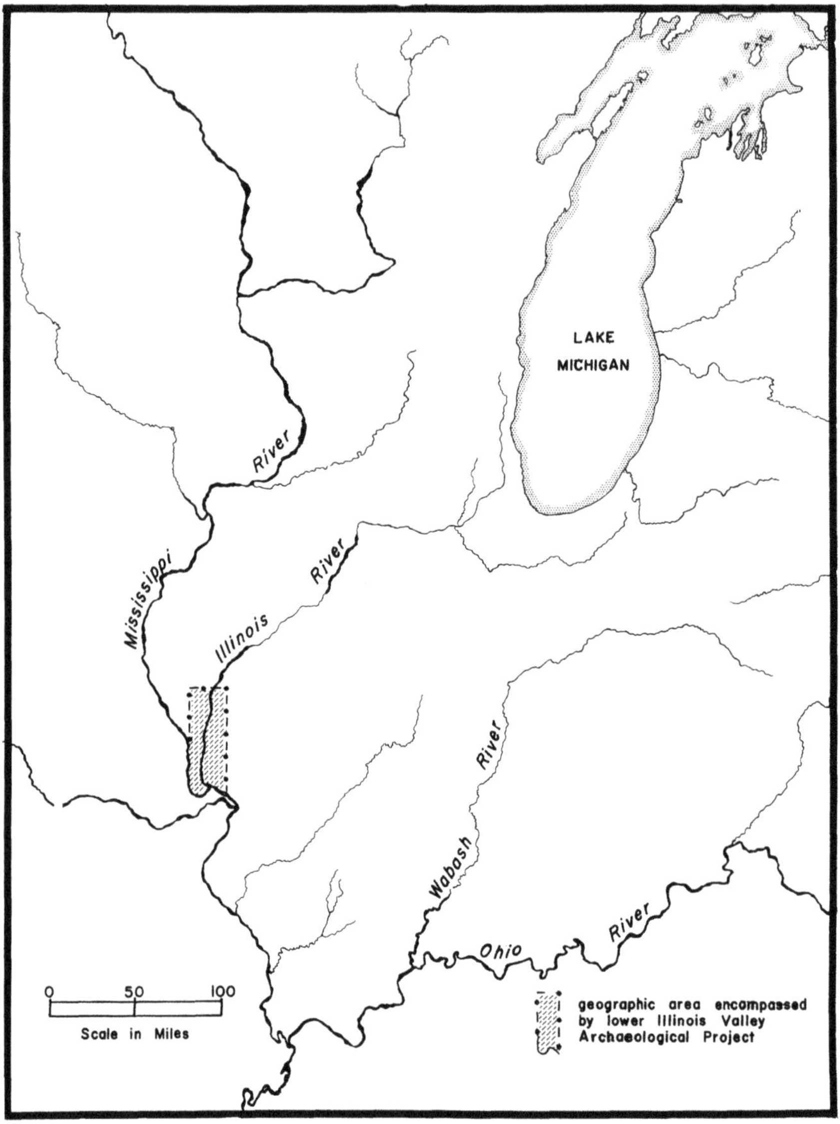

Figure 1. Lower Illinois Valley Archeological Project.

region. These plant distributions play an important role later in this paper in interpreting Woodland subsistence and settlement.

The hydrology and physiography of the lower Illinois, and in particular their relationship to the flora, are essential for understanding Woodland adaptations here. In this region the Illinois Valley is a broad, north-south–oriented trench that has cut deeply into Mississippian limestones. The lower Valley ranges from 3.5 to 5 miles in width and is bordered by perpendicular bluffs along both its eastern and western margins.

The Illinois River is a sluggish stream with a gradual gradient. Accordingly, it has not cut a deep channel, and natural levees that have a flood-controlling function are poorly developed along its banks. In this region the river hugs the western bluff line. Between the river and the bluffs on the opposite or eastern side of the valley stretches a broad alluvial bottomland which, prior to recent drainage, supported a dense forest of cottonwood, willow, and other water-tolerant trees, interspersed with sloughs and shallow lakes. Except for a narrow terrace along the eastern edge of the valley, this bottomland spans the entire breadth of the valley floor (cf. Fig. 4). The lakes were shallow catchbasins refilled almost annually by the spring floods. Through the summer months these lakes gradually evaporated and shrank, creating extensive mud-flats that provided an ideal habitat for local seed-bearing plants such as *Chenopodium, Polygonum, Iva,* and *Amaranthus* spp. The extensiveness of these backwater lakes is attributable to the gradual gradient, shallow stream bed, and minimal levee development characteristic of the lower reaches of the Illinois River. These, together with waters backing up from the Mississippi River into the Illinois Valley during periods of high water, resulted in prolonged floods in the lower Illinois. The sustained and almost annual flooding and subsequent gradual recession of the waters created a saturated floodplain dotted with shallow lakes and puddles, each with its captive fish population and a bottom formed of newly deposited silt.

Within the valley floor, adjacent to and paralleling the eastern bluff line, was a wet prairie covering the narrow corridor of higher ground previously mentioned.

The talus slope at the base of the bluffs along the valley margins, as well as the slopes of the tributary stream valleys cutting through the bluffs and leading into the Illinois from both east and west (cf. Fig. 4), were and are today covered by an oak-hickory forest. Above this "Hillside-Talus Slope Zone," as defined by Allison (1966), and extending from several hundred yards to more than a mile away from the Illinois Valley is a heavily dissected terrain. Like the Talus Slope Zone, this landscape supported a heavy and predominately oak-hickory forest. Beyond this upland forest belt, and still farther from the valley, began the high grass prairie which formed the predominant vegetation over an extensive area immediately south of the western Great Lakes. The Illinois River Valley and bordering uplands present a picture, then, of a narrow biome differentiated internally into a number of small-scale plant associations and cutting through a vast prairie landscape.

To analyze what, if any, change occurred in subsistence and settlement as part of a hypothesized general change in cultural system between the

Early and Middle Woodland periods in the lower Illinois Valley, it is necessary to describe and compare the material remains associated with Black Sand and the later Havana and Pike-Hopewellian phases.

The interpretations presented here are based upon data recovered and analyzed through December, 1965. These are preliminary impressions of incomplete studies; many changes in the interpretations presented here can be expected when the analyses of artifacts, faunal, and floral materials are completed.

Description of Black Sand Phase Sites in the Lower Illinois Valley

DISTRIBUTION

Black Sand living sites tend to be scattered along a series of low sand ridges situated in the Illinois Valley bottomlands and roughly paralleling the river (Fig. 2). In the main, these sand ridges, which in some cases run continuously for miles, appear to be shorelines of extinct river channels. They represent the highest ground in the floodplain.

Black Sand sites are located on the crest of these sand ridges, as well as on the upper few yards of slope leading into what was formerly the river; they are *not* located back from the immediate edge of what was then or formerly the river shore.

SIZE AND GROSS FORM OF SITES

Surface survey indicates Black Sand living sites on the old river beaches take two different forms: (1) small scatters of debris with definable limits; the area of scatter ranges from 0.5 to 2 acres; (2) continuous linear scatter; a light density of debris spread along the crest of a sand ridge for considerable distances. We might guess that the continuous linear scatter reflects repeated reoccupation or continuing occupation over some time of the same *locality* (that is, the sand ridge) but not reoccupation of a *specific site locus*. Stated differently, the continuous linear scatter reflects frequent shifting of the settlement without intention of confining occupation to a few spatially-bounded site locations. The debris left from many reoccupations or a continually shifting occupation gives the illusion of a single, long, shoreline community. It is our guess that the occasional small Black Sand site found on these same beaches reflects the true size of the local aggregate.

The predominance of a continuous scatter of Black Sand debris along the old river shorelines suggests: (1) intensive occupation of a single microenvironment, but not confinement of settlement for long periods to a specific site locus in that microenvironment; and (2) since the shoreline settlement was temporary and shifting, permanent constructions such as reuseable house frames and storage pits were not built there. It can be guessed that if constructions made for long-term use characterized these

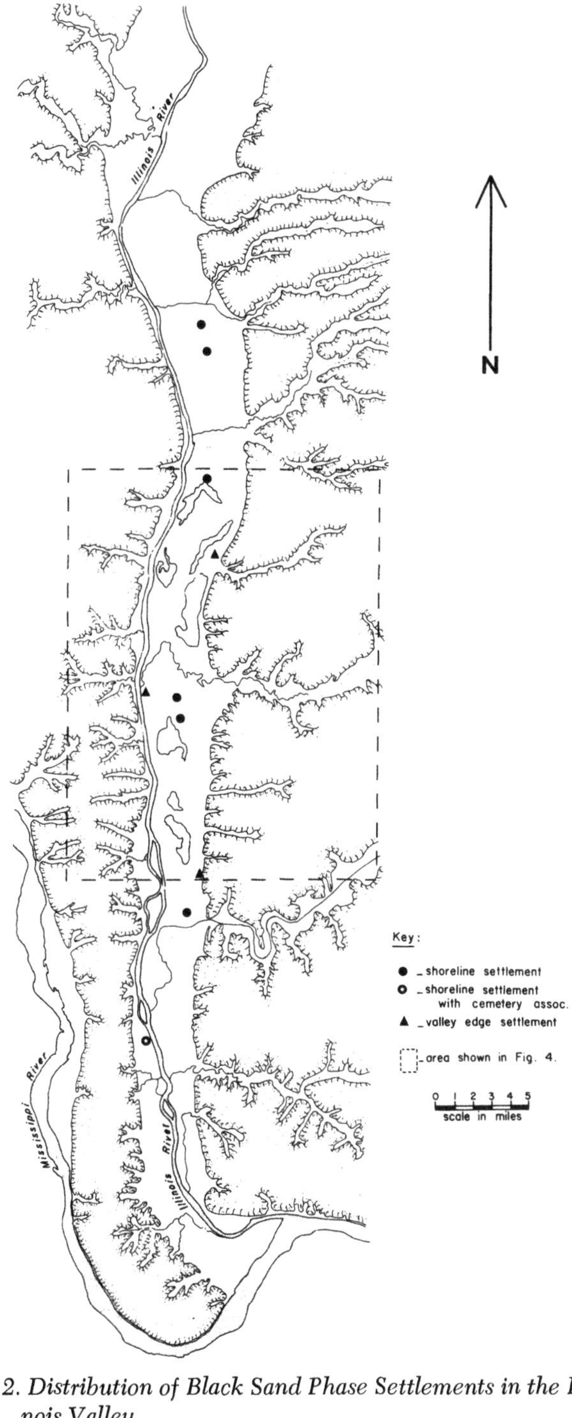

Figure 2. Distribution of Black Sand Phase Settlements in the Lower Illinois Valley.

shoreline communities, a higher frequency of sites with definable boundaries would occur.

INTERNAL STRUCTURE OF THE SITES

Survey data. Surface survey indicates a *very light* scatter of debris characterizes these Black Sand shoreline sites. Sherd densities are particularly *low,* while chert debris occurs in relatively *high* densities. A recent study of chert sources indicates exclusively local raw material on these sites. Mussel shell and animal bone are almost nonexistent on the surface, and burnt limestone—characteristic hearth stone in this region of natural limestone deposits—is scarce. Hand-size cobbles of crystalline rock, most often used in hammer and grinding activities, occur in high frequency. The soil of these Black Sand sites shows no sign of organic staining.

Excavation data. To date, Peisker represents the only excavated Black Sand habitation site in the lower Illinois Valley. Luckily, this site was protected against later disturbances by a Hopewellian burial mound built over it. Peisker was completely excavated in 1962 and 1963 by Gregory Perino of the Gilcrease Institute of Indian History and Art (Tulsa, Oklahoma), with intermittent help by the writer. This site was no more than an acre in area. Conforming to the surface survey evidence for Black Sand sites, densities of most classes of artifacts were light. A hunting-butchering tool kit was well-represented by the high frequency of projectile points and flake knives. Pebble manos and hammerstones also occurred in high frequencies. Recognizable imported chert was absent. It is notable that so-called "ceremonial items" (or, better, artifacts whose primary functional context was probably the social rather than technological) were also absent from the site.

Food remains included a wide range of land mammals; except for white-tail deer, high frequencies of bone from any one or two animal species were lacking. Flotation sampling of feature contents enabled retrieval of moderate densities of wood charcoal, but charred nut shells provided the sole evidence for plant foods.

Small, basin-like pits were found whose frequent charcoal contents indicate they were fire features of some sort. If cooking features, they were more likely roasting pits than earth ovens. Earth ovens are usually deep and steep-sided, and might be expected to contain fire-altered stone; none of these characteristics describes the Peisker features. Storage pits and houses are other feature types notably absent at this site.

A small cemetery occurred within the settlement precincts. A few primary and secondary burials were found in simple unprepared pits in the old beach; grave goods were absent except for red ochre associated with some skeletons. There was no evidence of differentiation between burials that might be associated with status.

Description of Middle Woodland Habitation Sites in the Lower Illinois Valley

DISTRIBUTION

Middle Woodland habitation sites are, with a few exceptions, concentrated at the base of the steep bluffs that define the eastern and western margins of the Illinois Valley (Fig. 3). These sites lie within Allison's Hillside–Talus Slope Zone with its dense and predominantly oak-hickory forest. The terrain is high and well-drained—not even exceptional floods in recent times have reached this elevation. The majority of these bluff-base sites are located along the *western* side of the valley; perhaps the bluffs here afforded protection against severe and prevailing westerly winds during the winter months. Proximity to the river, if it occupied its present channel, may also have been a factor favoring occupation of the western bluff-base.

Detailed analyses of prehistoric hydrology and physiography in the lower Illinois remain to be undertaken, but a few observations on the relationship of Middle Woodland bluff-base sites to water sources and land forms today are pertinent. First, the majority of Middle Woodland bluff-base settlements were situated at the junction of a secondary stream valley with the Illinois Valley. Inspection of these localities indicates most have three characteristics in common: (1) the tributary valley supports a perennial stream—even during dry months the drainage system of the small valley is extensive enough to maintain some minimum water level; (2) the river *today* passes close by the mouth of these secondary valleys; and (3) the floodplain in the lower reaches of the tributary valley is broad; heavy, swift run-off from the hill-country drained by the stream would have resulted in frequent floods and consequent silt deposition over extensive areas of the floodplain at the mouth of the secondary valley.

The great majority of Middle Woodland habitation sites in the lower Illinois occupy a bluff-base position, but there are a handful of sites on the old river shorelines in the valley floodplain. Not a single site is known from any of the tributary valleys leading into the Illinois, the upland forest bordering the Illinois Valley, or the prairie zone beyond (cf. Figs. 3 and 4). In short, Middle Woodland sites are located entirely within the trench of the Illinois Valley itself; they do not occur even several hundred yards outside the limestone bluffs that define its margins.

NUMBER AND SIZE OF SITES

The number of habitation sites increases sharply from Early to Middle Woodland periods in the lower Illinois. There are ten documented Early Woodland habitation components in the region, 25 Middle Woodland

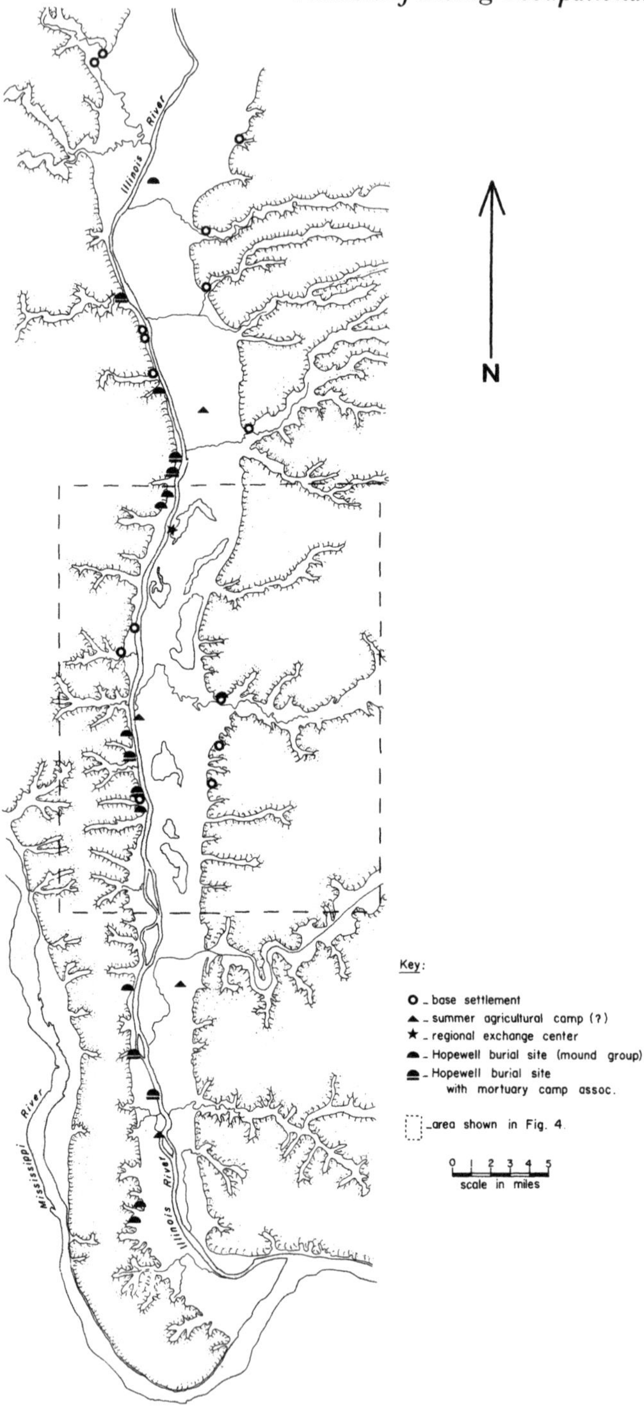

Figure 3. Distribution of Middle Woodland Settlements in the Lower Illinois Valley.

ones. This increase in frequency of living sites is believed to reflect both a change in settlement system, with a greater number of settlement types occupied by a single Middle Woodland local group within the span of a complete settlement cycle, and an absolute increase in population size in the region. The population increase cannot be measured until controlled sampling of all recognized microenvironments has been completed and both Early and Middle Woodland settlement systems are understood. Then, comparison of the size and number of examples of the settlement type believed to have been occupied by the *Maximum Local Aggregate*[3] chaaracteristic of a single *Maximum Subsistence-Settlement Unit*[4] can be used to estimate relative population densities here during the Early and Middle Woodland periods.

Certainly the increased frequency of living sites cannot be attributed to the concealing or destruction of Early Woodland sites; quite the contrary, Early Woodland sites are concentrated on natural levees most of which have *not* been covered or destroyed in any way. Middle Woodland habitation sites, on the other hand, because they are largely situated at the bluff base, are in position to be covered by sheet wash carried down from the bluff above. Test excavation indicates most bluff-base sites have been partially covered by recent sheet wash, and by chance two sites have been discovered that were completely covered by sterile overburden. It is clear that extensive sheet erosion has concealed entirely some bluff-base Middle Woodland settlements, and therefore the number of these sites is expected to be greater than the present survey evidence indicates.

Bluff-base Middle Woodland sites tend to have an area of scatter ranging from 2.5 to 8 acres. Even the smaller bluff-base sites are larger than any known Black Sand habitation site with definable boundaries. Middle Woodland bluff-base sites reveal a heavy scatter of debris; sharp increases are noted over Early Woodland in the density of all stone artifact types relating to exploitative and maintenance tasks, and in the density of sherds, faunal debris, and hearth stone. The soil within the site area is usually dark-stained, reflecting its high organic content. The site limits, in contrast to Black Sand, are sharply defined by the color differences between the organically stained habitation area and the unstained soil around it.

INTERNAL STRUCTURE OF SITES

To date, Apple Creek is the only extensively excavated Middle Woodland bluff-base site in the lower Illinois Valley. Snyder's Site in the Mississippi

[3] A *Maximum Local Aggregate* consists of the maximum number of people who together occupy a single settlement at *some* time during a total settlement cycle.

[4] A *Maximum Subsistence-Settlement Unit* includes all those people integrated at one or more intervals in the functioning of a single example of a subsistence-settlement system. It may or may not be synonomous with a Maximum Local Aggregate, depending on the system. It sometimes occurs that people who at no time in the subsistence-

Valley a few miles to the west is similarly located and was excavated by the writer in 1960.

At Apple Creek there is a major *early* Late Woodland occupation belonging to the newly defined White Hall phase. White Hall dates from about A.D. 400 to 700.[5] It immediately post-dates the Pike-Hopewellian phase of the Middle Woodland period (dated *ca.* A.D. 100 to 400). The succeeding is a composite description of the internal structure of the Apple Creek settlement compiled from the materials associated with both Middle and early Late Woodland occupations. Analysis of the Apple Creek materials has not yet proceeded far enough to enable division of excavated materials between these two successive occupations, nor is it yet possible to demonstrate the association of specific artifact and feature types in arriving at a definition of tool kits, activity areas, and areas of social distinction. However, the kind and quantity of artifact and feature types, together with food remains recovered are themselves illuminating.

Tools belonging to a hunting-butchering tool kit occur in very high frequency, as do pebble hammer-grinding stones. Manufacturing tools also occur in large numbers. These include tools to make items of exploitative technology and others to make products not directly associated with food procurement and preparation (for example, clothing). Items of recreational equipment (for example, deer phalanges drilled for use in the cup-and-pin game) are also frequent.

Noteworthy is the high frequency of artifacts fitting L. R. Binford's (1962, p. 219) definition of "sociotechnic" items. These artifacts are believed to have their primary functional context in the social subsystem where, for example, they might serve to symbolize and communicate status of the person identified with the object. At Apple Creek these would include drilled bear canine teeth, pottery earspools and figurines, fragments of platform pipes (some converted into pendants), and perhaps obsidian lamellar flakes. Mica flakes recovered in the excavations suggest that sheets of this mineral—a characteristic Hopewellian grave good in this region—were cut and shaped by the Middle Woodland occupants. This perhaps reflects *manufacture* as well as use of these status goods in the Apple Creek community.

An exceedingly high density of structural features occurred at Apple Creek. Most numerous were deep, cylindrical storage pits and earth ovens. Earth ovens were characteristically filled in part with a mass of burnt limestone chunks. Quantities of this burnt rock were dispersed

---

settlement cycle are members of a common residence unit (such as a nucleated community) belong to a single *Maximum Subsistence-Settlement Unit.* This would be the case in some redistributive systems.

[5] Apple Creek is the type site for White Hall. Characteristic White Hall pottery styles are sufficiently distinctive to warrant the separate phase designation, yet they are similar enough to Weaver in the central Illinois Valley, and other early Late Woodland regional variants in the Midwest, to indicate contemporaneity with them. Radiocarbon evidence confirms this estimate of White Hall dating.

through the midden and littered the site surface. At Apple Creek more than 600 of these and other features were located in some 18,500 square feet of excavated site surface; this is equivalent to one storage-refuse pit or earth oven per 5 x 6-ft. area of site surface. As a further indication of the magnitude of storage and cooking facilities at Apple Creek, total volume of these features exceeds an estimated 10,000 cubic feet.

One complete Middle Woodland house, 40 feet in diameter, was excavated at Apple Creek. Holes defining the perimeter of the building ranged from 6 to 16 inches in diameter, suggesting that posts of the exterior supporting wall were both large and permanent. In turn, this suggests the building was constructed for use over some period of time. Remains associated with this building indicate it served as a domicile.

By-products of living, particularly food remains, excavated at Apple Creek also reflect Middle and early Late Woodland subsistence practices. Quantities of animal bone were recovered; Paul W. Parmalee (ethnozoologist at the Illinois State Museum) and Andreas A. Paloumpis (icthyologist at Illinois State University) have almost completed identification of these materials. A diverse local fauna is represented, but it is noted that bone from the white-tail deer, wild turkey, and various migratory waterfowl species occurs in high frequencies. In addition, Paloumpis (1966) has analyzed almost 30,000 fish bones from the site. Lawrence Kaplan (University of Massachusetts) and Richard A. Yarnell (Emory University) are working with quantities of carbonized plant remains from Apple Creek. These were recovered almost entirely by means of water and chemical flotation processes (Struever, 1965b). Over 36,000 fragments of hickory nut shell from 189 earth ovens, surface hearths, and storage-refuse pits have been identified, together with more than 4,200 fragments of acorn shell from 140 features. Seeds of commensal plants are represented by some 1,800 charred *Polygonum* seeds, 230 *Chenopodium*, and 160 *Iva* seeds (Lawrence Kaplan, personal communication).

Food remains associated with Middle and early Late Woodland occupations at Apple Creek, while reflecting exploitation of a broad range of local fauna, show major reliance on deer, turkey, ducks and geese, and fish. Aside from one *Lagenaria* seed and four seeds of *Cucurbita pepo* (Hugh C. Cutler, personal communications), no certain cultigens have been identified from Apple Creek. The evidence indicates reliance on hickory nuts and acorns in season, with the seeds of pigweed, lamb's-quarter, and other local plants still of indeterminate importance.

At the Newbridge site, three miles from Apple Creek, the writer recovered a mass of carbonized *Chenopodium* and *Polygonum* seeds from a White Hall phase pit. The seed mass was entirely free of leaves, stems, or other plant debris and had all the appearances of food that had been burnt and discarded in the process of cooking. While nothing comparable was recovered from any feature at Apple Creek, the Newbridge *Chenopodium-Polygonum* seed mass suggests these seed-bearing plants played a role in the White Hall subsistence economy.

Discussion thus far has centered entirely on the number, distribution, and internal structure of Middle Woodland sites located at the base of the talus slope along the margins of the Illinois Valley. The majority of Middle Woodland habitation sites occupy this bluff-base position, but survey to date also reveals five sites on the old river shorelines in the Illinois Valley floodplain. Unfortunately none has been excavated.

One of these five floodplain sites is different from all other known Middle Woodland sites in the lower Illinois Valley. This site covers a minimum of twenty acres and its surface is littered with an incredibly high density and diversity of cultural materials. The size of the Mound House site sets it apart from the other 24 Middle Woodland habitation sites known in this region. None of these 24 covers an area more than one-third that of Mound House. This site has not yet been excavated, and little can be said of its internal structure. However, debris collected from its surface suggests it may represent a unique example of one settlement type in the Middle Woodland settlement system of this region.

Large quantities of imported raw material and finished goods made from this material have been collected from its surface. Copper celts and earspools, drilled bear canine teeth, platform pipe fragments, and other typical Hopewellian status items are found in numbers. Artifacts or unaltered bits of obsidian, mica, marine shells, and copper reflect participation of the inhabitants in an exchange system bringing raw materials from distant sources into the Illinois Valley. The diversity and density of this exotic material are additional characteristics that set Mound House apart from the other Middle Woodland sites in the region. The site appears to represent some sort of trade or exchange hub, and perhaps served as a center of within- and between-region interaction, in which exchange activities took place articulating local Middle Woodland groups with each other and, in turn, with groups outside the region.

The Peisker site, described earlier in this paper, is both the location of the one excavated Black Sand component in the lower Illinois Valley, and also the site of a group of three Hopewellian burial mounds. These mounds were recently excavated by the Gilcrease Institute under Gregory Perino. Altogether they yielded five log crypts in each of which occurred from seven to twelve adult human skeletons with typical Hopewellian artifacts in association.

Alongside these mounds was a Middle Woodland habitation site which the writer excavated. The artifacts recovered here suggest this living site belonged to the same cultural group that was responsible for the mounds.

This Middle Woodland occupation site situated adjacent to the Peisker mounds is markedly different in size and internal structure from the aforementioned bluff-base settlement as represented by Apple Creek. Evidence recovered indicates the site was not occupied primarily to perform tasks relating to the subsistence economy. Rather, activities relating to maintenance and reinforcement of social integration of the group, centering about mortuary ceremonialism, appear to characterize the occupation. The excavated materials indicate exploitative and maintanence activities connected with subsistence were singularly unimportant at this site. Evidence to support this interpretation is of several kinds:

1. Low densities of faunal material occurred, even though bone was moderately well preserved.
2. Extensive flotation sampling produced quantities of charcoal flecks from the midden, but little analogous to the nut shells and seeds recovered at Apple Creek. The widespread occurrence of wood charcoal indicates this absence cannot be attributed to poor preservation.
3. A marked lack of storage-refuse pits and earth ovens in contrast to the great numbers of these features at Apple Creek.
4. Projectile points, scrapers, knives, manos and metates and other food preparation tools were scarce.
5. Manufacturing tools of all kinds were almost totally absent.
6. Woodworking tools (for example, celts) and stone or shell hoes were rare.
7. Sherds from what were likely culinary or storage vessels were numerous.

In brief, the combined evidence from Peisker indicates that little, if any, food was collected, processed, or stored on this site. The occurrence of hearths in numbers and pottery vessels caked with char suggest that food was prepared and eaten on the site, but it may well have been carried here from another settlement. House remains were absent.

In contrast to the scarcity of artifacts and features associated with subsistence activities, numbers of typical Hopewellian status items were recovered. These comprise a high proportion of the total artifact assemblage, when compared against assemblages from known bluff-base sites.

Taken together, this evidence suggests that Peisker represents a specialized Middle Woodland mortuary camp. Data in support of this conclusion are: (1) the large number of status items, all common Hopewellian burial associations; (2) two apparent ritual features—one a cache of status items and the other remnants of a structure that was apparently built and burned several times; (3) a small area within the habitation site in which status artifacts were concentrated; (4) Hopewellian burial mounds in immediate proximity; (5) paucity of evidence for exploitation, preparation, and storage of food and manufacture of tools and other goods; and (6) the absence of houses or other permanent constructions.

The Gilcrease Institute excavations uncovered a total of five log crypts in the three mounds. Each tomb apparently served as a mausoleum into which bodies were placed; burial occurred soon enough after death that decomposition had *not* progressed to the point where bone articulations were disturbed. It would appear that each log crypt was reopened at intervals to receive a new body. Only occasional burials occurred in the mound fill or around the mounds.

In sum, the materials from the living area and the mounds appear to be the remnants of multiple, short-lived occupations associated with the burial of select dead. Activities involved were earthwork and tomb construction, mortuary ritual, and interment of the body.

A Black Sand Subsistence-Settlement System in the Lower Illinois Valley

The totality of evidence from which to interpret Black Sand subsistence and settlement is relatively sparse compared to that available for the succeeding Middle and early Late Woodland periods. However, certain generalizations can be made.

Settlement was concentrated in the alluvial floodplain of the Illinois River, specifically on the shorelines of old river channels and perhaps on the banks of floodplain lakes. Occasional Black Sand sites are found on sand ridges located near the bluffs at the valley edge, but *none* are known from the base of the bluff talus slope itself or outside the Illinois Valley proper (that is, within the secondary stream valleys, in the dissected uplands adjacent to the river, or on the prairie beyond).

The preponderance of Black Sand habitation sites in the Illinois Valley floodplain may reflect heavy dependence on riverbottom flora and fauna. The faunal remains recovered at Peisker indicate Black Sand groups exploited a wide range of *land* animals. Location of habitation sites on the river shoreline may relate to fishing, but the faunal materials do not confirm this. Fish remains were rare. It is important to know, in this connection, whether the sand ridges were, at the time of occupation, the shoreline of an existing river or the shoreline of an abandoned stream channel. Immediate proximity of sites to river channels does not necessarily indicate Black Sand groups depended heavily on river foods; occupation of the natural levees may reflect effort to settle on the highest available ground in the floodplain.

Perhaps most important of all, there is no evidence that Black Sand groups depended heavily on one or a few animal species.

No evidence for plant cultivation was found, whether of tropical or local plant types. Admittedly, carbonized plant remains have been actively sought at one site only. Plant remains at Peisker indicate use of nuts, but preliminary inspection reveals few, if any, seeds from such local plants as *Chenopodium, Polygonum,* and *Iva.*

In sum, diversified collecting of river-bottom fauna, and perhaps plant foods, characterizes Black Sand subsistence.

Our sample of Black Sand sites is too small to determine if settlement size has one or more than one mode. If further survey confirms the present suggestion that *bounded* Black Sand habitation sites are uniformly small (about 0.5 to 2 acres in area), it may be possible to infer that fusion and fission of the Maximum Local Aggregate did not occur in the course of the settlement cycle.

The sites tend to be linear in form and to hold to the crest of the natural levees. Continuous scatters of debris, in at least one case extending for a mile or more, are thought to reflect intensive occupation of the shoreline zone with shifting, impermanent settlement characteristic. Apparently no attempt was made to occupy for long periods or to continually reoccupy a specific site location, and it is inferred that constructions made for long-term use were not part of these communities. Excavation at Peisker confirms this interpretation, since no evidence of houses or other permanent constructions was recovered here. The absence of storage pits supports the view of a shifting residence pattern.

It will be recalled that there was no evidence at Peisker for Black Sand natural food harvests. It can be inferred that harvest of natural food "crops" with concomitant surpluses would have resulted in storage; in turn, the latter would make continued occupation or seasonal reoccupation of a single site adaptive. We have seen that the combined survey and excavation data from Black Sand sites reveal the absence of all three—that is, natural food harvests, food storage, and long-term residence at one site.

In sum, one, and perhaps two, Black Sand settlement types are recognizable. One, the *Shoreline Settlement,* was temporary and shifting. Local Black Sand groups used an existing or former river shoreline as a base of operations from which to exploit resources in the riverbottoms surrounding it. These sand ridges and adjacent bottomlands fall within Allison's Floodplain Forest and Backwater Lakes Zones, two microenvironments with the highest productive potential of any in the lower Illinois Valley region in terms of the density and diversity of natural food resources.

Seasonally, local groups may have moved nearer the bluffs at the valley edge to exploit ripening nuts, and these sites, none of which have been excavated, would represent a possible second settlement type (cf. Fig. 2).

Middle Woodland Subsistence-Settlement System

Middle Woodland sites in the lower Illinois Valley, then, have three characteristic locations: (1) at the base of the talus slope along the valley margins; (2) on river shorelines in the Illinois Valley floodplain; and (3) immediately proximal to a Hopewellian burial site. Figure 3 shows this distribution clearly. Furthermore, it has been seen that in structural terms the floodplain sites can be separated into two types, with Mound House a unique example of one type.

The totality of evidence supports the interpretation that the bluff-base Middle Woodland site represents a community occupied continuously or intermittently over a long time span. It reflects an adaptation characterized by a high level of residential stability.

Differentiation in soil color alone suggests that the bluff-base site is the remains of a discrete, bounded settlement. The internal structure of the community, as seen at Apple Creek, supports the idea of long-term residence. High frequencies of storage pits and a house with heavy supporting framework are seen as evidence for permanent constructions. The artifactual evidence indicates that tool manufacturing was important at this site, and that recreational activity was part of the daily life of the local inhabitants. The occurrence of artifacts associated with manufacturing and recreational activities itself suggests sustained occupation of the site. Ethnographically in the eastern Woodlands it was during the long winter occupations that the bulk of tool manufacturing and repair, as well as games and other entertainment took place.

In sum, bluff-base sites like Apple Creek provide evidence of sustained occupation of a specific site locus. The site may have been occupied year-round, or for a span of several months each year.

The analyses of the food remains from Apple Creek indicate heavy dependence on white-tail deer, wild turkey, migratory waterfowl, and fish. Large quantities of hickory nut and acorn shell indicate these were collected in quantity, while smaller numbers of charred smartweed, lamb's-quarter, and marsh-elder seeds suggest they *may have been* exploited at the time the site was occupied. Noteworthy here is the apparent selectivity in natural foods exploited. From the various Apple Creek data it is inferred that the bluff-base settlement was occupied during all or part of the fall, winter, and spring.

Because none have been excavated, the Middle Woodland sites located on the sand ridges in the flood-plain—sometimes three or more miles from the nearest bluff-base site—remain a mystery.

It may be noteworthy that these sites are located in the microenvironment where the backwater lakes occur with their shorelines of rich alluvial silt.

The Mound House site, from the surface evidence alone, is distinguishable from all other known Middle Woodland sites in the lower Illinois. Its size is several times that of the next largest Middle Woodland site. Its surface yields an unequaled density and diversity of debris; and the materials collected there include a high proportion of imported raw materials used exclusively in making Hopewellian sociotechnic items.

The Peisker Middle Woodland component is different from Apple Creek and any of the aforementioned sites. High densities of animal bone are lacking. Occupations of the site may have been of short duration, since storage pits and other features interpreted as permanent constructions are lacking. Tools of exploitative and maintenance technology relating to subsistence are scarce, while manufacturing tools and recreational paraphernalia are absent. That food was prepared and cooked on the site is indicated by bone fragments, apparent roasting pits, and char-covered sherds from culinary vessels.

Noteworthy in this Middle Woodland occupation site at Peisker was direct evidence for ceremonial-mortuary activity. This was reflected in the high proportion of sociotechnic artifacts, the occurrence of two ritual features and a possible ceremonial precinct (inferred from the localization of sociotechnic artifacts on the site), and the immediate proximity of the occupation area to five log mausoleums covered by earth mounds. Each tomb contained a few adult burials with associated Hopewellian goods.

Middle Woodland Culture Change: An Explanatory Model

What model most economically explains the observed structural changes between the Early and Middle Woodland archeological complexes described here?

The following hypothesis suggests that a shift in subsistence-settlement system occurred between Early and Middle Woodland times. Changes also occurred in social organization, reflecting different integrative requirements created by higher population densities, larger local aggregates, and changes in the manner of segmenting and partitioning the population required for performing the new subsistence tasks.

It is inferred that a marked change in ecological adaptation occurred in the lower Illinois Valley about the time of Christ. Caldwell (1958, p. 31) has noted that following the establishment of primary forest efficiency in the eastern Woodlands by Late Archaic times (*ca.* 2500 to 1000 B.C.), the hunting-gathering pattern continued, and in favored areas it was characterized by more "specific adjustments to regional resources." The lower Illinois Valley is seen as one such "favored area" and here collecting of natural foods reached a new high level of efficiency by at least the Hopewell phase of the Pike tradition (Middle Woodland period, *ca.* A.D. 100 to 400).

This new subsistence base can be termed *Intensive Harvest Collecting.* Intensive Harvest Collecting denotes an adaptation centering on exploitation of *selected, high-yielding* natural food resources characteristic of certain biomes that have a sharply restricted geographic distribution within the woodlands of northeastern United States.

Two factors are seen as essential to the biomes in which Intensive Harvest Collecting is feasible: (1) natural food products must occur in large, concentrated populations and lend themselves to harvesting (that is, they can be collected in quantity with relatively small labor output); and (2) the plant and animal populations from which these food products are derived must be regularly renewed.

At least five resources available to Woodland groups in the lower Illinois Valley meet these criteria: (1) nuts and acorns; (2) the seeds of commensal plants such as *Iva* (marsh-elder), *Polygonum* (smartweed), and *Chenopodium* (lamb's-quarter); (3) white-tail deer; (4) migratory waterfowl; and (5) certain species of fish. All five resources can be efficiently exploited by means of a simple harvest technology. Annual fall nut crops, with hickory nuts and acorns especially important, have their highest productive potential in the Hillside-Talus Slope and Upland Forest zones occupying the steep slopes and dissected uplands along the margins

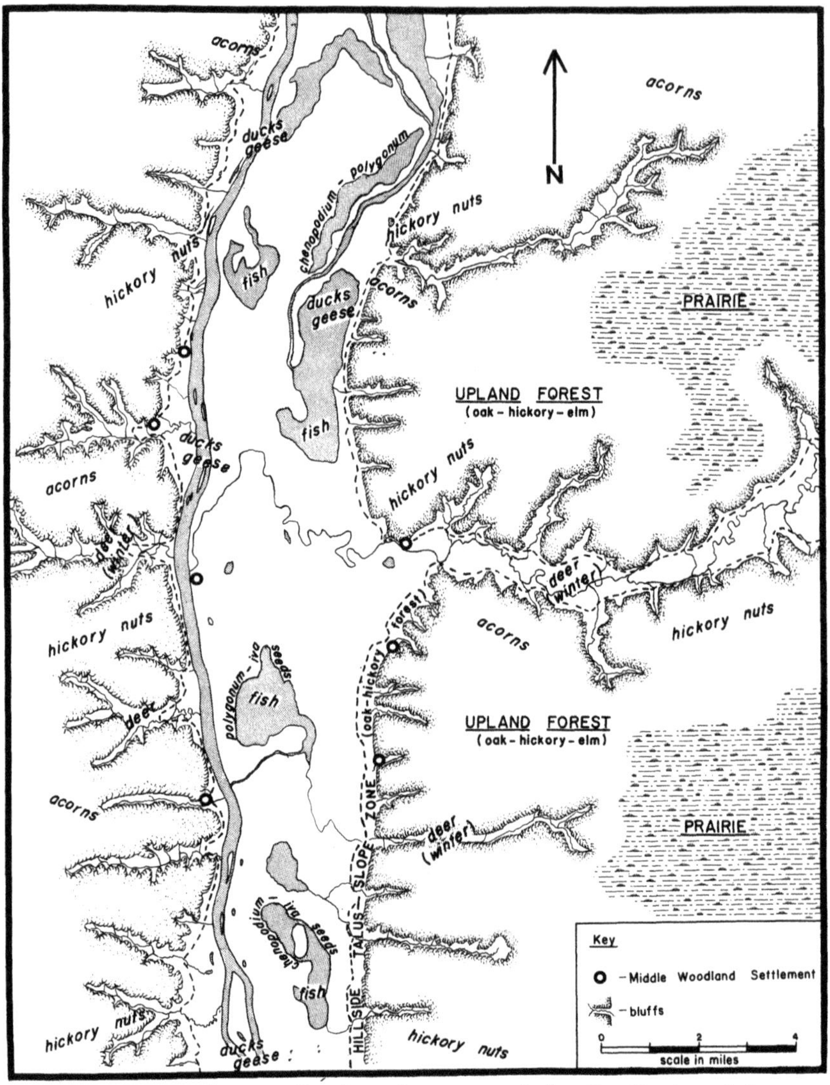

Figure 4. Middle Woodland Settlements and the distribution of harvestable natural foods.

of the Illinois and secondary stream valleys (Allison, 1966). *Chenopodium* and the other seed-bearing plants mentioned above colonize natural scars in the mantle of vegetation. In the valley bottomlands, spring floods are constantly opening new areas of soil, the most extensive of which are the mud-flats bordering permanent floodplain lakes and the silt deposits remaining after temporary catch-basins of floodwater have entirely evaporated. It may be that here, naturally or through man's intervention, grew stands of lamb's-quarter and other plants whose carbonized seeds at Apple Creek, Newbridge, and other sites attest to their economic importance. Indeed, Allison's (1966) botanical study highlights the localization of these species on the floodplain lake shorelines.

During the winter deer tend to move out of the Illinois Valley floodplain and into the valleys of feeder streams and into the forested areas of the talus slope and adjacent uplands where browse is more plentiful. Here, by various ambush and drive techniques, large numbers might be killed. The Illinois Valley is an important waterfowl migration route, part of the Mississippi flyway. Ducks and geese move along this narrow corridor twice annually. The migrating birds stay largely within the confines of the river valley, feeding and resting on the floodplain lakes. On these lakes, by means of cast nets or other trapping devices, it was feasible for Middle Woodland hunters to harvest these birds. In the early twentieth century, market hunters using different techniques have demonstrated this all too successfully. Paloumpis (1966) demonstrates that on the basis of both species composition and size range within species determined on fish remains from the Apple Creek site, entire fish populations characteristic of riverbottom lakes were apparently collected by the Middle and/or early Late Woodland residents. Possible techniques for harvesting fish in this situation would include use of natural poisons, draining the lake, and stunning the fish by stirring up the muddy bottom and thus reducing the oxygen level of the water.

In short, the food remains from Apple Creek suggest selective exploitation of those natural plants and animals that could be harvested efficiently and with resulting high yields. This change in subsistence practices appears to have begun in Middle Woodland and continued into White Hall times (at least to A.D. 700).

With these changes in subsistence there occurred a concomitant shift in settlement. From the survey and excavation data, four settlement types can be tentatively recognized constituting a Middle Woodland settlement system. The *Base Settlement* is represented by Apple Creek and all those sites located at the talus slope along the sides of the Illinois Valley. The valley-edge lies midway between *all* the microenvironments in which occur one or more of the aforementioned harvestable natural foods. Inhabitants of the Base Settlement had immediate access to all five resources. It is guessed that these resources were exploited in season from this site, and also that processing and storage of these foods constituted major tasks performed in these communities. These foods are available at various times from fall through early spring, and it is hypothesized that valley-edge settlements were occupied continuously during this period.

The few Middle Woodland sites on the sand ridges in the floodplain may represent *Summer Agricultural Camps.* These sites are located proximal to former lake shorelines which provided the only extensive soil areas on which plant cultivation could be practiced, given a simple hoe technology. Until one of these floodplain sites is excavated, little more can be said to support the thesis that these sites were occupied primarily during the summer to perform agricultural tasks. There is some suggestion from the pollen evidence that Apple Creek was abandoned during the summer (Schoenwetter, 1964). During this period the occupants may have moved into the floodplain, setting up temporary camps on the sand-ridge shorelines of the river and lakes to carry on agricultural activities nearby. Summer and early fall were seasons in which inhabitants of the bottomlands were relatively safe from the floods that regularly inundated the valley floor.

The Mound House site is a unique example of the third tentative Middle Woodland settlement type: the *Regional Exchange Center*. Here, finished goods and raw materials characteristic of the Hopewell Interaction Sphere (Caldwell, 1964; Struever, 1964) may have entered the lower Illinois Valley and been exchanged for local products (pearls?). At Mound House, members of the local Middle Woodland groups throughout the lower Illinois Valley area may have congregated periodically to trade and carry on ritual activities by means of which these foreign imports—copper, mica, marine shells, obsidian, etc.—were distributed over the region, eventually to become burial goods in status graves covered by earth mounds that occur in small groups scattered along the valley margins.

The fourth Middle Woodland settlement type here is the *Mortuary Camp*. These small habitation sites proximal to Hopewell mound cemeteries appear to represent short-lived, specialized occupations undertaken to perform mortuary tasks. The archeological evidence from Peisker, the only excavated example of this settlement type, reflects activities relating both to mortuary tasks themselves and to maintenance of the participants engaged in this work.

Conclusions

This paper attempts to demonstrate a major change in subsistence-settlement systems from Early to Middle Woodland periods in the lower Illinois Valley. The new subsistence pattern involves the intensive "harvest" exploitation of select natural food resources, with possible cultivation of local seed-bearing plants along the shorelines of riverbottom lakes. The resulting higher levels of economic productivity were accompanied by population expansion (documented by the marked increase in total number and size of habitation sites). Population expansion, combined with new patterns of segmenting and partitioning the population necessitated by the harvest-collecting technology, created new integrative requirements. Now perhaps larger numbers of people were organized into a single sociopolitical system. Differential access to goods and services, so apparent in Hopewell burial sites in the lower Illinois Valley, reflects increased status differentiation. Imported raw materials and craft items fashioned from them occur with relatively few burials interred in tombs or mausoleums. These constructions involved major outlays of labor; one Hopewellian mound in the lower Illinois is built from more than an estimated one million cubic feet of soil. Associated with these inferred changes in social structure is the extension and intensification of long-distance trade which, for the first time on any scale, brought exotic raw materials and finished goods into the region. Again, for the most part these imported goods appear archeologically as burial associations with selected individuals.

How can this episode of culture change—at this time and place—be explained? David Aberle (personal communication) reminds us that cultures do not *necessarily* maximize the exploitative potential of their environment. It is only in certain, still-to-be-defined coping situations involving particular relationships of culture to other cultures and culture to biophysical environment that "maximizing adaptations" occur. It remains to be determined what changing selective pressures provided the impetus for maximization of productivity based on collecting, as documented here for Middle and early Late Woodland in the lower Illinois Valley. It is important only to reaffirm that it is in the nature of the shifting coping situations during Early Woodland and initial phases of Middle Woodland that we must seek an explanation for the culture changes described here.

Whatever the shifting selective pressures from Early to Middle Woodland times in the lower Illinois Valley, they were not present equally—or at least did not produce the same results—throughout the entire western Great Lakes—Riverine area. Judging from the distribution of Hopewellian goods and mortuary sites, the shift in adaptation described here—involving changes in the structure of subsistence and settlement, an increase in population density, increased social complexity, and participation in long-distance trade—appears to have been a localized phenomenon confined largely to the central and lower Illinois Valley, sections of the central Mississippi Valley, and a few other localities.

Increased economic productivity is regarded as prerequisite to the other manifestations of change noted here. To the extent that increased productivity was dependent on an intensification of collecting like that inferred here for the lower Illinois Valley, it is not surprising that major culture change during Middle and early Late Woodland was *geographically restricted* in the western Great Lakes area. The complex of potentially harvestable natural resources described here for the lower Illinois have a very *limited* distribution. Paloumpis (1966) demonstrates that fish in riverbottom lakes of the central Mississippi drainage have an exceedingly high biomass; furthermore, he points out how restricted within the Great Lakes area are broad floodplain situations with extensive backwater lakes. Waterfowl migration routes within the Mississippi flyway are narrow corridors along which great flights of ducks and geese move seasonally. Outside these routes, which follow certain major river valleys, waterfowl numbers diminish sharply. Cleland (1965) points out that deer prefer deciduous forest "edges," that is, places where forest borders on scrub and grassland, and Taylor (1956, p. 137) notes that white-tail deer have always produced their largest populations where edges are most extensive. One such edge situation is the forest-grassland ecotone, an example of which is the strip of forested uplands bordering the Illinois and other river valleys that dissect the long-grass prairie south of the western Great Lakes. It can be expected that this forest-grassland zone supported a dense deer population in prehistoric times.

The northern boundary of the temperate deciduous forest lies in southern Illinois and Indiana. North of it, and extending into southern Wisconsin and Michigan, lies the prairie peninsula. Within the prairie peninsula nut crops were restricted to the narrow strips of forest bordering stream courses. The dissected terrain adjacent to the Illinois Valley and feeder streams leading into it supported a heavy oak-hickory forest with excellent potential for nut production. And, finally, large stands of *Chenopodium* and similar seed-bearing plants occur only where stable plant associations are prohibited from forming over extensive areas. The most extensive areas of this kind in the eastern Woodlands occur in the broad river floodplains.

Intensive Harvest Collecting, then, is a subsistence type that, given certain selective pressures, may develop in an ecological context supporting a number of particularly high-yielding natural food resources. In the western Great Lakes area these conditions are found in certain broad river valleys only. These valleys have extensive floodplains with a shallow river channel, low gradient, and poorly developed natural levees. Flooding is an annual occurrence. These valleys have a high productive potential in fish, a fact traced to the great expanse of backwater lakes with their high biomass and fish populations that are renewed through regular flooding (Paloumpis, 1966). These same conditions create extensive areas of raw soil on which seed-bearing chenopods, marsh elder, and other plants flourish. During the spring and fall, waterfowl migrate along certain of these valleys. Heavy forests along the valley margins produce nut crops and provide maximal conditions for support of a dense white-tailed deer population (Cleland, 1965).

It is interesting that culture change during the Middle Woodland period in the western Great Lakes area appears most marked in localities where this convergence of high-yielding populations of several plant and animal species seems to have existed. Hopewell burial sites have their greatest density in areas characterized by such an environment. It can be hypothesized that, were the evidence available, these same areas would also disclose significant population expansion and extensive participation in the Hopewell "interaction sphere," or trade system, during the Middle Woodland period.

This is not to imply that *all* culture change during Middle Woodland in eastern United States was based on this *particular* shift in subsistence practices. Rather, it might be expected that marked regional variability in both ecological conditions and selective pressures gave rise to a complex mosaic of regional developments. Each was characterized by greater or lesser rates and varying types of change and influenced in varying ways by occurrences in contiguous and non-contiguous regions. David Aberle (personal communication) cautions that developments in any one region must be understood in terms of changes in the total environmental context of a culture, and this context includes the whole sphere of between-culture interaction in which the group under investigation resides. Therefore, the eventual explanation of the accelerated culture change in Middle Woodland groups of the lower Illinois Valley may lie more in a response to significant culture change occurring in southern Ohio, the Gulf Coastal Plain, or elsewhere, than in the changing availability of fish, chenopods, hickory nuts, deer, and ducks in the lower Illinois Valley, or in a new realization that these resources could be collected on a large-scale by means of new techniques.

In short, it may well be to changes in the *social* environment of these Illinois Valley Middle Woodland groups that we will eventually ascribe the changes in subsistence, settlement, population density, and social structure that are only now beginning to emerge from the archeological record.

References

ALLISON, APRIL L. 1966. Reconstruction of pre-modern vegetation in the lower Illinois Valley: a study of floral communities and their distribution with reference to prehistoric cultural-ecological adaptations. (Unpublished).

BINFORD, LEWIS R. 1962 Archaelogy as anthropology. *American Antiquity,* 28(2): 217–25.

BINFORD, LEWIS R., and SALLY R. BINFORD. 1966. A preliminarv analysis of functional variability in the Mousterian of Levallois facies. *American Anthropologist,* 68(2), Part 2: 238–95.

CALDWELL, JOSEPH R. 1958. Trend and tradition in the prehistory of the eastern United States. American Anthropological Association, Memoir No. 88.

——. 1964. Interaction spheres in prehistory. In Joseph R. Caldwell and Robert L. Hall (Eds.), *Hopewellian studies. Scientific Papers,* 12 (6): 133–43. Springfield: Illinois State Museum.

CALDWELL, JOSEPH R., and ROBERT HALL (Eds.). 1964. *Hopewellian studies. Scientific Papers,* Vol. 12. Springfield: Illinois State Museum.

CLELAND, CHARLES E. 1965. The evolution of subsistence patterns in the eastern United States. (Unpublished.)

PALOUMPIS, ANDREAS A. 1966. Prehistoric utilization of fish populations in the lower Illinois Valley. (Unpublished.)

SCHOENWETTER, JAMES. 1964. Pollen studies in southern Illinois. Unpublished report to M. L. Fowler, Southern Illinois University, as part of research undertaken under the auspices of the National Science Foundation (G188) and the Illinois Archaeological Survey.

STRUEVER, STUART. 1964. The Hopewell interaction sphere in Riverine-western

Great Lakes culture history. In Joseph Caldwell and Robert L. Hall (Eds.), *Hopewellian studies. Scientific Papers,* 12(3): 85–106. Springfield: Illinois State Museum.

——. 1965a. Middle woodland culture history in the Great Lakes-Riverine area. *American Antiquity,* 31(2): 211–23.

——. 1965b. The flotation process for recovery of plant remains. Southeastern Archaeological Conference, *Bulletin* 3: 32–35.

Taylor, Walter P. 1956. *The deer of North America.* Harrisburg, Pa.: Stackpole Press.

Turner, Lewis MacDonald. 1931. Ecological studies in the lower Illinois River Valley. Unpublished Ph.D. dissertation, University of Chicago.

Winters, Howard D. 1966. The Riverton Culture. Unpublished Ph.D. dissertation, University of Chicago.

Post-Pleistocene Adaptations

This paper will examine some of the major assumptions underlying the current systematics of the archeological remains of the post-Pleistocene period. The paper falls into three parts: (1) a brief survey of the history of research on the immediately post-Pleistocene period, with particular attention to the conditions affecting research orientation and, consequently, systematics; (2) an assessment of the utility of current concepts, schemes, and arguments which are advanced to explain cultural events of the post-Pleistocene period; and (3) the outlining of a different approach for understanding the nature and extent of cultural changes occurring during the period.

The archeological remains of the immediately post-Pleistocene period are generally termed Mesolithic. They are characterized over wide areas by the appearance of small, highly specialized flint implements; these occur frequently on later sites in the coastal and riverine regions in the context of the systematic exploitation of aquatic resources.

Until 1892, there was widespread agreement among European scholars that there was a break, or "hiatus," in the archeological record between the Paleolithic and Neolithic epochs (Brown, 1893; G. de Mortillet, 1885, pp. 479–84; Breuil, 1946, p. 25).

> It has generally been assumed that a break occurred between the periods during which this country, and in fact the continent of Europe, was inhabited by Palaeolithic Man and his Neolithic successors, and that the race or races of Palaeolithic folk who hunted the elephant, rhinoceros, cave bear,

hippopotamus, reindeer, *ursus*, bison, etc., were completely seperated as by a chasm from the agricultural people, the herdsmen with their oxen and sheep, and the tillers of the soil of the so-called Neolithic epoch, implying that man in Britain had changed suddenly from the low savage hunter to a half-civilized farmer and drover (Brown, 1893, p. 66).

A. C. Carlyle who conducted archeological investigations in the Vindhya Hills of Central India between 1868 and 1888 was the first to use the term "mezolithic." Carlyle was also one of the early questioners of the validity of the hiatus between the Paleolithic and Neolithic. Carlyle's excavations yielded typical crescents, trapezoids, and other geometric microliths; it was asserted that these implements were found both with late Paleolithic tools and pottery. This led him to propose that there was no hiatus in India and that the microliths constituted an intermediate industry to which he applied the term "mezolithic." These materials were exhibited in England in 1888 at the Royal Albert Hall.

Carlyle's findings served to stimulate John Allen Brown who published an article summarizing Carlyle's work (Brown, 1889). In this article, Brown asked if there had been similar microlithic forms found in the British Isles, pointing out that they were already reported from Tunis, Egypt, Italy, Palestine, France, Portugal, and the Crimea. Brown's main concern was with documenting the widespread occurrences of microliths, and he offered no chronological interpretation. Wilson (1894) reported that in 1892, the U.S. National Museum acquired much of Carlyle's material, and he proposed the acceptance of the Mesolithic as a transitional period between the Paleolithic and Neolithic.

The following year Brown published an extensive paper (Brown, 1893) in which he discussed the problem of the hiatus. He went on to argue in favor of an unbroken continuity between the Paleolithic and Neolithic, setting forth four stages: Eolithic, Paleolithic, Mesolithic, and Neolithic. He based this four-fold division on the transformational sequence of axes, from the crude forms of the "Drift" to the well-made polished types of the Neolithic. He documented finds of "intermediate" forms and used a scale of crude to fine as evidence for historical continuity, citing Pitt-Rivers' argument that such a transformational sequence indicated historical continuity (see Pitt-Rivers, 1906, pp. 20–44). Occupation of the same caves by Paleolithic and Neolithic populations is cited as further support for the claim of continuity.

The following year, Boyd Dawkins challenged Brown's views:

> I shall first of all address myself to the point as to continuity in this country. Is there any evidence that the Palaeolithic shaded off into the Neolithic age in this country without any such break as I have mentioned above? Next, I shall examine the facts bearing on the point outside of the British Isles, premising that the evolution of the Neolithic from the Palaeolithic stage of culture in some part of the world may be accepted as a high probability, although we may be unable to fix with precision the land where this transition took place (1894, p. 243).

Dawkins went on to question the validity of the reasoning behind the claims for continuity and concluded: "The exploration of caverns has not, I submit, yet resulted in establishing a 'continuity' but simply a sequence" (1894, p. 274).

The English literature of the early 1890's is full of arguments on these issues, and similar questions were also occupying continental scholars. The formal changes in the archeological record were the subject of controversy, both with regard to the meaning of the observed changes and the reality of a hiatus. Lartet and G. deMortillet claimed as early as 1872 that the apparent break in the archeological record was in reality simply a gap in knowledge and did not represent a period during which Europe was not occupied (Piette, 1895b, pp. 235–36). Cartailhac, on the other hand, stated that the hiatus consituted a major break in the occupancy of the continent. In 1875 the Congress of Prehistory held a meeting at Nantes, and an argument was presented which attempted to disprove Cartailhac's position by pointing to formal similarities between the flints from Solutré and those of the Neolithic period (Piette, 1895b, p. 238).

Shortly after this, artifacts were found which were dated to the period between the remains of the Magdalenian, or "reindeer," period and that of the Lake Dwellers, the Robenhausian. In 1879 Vielle discovered microliths at Fère-en-Tardenois (1890, p. 961). Almost ten years later Piette made his discoveries at Mas d'Azil where microliths were found in association with modern fauna. The deposits in question overlay the Magdalenian and lacked the features then considered diagnostic of the Neolithic (Piette, 1895a). These finds were followed by surveys of locations with microliths (A. deMortillet, 1896), and there was a proliferation of names for these industries which were said to fill the hiatus (see Coutil, 1912). New excavations were also carried out (deLoe, 1907; Herve, 1899).

In the years following World War I, there was a marked increase of interest in the post-Pleistocene period, and a number of regional syntheses were made (Kozlowski, 1926; Clark, 1932, 1936; Childe, 1931, 1937). Further, there was an extension of European terms to non-European materials which were considered intermediate between the Paleolithic and Neolithic (Garrod, 1932, 1937). Some general works also appeared in which data from various regions were summarized and compared (Obermaier, 1916; Osborn, 1919; deMorgan, 1924; MacCurdy, 1924; Menghin, 1927). Specific syntheses of the Mesolithic period proper have appeared (Burkett, 1925; Gimbutas, 1956, 1963). In these various summary and interpretive writings, there are several distinct lines of reasoning, leading to a diversity of opinion as to the historical significance of the archeological record.

One line of argument sought to demonstrate that the Mesolithic represented a way of life, and a subsistence base, intermediate in a developmental sequence between the reindeer hunters of the terminal Pleistocene and the food-producing villagers of the Neolithic. For example, Piette claimed that there was evidence for the domestication of the horse by the

Solutreans, reindeer by the Magdalenians, and cattle by the occupants of Mas d'Azil who also, according to Piette, domesticated plants (Piette, 1895b). Less extravagant claims have recently been made for the transitional nature of the Baltic materials (Troels-Smith, 1953) and those from Central Europe (Pittioni, 1962). Few workers, however, have seriously considered the European Mesolithic as a stage transitional to the later food-producing societies.

Other workers were more concerned with the problem of the continuity (or lack of it) between the human groups responsible for the Paleolithic and Mesolithic. Osborn (1919, p. 457) saw in each change in form of archeological assemblages evidence for the invasion of new "races." Others argued that the presence or absence of discrete traits was diagnostic of population stability or change. For example, Grahame Clark (1932, p. 2) and Menghin (1927) based their claims for historical continuity between the Paleolithic and Mesolithic on the continued use of core tools. Obermaier (1924, p. 324), on the other hand, viewed the shift to the exploitation of aquatic resources in Ertebølle and the Auterian as justifying the postulation of movement of new people into Western Europe. DeMorgan (1924, p. 74) saw the adoption of microliths and the loss of graphic arts as "revolutionary" and as proof of a major break in historical continuity. Childe (1925, p. 2), Clark (1932, p. 1), Gimbutas (1956) and Braidwood (1963) are in general agreement that the Mesolithic of Europe is a continuation of the Paleolithic way of life and that the observed archeological changes can be related directly to the major climatic changes of the post-Pleistocene period. These authors do differ, however, on the degree to which changes in the form of archeological assemblages can be explained by reference to new populations or to "influences" from other cultures.

We have attempted to show in this brief historical survey that Mesolithic research has been characterized by a series of changing questions and that the answers to any one question have tended to generate new questions. The initial problem was to determine whether or not Europe was occupied between the end of the Paleolithic and the beginning of the Neolithic. The affirmative answer to this problem led to the question of historical continuity. Consideration of this problem necessitated consideration of the criteria for evaluation of formal archeological variations in terms of their meaning for population change or lack of change. There was considerable diversity of opinion on this question.

Although problems of interpretive theory and method were never solved (see the papers by S. R. Binford and J. Sackett, this volume), they began to occupy scholars less and less as more detailed knowledge of the archeological record accumulated. Local sequences were worked out, and a more limited geographical perspective led to greater conservatism in interpretive viewpoints. Most recent workers have used a diffusionist model for interpreting geographic variations in archeological data, with the postulation of actual movement of peoples playing a minor role (see, for example, Waterbolk, 1962). The problem of historical continuity *vs.* population movement has not been so much solved as circumvented; this circumvention has involved two means: first, application of one's own criteria to an extremely detailed sequence in a very limited area making it almost impossible for other workers to judge interpretations offered; and second, stressing certain widespread "traits" in macroregional syntheses, traits which are usually so generalized that one might question their relevance to the measurement of detailed changes in culture history.

The work of the past 100 years has resulted in the accumulation of sufficient data to justify some generalizations made by workers in the field of European Mesolithic studies. Some of the generalizations made in distinguishing the Paleolithic from the Mesolithic are:

1. *There was a major shift in the centers of population growth in Western Europe.* "During the Upper Magdalenian, the density of population was relatively high in France, as evidenced by the great number of sites occupied for the first time, and by the richness of the sites. . . . The end of the glacial times was fatal to this striking human expansion. The disappearance of the cold fauna and the replacement of the steppe, rich in game, by forests was followed by the demographic recession and breakup of the Upper Paleolithic cultures resulting in the traditions which are grouped together under the general name of Mesolithic" (deSonneville-Bordes, 1963a, p. 354; see also deSonneville-Bordes, 1960, 1963b; and Sackett's paper, this volume).

2. *There was a major change in the form of stone tools.* "Small, geometric flints became very common, and the bow and arrow became widespread during the immediately post-Pleistocene period. The changes have occasionally been taken as defining features of the Mesolithic" (Childe, 1956, p. 96, see also Gabel, 1958, p. 658).

3. *There is greater geographic variety in cultural remains suggesting more specific responses to local environmental conditions.* See deMorgan, 1924, p. 74, Garrod and Bate, 1937, p. 121, Braidwood and Willey, 1962, p. 333, Schwabedissen, 1962, p. 260, Pittioni, 1962, p. 218; deSonneville-Bordes, 1960, p. 497–500; 1963 for specific statements of this generalization.

4. *There was a marked increase in the exploitation of aquatic resources and wild fowl.* This statement scarcely requires documentation since it is practically a definiens of the Mesolithic (cf. Gabel, 1958, p. 661).

5. *There was a "trend" toward small game hunting.* Braidwood (1962, p. 332) notes that this phenomenon has traditionally been explained as a response to the extinction of large mammals at the close of the Pleistocene. He points out, however, that this trend occurs before the end of the Pleistocene and characterizes Africa and India as well as Europe (see also Gimbutas, 1956, p. 14).

6. *The Mesolithic represents cultural degeneration when compared*

with the Upper Paleolithic. This is generally cited in the context of discussions of the Western European materials and the loss of graphic arts (see Osborn, 1919, p. 456; deMorgan, 1924, p. 73; Clark, 1932, p. 1; Sollas, 1924, p. 595; deSonneville-Bordes, 1960, p. 498). Reference is also made to the less prestigeful activity of fishing and shellfish collecting, as opposed to reindeer hunting (Osborn, 1919, p. 457).

These generalizations which summarize archeological observations have been conceived by most European scholars in the following manner (see Clark, 1962, p. 100):

1. There are major changes in cultural remains which serve to differentiate the cultural systems of the terminal Pleistocene from those of the immediately post-Pleistocene period.

2. This immediately post-Pleistocene period is further characterized by major changes in pollen profiles, fossil beach lines, and the geomorphology of major drainage systems.

3. The demonstrable correlation between the dramatic cultural and environmental changes at this time is evidence for the systematic articulation of cultural and environmental systems.

Therefore:

a) Archeological differences observed between the terminal Paleolithic and the Mesolithic can be explained by reference to environmental changes.

b) Differences not explained by reference to environmental changes are the result of new social contacts; such social contacts were a result of movement of populations in response to local climatic deterioration (for example, the "desiccation" of North Africa cited by Clark, 1936, p. xiv).

This argument is a relatively straightforward mechanistic approach and is completely compatible with a materialistic, systemic approach to the understanding of cultural change. The extent to which this approach might be questioned and the particulars of its application tested depends upon the degree to which: (1) equally radical changes in culture can be demonstrated in the absence of analogous environmental changes, and/or (2) major environmental changes can be demonstrated to vary independently of analogous changes in cultural systems.

Such test situations can be found either at a contemporary time period outside the area directly affected by the retreat of glacial ice or in the same regions under similar environmental conditions at a different time period. Researchers concerned with the initial appearance of food production, as well as those workers operating in a variety of non-Western European regions, are the ones to whom we now turn for an evaluation of the explanatory approach commonly used on Western European materials.

The shift from food-procurement to food-production has been examined by many scholars; Childe termed this change the Neolithic Revolution. In *The Dawn of European Civilization* (1925) Childe suggested that the investigation of the origins of the Neolithic and its spread into Europe would be a major step in the understanding of the post-Mesolithic history of Western Europe. In his *New Light on the Most Ancient East* (1952) Childe offered a model to explain the beginnings of the Neolithic Revolution. Until this point, several other workers had considered the problems of understanding the conditions surrounding the origins of agriculture, and some offered idealistic progressions of conditions under which man would have gained sufficient knowledge of plant and animal biology to permit cultivation (Darwin, 1875, pp. 326–27; Roth, 1887). Others offered mechanistic generalizations about the conditions under which man would have been most likely to have implemented his knowledge (Tylor, 1881, p. 214; deCandolle, 1959). Childe's consideration of the problem was the most influential, since he presented a series of propositions specific enough to be tested through the collection of paleoenvironmental and paleoanthropological data:

> Food production—the deliberate cultivation of food plants, especially cereals, and the taming, breeding and selection of animals. . .was an economic revolution. . .the greatest in human history after the mastery of fire. . . . The conditions of incipient desiccation. . .would provide the stimulus towards the adoption of a food-producing economy. Enforced concentration by the banks of streams and shrinking springs would entail an intensive search for means of nourishment. Animals and men would be herded together in oases that were becoming increasingly isolated by desert tracts. Such enforced juxtaposition might promote that sort of symbiosis between man and beast implied by the word domestication (Childe, 1951, pp. 23-25).

If it was Childe who first provided a set of testable propositions as to the conditions under which food-production was achieved, it was Braidwood who actively sought the field data to test Childe's propositions. For a short history of the Iraqi-Jarmo project, the reader is referred to Braidwood and Howe (1960, pp. 1–8); we shall simply summarize the findings of Braidwood and his co-workers with specific reference to the validity of the oasis theory and to the materialistic approach to the understanding of culture change. In discussing the oasis theory Braidwood states:

> So far this theory is pretty much all guess-work, and there are certainly some questions it leaves unanswered. I will tell you quite frankly that there are times when I feel it is plain balderdash (1951a, p. 85).

Braidwood also questioned the relevance of the postulated environmental changes to the origins of food-production:

> There had also been three earlier periods of great glaciers, and long periods of warm weather in between. . . . Thus the forced neighborliness of men, plants and animals in river valleys and oases must also have happened earlier. Why didn't domestication happen earlier too, then? (1951a, p. 86).

Braidwood has made the above point on numerous occasions, but it is in more recent publications (Braidwood and Willey, 1962, p. 342) that the comment is less directly aimed at the oasis theory and more toward questioning the role of environmental change in bringing about food-production.

Braidwood's work in the "hilly flanks" zone of the Fertile Crescent was carried out over a number of years and involved the collaboration of a number of scientists from the fields of zoology, paleontology, geology, palynology, paleobotany, etc. Their investigations had been directed toward the identification of the physical effects of domestication on plants and animals and the documentation of the environmental events of the period between 10,000 B.C. and the appearance of "settled village life." The climatological-environmental results have allowed Braidwood to generalize:

> It seems most unlikely that there was any really significant difference between then and now in the general land forms and rainfall patterns (1952b, p. 11).
>
> In southwestern Asia. . .our colleagues in the natural sciences see no evidence for radical change in climate or fauna between the levels of the Zarzian and those of the Jarmo or Hassunah phases (Braidwood and Howe, 1960, p. 181).

Discussing specifically the relationship between environmental change and the beginnings of food-production, Braidwood states:

> We do not believe that the answers will lie within the realm of environmental determinism and in any direct or strict sense . . . we and our natural-science colleagues reviewed the evidence for possible pertinent fluctuations of climate and of plant and animal distributions. . .and convinced ourselves that there is no such evidence available. . .no evidence exists for such changes in the natural environment. . .as might be of sufficient impact to have predetermined the shift to food production (Braidwood and Howe, 1960, p. 142)

Thus Braidwood argues that: (1) environmental conditions analogous to those at the close of the Pleistocene had occurred previously without having brought about food-production, and (2) there is no evidence to support major climatic changes in the Near East of sufficient magnitude to have "predetermined the shift to food production." These observations are not only directed against the oasis theory but also against the argument that food-production constituted an alternative adaptation to changed environmental conditions at the close of the Pleistocene. Braidwood also argues against the causative role of environmental change in his consideration of the applicability of the term Mesolithic to non-European areas (Braidwood and Willey, 1962, p. 332). Garrod (1932) called the Natufian of Israel a Mesolithic industry, and the appropriateness of this terminology has been questioned by Braidwood:

> . . .the usual conception of the Mesolithic is as a cultural readaptation to post-Pleistocene environments but the conception has become an awkward

> one, on a world wide scale, since as we have just seen, there is evidence that the same trends toward readaptation and intensification of collecting activities had begun to manifest themselves in certain areas before the conventional date for the end of the Pleistocene. One of us is of the opinion that there was no Mesolithic sensu stricto, in southwestern Asia, at least (Braidwood and Willey, 1962, p. 332).

There is also increasing evidence that there were cultural changes parallel to those occurring in Western Europe in regions where there were no correlated major climatic changes (see, for example, Perrot, 1962, pp. 147, 151–53).

Braidwood presents a strong case that there was major cultural change in areas where environmental change was minor or absent, as well is in areas such as Western Europe where environmental change was marked. This, together with the fact that earlier interglacial warm periods were not accompanied by drastic cultural changes of analogous form, is sufficient to invalidate the argument that the magnitude of environmental and cultural change can be expected to vary directly in a simple stimulus-response pattern. These data also raise questions about the positive correlations claimed for the form of environmental and cultural changes.

Braidwood, however, is not completely consistent in his application of these findings. He argues *against* the causative role of environmental change in the Near East, yet *for* such an explanation for the cultural changes observed in Western Europe (Braidwood and Willey, 1962, p. 341). We do not propose here that there is no relationship between environmental and cultural change in Western Europe but rather argue against the direct and simple causative role of environmental change in view of Braidwood's own findings. What we must seek is a set of explanatory variables which will be valid on a world-wide scale at the terminal- and post-Pleistocene periods.

If Braidwood rejects environmental change as the principal explanation in the Near East, what does he propose instead? After apologizing for Childe's "materialistic philosophy of history" (Braidwood and Howe, 1960, p. 7), Braidwood offers his "nuclear zone" theory:

> In my opinion there is no need to complicate the story with extraneous "causes." The food producing revolution seems to have occurred as the culmination of the ever increasing cultural differentiation and specialization of human communities. Around 8,000 B.C. the inhabitants of the hills around the fertile crescent had come to know their habitat so well that they were beginning to domesticate the plants and animals they had been collecting and hunting. . . . From these "nuclear" zones cultural diffusion spread the new way of life to the rest of the world (1960a, p. 134).

A nuclear zone is defined as follows:

> A region with a natural environment which included a variety of wild plants and animals, both possible and ready for domestication . . . (Braidwood, 1963, p. 106).

In his statements Braidwood proposes that cultivation is the expected, natural outcome of a long, directional evolutionary trend, limited only by the presence in the environment of domesticable plants and animals. This is clearly an orthogenetic argument (see Simpson, 1949, pp. 130–59 for a critical discussion of orthogenesis). The vital element responsible for the directional series of events appears to be inherent in human nature; it is expressed by Braidwood in such phrases as "increased experimentation" (1963, p. 106) and "increased receptiveness" (1963, pp. 97–98, 137–38). These behavioral traits made it possible for man to "settle into" his environment (Braidwood and Reed, 1957, p. 20), and they serve as the basis for Braidwood's taxonomy of subsistence-settlement types (1960b, pp. 143–51) in which three long-run trends can be seen: (1) increased localization of activity within the territory of a group, (2) more specific exploitation of the habitat, and (3) increased group size. (For a playful treatment of Braidwood's frame of reference see Binford and Binford, 1966.) It is when we have these trends, based on inherent human nature, operating in the context of a "nuclear zone" that things begin to happen:

> Now my hunch goes that when this experimentation and settling down took place within a potential nuclear area . . . where a whole constellation of plants and animals possible of domestication were available . . . the change was easily made . . . (Braidwood, 1963, p. 110).

The explanation for absence of food production during earlier interglacial periods is that: "culture was not ready to achieve it" (Braidwood and Willey, 1962, p. 342).

It is argued here that vitalism, whether expressed in terms of inherent forces orienting the direction of organic evolution or in its more anthropocentric form of emergent human properties which direct cultural evolution, is unacceptable as an explanation. Trends which are observed in cultural evolution require explanation; they are certainly not explained by postulating emergent human traits which are said to account for the trends.

In summary, post-Pleistocene research began with the question of whether or not Western Europe was populated between the close of the Pleistocene and the first appearance of the later Neolithic settlements. When this question was answered affirmatively, emphasis shifted to the question of continuity—were the "intermediate" populations indigenous or were they intruders? In seeking to solve this problem scholars were involved in the methodological question of what archeological data could be cited as proof or disproof of continuity. As local sequences became better documented, this question was dropped, and there was an increasing tendency to view variability as a direct response to local environments which had radically changed with the retreat of the ice. This stimulus-response reasoning was generalized not only for the European foraging adaptation but was also used to explain the origins of food-production (the propinquity or oasis theory). Field investigation in the relevant parts of the Near East showed that dramatic environmental change did not characterize the crucial periods of time. The oasis theory has fallen into disfavor, and Braidwood's nuclear zone theory has tended to replace it. We have sought to demonstrate in our analysis that this theory is based on a kind of vitalism and a postulation of causal factors which are incapable of being tested. We also propose that current explanations for the form and distribution of post-Pleistocene cultures in Europe are implicitly, and often explicitly, based on simple and direct environmental determinism which the data from non-European parts of the world tend to refute. What follows is an examination of post-Pleistocene data within a different theoretical framework and the formulation of explanatory hypotheses which, it is hoped, are both more generally applicable and also testable.

If our aim is the explanation of cultural differences and similarities in different places and at different times, we must first isolate the phenomena we designate "cultural." Culture is all those means whose forms are not under direct genetic control (that is, extrasomatic [White, 1959, p. 8]) which serve to adjust individuals and groups within their ecological communities. If we seek understanding of the origins of agriculture or of "the spread of the village-farming community," we must analyze these cultural means as adaptive adjustments in the variety of ecosystems within which human groups were participants.

Adaptation is always a local problem, and selective pressures favoring new cultural forms result from non-equilibrium conditions in the local ecosystem. Our task, then, becomes the isolation of the variables initiating directional change in the internal structuring of ecological systems. Of particular importance is understanding the conditions which favor the rearrangement of energy-matter components and their linked dependencies in a manner which alters the effective environment of the unit under study.

The term "effective environment" (Allee *et al.*, 1941, p. 1) designates those parts of the total environment which are in regular or cyclical articulation with the unit under study. Changes in the effective environment will produce changes not only in the boundaries of the ecological community but also in the internal organization of the community. Both of these changes in turn set up conditions favoring adaptive adjustments among the components of the community. In dealing with sociocultural systems and in trying to understand the conditions under which such systems undergo adaptive change, we are necessarily concerned with the effective environment of a given system.

> Cultural systems relate man to habitat, and an equilibrium can be established in this relationship as in others. When an equilibrium has been established culturally between man and habitat, it may be continued indefinitely until it is upset by the intrusion of a new factor (White, 1959, p. 284).

If we hope to understand culture change in general, and the changes of the post-Pleistocene period in particular, we must seek the conditions which have brought new factors into play in the effective environments of the cultural systems at the close of the Pleistocene.

Before undertaking our analysis, one further distinction needs to be made—the distinction between functional and structural differences in ecological niches. *Functional differences* are those which result from differences in the form of the elements of a system and which do not necessarily imply differences in the kind of articulation which exists between a cultural system and the ecological community of which it is a part. *Structural differences* refer to communities made up of non-analogous components which are integrated in different ways. In citing functional variability between niches, we are referring to differences in the form of the gross environment in which ecological communities occur; in such cases there would be no necessary structural differences in the organization of the ecological communities of the system, but only in the form of their environments. A case in point might be two cultural systems, both of which are solely dependent upon terrestrial resources within their home ranges and neither of which possesses the technological means for food storage or circulation beyond the locus of procurement. If one such system were located in a tropical rain forest and the other in a temperate deciduous forest, we would observe numerous formal differences between the cultural elements in the two systems, yet both can be said to occupy similar ecological niches within their habitats. Despite obvious differences in raw materials, the form of implements, differences in phasing of activities, and even in social organization, all such differences are explicable directly by reference to differences in gross environment. Therefore, we would term these differences functional, not structural.

Structural differences in ecological niches, on the other hand, refer to differences in the modes of integration between cultural and other components within ecological communities. Such differences imply a different set of relationships between the cultural unit and the variables in the gross environment with which the cultural unit is articulated. Cultural systems which occupy different ecological niches would therefore have different effective environments. An example of two cultural systems in the same gross environment but occupying different ecological niches would be the commonly occurring case where horticulturalists and hunters and gatherers live side by side. Each cultural group is in articulation with quite different elements of the gross environment and is integrated with the environment differently. Such cultural systems would be subject to qualitatively different types of selective pressure.

We would argue that understanding the selective pressures favoring the adoption of adaptive means as radical and as new as animal husbandry and cultivation in the post-Pleistocene requires the application of the ecological principles outlined above. A first step would be to determine whether food-production constitutes a functional variant of analogous ecological niches in different environments, or whether it is a structurally new adaptive means in an ecological niche not previously occupied by cultural systems.

Braidwood's nuclear zone theory is an argument for the former interpretation; the differences between the post-Pleistocene cultures in the hilly flanks and elsewhere are explicable by reference to formally unique elements in the plant and animal populations of the piedmont regions of the Near East. Childe's position is a statement of the latter interpretation, and he cites changes in the physical environment as the cause for bringing about new structural relationships between plants, animals, and men. Our argument also favors the second interpretation but with demographic, rather than gross environmental, variables responsible for the generation of pressures favoring new ecological niches.

> At certain times and places in the course of culture history, the threat of a diminished food supply, coming from an increase of population through immigration, or from a decline in local flora due to climatic or physiographic change, was met by various measures of cultural control over plant life, which collectively, we call agriculture (White, 1959, p. 285).

White's citation of population increase through immigration as a relevant variable in explaining the appearance of agriculture is a radical departure from traditional interpretations.

In the traditional approach, changes and variation in the available food supply have been cited as the major factors which regulate population equilibrium systems (Childe, 1958, p. 98; Dumond, 1965, p. 310).

> Man must eat to live at all; food is perhaps the one absolute and overriding need for man. In early and primitive societies the quest for food was and is the most absorbing preoccupation for all members of the group. The enlargement of the food-supply was therefore presumably the indispensable condition for human progress (Childe, 1944, p. 12).

> The community of food-gatherers had been restricted in size by the food supplies available (Childe, 1951, p. 61).

Similar statements have been made by Braidwood (1963, pp. 121–22), among others.

The inference about population dynamics to be made from these statements is that populations will grow until the food requirements of the group begin to exceed the standing crop in the local habitat. No population could ever achieve a stable adaptation, since its members would always be under strong selective pressure to develop new means of getting food. This assumption of the available food supply as the critical variable in population dynamics has prevented consideration of population variables themselves as possible sources of disequilibrium.

Recent studies in demography have argued strongly against the direct control of population density by the availability of food.

> We have the strongest reasons for concluding . . . that population density must at all costs be prevented from rising to the level where food shortage begins to take a toll of the numbers—an effect that could not be felt until long after the optimum density had been exceeded. It would be bound to result in chronic over-exploitation and a spiral of diminishing returns (Wynne-Edwards, 1962, p. 11).

> Long term population equilibrium . . . implies some kind of restraint. . . . "Food supply" offers a quick answer, but not, I think, the correct one. At any rate, a forest is full of game for an expert mouse-hunter, and a Paleolithic man who stuck to business should have found enough food on two square kilometers instead of 20 or 200. Social forces were probably more powerful than mere starvation in causing men to huddle in small bands (Deevey, 1960, p. 6).

Most demographers agree that functional relationships between the normal birth rate and other requirements (for example, the mobility of the female) favor the *cultural* regulation of fertility through such practices as infanticide, abortion, lactation taboos, etc. These practices have the effect of homeostatically keeping population size below the point at which diminishing returns from the local habitat would come into play. (See Carr-Saunders, 1922; Wynne-Edwards, 1962, 1964; Birdsell, 1958, 1968; Deevey, 1960; Hainline, 1965; Dumond, 1965; and Halbwachs, 1960).

The arguments of demographers are supported by a number of recent ethnographic studies which document the abundance of food available to even marginal hunters. Some cases of importance are J. D. Clark (1951) on the Barotse, Lee (1965) on the !Kung Bushmen, Woodburn (1968) on the Hadza, and Huntingford (1955) on the Dorobo. Similar conditions of relative abundance have been reported for Australia. For example, life on the Daly River in the Northern Territory led McCarthy (1957, p. 90) to generalize: "for the uncontaminated bush native the food problem hardly exists." Ease in food procurement is also reported for Arnhemland (McCarthy, 1957, p. 90; McCarthy and McArthur, 1960, pp. 145–93). Quimby has described the truly impressive quantities of food obtained in the course of a single year by a Chippewa family in the Lower Peninsula of Michigan in 1763 (Quimby, 1962, pp. 217–39). In a quantitative study of food intake by the Onge hunters of Little Andaman, Bose (1964, p. 306) states: "The region surrounding Tokebuea can supply more food than the requirement of the local people."

These data suggest that while hunting-gathering populations may vary in density between different habitats in direct proportion to the relative size of the standing food crop, nevertheless within any given habitat the population is homeostatically regulated *below* the level of depletion of the local food supply.

There are two corollaries of the assumption that population size is regulated almost exclusively by food supply which we also need to examine. The first corollary is: *Man would be continually seeking means for increasing his food supply.* In other words, there would be ubiquitous and constant selective pressure favoring the development of technological innovations, such as agriculture, which serve to make larger amounts of food available to a group. There is a large body of ethnographic data which suggests that this is not the case.

Carneiro (1957) in his study of the Kuikuru, who are horticulturalists, demonstrated that these people were capable of producing several times the amount of food they did. A small increment in the amount of time devoted to planting and harvesting would have brought about substantial increases in the available food, yet the Kuikuru chose not to do this. Enough food was produced to meet local demands, and it was at that point that production stopped. Equilibrium had been reached, and neither population nor production increased.

In writing about the Southeastern United States, Caldwell concerned himself with the question of why no effective early prehistoric agriculture was developed in the region. He concluded:

> We have suggested that so many natural foods were available that to place any reliance on cultivation . . . might have seemed risky or irrelevant. The hunting-gathering pattern was developed to a peak of efficiency and jelled, so to speak, in the very heart of eastern cultures (1958, p. 72).

If we recognize that an equilibrium system can be established so that populations are homeostatically regulated below the carrying capacity of the local food supply, it follows that there is no necessary adaptive pressure continually favoring means of increasing the food supply. The question to be asked then is not why agricultural and food-storage techniques were not developed everywhere, but why they were developed at all. Under what set of conditions does increasing the supply of available food have adaptive advantage?

The second corollary to be examined concerns leisure time: *It is only when man is freed from preoccupation with the food quest that he has time to elaborate culture.* A fairly representative statement of this corollary has been made by Childe (1951, p. 61) and is cited above. Also, Braidwood writes:

> Proper village life now came into being, and with it a completely new kind of technology. This latter depends on the fact that time now became available for pursuits other than that of simply collecting food (Braidwood and Braidwood, 1950, p. 189).

Braidwood reiterates the same argument in more detail in another place (1963, pp. 121–22). The view of the hunter constantly involved in scrounging a bare subsistence and existing on the brink of starvation has recently received some rather pointed comments by Sahlins:

> Almost totally committed to the argument that life was hard in the Paleolithic, our text books compete to convey a sense of impending doom, leaving the student to wonder not only how hunters managed to make a living but

> whether, after all, this is living. The spectre of starvation stalks the stalker in these pages. His technical incompetence is said to enjoin continuous work just to survive, leaving him without respite from the food quest and without the "leisure time to build culture" (1968).

There is abundant data which suggests not only that hunter-gatherers have adequate supplies of food but also that they enjoy quantities of leisure time, much more in fact than do modern industrial or farm workers, or even professors of archeology. Lee (1965), Bose (1954), McCarthy and McArthur (1960), and Woodburn (1968) have shown that hunters on a simple level of technology spend a very small percentage of their time obtaining food. On these grounds we can reasonably question the proposition that cultural elaboration is caused by leisure time which is available for the first time to agriculturalists.

In rejecting the assumption that hunter-gatherer populations are primarily regulated by the available supply of food, we put the problem of the development of new types of subsistence in a different light. As long as one could assume that man was continually trying to increase his food supply, understanding the "origins of agriculture" simply involved pinpointing those geographic areas where the potential resources were and postulating that man would inevitably take advantage of them. With the recognition that equilibrium systems regulate population density below the carrying capacity of an environment, we are forced to look for those conditions which might bring about disequilibrium and bring about selective advantage for increased productivity. According to the arguments developed here, there could be only two such sets of conditions:

1. A change in the physical environment of a population which brings about a reduction in the biotic mass of the region would decrease the amounts of available food. The previous balance between population and standing crop is upset, and more efficient extractive means would be favored. This is essentially the basis for Childe's propinquity theory.

2. Change in the demographic structure of a region which brings about the impingement of one group on the territory of another would also upset an established equilibrium system, and might serve to increase the population density of a region beyond the carrying capacity of the natural environment. Under these conditions manipulation of the natural environment in order to increase its productivity would be highly advantageous.

The remainder of this paper is devoted to the exploration of this second set of conditions. The first step of our analysis is to build models of different types of population systems under different conditions. One such type of system is termed a *closed population system* (Hyrenius, 1959, p. 476) in which a steady state is maintained by internal mechanisms limiting numbers of offspring at the generational replacement level. Techniques such as abortion, contraception, abstinence, and infanticide serve to lower the birth rate and increase the mortality rate so that a given population would be homeostatically regulated at a given size or density.

The second type of system, the *open population system*, is one in which size and/or density is maintained by either the budding off of new groups or by the emigration of individuals. This would be an *open system of the donor type*. If the size or density of the system is altered through the introduction of immigrants from other population groups, we have an *open system of the recipient type*.

Given these two types of population systems—closed and open, the latter including two sub-types, recipient and donor—we can begin to analyze differences in the ways in which the two system types can be articulated in a given region.

Closed Systems

We can identify the population of a region as a whole as a closed system, yet find that within the region there would be some variability in optimum group size as a response to geographical differences in the regional distribution of resources. Further, each local group within the region may operate periodically as an open system, since we would expect some variability in the degree to which local groups have achieved equilibrium. There would therefore be some redistribution of population between groups which would promote a more uniform and steady density equilibrium system over the region as a whole.

We would expect selection favoring cultural means of regulating population to occur in situations where the density equilibrium system for the region as a whole was in fact a closed system, and where there were significant imbalances in the losses and recruits for the local subsegments of the regional population. There would be differential selective advantage for cultural regulation of population growth between two closed population systems in different environmental settings if there were discrepancies between the actual birth and death rates on the one hand and the optimal rates for maintaining population size on the other.

Open Systems, Donor Type

We would expect to find this type of population system in areas which are not filled to the point at which density dependent factors are brought into play. The peopling of a new land mass, such as the New World or Australia, would be an example of such a situation in which there would be positive advantage for this type of system.

The rate of expansion of open donor systems into uninhabited territory has been discussed in the literature, and models for this type of expansion have been built (Bartholomew and Birdsell, 1953; Birdsell, 1957, 1958, 1968; Yengoyan, 1960). Birdsell has made two observations which are particularly relevant here. First, the budding off of new groups occurs *before* optimum local population size has been reached (Birdsell, 1957, p. 54). This observation demonstrates the role of emigration in bringing about and maintaining equilibrium and also shows that the unit on which selection for emigration operates is a subunit of the local population, since conditions favoring segmentation appear before the regional population is under pressure from density dependent factors.

Second, the adaptation of any given sociocultural system will determine in part the locus of selection within the social system and the particular selective advantages for different fertility rates. Birdsell writes:

> In a population stabilized at the carrying capacity of its given environment, some limitation on procreative activities naturally filter down to the level of the biological family. These may be examined most profitably in terms of the requirements which affect the spacing of the natal survivors. Generalized hunters with their requirements of high mobility present the most exacting model. Australian data indicate that the inability of a mother to carry more than one child at a time together with her female baggage impose the first insurmountable barrier to a large number of children. Strongly reinforced by an equally limiting incapacity to nurse more than one child simultaneously imposes a minimum of a three-year spacing upon children designed for survival. Since human female reproductive physiology does not reliably prevent conception while still nursing, children are frequently conceived and born which cannot be reared. The result is systematic infanticide (1968).

We have seen that two frequent means of maintaining homeostasis are emigration and cultural regulation of births and deaths. The relative importance to any group of one of these means *vs.* the other will be conditioned by such factors as mobility requirements of the group. Another conditioning factor would be the type of articulation between segments of the population which can directly affect the ease with which budding-off can occur. A third factor would be the degree to which the region as a whole is occupied which would affect the expectations of success in the establishment of daughter communities.

Open Systems, Recipient Type

This type of system could occur under only two sets of conditions; the first would be where there is the expansion of a donor system into an uninhabited region. The frontier of the region would contain a number of population units which could, for a short time, serve as recipient systems. Their change from recipient to donor systems would depend upon the extent to which optimal densities were achieved locally and the frontier continued to advance.

The second set of conditions promoting systems of the recipient type is more relevant to the consideration of early agricultural developments.

This is the situation in which two or more different kinds of sociocultural systems occupy adjacent environmental zones. If the adaptation of one sociocultural unit is translatable into the adjacent environmental zone, it may expand into that zone at the expense of resident systems. Cases of this type have been cited by Kaplan (1960) as examples of the Law of Cultural Dominance, and a specific instance referred to by Sahlins are the Tiv and the Nuer (1961). We would expect expansion of the dominant system until the zone to which the system was adapted was occupied; at this juncture there would be selection for increased efficiency of production and/or for increased regulation of the birth rate.

A different kind of situation would obtain in the case of sociocultural systems occupying adjacent zones if the adaptation of the more rapidly growing group is not translatable into the adjacent zone. Population growth within the area occupied by the parent group might well be so great that daughter communities would frequently be forced to reside in an environment which is incompatible with their particular cultural adaptation. There could be a number of effects under these circumstances.

From the standpoint of the populations already in the recipient zone, the intrusion of immigrant groups would disturb the existing density equilibrium system and might raise the population density to the level at which we would expect diminishing food resources. This situation would serve to increase markedly for the recipient groups the pressures favoring means for increasing productivity. The intrusive group, on the other hand, would be forced to make adaptive adjustments to their new environment (for an example of this situation see L. R. Binford, 1968). There would be strong selective pressures favoring the development of more efficient subsistence techniques by both groups.

It should be pointed out, however, that such advantage does not insure that these developments will inevitably occur. In many cases these problems are met by changes which might be called regressive in that the changes in adaptation which occur may be in the direction of less complex cultural forms. Examples of this sort of change can be seen among the hunter-gatherers of the non-riverine tropical forest zones in South America. Steward and Faron write of the Siriono and Guayaki:

> These Indians retreated . . . to inaccessible regions where they largely abandoned horticulture to rely on a predominantly hunting and gathering subsistence. Other enclaves of nomads isolated in the tropical forests and interfluvial regions may also have experienced similar deculturation (1959, p. 378).

Lathrap has offered the possibility that perhaps all of the less sedentary South American groups are "the degraded descendants of peoples who at one time maintained an advanced form of Tropical Forest Culture" (1968).

While in these examples the adaptations along population frontiers were in the direction of less complexity, it is in the context of such situations of stress in environments with plant and animal forms amenable to manipulation that we would expect to find conditions favoring the development of plant and animal domestication. Such situations would be characterized by disequilibrium between population and resources which, in turn, would offer selective advantage to increases in the efficacy of subsistence technology. Rather than seeking the locus for the origins of agriculture in the heart of a "natural habitat zone," we would argue that we must look to those places where a population frontier or adaptive tension zone intersects a "natural habitat zone." This means that archeological investigations might well concentrate on those areas within the natural habitat zone where there is an archeologically demonstrated major shift in population density. The presence of such a shift might well indicate a population frontier where rapid evolutionary changes were taking place.

Another archeological clue to be exploited is the degree to which settlements are characterized by sedentism. The frontier zones would be expected between regions which differed widely in the degree of sedentism practiced by resident groups. In those areas with highly sedentary population, problems of transport of young and belongings would be reduced. Reduced mobility of social units in general and in the daily routines of females in particular would in turn reduce the selective advantages accruing to cultural means of controlling population growth. Therefore, under conditions of increased sedentism we would expect population growth. A consequence of such growth would be the increased relative importance of emigration as a mechanism for maintaining the local group within optimal size and density limits.

Therefore where there is a marked contrast in degree of sedentism between two sociocultural units within a relatively restricted geographical region, there would be a tension zone where emigrant colonies from the more sedentary group would periodically disrupt the density equilibrium balances of the less sedentary group. Under these conditions there would be strong selective pressure favoring the development of more effective means of food production for both groups within this zone of tension. There would also be increasing pressures against immigration, given the failure to develop more effective extractive technologies.

It is proposed here that it was in the selective context outlined above that initial practices of cultivation occurred. Such selective situations would have been the consequence of the increased dependence on aquatic resources during the terminal and immediately post-Pleistocene period. Not all portions of rivers and shorelines favor the harvesting of fish, molluscs, and migratory fowl; it is with the systematic dependence on just these resources that we find archeological remains indicating a higher degree of sedentism in both the Archaic of the New World and the terminal Paleolithic and Mesolithic of the Old World. This hypothesis is lent strong support by the fact that it is also in the terminal Paleolithic-Mesolithic and Archaic that we find, associated with increased sedentism, evidence for marked population growth and for the development of food-storage techniques, the latter being functionally linked to the highly seasonal nature of migratory fowl and anadromous fish exploited as food crops (for an example of the importance of anadromous fish see L. R. Binford, 1964).

Since the systematic exploitation of these food sources (and of markedly seasonally available terrestrial forms as well—for example, reindeer) characterized adaptations of this time range in a wide variety of environments, we would expect that tension zones, with their concomitant selective pressures favoring increased subsistence efficiency, would be widely distributed also. This expectation is in accord with the empirical generalizations that: (1) There were a number of independent loci of the development of cultivation techniques—the Near East, Asia, and the New World—and all the developments of these techniques occur within the time range in question; and (2) These loci were distributed across widely different environmental types—root crops in the tropics and cereals in semi-aridlands, for example.

The widespread nature of conditions favoring increased subsistence efficiency also accounts for the rapid transmission and integration of contributing innovations from one cultural system to another. Many authors have cited the rapid "diffusion" of cultural elements as characterizing the immediately post-Pleistocene period.

Finally, in the traditional view the "Neolithic Revolution" is characterized by the appearance of a number of traits which are thought to be linked to the shift to food production. The manufacture of ceramics and textiles, relatively permanent houses, and craft specialization are only a few of those frequently cited (cf. Braidwood, 1963, pp. 122-23). These traits constitute part of the definition of the "village farming way of life," and the assumption is that they originated in the "nuclear area" from which they spread as a complex, the spread being achieved by diffusion, stimulus diffusion, and/or migration. As more data have been accumulated, it becomes increasingly clear that these traits are not mutually dependent; indeed, it seems to be quite clear that ceramics, for example, were first used in the Old World in coastal Japan (Griffin, 1961, p. 92), with a cluster of radiocarbon dates averaging *ca.* 7000 B.C. This is about the same time that effective grain agriculture was initially practiced in the Near East (Mellaart, 1961, 1963; Hole, 1966; Young and Smith, 1966), and the occupations in question have yielded no ceramics. Given our model, such traits insofar as they are functionally linked to sedentism and/or food production would be expected to appear in a variety of regions as the result of numerous independent but parallel inventions.

Further utility for the model presented here can be shown by the degree to which it provides explanatory answers for a series of questions posed by Braidwood and Willey—questions which cannot be satisfactorily answered within the traditional framework.

> Why did incipient food production not come earlier? Our only answer at the moment is that culture was not yet ready to achieve it (Braidwood and Willey, 1962, p. 342).

We believe that a more complete answer is possible. The shift to the exploitation of highly seasonal resources such as anadromous fish and migratory fowl did not occur until the close of the Pleistocene. This shift, probably linked to worldwide changes in sea level, with attendant increase in sedentism, established for the first time conditions leading to marked heterogeneity in rates of population growth and structure of the ecological niche of immediately adjacent sociocultural systems. This new set of conditions brought about, in turn, conditions favoring improved subsistence technology. It was not that culture was unready, but rather that the selective conditions favoring such changes had not previously existed.

> What were the . . . cultural conditions favoring incipient cultivation or domestication? Certainly there is nothing in the archeological record to indicate that those few instances of cultural build-up and elaboration, as manifested by the varying art styles of the upper paleolithic from western Europe into Siberia . . . provided a favorable ground for incipient food production. On the contrary, those instances of incipient cultivation or domestication of greatest potential are found in contexts of a much less spectacular character (Braidwood and Willey, 1962, p. 343, see also Willey, 1966, pp. 141–42).

According to our model, we would *expect* to find the selective situation favoring "incipient cultivation" in "contexts of a much less spectacular character"—in those tension zones where less sedentary populations are being moved in on by daughter groups from more sedentary populations. These are the areas where the development of greater productive means is most advantageous.

> The perplexing question of what kinds of natural environmental settings were most propitious for the early development of incipient food production is by no means solved. Nevertheless, the data on hand suggest that generally semi-arid regions . . . with adequate but not overabundant collectible food resources were the hearths of the most important beginnings of cultivation and domestication (Braidwood and Willey, 1962, p. 342).

If we look at the semi-arid areas where the crops referred to (wheat and barley in the Old World; maize in the New World) were developed, it turns out that they are adjacent to areas which already supported settled (that is, sedentary) villages whose populations depended in large part upon aquatic resources. The Natufian of the Near East (Kenyon, 1959; Perrot, 1960, 1962) and the coastal settlements of Mexico and Peru

(Willey, 1966, p. 144; see also Flannery and Coe, this volume) are cases in point.

The explanation of the distribution noted above of the hearths of domestication of most economically significant crops within semi-arid regions lies in the nature of the seeds produced by the plants in such regions. Seeds of xerophytic plants normally have low moisture requirements and can therefore remain viable without being subject to rots which attack many other kinds of seeds. Their economic value also lies in the fact that semi-arid regions are areas with low diversity indices (Odum, 1954, p. 281), which means that there will typically be many individuals of a given species within a very limited space.

We would like to note in passing that the post hoc evaluation of some "beginnings of cultivation" as "most important" (because of the ultimate economic significance of the crops produced) and the limitation of question-asking to these instances has served to prevent the recognition of the general conditions under which cultivation may have been initiated.

> *How* did the new elements spread into Europe; how shall we conceptualize the nature of the cultural mechanisms of "diffusion" and the spread of new "influences" through a vast area of already functioning cultural and environmental adaptations? (Braidwood and Willey, 1962, p. 347).

While wheat and barley might have constituted "new influences" in Europe, it has been suggested above that cultivation arose as a response to similar pressures many times and in many places. Given the existence of the selective situation favoring food production and the response to this adaptive situation occurring in a number of places, including Europe, the adoption of easily storable high-yield crops such as wheat and barley becomes readily understandable. However, it is important not to confound the adoption of specific crops with the "spread of the village-farming way of life."

If the model presented here has value above and beyond that of a logical exercise, it must be tested by the formulation of hypotheses and the collection of data. While the outlining of a program of research is beyond the scope of and irrelevant to the aims of this paper, a few predictions follow which, if borne out by field research, would empirically validate some of our assertions.

1. Evidence for the initial domestication of plants and animals in the Near East will come from areas adjacent to those occupied by relatively sedentary forager-fishers. One such area is that adjacent to the Natufian settlements in the Jordan Valley. These settlements have yielded evidence of heavy dependence upon fish and migratory fowl (Perrot, 1960, p. 20) and the architecture suggests a sedentary way of life. The areas just beyond these villages would have received "excess" population and would therefore have been areas of disequilibrium in which adaptive change would have been favored. Intermontane valleys and foothills which sup-

ported migratory hunters far removed from the kind of villages described above will not yield information on the earliest transition to dependence on food production, regardless of the density of wild ancestors of domesticates.

2. Evidence for independent experimentation leading to the development of agriculture as well as animal domestication will be found in European Russia and south-central Europe. We would expect the relevant areas to be adjacent to those where there was effective exploitation of anadromous fish and migratory fowl. Such areas appear to be the rivers flowing into the Black Sea (Clark, 1948b, p. 50).

3. As further research is carried out in Europe, Asia, and the New World, there will be evidence for numerous independent innovations paralleling forms appearing in other areas. Post-Pleistocene adaptations are viewed as the result of the operation of local selective pressures, and the development of food production is one instance of such adaptations. Parallel innovations can be expected where structurally similar ecological niches were occupied, regardless of differences in the general form of the environment.

In conclusion, it is hoped that the theoretical perspective offered here will serve to generate a new series of questions, the answers to which may increase our understanding of the major cultural changes which occurred at the close of the Pleistocene.

References

ALLEE, W. C., A. E. EMERSON, O. PARK, T. PARK, and KARL P. SCHMIDT. 1949. *Principles of animal ecology*. Philadelphia and London: W. B. Saunders.

BARTHOLOMEW, GEORGE A. JR., and J. B. BIRDSELL. 1953. Ecology and the protohominids. *American Anthropologist*, 55(2): 481–98.

BINFORD, LEWIS R. 1964. Archaeological and ethnohistorical investigations of cultural diversity. Microfilm, Ph.D. dissertation, University of Michigan.

——. 1965. Archaeological systematics and the study of culture process. *American Antiquity*, 31(2): 203–210.

——. 1968. An ethnohistory of the Nottoway, Meherrin and Weanock Indians of southeastern Virginia. *Ethnohistory*, Vol. 14, No. 3–4 (whole number).

BINFORD, LEWIS R., and SALLY R. BINFORD 1966. The predatory revolution: a consideration of the evidence for a new subsistence level. *American Anthropologist*, 68(2), Part 1: 508–512.

BIRDSELL, JOSEPH B. 1953. Some environmental and cultural factors influencing the structuring of Australian aboriginal populations. *American Naturalist* (Supp.; May–June) 87(834): 171–207.

——. 1957. Some population problems involving Pleistocene man. *Cold Spring Harbor Symposia on Quantitative Biology*, 22: 47–69.

——. 1958. On population structure in generalized hunting and collecting populations. *Evolution*, 12(2): 189–205.

——. 1968. Some predictions for the Pleistocene based upon equilibrium systems among recent hunters. In Richard B. Lee and Irven DeVore (Eds.), *Man the hunter*. Chicago: Aldine Publishing Company.

Bose, Saradindu. 1964. Economy of the Onge of Little Andaman. *Man In India*, 44(4): 298–310.

Braidwood, R. J. 1951a. *Prehistoric men*. (2d ed.) Popular Series, Anthropology No. 37, Chicago: Chicago Natural History Museum.

——. 1951b. From cave to village in prehistoric Iraq. *Bulletin of the American Schools of Oriental Research*, 124: 12–18.

——. 1952a. From cave to village. *Scientific American*, 187(4): 62–66.

——. 1952b. The Near East and the foundations for civilization. (Condon Lectures.) Eugene: Oregon State System of Higher Education.

——. 1960a. The agricultural revolution. *Scientific American*, 203: 130–41.

——. 1960b. Levels in prehistory: a model for the consideration of the evidence. In Sol Tax (Ed.), *The evolution of man* (Vol. 2 of *Evolution after Darwin*). Chicago: University of Chicago Press.

——. 1963. *Prehistoric men*. (6th ed.) Popular Series, Anthropology No. 37, Chicago: Chicago Natural History Museum.

Braidwood, R. J., and Linda Braidwood. 1950. Jarmo: a village of early farmers in Iraq. *Antiquity*, 24(96): 189–95.

Braidwood, R. J., and Charles A. Reed. 1957. The achievement and early consequences of food production. *Cold Spring Harbor Symposia on Quantitative Biology*, 22: 19–31.

Braidwood, R. J., and Gordon Willey. 1962. Conclusions and afterthoughts. In R. J. Braidwood and G. R. Willey (Eds.), *Courses toward urban life* Chicago: Aldine Publishing Company.

Braidwood, R. J., and Bruce Howe. 1960. *Prehistoric investigations in Iraqi Kurdistan*. Oriental Institute Studies in Ancient Oriental Civilization, no. 31. Chicago: University of Chicago Press.

——. 1962. Southwestern Asia beyond the lands of the Mediterranean littoral. In R. J. Braidwood and G. R. Willey (Eds.), *Courses toward urban life*. Chicago: Aldine Publishing Company.

Breuil, H. 1921. Observations suivantes: M. Cartilhac, La question de l'hiatus entre le Paléolithique et le Néolithique. *L'Anthropologie*, 31: 349–55.

——. 1946. The discovery of the antiquity of man. *Journal of the Royal Anthropological Institute of Great Britain and Ireland*, 75(1): 21–31.

Brown, John Allen. 1888. On some small highly specialized forms of stone implements, found in Asia, North Africa, and Europe. In *Journal of the Royal Anthropological Institute of Great Britain and Ireland*, 18(2): 134–39.

——. 1892. On the continuity of the Palaeolithic and Neolithic periods. *Journal of the Royal Anthropological Institute of Great Britain and Ireland*, 22(1 and 2): 66–98.

Burkitt, M. C. 1925. The transition between Palaeolithic and Neolithic times, i.e. the Mesolithic period. *Proceedings of the Prehistoric Society of East Anglia*, 5(1): 16–33.

Caldwell, Joseph R. 1958. Trend and tradition in the prehistory of the eastern United States. *Memoir no. 88*, American Anthropological Association, vol. 60(6), Part 2. Springfield: Illinois State Museum.

Carneiro, Robert. 1957. Subsistence and social structure: an ecological study of the Kuikuru Indians. Ph.D. dissertation, University of Michigan. (Mimeographed.)

Carr-Saunders, A. M. 1922. *The population problem: a study in human evolution*. Oxford: Clarendon Press.

CHILDE, V. GORDON. 1925. *The dawn of European civilization.* New York: Alfred A. Knopf.
——. 1931. The forest cultures of northern Europe: a study in evolution and diffusion. *Journal of the Royal Anthropological Institute of Great Britain and Ireland,* Vol. 61, Part 2: 325–48.
——. 1937. Adaptation to the postglacial forest on the north Eurasiatic plain. In G. G. McCurdy (Ed.), *Early man.* Philadelphia and New York: J. B. Lippincott.
——. 1944. *Progress and archaeology.* The Thinkers Library, No. 102. London: Watts and Co.
——. 1951. *Man makes himself.* New York: Mentor Books, New American Library.
——. 1952. *New light on the most ancient East.* London: Routledge and Kegan Paul. (4th ed.)
——. 1956. The new Stone Age. In Harry L. Shapiro (Ed.), *Man, culture, and society.* New York: Oxford University Press.
CLARK, J. DESMOND. 1951. Bushmen hunters of the Barotse forests. *The Northern Rhodesia Journal,* 1(3): 56–65.
——. 1962. Africa south of the Sahara. In. R. J. Braidwood and G. R. Willey (Eds.), *Courses toward urban life.* Chicago: Aldine Publishing Company.
CLARK, J. G. D. 1932. *The Mesolithic age in Britain.* Cambridge, England: The University Press.
——. 1936. *The Mesolithic settlement of northern Europe: a study of the food gathering peoples of northern Europe during the early post-glacial period.* Cambridge, England: The University Press.
——. 1948a. Fowling in prehistoric Europe. *Antiquity,* 22(8): 116–30.
——. 1948b. The development of fishing in prehistoric Europe. *The Antiquaries Journal,* 28: 45–85.
——. 1963. A survey of the Mesolithic phase in the prehistory of Europe and Southwest Asia. *Atti de 6 Congresso internazionale delle Scienze preisstoriche e Protostoriche,* 1: 97–111. Rome: Collegio Romano.
COUTIL, L. 1912. Tardenoisien, Capsien, Getulien, Ibero-Maurusien Intergetulo-Néolithique, Tellien Loubirien, Geneyenien. *Congrès International d'Anthropologie et d'Archéologie préhistorique,* 14th session, 1: 301–336. Geneva.
CUMONT, M. 1907. Quelques mots au sujet de Tardenoisien et de la transition du Paléolithique au Néolithique. *Sociéte Royale Belge d'Anthropologie et de Préhistoire, Bulletin,* 26: ccv-ccviii.
DARWIN, CHARLES R .1875. *The variation of animals and plants under domestication,* Vol. 1. (2d ed.) London: Murray and Sons.
DAWKINS, WILLIAM BOYD. 1894. On the relation of the Palaeolithic to the Neolithic period. *Journal of the Royal Anthropological Institute of Great Britain and Ireland,* 23: 242–54.
DECANDOLLE, ALPHONSE L. P. P. 1959. *Origin of cultivated plants.* (Reprint of the 2d ed., 1886.) New York: Hafner.
DEEVEY, EDWARD S., JR. 1960. The human population. *Scientific American,* 203(1): 194–204.
DIGBY, ADRIAN. 1949. Technique and the time factor in relation to economic organization. *Man,* 49: 16–18.
——. 1962. Time the catalyst: or why we should study the material culture of primitive peoples. *The Advancement of Science,* 19(80): 349–57.
DUMOND, D. E. 1965. Population growth and cultural change. *Southwestern Journal of Anthropology,* 21(4): 302–324.

DURKHEIM, EMILE. 1897–98. Morphologie sociale, *L'année sociologique,* 2: 520–21.

GABEL, W. CRIEGHTON. 1958a. The Mesolithic continuum in western Europe. *American Anthropologist,* 60(4): 658–67.

——. 1958b. European secondary Neolithic cultures. *Journal of the Royal Anthropological Institute of Great Britain and Ireland,* 88(1): 97–107.

——. 1960. Seminar on economic types in pre-urban cultures of temperate woodland, arid, and tropical areas. In *Current Anthropology,* 1(5–6): 437–38.

GARROD, D. A. E. 1932. A new Mesolithic industry: the Natufian of Palestine. *Journal of the Royal Anthropological Institute of Great Britain and Ireland,* 62(2): 257–69.

GARROD, D. A. E., and D. M. A. BATE. 1937. *The Stone Age of Mount Carmel, excavations at the Wadi El-Mughara,* Vol. 1. Oxford, England: Clarendon Press.

GIMBUTAS, MARIJA. 1956. *The prehistory of eastern Europe.* In Hugh Hencken (Ed.), Harvard University, Bulletin No. 20. Cambridge, Mass.: American School of Prehistoric Research, Peabody Museum.

——. 1963. European prehistory: Neolithic to the Iron Age. In Bernard J. Siegel (Ed.), *Biennial Review of Anthropology 1963,* Stanford: Stanford University Press.

GRIFFIN, JAMES B. 1961. Comments in Edmonson: Neolithic diffusion rates. *Current Anthropology,* 2(2): 92–93.

HALBWACHS, MAURICE. 1960. *Population and society, introduction to social morphology.* Translated by Otis Duncan and Harold W. Pfautz. Glencoe, Ill.: The Free Press.

HAINLINE, JANE. 1965. Culture and biological adaptation. *American Anthropologist,* 67(5), Part 1: 1174–97.

HERVE, GEORGES. 1899. Populations Mesolithiques et Néolithiques de l'Espagne et du Portugal. *Revue Mensuelle de L'Ecole d'Anthropologie de Paris,* 9(Series no. 1): 265–80.

HOLE, FRANK. 1966. Investigating the origins of Mesopotamian civilization. *Science,* 153(3736): 605–611.

HUNTINGFORD, G. W. B. 1955. The economic life of the Dorobo. *Anthropos,* 50: 605–684.

HYRENIUS, HANNES. 1959. Population growth and replacement. In P. M. Hauser and Otis Duncan (Eds.), *The study of population: an inventory and appraisal.* Chicago: University of Chicago Press.

KAPLAN, DAVID. 1960. The law of cultural dominance. In Marshall D. Sahlins and Elman R. Service (Eds.), *Evolution and culture.* Ann Arbor: University of Michigan Press.

KENYON, KATHLEEN M. 1959. Some observations on the beginnings of settlement in the Near East. *Journal of the Royal Anthropological Institute of Great Britain and Ireland,* 89: 35–43.

KOZLOWSKI, LEON. 1926. L'Époque Mésolithique en Pologne. *L'Anthropologie,* 36: 47–74.

LATHRAP, DONALD W. 1968. The hunting economies of the Tropical Forest Zone of South America: an attempt at historical perspective. In Richard B. Lee, and Irven DeVore (Eds.), *Man the hunter.* Chicago: Aldine Publishing Company.

LEE, R. B. 1965. *Subsistence ecology of !Kung Bushmen,* Microfilm. Ph.D. dissertation, Berkeley: University of California.

DE LOE, BARON A. 1908. Contribution à l'étude des temps intermédiares entre le Paléolithique et le Néolithique, *XIII Congrès International d'Anthropologie et d'Archéologie préhistorique, Monaco, 1907*, 1: 422–23.

McCarthy, Frederick D. 1957. Habitat, economy, and equipment of the Australian aborigines. *The Australian Journal of Science*, 19: 88–97.

——. and Margart McArthur. 1960. The food quest and the time factor in aboriginal economic life. *Records of the American Australian Scientific Expedition to Arnhemland*, 2: 145–94. Parkville, Australia: University of Melbourne, University Press.

MacCurdy, George Grant. 1924. *Human origins: a manual of prehistory*. (2 vols.) New York: D. Appleton.

Mellaart, James. 1961. Excavations at Hacilar: 4th preliminary report. *Anatolian Studies*, 11: 39–75.

——. 1963. Excavations at Catal-Hüyük 1962: 2d preliminary report. *Anatolian Studies*, 13: 43–103.

Menghin, Oswald. 1925. Die mesolithische Kulturentwicklung in Europa. *Deutsches Archäologisches Institut*, Röm.-Germ., Komsn. Bericht., 17: 154.

deMorgan, Jacques Jean Marie. 1924. *Prehistoric man: a general outline of prehistory*. New York: Alfred A. Knopf.

deMortillet, Adrien. 1896. Les petits silex taillés, à contours géométriques trouvés en Europe, Asie et Afrique. *Revue de l'Ecole d'Anthropologie*, 6: 376–405.

deMortillet, Gabriel. 1885. *Le préhistorique, antiquité de l'homme*. (2d ed.) Paris: C. Reinwald.

Obermaier, Hugo. 1925. *Fossil man in Spain*. New Haven: Yale University Press.

Odum, Eugene P., and H. T. Odum. 1959. *Fundamentals of ecology*. (2d ed.) Philadelphia: W. B. Saunders.

Osborn, Henry Fairfield. 1919. *Men of the Old Stone Age, their environment, life and art*. (3d ed.) New York: Charles Scribner.

Perrot, Jean. 1960. Excavations at 'Eynan ('Ein Mallaha). Preliminary report on the 1959 season. *The Israel Exploration Journal*, 10(1): 14–22.

——. 1962. Palestine-Syria-Cilicia. In R. J. Braidwood and G. R. Willey (Eds.), *Courses toward urban life*. Chicago: Aldine Publishing Company.

Piette, Ed. 1895a. Études d'ethnographie préhistorique. *L'Anthropologie*, 6: 276–92.

——. 1895b. Hiatus et lacune vestiges de la période de transition dans la grotte du Mas-d'Azil. *Bulletin de la Société d'Anthropologie de Paris*, 6(4th series): 235–67.

Pittioni, Richard. 1962. Southern middle Europe and southeastern Europe. In R. J. Braidwood and G. R. Willey (Eds.), *Courses toward urban life*. Chicago: Aldine Publishing Company.

Pitt-Rivers, A. Lane-Fox. 1906. *The evolution of culture and other essays*. Edited by J. L. Myres. Oxford: Clarendon Press.

Quimby, George I. 1962. A year with a Chippewa family, 1763–1764. *Ethnohistory*, 9(3): 217–39.

Roth, H. Ling. 1887. On the origin of agriculture. *Journal of the Royal Anthropological Institute of Great Britain and Ireland*, 16(2): 102–136.

Sahlins, Marshall. 1958. *Social stratification in Polynesia*. Seattle: University of Washington Press.

——. 1961. The segmentary lineage: an organization of predatory expansion. *American Anthropologist*, 63(2), Part I: 322–45.

——. 1968. Notes on the original affluent society. In Richard B. Lee and Irven DeVore (Eds.), *Man the hunter*. Chicago: Aldine Publishing Company.

SCHWABEDISSEN, HERMAN. 1962. Northern continental Europe. In R. J. Braidwood and G. R. Willey (Eds.), *Courses toward urban life.* Chicago: Aldine Publishing Company.

SIMPSON, GEORGE GAYLORD. 1949. *The meaning of evolution.* New Haven: Yale University Press.

DE SONNEVILLE-BORDES, DENISE. 1960. *Le Paléolithique supérieur en Périgord,* 2. vol. Bordeaux: Imprimerie Delmas.

——. 1963a. Upper Paleolithic cultures in western Europe. *Science,* 142 (3590): 347–55.

——. 1963b. Le Paléolithique supérieur en Suisse. *L'Anthropologie,* 67 (3–4): 205–268.

SOLLAS, W. J. 1924. *Ancient hunters, and their modern representatives.* New York: Macmillan.

STEWARD, JULIAN H., and LOUIS C. FARON. 1959. *Native peoples of South America.* New York: McGraw-Hill.

TROELS-SMITH, JORGEN. 1953. Ertebølle culture-farmer culture, results of the past ten years' excavations in Asmosen Bog, West Zealand. *Aarboger for nordisk Oldkyndighed of Historie,* pp. 1–62. Copenhagen.

TYLOR, E. B. 1881. *Anthropology.* London: Henry Holt.

VAVILOV, N. I. 1951. The origin, variation, immunity and breeding of cultivated plants. *Chronica Botanica,* Vol. 13, No. 1/6.

VIELLE, EDMOND. 1890. Pointes de fleches typiques de Fère-en-Tardenois (Aisne). *Bulletin de Société Anthropologique de Paris,* 1(6th series): 959–64.

WATERBOLK, H. T. 1962. The lower Rhine Basin. In R. J. Braidwood and G. R. Willey (Eds.), *Courses toward urban life.* Chicago: Aldine Publishing Company.

WHITE, LESLIE A. 1959. *The evolution of culture.* New York: McGraw-Hill.

WILLEY, GORDON R. 1966. New World archaeology in 1965. In *Proceedings of the American Philosophical Society,* 110(2): 140–45.

WILSON, THOMAS. 1894. Minute stone implements from India. In *Report of the U.S. National Museum, 1882.* Washington, D.C.: U.S. Government Printing Office.

WOODBURN, JAMES. 1968. Background material on the Hadza of Tanzania. In Richard B. Lee and Irven DeVore (Eds.), *Man the hunter.* Chicago: Aldine Publishing Company.

WYNNE-EDWARDS, V. C. 1962. *Animal dispersion in relation to social behaviour.* Edinburgh: Oliver and Boyd.

——. 1964. Population control in animals. *Scientific American,* 211(2): 68–74.

YENGOYAN, ARAM A. 1960. Preliminary notes on a model of the initial populating of the Philippines. *Anthropology Tomorrow,* 6(3): 42–48.

YOUNG, T. C., and P. E. L. SMITH. 1966. Research in the prehistory of central western Iran. *Science,* 153(3734): 386–91.

PART IV

Discussion

The anthropologists whose comments constitute this section of the book were invited to comment only on certain portions of the complete symposium at Denver. The comments of Lee, DeVore, and Fried were made with reference to the papers of S. R. Binford, Sackett, L. R. Binford, Winters, and Hole. The comments of Dozier, Aberle, and Harris were made with reference to the papers of Flannery and Coe, Longacre, Hill, Whallon, and Deetz. The purpose of soliciting the comments of these non-archeological anthropologists was to get their response to the kinds of approaches used and to insure that there would be the very essential feedback maintained between students of living cultures and students of extinct ones. Their comments were especially gratifying in that they went far beyond the content of the symposium papers and further elucidated the nature of the relationship between anthropological subdisciplines.

Comments by Richard B. Lee

As a social anthropologist who has been interested in problems of archeological reconstruction and more generally in the problems of the evolution of human behavior, I hope to offer one or two suggestions about how social anthropology can be of use to the archeologist and how the archeologist can make richer inferences from his own data.

First of all it appeared to me in listening to several of the papers that perhaps this symposium entitled "Social Organization of Prehistoric Communities" had been misnamed. Sally Binford's and Sackett's papers were intriguing examples of the current highly sophisticated methodologies

I felt that they stopped far short of inferences about social organization. Perhaps these papers should have been put into a symposium entitled "Human Behavior Patterns of Archeological Significance."

On the other hand, L. R. Binford's concluding paper is a strange bedfellow because it goes far beyond the discussion of social organization to a consideration of total socioecological adaptation in the post-Pleistocene. Thus, he considers one of the basic questions that informs the humanities: the transformation of the human condition brought about by the onset of agriculture and animal domestication. So, in this respect it goes beyond the scope of the symposium, and of course it raises exciting questions for many of us.

I am going to make two comments now on the Paleolithic materials. First of all, I think that we need for this earlier period the kind of synthesis that Lewis Binford has offered us for the later post-Pleistocene period. One of the important ways that social anthropologists can assist in this task is to get down to the long overdue job of developing a general statement about the ecology, subsistence, and social organization of contemporary hunting and gathering peoples.[1]

Another way that we can assist is to undertake more ethnographic studies of hunting and gathering peoples, with archeological questions in mind. DeVore and I attempted to do this between 1963 and 1965 in our research among the !Kung Bushmen of Bechuanaland. What we found may be of interest to archeologists. We were impressed that the !Kung have a very substantial subsistence base largely made up of vegetable foods and small mammals, but that there would be *almost a total loss of this evidence to the archeologist.* !Kung campsites are subject to very rapid destruction, and after ten or fifteen years the evidence of the settlement pattern disappears and the evidence for the substantial vegetable food base rots away. Therefore, by doing Bushman archeology, I think one would radically underestimate the level of their subsistence. One would infer that life among the Bushmen must have been nasty, brutish, and short, whereas it is in fact delightful, as DeVore and I can attest.

This leads into a second point about the synthesis that is yet to be done on the subsistence and ecology of contemporary hunting and gathering peoples. One thing that we can say right off concerns the importance of meat. In the world ethnographic sample of food-gathering societies, only the Eskimos are primarily mammal eaters, and we are not even sure about them because fish among the Eskimo may have been of equal importance with mammals. *Virtually all the rest of the societies in the sample have a subsistence base primarily of vegetable foods and/or marine resources.* This is a very marked contrast to the Paleolithic peoples. The latter appear to be much more successful big game hunters,

[1] An attempt at synthesizing hunter-gatherer materials was made by an international panel of scholars at the symposium, "Man the Hunter," Chicago, April 6-9, 1966 (Chicago: Aldine Publishing Company, 1968).

and, I would think that the Dordogne cultures, for instance, would fall quite outside the range of variation of known food-gathering peoples. In light of this, I think that the archeologists could be much more intrepid in their reconstruction of Paleolithic social organization. What their material suggests to me is very substantial group sizes and a high level of social complexity for late Paleolithic man.

One starts with the question: What are the implications of the regular hunting of large numbers of large mammals? First of all, it requires a high level of social organization to organize a game-drive or to attack and kill an animal as large as an elephant. Second, and even more important, it requires a large number of people to butcher, transport, cook, and consume the many thousands of pounds of meat that would be derived from such hunting activities.

The contemporary !Kung Bushmen are a case in point. They live in small groups of ten to thirty people, and they specialize in hunting small mammals non-cooperatively. Practically all the mammals they kill can be consumed within the local group. However, when a large animal, such as a gemsbok or wildebeeste is killed, providing 200 to 300 pounds of meat, visitors from far and wide come in to consume and to share in the good fortune of the local group. I would predict, if large game were regularly killed by the !Kung Bushmen, that instead of people visiting back and forth every second day, the present small groups would tend to combine into substantially larger groups, simply in order to consume the meat that is available. Let us make a simple calculation: one gemsbok with 250 pounds of meat, will in fact feed forty !Kung Bushmen for three days. An elephant yielding ten times as much meat as a gemsbok would provide, instead of 120 man-days of meat, something on the order of 1,200 man-days of meat! This quantity of meat would feed 400 people for three days. Such a calculation would necessarily imply much larger groups for Paleolithic hunters than, for instance, occur among the !Kung Bushmen, and these larger groups would display much greater residential stability.

I am reminded of the old chestnut about the Eskimo hunter who goes out on the iceflows, and by a great stroke of fortune manages to harpoon and kill a whale. By organizing his dog team and by dint of great effort he manages to drag this enormous carcass back to the igloo. He knocks on the door of the igloo, and he calls to his wife, "Dear, dear, come and look what I have." His wife crawls out of the igloo, takes one look at this hulk, and says, "You clean it, and I'll eat it!" In other words, Paleolithic archeologists would do well to consider Brecht's dictum: "Erst kommt die Fressen, dann kommt die Moral."

Finally I want to propose that we should offer as an option in the graduate anthropology program something called "interpretive archeology." In this scheme, each archeology graduate student would be required to spend three to six months doing an ethnographic field study, preferably after he has had archeological field experience and preferably that have been developed for the analysis of Paleolithic assemblages, but in a living culture that is somehow related to his archeological work or related to the kinds of interpretive problems he is dealing with. Personally, I can't help feeling, for instance, that if every African prehistorian spent a field season working with the Kalahari Bushmen (or with Australian aborigines), this experience would immeasurably enrich his understanding of all levels of African prehistory. I cite as an example Francis van Noten, a Belgian archeologist, who first excavated an early Bushman site with a carbon date of 4700 BP, and then came to our field station at Dobe, Bechuanaland, where he spent three weeks studying Bushman settlement patterns. At the end it was not possible for him to say "I learned this, this, and this," but the experience certainly enlarged his understanding at an intuitive level.

Here is an example of another kind of ethnographic project that archeologists could usefully carry out. Deetz's paper considers the problem of how residence and descent rules may be inferred from archeological evidence. It would seem to me that an archeology graduate student could very usefully go into an ethnographic field situation and study the actual fit between the observed post-marital residence pattern and the distribution of stylistic techniques and technology. My guess is that no discernable correspondence could be demonstrated between, for example, an uxori-matrilocal rule of residence and the spatial distribution of pottery types, but I would be delighted to be proven wrong!

Comments by Irven DeVore

As a non-archeologist, I warmly applaud the shift in emphasis in archeological thinking in recent years as evidenced, for example, by the papers in this symposium. In the past we were presented with lithic industries which, to judge by their descriptions, were copulating, hybridizing, evolving, adapting, and producing offspring. The modern emphasis on the meticulous excavation of living floors is not only an exciting development within archeology, but is also rapidly creating an atmosphere in which the ethnographer and the archeologist may enter into useful discourse.

I want to amplify some of the points Richard Lee made with regard to the Bushmen study and archeological interpretation. I trust it is unnecessary to state that we view the Bushmen study not as a study of living Paleolithic fossils but as an opportunity to test some assumptions about correlations between observed behavior patterns and the artifactual materials that are left behind to reveal those patterns.

RECONSTRUCTION OF SUBSISTENCE ACTIVITIES

Sally Binford has called attention to the analysis of "tool kits" as a means of revealing much more about the actual hunting activities of hominids than is possible from the interpretation of either tool types or total assemblages. That the ability to reconstruct the activity of a hunter or hunters at a given time and place would yield extremely important information is obvious, but what can then be made of this information to predict the entire subsistence pattern is less straightforward.

Lee has carefully documented the tool kit that a Bushman hunter uses in pursuit of game, and it is a very complex kit (Lee, 1965). When a hunter leaves in the morning he may well be carrying a spear, a bow and arrows, a digging stick, a throwing stick, and a flexible 12–14-ft. pole used for snagging spring hares in their underground burrows. Under his arm will be a pouch containing snares, an arrow-poison kit, gum mastic, fire sticks, a knife, an ostrich eggshell canteen, and so on. Hunting is a complex activity; even though you may hunt for days or weeks without killing an animal, you must be prepared to kill or capture anything from a hare to a 2,000-lb. eland. A woman's kit is far simpler; a pair of stones to crack mungongo nuts, a leather pouch to carry foodstuffs, and a digging stick comprise the essentials. If these two kits are projected backward in time to a pre-iron period, all of the woman's kit would have disintegrated in an excavation site except the stones, but the range of chipped stone projectiles and cutting edges would be impressive. The abundance and complexity of the hunting artifacts would suggest that hunting had been the basis of the economy (and that the nut-cracking stones were used to extract marrow). Quite the opposite is the case, but it happens that the important nut-and-vegetable subsistence of the Dobe area Bushmen is extracted by a very simple, largely perishable, tool kit.

That the ordinary site yields only a small, imperishable fraction of a culture's total impedimenta will hardly be greeted by archeologists as a revelation, but I am suggesting something more. Increasingly large samples of the "hunting artifacts" and bone debris on the living floors of early man will naturally lead to more sophisticated analyses of hunting techniques and the prey animals, but these data may also divert attention from consideration of the broader aspects of subsistence. Bushmen groups orient to vegetable supplies and water, and after these requirements are met the hunters find what game they can in the area. Lee has already mentioned the importance of vegetable and marine resources in the subsistence of living hunter-gatherer peoples, and a comparably vegetarian diet is universal among Old World monkeys and apes. Even though both primates, and, with rare exceptions, living hunter-gatherers depend heavily on a vegetable subsistence base, our textbooks treat human prehistory as a series of stages of more and more efficient *hunting*. Yet it seems unlikely that the women, the young, and the aged sat idly by during more than a million years of male hunting activities. We believe that a more balanced view of living hunter-gatherers will offer a better perspective on prehistory.

LIVING FLOORS

Archeologists now speak of "activity specific" areas within a living site as early as the Middle Pleistocene at such sites as Ambrona and Torralba.

Lee has already pointed to the necessary size and presumed complexity of a social group capable of routinely killing elephants, and in these Spanish sites there is evidence of some 40–50 butchered elephants (Butzer, 1964). The Dobe Bushmen will not tackle an elephant, but their campsites can reveal much more to the archeologist than the ethnographic literature implies. As everyone knows from the literature, and a brief visit would confirm the impression, a Bushman campsite is disappointingly ephemeral—a series of flimsy grass huts around campfires. But it is soon apparent to the observer that the Bushmen are carrying out a series of activities whose diversity is comparable to those in middle-class suburbia. These activities can be described in objective terms (eating, sleeping, defecation, etc.), but for the present illustration suffice it to say that in these simple hunter-gatherer camps one finds the functional equivalents of a bedroom, a kitchen, a sitting room, bathroom, storage closet, pantry, den, doghouse, and even a patio barbecue pit. The "den" is the dance circle where Bushmen gather with visitors. Wart hogs and other such delicacies may be cooked in the skin and this tends to be a smelly business. The sensible chef digs his roasting pit (his "barbecue pit") some twenty yards outside the camp circle. These routine activities, then, tend to occur in specific areas, and these areas can be plotted by their characteristic debris.

The relocation of a campsite may owe more to olfactory considerations than is sometimes appreciated. As L. R. Binford has already mentioned, people defecate and the accumulation of these waste products may become noisome. Thus the Bushmen may move a camp, not for some tidy ecological reason such as shifting game herds or drought, but because, as they say, "the place stinks." Even hunting success may create problems. A typical reconstruction depicts the hunters camped beside a dead elephant, happily hacking away. This may be reasonable in near-freezing weather, but it is intolerable in the tropics. In 1964 an elephant was killed in the Masai Amboseli Reserve, Kenya. After 24 hours in this climate the bubbling carcass could be both heard and smelled for hundreds of feet in all directions; the smell of putrefaction could scarcely be borne at 1,000 yards downwind, and the winds were variable. Presumably our ancestors were not oblivious to this situation, and one might postulate an olfactory theory of shifting human occupation. Perhaps this will serve as an example of the "intuitive level of understanding" Lee is asking archeologists to seek in the ethnographer's camp.

A dead elephant is outside the experience of most of us, whether archeologist or otherwise. What amazed me was the number of animals attracted to this mountain of rotting flesh. There were thirteen lions (who seemed as eager to eat people as to work at the carcass), a great many hyenas and jackals, and over 350 very persistent vultures and marabou storks. From the simple fact of a dead elephant, then, one can make some calculations about the size of the group that could be supported by its flesh, the minimum number of adults necessary to separate an individual from an angry and protective herd, surround and dispatch it (and then fight off competing predators); and, perhaps, arrive at some notion of the effect of the carcass on the location of the campsite.

CONCLUSION

The methodological expertise evident in these symposium papers is the envy of social anthropologists. One is struck not only by the impressive amount of material being excavated, preserved, and analyzed, but also by the amount of information derivable from these efforts. As archeologists go beyond the analysis of tool types and assemblages to reconstruction of the tool makers and their life patterns, they will increasingly engage the interest of their colleagues. While the social anthropologist may be scandalized by reconstructions of ancestral systems of residence and descent, he should recognize that contemporary studies in social anthropology have not always offered archeologists a very wide range of alternatives for dialogue. Indeed I would echo Lee's statement that, bold as archeologists may now consider themselves to be, I feel they are being unnecessarily timid, and wish they would extend their reconstructive necks still further.

I realize that a predictable result of this widespread sticking-out-of-necks would be wholesale decapitation. As an alternative, I would hope that archeologists could offer not one, but a range of possible interpretations and models based on their data—models which would be at least in some respects empirically verifiable independent of archeological evidence. In a different context, S. L. Washburn suggested one way in which these alternatives could be offered. This would involve not only making a clear distinction between the *data* from an excavation and the *interpretation* of these data, but would also involve giving some sort of confidence limits to interpretations and reconstructions. Crudely, the prehistorian could say that on the basis of material "A," I place considerable (90 per cent?) confidence in the conclusion that "X" is true, but the interpretation of material "B" is much less straightforward and I would suggest at only the "20 per cent level" that "Y" occurred. This approach has the advantage of taking the more controversial aspects of archeology out of the realm of personal invective and ad hominem argument, while at the same time allowing us to discuss the necessarily controversial aspects of reconstruction which will surely continue to be of the most interest to the profession at large.

References

Butzer, Karl W. 1964. *Environment and archeology*. Chicago: Aldine Publishing Company.

Lee, Richard B. 1965. *Subsistence ecology of !Kung Bushmen*. Unpublished Ph.D. thesis. Berkeley: University of California.

Comments by Morton H. Fried

I will be brief because my expertise falls far short of that displayed by the other discussants, not to mention the speakers. I am going to make six points, all quite brief and programmatic. My comments, of course, represent only one sociocultural anthropologist's reaction to what some archeologists are doing at the present time. Since I am considering certain aspects of that work which I consider exciting and of which I approve, my message should be scanned for encouragement rather than wisdom.

First, what have some archeologists been up to recently? Well, they have been getting wordy, as prolix as their sociocultural brethren, and this does not excite me, although I am in no position to disapprove. Actually, my first point is somewhat more serious, for I would like to note and loudly cheer the continued collapse of archetypal thinking among archeologists. Almost gone are such procrustean notions of my youth as the core cultures or the flake cultures. I must confess now to having harbored certain subversive images when I was a graduate student and forced to submit to a number of archeology courses. One image involved an ancient hominid type who I imagined squatting over his work as he bashed out a stone tool. After laboring long and intently he rose and with an expression of ineffable sadness chucked away the neat object of his labors. One close enough to hear and understand him would have caught his plaintive remark: "I'm not allowed to use that, it's flake and I'm core."

These papers have universally shown disdain for the rigid categorical thinking that mars much of the earlier archeology and makes it incompatible with what we know about the dynamics of culture. While culture has its own laws of conservation, it is an unusually volatile realm and the notion of static, homogeneous archeological cultures is impossible to fit with current theoretical models of culture. As a by-product, we also vitiate the requirement that major cultural changes in the remote past occurred to the tune of genocide, which may be seen ultimately as a projection of the world we know into the past we must reconstruct.

Second, these papers universally avoid anything that might be called, for want of a better term, "organic thinking." Nowhere, I believe, is there a reference to "race" or even ethnic groups or populations. What we are told about is culture, the dynamics of culture, and social systems and the dynamics of such systems. This is closely linked to the first point that I made, for the archeological emphasis is located in the realm of culture and not in some hypothetical realm of racial biology. Fundamentally, the intrinsic assumption is that ideas can spread wide and more or less rapidly depending upon sociocultural circumstances. Acting upon assumptions such as this, we can see that there is no theoretical gulf between archeologists and sociocultural anthropologists, but essentially a difference of data.

My third observation has to do with archeological method. Those of us who have not had a primary investment in archeology but who have dutifully kept contact by reading monographs or serving on dissertation committees have sometimes been pained by the detailed empiricism of the field archeologist. But now the painstaking methods of recovery and reporting are beginning to pay off: fellows, you were right! Intricate, comprehensive summaries of living floor contents are infinitely more meaningful and useful than the intuitive epitomizations that take us back to archetyping. Dependence upon itemization of the contents of living floors, however boring to the reader in quest of the fast generalization, has its rewards. Those who pursue this method, I believe, are on the verge of revolutionizing our detailed understanding of the logic and flow of prehistory. This is being done by constantly increasing the probability coefficients of statements that were originally made as speculations, and the increasing reliability of these statements is a direct function of the energy that has been put into site inventories, or so it would seem to an observer from outside.

My fourth point is that archeology, like certain other fields, is now in possession of a "synthetic theory." I mean by this exactly what Julian Huxley meant when he applied it to biology: you have come upon a theory and a method that are the integrated product of several disciplines. Like biology, archeology has had its wedding with statistics and with ecology.

This leads me to the fifth point, which acknowledges the mutual relations between archeology and comparative ethnography. I use the latter phrase instead of ethnology, because it better conveys the emphasis upon the detailed inventory, which is parallel to the detailed inventory of living floors already mentioned. I should also like to endorse Mr. Lee's suggestions about ethnographic training for archeologists, even at the risk of further elaborating the graduate program. In all of this, however, I think a distinction should be drawn between an archeology informed by comparative ethnography and an archeology dominated by sociocultural anthropology. Obviously, the data of archeology and the discipline-specific theories of archeology must take first place in this exchange.

Since the question has been raised, I cannot refrain from commenting on the relation between archeology and contemporary ethnographic experience. Everyone is aware that contemporary marginal cultures occupy environmental niches that are in most cases probably quite different from those occupied by the hunters and gatherers of the past. What is more, certain processes of sociocultural development, particularly in the area of polity, are probably much different under derived and induced conditions, as opposed to those which transpired under pristine conditions. This is not to say that Bushman culture cannot reflect things of great value and interest to the archeologist, but does suggest that the reflecting edge must be held at the proper angle to avoid distortion.

Finally, my last point has to do with an ancient philosophical conflict presently reviving once again in more than one subdiscipline of our anthropological complex. It seems to me, in the conflict between materialistic and idealistic approaches, that the archeologists have swung back to the former. Some may argue that archeologists never really departed from materialism, since their data are of such nature as to encourage a materialistic approach. We did not hear in the preceding comments very much about ideas, values, or desires; we did hear about stinking elephant carcasses and how camps will be moved to avoid them. We heard about the contents of tool kits and their limitations, and things of this kind. While I am certainly not willing to cast out the humanistic approach with its various benefits, I think that there is a time for various research strategies and that this is the time to stress the painstaking recovery and description of whole sites which are then presented in their complexity rather than as epitomes of limited value and less limited error.

Comments by Edward P. Dozier

I am not going to comment on methodology or techniques explored or expressed in the papers of the participants. I want, instead, to say something about social units and the types which may occur in prehistoric sites.

I note that our speakers have searched for, or have tried to infer only unilinear type organizations in the sites that they have worked. This is probably because they are dealing with the former habitations of simpler societies and, therefore, do not expect to find other types of social units. Or, perhaps, they have simply taken a cue from social anthropologists who have devoted so much attention to the study of kinship units. However, I feel strongly that non-kinship units were present in some of the groups reported on, particularly those in Mesoamerica. I think that a search for non-kinship units should be made in these groups. What the social anthropologist is particularly concerned with is: "What are the corporate aspects of the particular prehistoric society?" I believe this is the same question—or at least related to it—that Deetz raised in his paper. As far as kinship organizations are concerned, we are restricted essentially to two broad types of social units: unilinear organizations or ramified, bilateral descent groups. We cannot assume, however, that given evidence of corporateness in house or ceramic remains we are dealing with kinship units. We must still resolve this either by reference to surviving groups in the area, or by other means, for corporateness may exist in kinship units as well as in non-kinship units.

In many of our societies today, in North America as well as in Mesoamerica, non-kinship sodalities are extremely important; these organizations provide integrative functions and have corporate features. The fact that these units are represented in living indigenous peoples in the neighborhood of some of the sites reported in the symposium would indicate that they have deep historical roots.

As a social anthropologist, non-kinship organizations are the kind of units I would like to have archeologists look for. This is simply because I believe that particularly in Mexico, but also in parts of the Southwestern United States, such units are of primary importance among the contemporary Indian populations. I would like to make a plea to social anthropologists that we begin to study non-kinship organizations with the same fervor we have devoted to kinship units. If we do this, we will have a model for the archeologists to aim at and, hence, to have them seek evidence for both types of social structures.

Comments by David F. Aberle

My general remarks and specific comments are restricted to the papers that were read at the session for which I was asked to serve as a discussant: those by Flannery and Coe, Struever, Longacre, Hill, Deetz, and Whallon. The papers are characterized by freshness, enthusiasm, sophistication in the use of quantitative methods, and an informed and sensitive use of the concepts of social anthropology and of cultural ecology as applied to ethnographically recorded cultures. They afford a promise of new, cooperative intellectual endeavors requiring the collaboration of archeologists and ethnologists and providing rewards for both. And they also open the possibility of a kind of sequential analysis that is often difficult in ethnology for lack of adequate historical information. In this respect, archeology may well advance ethnological thinking, whereas in some other respects, archeology depends on ethnological theory.

There are two problems about work of the sort represented in these papers. The first lies in the area of methods. These papers show more sophisticated use of statistics than is characteristic of a good deal of work in ethnology, but in the drafts I saw some did not make entirely clear why a particular statistic was chosen, nor what it did. In ethnology (and in archeology, for that matter), although the situation is changing, there are a good many of us who have little enough background in statistics. As a result, data analysis surrounded by a sufficient number of tables is likely to be accepted because of the figures, whether they are understood or not, or rejected in spite of the figures, because they are not understood. It behooves those who use novel or complex statistics to inform us quite carefully as to what they are doing, and why, so as to maximize the chance for the spread of the techniques and for their critical evaluation.

The second problem lies in the area of theory, or perhaps of concepts, since theory in ethnology has a limited development at present.[1] On the one hand, the archeologist will have to keep very much abreast of current

[1] By "theory" I refer to generalized propositions stating relationships between two or more classes of phenomena.

theory and concepts, or we will have the usual spectacle of the use of ideas outworn in one field as the basic assumptions of another. This is a familiar problem to anthropologists in general: many economists, political scientists, and psychologists start with working assumptions borrowed from the anthropology of twenty or more years ago and are startlingly invulnerable to efforts to update them. It is notable that the authors of these papers are relatively young and recently trained in ethnology. Petrifaction has had no time to set in, but it is an ever-present possibility. On the other hand, efforts to use the "fancier" types of ethnological concepts may lead to difficulties, particularly as these concepts demand moving several steps away from the data. As Morton Fried points out, there are advantages to a material perspective in this kind of work.

I come now to specific comments. The paper by Hill provides a finding surprising to me. He says that the pottery in the kivas was relatively uniform and he suggests therefore that each kiva was attached to a particular matrilocal cluster. In such modern matrilineal, matrilocal pueblos as the Hopi towns and Zuñi, kivas are made up of members of a number of clans, thus cross-cutting clan membership. If the kivas are in fact made up of unrelated men, married to matrilineally related women who form matrilocal clusters, this has escaped the attention of ethnographers. One might therefore expect that if these prehistoric pueblos moved in the direction of modern pueblos, later horizons would show less uniformity of kiva pottery. Whether or not data of this sort emerge, we find in the archeological picture a form of social organization that differs significantly from known ethnological types.

Whallon's illuminating paper brings out the point I referred to above about sequence analysis. And it also raises a point of significance about the interpretation of residence patterns. His paper shows increasing fixity of matrilocal residence over time. Now it is perfectly true that evidence of some degree of matrilocality at any one point of time is a poor basis for inferring matrilineal descent, whether the data are archeological or ethnological. There are at least four possible interpretations of such a pattern. The group may be moving toward matrilineality via matrilocality; it may have once been matrilineal but have lost matrilineal descent groups without losing a matrilocal bias; it may have a statistical preference for matrilocality without either a dogma of residence or a dogma of descent; or it may be matrilineal and matrilocal. But a pattern of increasing tendency over time toward matrilocality would seem to reduce us to two possibilities: that the system was matrilineal with increasing matrilocal preference, or that it was moving toward matrilineality via matrilocality. This at least reduces some of the static. Change over time, then, would seem a more powerful tool for social inferences than analysis of single sites in a restricted time range.

But Whallon's interpretation of his data does raise a problem: that of "fancy" theory. His interpretation is concerned with degree of corporateness. This is a concept exceedingly difficult to operationalize in ethnology, and perhaps of dubious value, since it tends to use a unidimensional quantitative concept to cover a multitude of dimensions (for example, inheritance, residential fixity, jural responsibility, sharing, joint economic activity, exclusive ritual activity, etc.). It would seem more profitable for the moment for him to remain somewhat closer to his data, which do indicate more fixity of residence and perhaps a larger number of people in the fixed clusters. I would be reluctant to use a statistical measure applied to artifacts to describe a condition (corporateness) that has yet to be satisfactorily quantified in ethnology.

With respect to Struever's paper, if indeed Hopewell is primarily non-agricultural and is based on what he calls the harvesting of wild resources, there is an interesting parallel with the Northwest Coast, where cultural elaboration is clearly based on just such harvesting. In Hopewell there is an elaboration of the mortuary pattern; in the Northwest Coast there is a considerable elaboration of the potlatch complex surrounding funerals. Indeed, up and down the Northwest Coast, and indeed among those Alaskan Eskimo groups with relatively abundant resources, whatever else is elaborated, feasting and prestations in connection with death show a rich development. Nor is this funerary elaboration simply a given of all relatively well-off cultures; it is not found, for example, in Pueblo culture, and there is no evidence that it was even at the climax of that culture.

The stimulating paper by Flannery and Coe does have some loopholes from the point of view of ethnological theory and data. The authors seem to assume to begin with that a kinship system is either unilineal and egalitarian or non-unilineal, ranked, and ramifying. As I see it, this is a misinterpretation of what Sahlins wrote, although a plausible (but I think incorrect) extrapolation from what Kirchhoff wrote.

Sahlins says, "A ramage then is a nonexogamous, internally stratified, unilineal—in Polynesia, patrilineal—descent group. Distance from the senior line of descent from the common ancestor is the criterion of stratification. By this definition, segments of a ramage are also ramages" (Sahlins, 1958, p. 140). He continues in a footnote: "At approximately the same time that Firth applied the term 'ramage' to this distinct type of organization, Paul Kirchhoff, in a brilliant paper, had isolated ramage organizations and called them 'conical clans' in contrast to the 'equalitarian clans' as one finds, for example, among the Iroquois" (Sahlins, 1958, p. 140). Elsewhere Sahlins speaks of "localized, discrete, patrilineal descent lines" as a contrast to ramified systems in Polynesia and continues, "The descent lines held titles. . . . Status did not depend—at least not in the same way as in the ramified system—on distance from the main line of descent, but rather on the traditional position of one's title in the territorial hierarchy of titles" (Sahlins, 1958, p. 181).

In a paper that "modifies, in places extends, and generally develops"

(1957, p. 291, n. 1) the interpretative sections of Sahlins, 1958, Sahlins changes his definitions and terms slightly. "A ramage is a common descent group internally ranked by a principle of genealogical seniority. Succession . . . is by rule of primogeniture. . . . Every line is ranked according to the respective birth order of ancestral figures, and every individual in a ramage holds a different rank—one precisely proportionate to his distance from the senior line. This is the outstanding indicative feature of ramages" (1957, p. 291). "A truncated descent line is a small localized common descent group. It differs from a ramage by absence of internal ranking according to genealogical principles. Although descent lines supply chiefs in territorial units, succession is determined primarily by leadership qualifications, not by rule of primogeniture. Correspondingly, distinction of senior and junior line is not made" (1957, p. 292). He continues by pointing out that villages involve sets of truncated descent groups. When a descent group within a village divides, genealogical ties eventually are forgotten. But descent groups of different villages are often affiliated by ties of ancestry. When this occurs, the different descent groups thus affiliated are not mutually ranked. Thus the fundamental political units of societies with ramages are the ramages themselves. The fundamental political units of societies with truncated descent lines are villages governed by councils of titled men, these offices being held by the leaders of the various descent lines. Villages in turn are grouped into districts ruled by similar councils (1957, pp. 292-93, paraphrased). "Neither exogamy nor endogamy are indicative features of ramages and truncated descent lines. Both are agamous" (1957, p. 293). Furthermore, these units may be either patrilineal or non-unilineal. "In the present discussion internal ranking and segmentary features of descent groups are at issue and 'ramage' and 'truncated descent lines' are discriminated principally by these criteria" (1957, p. 293). He continues, "Characteristics of lineality . . . are not features with which we are directly concerned at the moment" (1957, p. 293). Finally, the presence and absence of redistribution are not at stake. Both kinds of units redistribute (1958, *passim*; 1957, p. 295). It is clear throughout his 1957 paper that Sahlins' typology is oriented to Polynesian social forms, and that he is not concerned whether his typology can be carried over to other areas unchanged (cf. 1957, pp. 291, 299).

Flannery and Coe, however, say, "The first type of social organization was the 'descent line,' or simple 'unilateral exogamous clan' of Kirchoff. . . . These we might describe as corporate groups united by actual (or fictionalized) common descent through the male or female line, all members of a given lineage being regarded as equals. The second type of social organization was the ramified system, 'ramage,' or 'conical clan' of Kirchhoff . . . , which is not really a clan at all. . . . It is based not on unilateral descent but on primogeniture; individuals are ranked in status according to their distance from the direct line of descent from an ancestor at the apex of the ramified system" (Flannery and Coe, this volume, p. 274).

Thus they contrast egalitarian, exogamous, unilineal units with internally ranked, non-exogamous, non-unilineal units; they equate the former with Kirchhoff's equalitarian clan *and* Sahlins' descent line, and the latter with Kirchhoff's conical clan and Sahlins' ramage.

But Sahlins' contrasts do not involve unilineality versus non-unilineality, do not involve exogamy versus agamy, and do not involve egalitarianism versus ranking. They involve depth of genealogical reckoning, assignment of rank, and community composition. Neither group as defined for Polynesia is exogamous, and neither group is egalitarian. The "descent line" or "truncated descent line," however, does not assign rank on the basis of genealogical position. Its leaders, however, have rank within the descent group. The exogamous equalitarian clan of Kirchhoff appears only in a footnote; this unit is not used by Sahlins to analyze Polynesian data.

I now take a step beyond Sahlins' argument. Not only are there ramified unilineal and non-unilineal, agamous, genealogically ranked units in various parts of the world, but there are also at least the following: ramified, unilineal, genealogically ranked units exogamous in the main but with special, agamous marriages for those of high status, and unilineal, exogamous, genealogically ranked units, whose high-status figures contract marriages only with high-status figures from other units. Thus neither unilineality nor agamy are critical for the analysis of ramified, genealogically ranked units.

Now all of this does not undermine the analysis of Flannery and Coe. Their simple contrastive pair, however, does necessitate an unnecessarily complex argument to show that the lowland Maya were organized with patrilineal exogamous clans and redistribution and stratification. It is not that they have contructed an improbable model for the lowland Maya, but that they have found a problem in accounting for redistribution and stratification and exogamy as a package where no problem exists: there are many systems that combine all three features. They have not, then, used Sahlins' theory, either as stated in his 1958 book or in his 1957 article, with sufficient precision, nor have they taken into account living ethnographic examples that would have entitled them to arrive at the same conclusions with less elaboration. (There *is* a problem in accounting for the transition from egalitarian clans with little or no redistribution to less egalitarian units with considerable redistribution, but the problem is that of breaking out of egalitarianism, not out of unilineality or exogamy.)

They also argue—and this is a different point—that a system of reciprocity, as opposed to a system of redistribution, could not have adequately organized the exchanges of durable and perishable products in the Mexican highlands. They propose that two solutions were available for this: the market system of the Mexican highlands and a redistributive system.

Here they ignore ethnological evidence that indicates—unfortunately for the neatness of their theory—that exceedingly complex exchange systems involving basic foodstuffs can, in fact, be based on reciprocity. The trading system of Manus and the kula ring are cases in point (and the kula ring does not depend on redistribution, even though some of the systems involved in the kula ring were redistributive). Hence one can argue only that markets and redistribution are among the mechanisms that make possible the circulation of goods that they see as adaptive for the region, but not that these are the sole mechanisms. So far as I can see, we still have no empirically substantiated theory—in this paper or anywhere else—that will account for the origin of redistribution.

But the reason for raising these strictures is not to criticize Flannery and Coe. It is only to point out that the kind of archeological interpretation attempted in this and other papers in this volume will require constant interaction between ethnologist and archeologist; it is a concrete example of a general point raised earlier in my comments.

To turn briefly to Deetz's paper, it would appear that inferences about residence can be made with some security under some conditions, but not others. Inferences of matrilocal residence seem fairly secure. But evidence of clustering of attributes of equipment made by men could indicate either patrilocal or avunculocal residence, and the inferences about lineality to be made under these conditions would take one in opposite directions—toward patrilineality or matrilineality. Nor would the failure of women's implements to show clustering forbid us to consider matrilineality, since in avunculocal systems the co-resident women may be drawn from several descent groups.

Finally—although I am personally interested in inferences about residence and descent—it must be said that these variables are not always the most interesting ones. There is a sense in which such variables as ranking, hierarchy, organization, and so on, variables that cross-cut matriliny, patriliny, and non-unilineal descent groups, are of equal or greater importance, especially in the context of evolutionary and ecological considerations (cf. Fried, 1957, which introduces concepts for the comparison of unilineal units, many of which can, without strain, be used for non-unilineal ones as well).

Thus, to say that the Kaska and the Tsimshian resemble each other in being matrilineal is true enough, but what is omitted from consideration by that statement is the existence of organized, internally ranked, localized unilineal groups in the case of the Tsimshian and the absence of such units in the case of the Kaska. And many parallel instances could be cited. It is, of course, this sort of problem with which Flannery and Coe are concerned.

I return finally to analysis of sequence. This, it seems to me, is a peculiar strength available to archeology and not so often to ethnology. Insofar as ethnology examines a culture at a single point in time, problems arise as to whether particular features are, as it were, required by an ecological situation, or merely permitted. We do not know whether, given the technology, this is a "climax" culture or not. Increased time in the area alone, and time and increased population combined, might well produce changes, but we are often in no position to deal with these issues. What seems to emerge to some degree from Whallon's, Struever's, Longacre's, and Hill's papers, as well as from such important earlier work as that of Wedel on the Plains, is a picture of increased specialization of production, increased community size, decreased number of suitable locations, given the increased specialization and increased size, and perhaps increased competition for suitable sites. This parallel development for numerous areas invites further analysis and comparison and promises to provide us with new empirical and theoretical approaches in the areas of cultural evolution and ecology to which archeology will make a unique contribution.

References

FRIED, MORTON H. 1957. The classification of corporate unilineal descent groups. *Journal of the Royal Anthropological Institute,* 87: 1–30.

SAHLINS, MARSHALL D. 1957. Differentiation by adaption in Polynesian societies. *Journal of the Polynesian Society,* 66: 291–300.

——. 1958. *Social stratification in Polynesia.* Seattle: University of Washington Press.

Comments by Marvin Harris

I have to express my apologies for assuming to be able to contribute something here, suffering from the double handicap of not being an archeologist and not having had the opportunity to have read these fascinating papers before composing these comments. I am extremely motivated to encourage the type of analysis which has been attempted by the authors of these papers. I could comment on certain specific extrapolations from archeological data to social organization with respect to some of the individual papers which I have heard. For example, I think that the treatment of Marshall Sahlins' hypotheses concerning the distinctions between ramified and unilinear types of structures should have been brought up to date by reference to additional attempts to establish a more sophisticated typology of unilineal descent groups. Various other suggestions of this sort might be appropriate.

Let me, however, proceed to what I consider to be a more important type of comment which I personally can make, a comment on a much more general level. Actually, it is in the form of an exhortation: Archeologists, shrive yourselves of the notion that the units which you seek to reconstruct must match the units in social organization which contemporary ethnographers have attempted to tell you exist.

The problem in its widest scope, I think, is best understood in terms of the epistemological principles that are involved in an operational approach to definition. As archeologists, you have a number of observational procedures consisting of measuring instruments and the techniques through which you push these measuring instruments. Out of these operations you are capable of defining entities whose reality, I assure you, is every bit as well grounded as the entities which are now being discussed at great length by ethnographers dealing with contemporary sociopolitical systems. To set yourselves free, you have only to reflect upon the prodigious research effort now being expended by your colleagues in cultural anthropology upon the attempt to state the cognitive rules by which sociocultural systems are allegedly governed.

There is no need for you to enter into the trap which has snared generations of cultural anthropologists, by which they have been caught in the delusion that an understanding of the regularities of historical processes was to be derived from an analysis of the idea systems of surviving primitive societies. On the contrary, since you cannot legitimately hope to arrive at the sophisticated delusions of the componential and transformational techniques, I suggest that you abandon the attempt to reconstruct descent systems. What is being done by cultural anthropologists today is not be articulated with what is being done by archeologists; on the contrary, I am suggesting that you take the lead in the following sense:

You have knowledge of the material remains of populations, and thus you can develop techniques for measuring variations in the demographic and behavioral characteristics of such populations over long periods of time in relationship to specific complexes of biological, natural, and cultural features of their ecosystems.

What advantage is to be derived from attempting to use this knowledge for the identification of prehistoric patrilineal or matrilineal descent rules or similar cognitive phenomena? The really important questions which need answering are those which relate a population's pattern of material existence to its habitat over time periods sufficiently ample to shed light on the interaction between technology, economic behavior, and the "etic" organizations or groupings with which these are associated. The great strength of archeology is that it can deal with groups which are defined by the actual coming together and working together or living together of specific individuals at specific times and places. It does not have to and indeed cannot and should not deal with "emic" entities.

Ultimately, what we seek I presume in common, is the explanation of the differences and similarities in sociocultural phenomena. You are in a better position to provide such explanations because of your greater time span and because you can be relatively free from the mystifications which arise from the emic approach. You therefore ought not to permit your activities to be compressed into the narrow compass of attempting to link up with ethnographic data. Your operationally defined categories and processes are superior to the unoperational definitions and categories of much of contemporary cultural anthropology. It is for us in ethnology to find the equivalents of your units among our emically contaminated data. It is for us to link up descent rules, prestige formulations of stratification, ideal moral imperatives and all other subjective actor-oriented ethnographic categories with the durable and verifiable material conditions of sociocultural systems.

Contributors

David F. Aberle is Professor of Anthropology, University of British Columbia.

James E. Ayres is a graduate student in anthropology, University of Arizona.

Lewis R. Binford is Associate Professor of Anthropology, University of New Mexico.

Sally R. Binford is Associate Professor of Anthropology, University of New Mexico.

Michael D. Coe is Associate Professor of Anthropology, Yale University.

George L. Cowgill is Associate Professor of Anthropology, Brandeis University.

James Deetz is Professor of Anthropology, Brown University.

Irven DeVore is Associate Professor of Anthropology and Social Relations, Harvard University.

Edward P. Dozier is Professor of Anthropology, University of Arizona.

Kent V. Flannery is Assistant Professor of Anthropology, University of Michigan.

Morton Fried is Professor of Anthropology, Columbia University.

Marvin Harris is Professor of Anthropology, Columbia University.

James N. Hill is Assistant Professor of Anthropology, University of California at Los Angeles.

Frank Hole is Associate Professor of Anthropology, Rice University.

Richard B. Lee is Assistant Professor of Social Relations, Harvard University.

William A. Longacre is Associate Professor of Anthropology, University of Arizona.

James R. Sackett is Assistant Professor of Anthropology, University of California at Los Angeles.

Albert C. Spaulding is Professor of Anthropology and Dean of Letters and Sciences, University of California at Santa Barbara.

Stuart Struever is Assistant Professor of Anthropology, Northwestern University.

Robert Whallon, Jr., is Assistant Professor of Anthropology, University of Michigan.

Bobby Jo Williams is Assistant Professor of Anthropology, University of California at Los Angeles.

Howard D. Winters is Associate Professor of Anthropology, New York University.

Index

www.ingramcontent.com/pod-product-compliance
Ingram Content Group UK Ltd.
Pitfield, Milton Keynes, MK11 3LW, UK
UKHW022115190926
475702UK00013B/1447
9780202362373